Written in Water

Keats's Final Journey

Alessandro Gallenzi

New edition,
revised and expanded

ALMA CLASSICS

ALMA BOOKS LTD
Thornton House
Thornton Road
Wimbledon Village
London SW19 4NG
United Kingdom
www.almaclassics.com

Written in Water: Keats's Final Journey first published by
Alma Books Ltd in 2022
This new, revised edition first published in 2024
© Alessandro Gallenzi, 2022, 2024

Cover: nathanburtondesign.com

Alessandro Gallenzi asserts his moral right to be identified as the author of
this work in accordance with the Copyright, Designs and Patents Act 1988

Printed in Great Britain by CPI Group (UK) Ltd, Croydon CR0 4YY

ISBN: 978-1-84688-471-9

Contents

Written in Water

I am writing this on the Maid's tragedy which I have read since tea with Great pleasure—Besides this volume of Beaumont & Fletcher—there are on the tabl[e] two volumes of chaucer and a new work of Tom Moores call'd 'Tom Cribb's memorial to Congress[']—nothing in it—These are trifles—but I require nothing so much of you as that you will give me a like description of yourselves, however it may be when you are writing to me—Could I see the same thing done of any great Man long since dead it would be a great delight: as to know in what position Shakspeare sat when he began 'To be or not to be"—such thing[s] become interesting from distance of time or place.

JOHN KEATS
Letter of 14th February 1819 to
George and Georgiana Keats

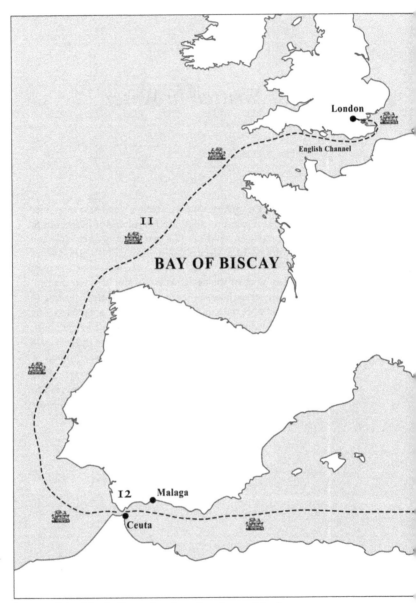

Route of the *Maria Crowther* from London to Naples

(Inset) 1. Departure from London (17th Sept. 1820); 2. Gravesend (17th–18th Sept.);
3. Off Dover Castle (19th Sept.); 4. Storm off the Brighton coast (20th Sept.); 5. Waiting for a wind at Dungeness (21st–23rd Sept.); 6. Landing at Portsmouth (28th Sept.);
7. Visit to the Snooks (28th–29th Sept.) and departure from Portsmouth (29th Sept.);
8. Becalmed off Yarmouth (30th Sept.); 9. Sailing past Handfast Point, landing on

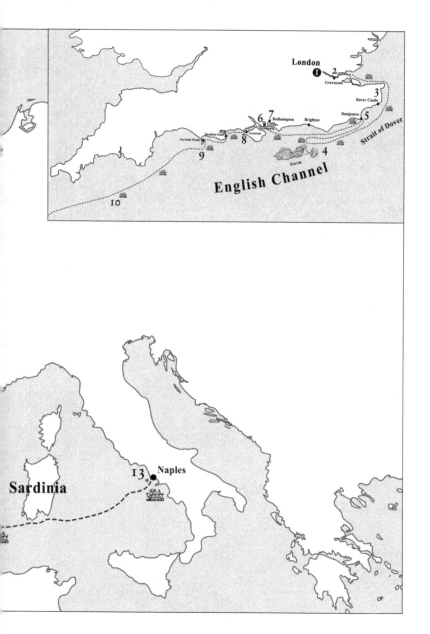

the Dorset coast and putting into Portland Roads (30th Sept.); 10. Clearing of the English Channel (1st–2nd Oct.?); (Map) 11. Encounter with two Portuguese men-of-war as the *Maria Crowther* crosses the Bay of Biscay (first week of Oct.); 12. Entering the Straits of Gibraltar and sailing past Ceuta and Malaga (16th Oct.); 13. Reaching the Bay of Naples (22nd Oct.)

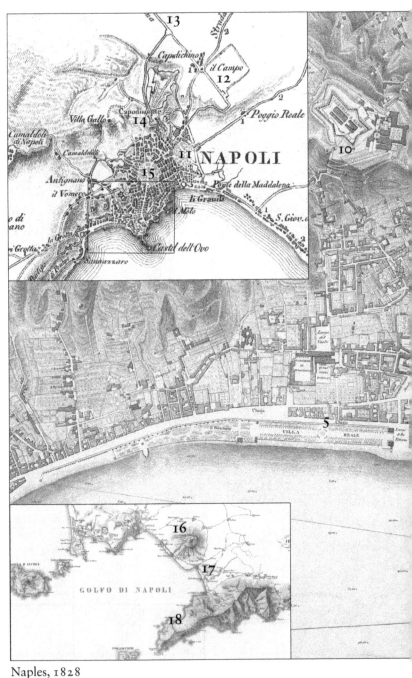

Naples, 1828

(Map) 1. The Hotel Villa di Londra on Strada S. Lucia and its courtyard; 2. Spring of sulphurous water; 3. Chiatamone and spring of ferrous water; 4. Castel dell'Ovo; 5. Riviera di Chiaia and Villa Reale; 6. Royal Palace, facing Piazza del Real Palazzo (now Piazza del Plebiscito) and the Church of San Francesco da Paola, still under construction in 1820;

7. Teatro San Carlo; 8. Mole; 9. Castel Nuovo; 10. Castel Sant'Elmo; (top-left inset)
11. Porta Capuana; 12. Campo di Marte (Field of Mars); 13. Road to Rome via Capua;
14. Royal Palace of Capodimonte; 15. Bourbon Museum (Studi); (bottom-left inset)
16. Mount Vesuvius; 17. Ruins of the ancient city of Pompeii; 18. Sorrento

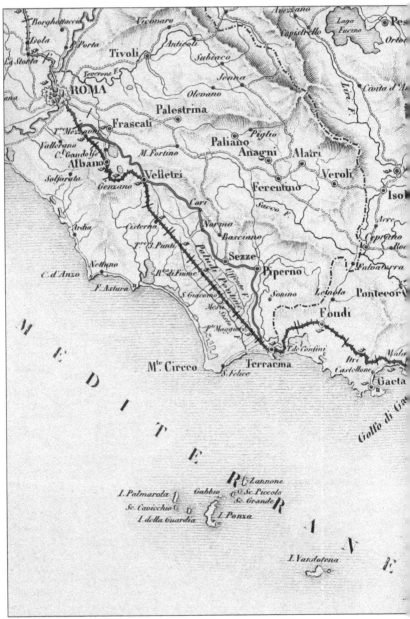

Routes from Naples to Rome

╫╫╫╫╫╫╫╫ Route via the Pontine Marshes (Paludi Pontine)

━━━━━ Alternative route from Terracina to Rome via Piperno avoiding the
Pontine Marshes (showing the two points where it could rejoin the
Appian Way after Albano)

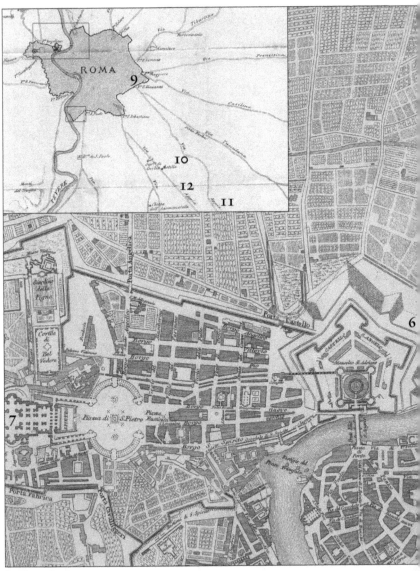

Rome, 1818

(Map) 1. Keats's lodgings at No. 26 Piazza di Spagna, by the Spanish Steps; 2. Pincian Mount public gardens; 3. Branch of Torlonia's bank; 4. Piazza del Popolo; 5. Piazza Navona; 6. Castel Sant'Angelo; 7. St Peter's Basilica; 8. Tiber; (top-left inset) 9. Lateran

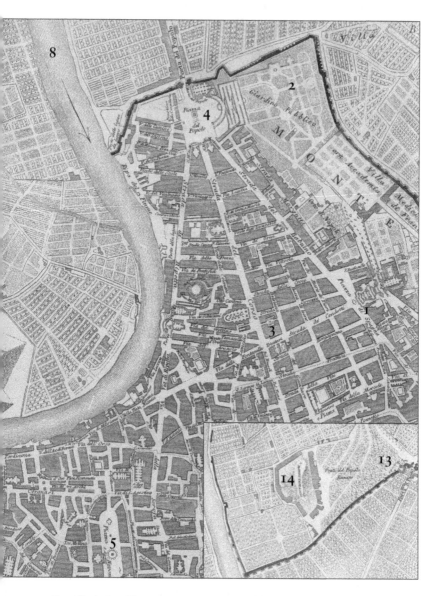

Gate (Porta San Giovanni); 10. Acqua Santa Baths; 11. Road to Naples via Albano (postal road, also called "new Appian Way"); 12. Old Appian Way; (bottom-right inset) 13. English burying place and grave of John Keats; 14. Mount Testaccio

Prelims

Route of the *Maria Crowther* from London to Naples: map and inset by the author

Naples, 1828: detail from *Pianta della città di Napoli*, engraved in the Reale Officio Topografico della Guerra in 1828; insets from an engraving by Nicola Ricci on a drawing by Giosuè Russo, from Andrea de Jorio, *Indicazione del più rimarcabile in Napoli e contorni* (Naples: Tipografia Simoniana, 1819), plate 1

Routes from Naples to Rome: *Viaggio da Roma a Napoli*, from Giuseppe Vallardi, *Itinerario d'Italia* (Milan: Pietro e Giuseppe Vallardi, 1832); the alternative route from Terracina to Rome via Piperno has been superimposed by the author

Rome, 1818: detail from *Pianta topografica di Roma moderna*, 1818, drawing and engraving by Pietro Ruga; the top-left inset has been retraced by the author from the topographic map *Dintorni e forti di Roma* included in Michele Marcani, *I forti di Roma* (Rome: Carlo Voghera, 1883); the bottom-right inset is a detail from Ruga's 1818 map

Text

p. 33: facsimile of an advert published in the *Public Ledger and Daily Advertiser* of 1st September 1820

p. 43: facsimile of a notice published in *Lloyd's List* of 8th April 1817

p. 46: facsimile of an advert published in the *Morning Chronicle* of 23rd September 1819

p. 58: notice published in the *Giornale generale del commercio* of 31st October 1820

Plates

1a. Keats's undated 'Testament': The Morgan Library & Museum. MA 214.2. Purchased by Pierpont Morgan, 1906. Photo: The Morgan Library & Museum, New York

1b, 1c. Keats's passport: MS Keats 7, Houghton Library, Harvard University

2a. Severn's watercolour of the *Maria Crowther*: image from *The John Keats Memorial Volume*, ed. G.C. Williamson (New York; London: John Lane, 1921), opposite p. 168

2b. 'Handfast Point, Dorsetshire / Studland Bay': Joseph Severn Watercolors (MS651,2), Z. Smith Reynolds Library Special Collections and Archives, Wake Forest University, Winston-Salem, North Carolina, USA

2c. 'Ceuta / Coast of Barbary': MS Eng 1460, Houghton Library, Harvard University

3. The 'Bright Star' sonnet: image from *The John Keats Memorial Volume*, op. cit., opposite p. 202

4a. 'Unknown Bay': Joseph Severn Watercolors (MS651, 3), Z. Smith Reynolds Library Special Collections and Archives, Wake Forest University, Winston-Salem, North Carolina, USA

£1 in 1820–21 = *c*.£85 of today

Kingdom of Naples
1 piastra = 12 carlins
1 ducat = 10 carlins
1 carlin = 10 grana
1 grano = 10 cavalli

(Allowing exchange fluctuations)
1 piastra = 4*s*. 6*d*.
1 ducat = 3*s*. 9*d*. or 45*d*.
1 carlin = 4.5*d*.
1 pound sterling = 53 ⅓ carlins

Papal States
1 zecchino = 20 ½ paoli
1 scudo = 10 paoli
1 paolo = 10 baiocchi
1 pound sterling = *c*.43 paoli

1 scudo (or crown) = *c*.12 carlins

Approximate population in 1820

Kingdom of Naples	5,000,000
Naples	350,000
Aversa	15,000
Capua	8,000
Mola and Castellone	5,000
Itri	4,000
Fondi	5,000
Kingdom of Sicily	1,785,000
Papal States	2,500,000
Terracina	5,500
Velletri	10,000
Genzano	4,000
Ariccia	1,250
Albano	5,000
Rome	135,000
Italy:	20,000,000

NOTE ON TRANSLITERATION

All the quotations are reproduced as they appear in the documents they are taken from. Italicized words in citations from printed transcripts of letters represent underlinings in the original. Editorial comments, additions or corrections (mine or by other editors) are indicated by square brackets and words censored by the writer or copyist by a series of *x*s. The notation [...] indicates an omitted word or passage within a quotation. Curly brackets ({}) enclose editorial insertions (mostly by other editors in published sources) to fill lacunae caused by tears, holes, frayed edges and the like. The author's above-line and marginal insertions are indicated in superscript, and legible deletions (when they are of any significance) in strikethrough. The date of letters written over a period of time is that in which they were started. Unless otherwise specified, translations from foreign-language sources are mine.

Preface to the Second Edition

The positive response from readers and reviewers to the first edition of this book has encouraged me to continue in my quest to get closer to the "posthumous" Keats. I consider this to be a work in progress, and I hope to be able to rectify mistakes and add further revelations in future editions.

The main changes from the first edition of *Written in Water* are the correct identification of the "Unknown Bay" (p. 135), previously named as the Bay of Chia in southern Sardinia, and the discovery of the name and exact location of the building in which the Albergo di Cicerone was housed (ibid.). A few small but significant corrections have been made throughout the book.

This is very much a book of details, and when I came across a manuscript fragment I had previously overlooked, containing a partial list of the books Severn and Keats had with them in Rome (SEV), I was forced to revisit some of the assumptions I had made. Most of the titles and authors in the list – some belonging to Severn (a Bible, a seven-volume edition of Shakespeare's works and the poems of Milton, Spenser and Tasso) and some owned by Keats (a copy of the New Testament, the *Divine Comedy* in three volumes, the tragedies of Alfieri and Cervantes's *Don Quixote*) – were already known to me through references in Severn's letters and memoirs, but three of the items in Keats's possession were a total surprise.

The first is a four-volume collection of "The Old English Poets" published by C. Chapple in 1820 (an advert in the *Monthly Literary Advertiser* of 10th August that year, a few weeks before Keats's departure from England, confirms that four volumes had been published so far, with a fifth, *Hero and Leander*, a poem left unfinished by Marlowe and completed by Chapman, forthcoming). The series comprised Thomas Sackville's poetical works and a three-volume edition of William Chamberlayne's heroic poem *Pharonnida* (his verse drama *Love's Victory* is included at the end of the third volume). This is a minor but interesting addition to our knowledge of what Keats read during his final months.

The second is simply listed as "Guide" by Severn. Beth Lau, in her 2016 essay 'Analyzing Keats's Library by Genre' (*Keats–Shelley Journal*, Vol. 65, pp. 126–51), thought it could be the popular *Picture of Italy: Being a Guide to the Antiquities and Curiosities of that Classical and Interesting Country* (1815) by Henry Coxe. However, I find it strange that Severn wouldn't identify the book by its author's name. The most plausible candidate, in my view, is Galignani's 1819 *Traveller's Guide through Italy*. I had already consulted this guidebook for my research, but a more thorough examination of it has yielded a wealth of additional information, such as the fact that it lists both Villa di Londra and the Albergo di Cicerone among its recommended inns.

The third book, listed as "Forsyth" by Severn, is *Remarks on Antiquities, Arts, and Letters during an Excursion in Italy in the Years 1802 and 1803* by Joseph Forsyth (1763–1815), first published by Cadell and Davies in 1813 (REM1) and later reprinted by John Murray in 1816 (REM2). It contains a detailed account of Pisa, its buildings, university, poets and climate, so it might have been purchased by Keats or given to him when he was mulling over the Shelleys' invitation. Shelley himself thought that the work was "worth reading" (PBSL, p. 89), and Byron presented a copy of it to the Italian poet Ippolito Pindemonte (BLJ, p. 233). The latter edition of the book, which is likely to be the one Keats took with him to Italy, is of particular interest, because it contains a long biographical note by Forsyth's son Isaac, from which the author emerges as a talented classical scholar suffering from a "tendency to pulmonary complaints". Leaving his native Scotland, Forsyth tried to fulfil his life's ambition: to tour through Italy. His main interests were the classics, architecture and Italian poetry (his pages on Alfieri must have piqued Keats's curiosity, because he bought an edition of his works soon after arriving in Rome). What is remarkable is that this is a tale of someone who had recovered from a lung disease, someone who had left his country in his late thirties and survived to be over fifty, after many vicissitudes on the Continent. We can imagine this book being presented to Keats as a gift by one of his well-wishing friends, in an effort to lift his spirits, cheer him on and give him some hope of restoring his health.

Sometimes small details can be very revealing.

The first edition of this book was written during the Covid pandemic of 2020–21, when access to libraries and archives was restricted or denied altogether to visitors and researchers. Most of my research had to be conducted remotely, and I have already expressed my debt of gratitude to all the institutions that enabled me to complete my first round of enquiries by supplying scanned documents by email.

Nothing, however, can replace research carried out in person. What escapes two-dimensional online reading may jump out when leafing through a book or a letter. Careful consultation of material contained in the same folders as the documents of interest may yield precious detail or evidence. Browsing through books, papers and archival records that are only in part relevant to the research in hand can lead to surprising connections, and these, in turn, to major new revelations.

With the full reopening of libraries, archives and museums at the end of the pandemic, I was able to conduct extensive research *in situ* or instruct assistants to consult material on my behalf.

A visit to Keats House in Hampstead provided a definitive answer to the question of where the poet found inspiration for the epitaph which gives this book its title. The chance to spend longer hours at the British Library allowed me to consult books that I had been able to read only in part or in snippets, prompting me to rewrite entire pages or notes. A trip to the Henry Moore Institute in Leeds produced some interesting findings about life in Rome at the time of Keats's death, urging me to reconsider some unwarranted generalizations and assumptions. As I looked for Doctor Clark's Roman address in the archives of the Wellcome Collection, a very interesting letter by William Ewing concerning Joseph Severn turned up, tucked away inside another. Searching through the catalogue of Eton College Library, I came across a short, unpublished account by Walter Severn, dating from September 1878, of conversations with his ailing father about his friendship with Keats, as well as notes about his fateful meeting, six years later, with William Sharp, which led him to commission *The Life and Letters of Joseph Severn*.

But the greatest discoveries awaited me in Rome. At the Archivio Storico Diocesano I was able to check, confirm, amend and add to the information W. Jackson Bate had been supplied by Vera Cacciatore, a former curator of the Keats–Shelley Memorial House, from the *Stati delle anime* registers. And after a tenacious search into the intricate depths of the Archivio di Stato di Roma – and only thanks to my brother Mirco's intuition and the kind assistance of several archivists working there – I was able to unearth what is probably the most significant addition to this book: the fact, more or less known but so far undocumented, that formal charges had been pressed against Keats by the local police before his death in Rome.

With the emergence of so many new documents – Anna Angeletti's handwritten petition, a letter by the governor of Rome, a report by the police health advisor, the eminent doctor Domenico Morichini – a fresh field of research at once opened in front of me, leading in many different directions and promising further revelations.

The search for the elusive footprints of historical truth continues.

Alessandro Gallenzi
– London, 23rd February 2024

WRITTEN IN WATER

Keats's Final Journey

Introduction

Had you been sitting here two hundred years ago, at this time of day, and looked across the Thames, you might have seen a brig gliding past on its way to Naples, carrying a dying poet and a young painter. It is impossible for us to know what the two passengers were thinking or feeling as they sailed towards the estuary, just as it is to visualize with any degree of accuracy what they saw along the banks from the deck of their ship, but through an effort of imagination, by an accumulation of detail, contextual historical evidence and logical reasoning, we can create a mental picture that, if not real, is at least a close approximation of reality.

I became interested in John Keats as a student in Italy. Looking through my diaries, I see I translated his 'Ode on a Grecian Urn' in 1988 and the beginning of his 'Ode to a Nightingale' in 1992. I believe I first tried my hand at a translation of 'On First Looking into Chapman's Homer' as early as 1986. My initial enthusiasm for Keats has not diminished: I have remained a faithful admirer of his poetry all my life, with frequent pilgrimages to his grave in Rome both before and after I moved to Britain in 1997, and although I accept that there are flaws in his writing, I don't think that these eclipse his merits as a poet.

Over the last few years I have had the privilege of curating an English edition of Keats's *Complete Poems* and publishing an Italian translation of his *Letters*, a book that has always been a particular favourite of mine. While annotating these volumes, I consulted a great number of reference books and resources, and was surprised to find that, when it comes to the last chapter of Keats's life – his "posthumous existence", as he himself called it[1] – the information is based in large part on secondary sources, such as the now-discredited *Life and Letters of Joseph Severn* by William Sharp (1892), if not on unverifiable inference and sheer guesswork.

The various "definitive" biographies of our poet are often at odds in their accounts. Nicholas Roe tells us that Keats woke on 17th September 1820, the day of his departure for Naples, "to fine weather and a fair wind", while Andrew Motion has him leaving "under an overcast sky".[2] Roe declares that Keats and Severn "cast off at seven", whereas Aileen Ward sets their departure at "mid-morning".[3]

Two days after his landing in Naples, Roe puts Keats in a carriage on the Strada di Toledo, "where the noisy life of Naples carried on with cries of 'Pane!', 'Panzarotti!', 'Acqua!' and 'Vino – Vino Rosso!'" and where the poet is supposed to have seen

men haggling over sardines; hungry children at pizza ovens; smoky stalls selling chestnuts; carpenters' benches and shoe-makers' stools; water- and lemonade-sellers; dogs, chickens and a pig in the gutter; corner kitchens with steaming pots; dung-carts, carts full of grapes and wagonloads of melons; a bagpipe player with dancing puppets; two lawyers, arm in arm, coming back from court; a monk begging; labourers with striped red caps; letter-writers at portable desks; and then a funeral bier, all crimson and gold, followed by mourners in masks and white gowns.[4]

This is all very colourful, and fits the stereotypical idea we may have of Naples and its inhabitants at that time, but it is not based on any actual first-hand account, letter or diary entry: if not altogether fabricated, it is pieced together from one or more coeval texts and placed there to suit the author's romantic notion, as well as the readers' expectation, of what Keats *may* have seen that day after getting off the *Maria Crowther*.

Does it matter whether it was sunny or cloudy when Keats left London – whether his ship weighed anchor earlier or later in the morning? I think it does, if there is a way of checking through primary sources. If that proves impossible, it is far better to remain silent. And is it acceptable for biographers to fill the inevitable gaps in a person's life with touches of the picturesque or frolics of the imagination? In my opinion, deduction is allowed, but only if accompanied by some relevant testimony or circumstantial evidence. It is true that biography should not be reduced to a dry scientific exposition of facts, but at the same time honest biographers should refrain from embellishing their subject if they cannot substantiate or document their claims.

With this in mind, I revisited what we know of Keats's last few months in Italy, a period in his life which has always struck me as of immense interest, and found the various accounts inadequate. Most of the biographies devote no more than thirty pages to the interval between his departure from England and his death – some of them, including Roe's, the most recent, fewer than twenty.

It is as if stepping out of his country Keats did indeed enter a sort of afterlife. This was, without a doubt, what the poet felt himself: in his first letter from Naples, he describes how the port "looks like a dream" and how he "do[es] not feel in the world" any more.[5] After making a final "awkward bow" in his bitter letter to Charles Brown from Rome,[6] Keats falls silent, and we hear his voice only through Severn's diary and letters. Yet he was far from dead: he may not at times have felt "at all concerned in the thousand novelties around [him]",[7] and have been forced to lie low for long spells because of his illness, but Severn tells us in his diaries and letters how he often revived and was able to stay through dinner, crack jokes, walk around, visit places, and even ride a horse. In short, he and his mind were very much alive until the very end.[8]

So, is it possible, after more than a century of scholarship and a dozen biographies, to add anything new to what has already been said about this period of Keats's life? A quick look through some archival material enabled me to find a number of documents that do not seem to have been consulted by previous researchers, perhaps because they are written in another language or stored in Italian archives. This prompted me to extend my research further, and I discovered that there is a vast quantity of papers and records that has gone untapped. I realized that, if I could not rewrite the story of Keats's last months in Italy, I could at least correct many of the mistakes made by previous biographers and fill some of the lacunae by using documentary evidence. All of a sudden some of the references in Severn's diaries and letters became clearer, new names and details emerged, and many of the elusive characters that appear in them took on a definite shape, offering a more vivid context and creating a fuller picture of the events.

That is why I have decided to write this book. I am not a professional scholar, nor do I pretend to be one, but I shall as far as possible use first-hand sources and question all the romantic assumptions that have been superimposed by previous biographers. The result, I hope, will not be an arid, unpoetic narration of facts, but a historical account that aims to be as close as possible to the truth – at least to the kind of truth that we, citizens of a far-removed world, can conjure up at a distance of two hundred years.

– London, 17th September 2020

BEFORE THE DEPARTURE

KEATS KNEW HE WAS A DYING MAN when he agreed to leave England for Italy. His medical training, the experience of losing his mother and his youngest brother to consumption, as well as his own sense of being born under an ill star, left him in no doubt: when he started coughing blood in February 1820, he knew he was doomed.

Yet death was perhaps the least of his worries at the time of his departure. Keats was not just in a bad way, but in a bad place too – "unmeridian'd, and objectless", as he had confided some time before to his friend Joseph Severn.[1] If he was prepared to face the voyage and almost certain death with the stoic attitude of a soldier marching up to a battery, it was the thought of the people and the situation he was leaving behind that was at the forefront of his preoccupations.[2]

His love for Fanny Brawne was as intense as it was fitful. After becoming engaged to her in secret towards the end of 1819, Keats had discovered the true nature of his disease and had tried to break off the arrangement the following February. Forced by illness to live apart from her, and unable to see her other than in fleeting appearances at the window, he had vented his spleen in a series of cruel, at times even insolent letters – not of the sort one writes to a nineteen-year-old sweetheart. He accused her of being fickle, flirtatious, self-centred – of preferring to go out and enjoy herself rather than to stay at home in sympathetic confinement. He became more and more possessive and para-noid, to the verge of obsession. It is easy to justify these letters as the product of a morbid state of mind, but the truth is that Keats, like every passionate, jealous young lover, wanted Fanny all for himself. "The persuasion that I shall see her no more will

9

kill me," he wrote to Charles Brown in a letter from Naples of 1st November 1820. "I cannot q—— My dear Brown, I should have had her when I was in health, and I should have remained well. I can bear to die—I cannot bear to leave her."[3] The idea of dying more than a thousand miles away from her, of being forgotten and replaced in her heart by another man, was "one thought enough to kill [him]".[4]

But Miss Brawne was not the only person Keats was loath to leave. Apart from his many friends – some of them very close, such as Charles Brown, who would have been the poet's companion of choice for his voyage – there was his seventeen-year-old sister, also called Fanny, the only family member still in England after the death of his brother Tom in December 1818 and his brother George's marriage and emigration to America in the summer of the same year. At the time of Keats's departure for Italy, Fanny was living in Walthamstow, in the home of her guardian, Richard Abbey. Much to the poet's frustration, Abbey had withdrawn her from school at the beginning of 1819, and was now making it as difficult as possible for him to see her, even objecting to his writing letters to her. Being the eldest brother, and no doubt feeling responsible for her, Keats must have been racked by guilt at abandoning his sister to the care of the strict and stuffy Abbeys until she came of age. His last thoughts, before closing his final letter in Rome, were still with her.

Keats's relationship with his brother George had been very strong before he left for Kentucky with his wife Georgiana. "George has ever been more than a brother to me," Keats wrote in August 1818, "he has been my greatest friend."[5] Although two years younger than the poet, George was taller and looked older. He had introduced John to many of those who would later become his friends. Being an active, enterprising and energetic young man, he had taken charge of the household's administration when the three brothers had been living together in London and later in Hampstead. He had acted as John's agent in his negotiations with his publishers and looked after all money matters on his behalf. In short, he had shielded his elder brother from life's practicalities. As Keats himself put it, "George always stood between me and any dealings with the world."[6] George's migration to America had been a great blow to him: now he had to fend for himself – to "buffet [the world]", "take [his] stand upon some vantage ground and begin to fight", "choose between despair & Energy".[7] Indolent and lackadaisical by nature, Keats always strove for energy and fell back on despair. Unlike his brother George, he didn't seem to know the value of money, and was rather careless with it. He gave out loans he could ill afford, landing himself in ever-deeper debt and being often forced to require, in his turn, his friends' financial assistance to get by.

In more recent times, Keats's close bond with his brother had weakened – and it was to do more with money than with George's absence from England. Over the years the two brothers had kept no accounts of the financial transactions between them, and often lent or gifted money to each other. Matters, however, came to a head in January 1820, when George rushed back from America in desperate straits following the failure of his early investments in Kentucky. He went to see Abbey, who was still controlling the purse strings of the Keats children's legacy, and persuaded him to liquidate Tom's inheritance. He also asked his brother to loan him a large portion of his own share. The details are not altogether clear – and this led to long and bitter disputes between George and his brother's friends after his death – but the fact is that of the £800 or so that was supposed to be divided in equal parts between the three surviving siblings only £70 ended up in Keats's pocket, which wasn't even enough to clear his debts.[8] As George returned to America in late January with the sizeable sum of £700, Keats's closest friends – among them Charles Brown and Fanny Brawne – railed against him for the way he had treated his elder brother, aware as he was of his poor health and reduced circumstances.[9] Since no more money was to be had from Abbey for the foreseeable future, Keats – who had spent most of his inheritance on his aborted medical studies – was forced to live off the generosity of his publishers and the charity of his friends until the end of his life. George was no doubt very fond of his brother, but he did not realize the profound implications his actions would have for the last year of Keats's life.

John's chronic lack of money helps to explain the restless, frantic, itinerant life he led in his final years. It is also a key to understanding his perpetual irresolution and some of the odd choices he made as he tried to juggle his literary ambitions, his financial constraints and his love interests.

Although Keats had decided to give up his medical training and devote himself to poetry at the end of 1816, there were many moments of misgiving later in his life, such as when he considered combining poetry with medicine, learning at the same time a little law, or going to Edinburgh and studying to be a physician, or looking for a position with an apothecary, or moving to Westminster to become a journalist and theatre reviewer, or working as a tea broker, or boarding an Indiaman as a ship's surgeon for a few years.[10] His dream, of course, was to earn his living through poetry and, if not sell tens of thousands of books like Lord Byron, at least be successful enough to be able to afford to travel abroad. "If [his] Books would help [him] to it," he wished to "take all Europe in turn".[11] Later, when he met Fanny Brawne, he dreamt he "might spend a pleasant Year at Berne or Zurich" with his beloved, or even emigrate to a remote island with her.[12]

The trouble was that Keats's success as an author was very much still "in nubibus" at the time of his departure for Italy, and there was very little chance anything might "shower" soon.[13] His poetical career had started off in the most inauspicious way. His first volume, *Poems* (March 1817), "launched amid the cheers and fond anticipations of all his circle", as Keats's friend Charles Cowden Clarke later recollected, rather than "creat[ing] a sensation in the literary world", turned out to be a failure.[14] The book was brought out by a new publishing house founded by Leigh Hunt's friend Charles Ollier and his brother James. In all likelihood, it was published on commission, as was common in those days for the works of little-known or first-time authors. On that basis, Keats was to pay for all the production and advertising costs – thought to be between £25 and £30 for a print run of 250 copies, not an insubstantial sum – and retain a 90 per cent share of the proceeds from any sales or subscriptions.[15] If the book enjoyed a moderate success, Keats would recover his costs, and in the event of selling out he would make a good profit, more than doubling his initial investment.

But the reality was very different. His association with the "Cockney School of Poetry" led by Leigh Hunt – to whom he addressed two sonnets in the collection, including the dedicatory one – and the radical circle of writers that gathered at Hunt's house in Hampstead and found expression in the columns of his weekly political journal, *The Examiner*, made the young poet an easy target for the censorial snub of the literary establishment. The appearance of Keats's *Poems* was met by a resounding silence, with the exception of a brief positive review in the *Monthly Magazine* and two longer ones penned by friends: one, by John Hamilton Reynolds in *The Champion*, full of praise – the other, by George Felton Mathew in the *London Review*, brimming with carping remarks and damning criticism:

> We cannot [...] advance for our author equal claim to public notice for maturity of thought, propriety of feeling, or felicity of style. But while we blame the slovenly independance of his versification, we must allow that thought, sentiment, and feeling, particularly in the active use and poetical display of them, belong more to the maturity of summer fruits than to the infancy of vernal blossoms.[16]

As Cowden Clarke wrote in his memoir, "The book might have emerged in Timbuctoo with far stronger chance of fame and approbation." Although "Keats had not made the slightest demonstration of political opinion," the fact that he was a protégé – or at least an associate – of Leigh Hunt "was motive enough with the dictators of that day to thwart the endeavours of a young aspirant".[17]

Whatever the reasons for the reviewers' indifference and the readers' lack of interest, sales were very poor, and well below everyone's expectations. This prompted immediate recriminations on the part of the author, who had squandered a large sum of money on the project, as well as questions about the publishers' handling of the volume's promotion. Although in the years that followed Charles and James Ollier went on to publish books by Hunt, Shelley, Lamb and others, their relationship with the young poet came to an abrupt end: not even two months had elapsed since the publication of *Poems* before they announced that they no longer wanted anything to do with Keats. In a tetchy letter to his brother George, who had perhaps overstepped the mark by demanding an account of the sales, they wrote:

> Sir,—We regret that your brother ever requested us to publish his book, or that our opinion of its talent should have led us to acquiesce in undertaking it. We are, however, much obliged to you for relieving us from the unpleasant necessity of declining any further connexion with it.[18]

The remaining stock was later transferred to Keats's new publishers, Taylor and Hessey, from whom it could still be purchased in 1824.[19]

This was not a good start for a young, ambitious writer, but Keats remained undeterred and began planning a long mythological poem, *Endymion*, which he hoped would be more popular with the reading public and find favour among the critics. This was to be published by Taylor and Hessey – who would later bring out the works of John Clare, William Hazlitt and Samuel Taylor Coleridge, among others – a firm with an already established reputation. Determined to succeed and wishing to avoid the distractions of the city, Keats borrowed money from his publishers against future sales and found himself a retreat on the Isle of Wight where he could live on the cheap and work away at his poem without interruption. Having set himself

the unenviable task of "mak[ing] 4000 Lines of one bare cir-
cumstance and fill[ing] them with Poetry", he got down to the
challenge – at first with dogged purposefulness, but then with
an increasing sense of pushing through treacle.[20] It wasn't so
much that he had grown tired of living away from the city, at
the expense of others, or that he was falling prey to his habitual
indolence: it was more that he was maturing as a poet, and being
a merciless critic of his own work he soon realized that his poem
was fuzzy, rather shapeless and written in antiquated-sounding
language which would be out of tune with current literary taste
and fail to resonate with a modern readership. He knew, deep
down, that rather than covering himself in poetical glory, he
was going to make a fool of himself.

But he was committed now, and he owed his publishers fifty
pounds and a 4,000-line poem.[21] So he pressed ahead and, against
his better judgement, published *Endymion* in May 1818. Trying
to pre-empt the inevitable criticism the poem would attract,
he appended a preface to the public – "a thing I cannot help
looking upon as an Enemy, and which I cannot address without
feelings of Hostility", as he wrote to his friend Reynolds.[22] The
first, longer version of this preface contained sentences such as:
"[T]his Poem must rather be considered as an endeavour than
a thing accomplish'd"; "I should have kept it back for a year or
two, knowing it to be so faulty"; "I here declare that I have not
any particular affection for any particular phrase, word or letter
in the whole affair."[23] His publishers and friends "all agree[d]
that the thing [was] bad", and persuaded him to make some
changes.[24] The preface he ended up publishing was a little more
subdued, but it still bristled with flippancy and self-deprecation:

Knowing within myself the manner in which this Poem has
been produced, it is not without a feeling of regret that I
make it public.

What manner I mean, will be quite clear to the reader,
who must soon perceive great inexperience, immaturity, and
every error denoting a feverish attempt, rather than a deed

accomplished. The two first books, and indeed the two last, I feel sensible are not of such completion as to warrant their passing the press; nor should they if I thought a year's castigation would do them any good;—it will not: the foundations are too sandy. It is just that this youngster should die away: a sad thought for me, if I had not some hope that while it is dwindling I may be plotting, and fitting myself for verses fit to live.

This may be speaking too presumptuously, and may deserve a punishment: but no feeling man will be forward to inflict it: he will leave me alone, with the conviction that there is not a fiercer hell than the failure in a great object. This is not written with the least atom of purpose to forestall criticisms of course, but from the desire I have to conciliate men who are competent to look, and who do look with a zealous eye, to the honour of English literature.

The imagination of a boy is healthy, and the mature imagination of a man is healthy; but there is a space of life between, in which the soul is in a ferment, the character undecided, the way of life uncertain, the ambition thick-sighted: thence proceeds mawkishness, and all the thousand bitters which those men I speak of must necessarily taste in going over the following pages.

I hope I have not in too late a day touched the beautiful mythology of Greece, and dulled its brightness: for I wish to try once more, before I bid it farewell.[25]

The poet's close circle of friends knew that this preface, with its apologetic, condescending tone, was a serious error of judgement. It smacked of false modesty – although Keats himself denied that there was "any thing like Hunt in it".[26] His dedication "to the memory of Thomas Chatterton" was another bad mistake: it was as if Keats were portraying himself as the new young genius misunderstood by the world – which sounded affected, if not downright infantile. All this didn't bode well for the book, but the ink had now dried on its pages, and Keats had to face the reading public and the critics once more.

And this time he was not granted the reprieve of silence and indifference: the mace of the literary establishment came down with full force, tearing the poem and its author to shreds. *Blackwood's Edinburgh Magazine* – which had already opened its skirmishes against Hunt and his young protégé in May, calling the former "the King of the Cockneys" and the latter "an amiable but infatuated bardling" – published a scathing review of *Endymion* in its August issue.[27] After a long personal attack on the "uneducated and flimsy strapling", the "fanciful tea-drinker", "good Johnny Keats", it proceeded to a detailed analysis of the poem, claiming that "it ha[d] just as much to do with Greece as it ha[d] with 'old Tartary the fierce'" and "ventur[ing] to make one small prophecy, that his bookseller will not a second time venture £50 upon any thing he can write". The review concluded with a blunt piece of advice for the poet which could have issued from the lips of his guardian Richard Abbey:

> It is a better and wiser thing to be a starved apothecary than a starved poet; so back to the shop Mr John, back to "plasters, pills, and ointment boxes," &c. But, for Heaven's sake, young Sangrado, be a little more sparing of extenuatives and soporifics in your practice than you have been in your poetry.

The comments of this anonymous reviewer must have hurt, but nothing could prepare Keats for the barbs and vitriol of another influential literary journal, the *Quarterly Review*, which printed a savage critique of *Endymion* in its issue for April 1818, published around 27th September.[28] Alongside the personal broadsides against Keats and the "Cockney School of Poetry", of which Hunt "aspire[d] to be the hierophant", the review contained a savage lambasting of the poem, which exposed all its stylistic and linguistic shortcomings. It started by picking holes in Keats's ill-judged preface, and went on to criticize the vagueness, diffuseness and disjointedness of the work itself. Then, giving a number of specific examples from Book I – the only one the reviewer confessed to having been able "to get through", despite "efforts almost as superhuman as the story itself" – it showed how the contrived rhyming appeared to dictate the narration, and listed various prosodic failings, as well as pointing out the bizarre use of nouns as verbs and verbs as nouns, and the creation of odd poetical neologisms.

This was more than a simple hatchet job: both the poem and its author had been altogether rubbished and ridiculed. It would be difficult to recover from such swingeing criticism. And, what was worse, Keats knew that it was well founded, though motivated in part by partisan bias. As he confessed to his publisher James Augustus Hessey early in October, he agreed with one of the commentators that *Endymion* was a "slipshod" work.[29]

It was only to be expected that many of the potential readers would accept the critical verdict of *Blackwood's* and the *Quarterly Review* and steer clear of the book. For a short while Keats and his friends entertained the hope that "the attempt to crush [him...] had only brought [him] more into notice"[30] – but they were wrong. The old publishing dictum that "any publicity is good publicity" did not hold true in this case. Sales were pitiful, and, after a brief stir of interest, came to a sudden stop. The book resulted in a loss of £130 for the publishers, and many of the original 500 copies printed ended up being remaindered after the poet's death.[31]

Were these negative reviews and the commercial failure of his first two books enough to "snuff out" Keats, as Byron wrote in a skittish stanza of his *Don Juan*[32] – and as many others, including Hunt and his friends, believed? Of course not. Any writer who has faith in his own talents, as Keats did, is able to learn from negative comments, shrug them off and move on. Critical approval can be a source of encouragement to most young authors, but in Keats's case his greatest spur was his own "domestic criticism".[33] "[W]hen I feel I am right," he wrote to Hessey, "no external praise can give me such a glow as my own solitary reperception & ratification of what is fine. [...] I was never afraid of failure; for I would sooner fail than not be among the greatest."[34] A few days later, still licking his wounds after the excoriating critique in the *Quarterly Review*, he had in part recovered his old self-assurance, and the matter had been settled in his mind: "I think I shall be among the English Poets after my death."[35]

This is not to say that Keats was not shaken by the reviews – on the contrary: they were a huge blow to his confidence. Coming at a time when he was embarking on an ambitious new project, the long Miltonian poem *Hyperion*, they must have insinuated the worm of doubt into every line he wrote, making him more self-conscious and more critical of his own poetry.

Keats wrote most of the poems for which he is remembered today during the last two years of his life. They tend to be short pieces not at first intended for publication. On the other hand, many of the longer works he wrote in the same period – such as the two *Hyperion* fragments, *The Cap and Bells* and *King Stephen* – remained incomplete and are all but forgotten today. The various upheavals that occurred in his personal life, including the death of his brother Tom and his own declining health, might help to explain why he decided to abandon them, but another factor must have been that Keats had become dissatisfied with them from an artistic point of view and, knowing their flaws, was reluctant to engage with the public and the critics after the failure of his "little book of verses" and *Endymion*, a poem "which [he] would willingly [have] take[n] the trouble to unwrite, if possible".[36] Explaining to his friend Reynolds why he had given up the revised version of *Hyperion*, he wrote: "[T]here were too many Miltonic inversions in it."[37] Even the works he did complete left him, more often than not, dissatisfied. Writing to his publishers' literary advisor Richard Woodhouse, he explained why he persisted in not publishing his poem *Isabella*:

It is too smokeable—I can get it smoak'd at the Carpenters shaving chimney much more cheaply—There is too much inexperience of life [written "live"], and simplicity of knowle[d]ge in it—which might do very well after one's death—but not while one is alive. [...] I intend to use more finesse with the Public. It is possible to write fine things which cannot be laugh'd at in any way. Isabella is what I should call were I a reviewer "A weak-sided Poem" with an amusing sober-sadness about it. [...] But this will not do to be public.[38]

Keats didn't just want to be a successful author. In the field of poetry, he aimed to surpass Spenser and Milton – in the field of tragedy, his ambition was "to make as great a revolution in modern dramatic writing as Kean ha[d] done in acting".[39] He was not interested in "a seat on the benches of a myriad aristocracy in Letters":[40] nothing short of being "among the English poets" would do for him. He was very conscious, as he started writing *Endymion*, that his first few lines were just a "Pin's Point", and "that so many of these Pin points [went] to form a Bodkin point (God send I end not my Life with a bare Bodkin, in its modern sense)," he quipped, alluding to Hamlet's soliloquy, "and that it requ[i]re[d] a thousand bodkins to make a Spear bright enough to throw any light to posterity".[41] The reference is of course to Shake*spea*re, whose achievements he hoped to emulate.

But he saw the process of establishing himself as an author as "nothing but continual uphill Journeying".[42] More than once in his poetry and in his letters he voiced his concern that he may not have enough time to achieve the grand objective he had set for himself.

> Oh, for ten years, that I may overwhelm
> Myself in poesy! So I may do the deed
> That my own soul has to itself decreed,

he had written as early as 1816 in 'Sleep and Poetry'.[43] His great-
est fear, as we have seen above, was not so much failure as "to be
so journeying and miss the Goal at last".[44] Keats was haunted by
this thought, and the last few months of his life were blighted,
more than anything else, by a strong sense of recrimination.
"God knows how it would have been—" he wrote to Brown in
his last letter from Rome.[45]

What made it all the more unpleasant for Keats is that he
could not carry out his journey to literary greatness at leisure
in the ivory tower of his own room: rather, it had to take place
under public scrutiny and under the constraint of time – which
he felt was against him. And although he claimed that he "never
wrote one single Line of Poetry with the least Shadow of public
thought", the damage he suffered to his purse and reputation
after the failure of his first two books must have rankled with
him, exacerbating his hostility towards the public and his dis-
gust for the literary world and the whole publishing process.[46]

Keats, in some ways, resembles another fame-obsessed poet,
Francesco Petrarca, who hoped to outclass Dante with his
terza-rima poem *Triumphs* and eclipse Virgil with his Latin epic
Africa. Petrarch devoted the greater part of his creative endeav-
ours to writing and revising these works over several decades.
Although he still considered them unfinished at his death, he
thought they would secure his posthumous fame. Instead, he
ended up being remembered for the "*rime sparse*" collected in
his *Canzoniere*, which he in fact renounced and deprecated.

But how did Keats rate his shorter works? Was he as dismiss-
ive as Shelley, who branded them as "insignificant enough",
"worth little", if compared to his fragmentary poem *Hyperion*?
We don't know. He didn't seem to have much confidence in
his two great odes, which he published in *Annals of the Fine
Arts*, a journal with a very limited readership, as if to shield
them from wider public notice.[47] His only comment on 'Ode
to a Nightingale' was that his brother George's copy was like
"an account of the b[l]ack hole at Calcutta on an ice bergh".[48]
I am not sure what we are to make of this remark. 'La Belle

Dame sans Merci' was published in *The Indicator* under the pseudonym "Caviare" – perhaps a sign of insecurity, perhaps a mischievous dig at his critics and the ignorant public, as if to say that "'Twas caviare to the general".[49] "Most of the Poems in the volume I send you," he wrote to Shelley just before his departure for Italy, referring to his final collection of poetry, which had been published the previous month and included some of his best work to date, "[...] would never have been publish'd but from a hope of gain."[50]

Even taking into account that these words, addressed as they were from an author to a rival poet, contain a certain swagger, there may be some truth in Keats's last statement. Unhappy with the reception of his first two books and his literary achievements so far, aware that his life would be cut short, preventing him from fulfilling his potential, during his last few months in England Keats turned in despair from "living to write" to "writing for a living". More anxious than ever for money, he wanted to show that he could be a commercial author if he only decided to put his mind to it: "I feel every confidence that if I choose I may be a popular writer," he wrote to his publisher John Taylor.[51] At the same time, he wished to take revenge on the literati and deride the gullibility and poor taste of the reading public. As he worked, in late 1819, on the unfinished fairy-tale burlesque *The Cap and Bells*, perhaps the last poem he ever wrote, Keats toyed with the idea of publishing it under the authorship of "Lucy Vaughan Lloyd", no doubt with the aim of hoaxing the literary world.

Just before that, Keats had tried to find instant success as an author for the stage, dashing out in less than three months a historical tragedy in verse, *Otho the Great*. It was a cooperative effort: his friend Charles Brown – who, a few years earlier, had written the comic opera *Narensky, or The Road to Yaroslaf*, which had been produced at Drury Lane in January 1814 and netted him £300 and a lifetime admission to that theatre – provided the subject, while Keats churned out the blank verse. Alongside the poet's declared ambition to make a great revolution in modern dramatic writing there was another one: "To upset the drawling of the blue stocking literary world".[52] And, as he angled for a new loan from his publisher, a further, less idealistic aim emerged: "To share moderate profits [from it]".[53] "If it succeeds," he explained to his brother George, "[it] will enable me to sell what I may have in manuscript to good advantage."[54] But Drury Lane wouldn't commit to staging the play until the following season, and Covent Garden rejected it. *Otho* was never performed, and Keats's hopes that his tragedy might prove to "be a bank to [him]" and "lift [him] out of the mire" soon vanished, together with his dream of becoming a dramatic beacon for his age.[55]

This is where Keats was when his illness took a turn for the worse during the early months of 1820. By July his doctor, George Darling, realizing that another winter in England would kill him, advised him to seek the milder climates of southern Europe in order to try to restore his health.[56] Shipping off a consumptive patient to another country was the remedy of choice in those days, but was seen by some as a risky and somewhat desperate measure. Contemporary medicine recommended it only for those in the very early stages of the disease, as a kind of preventive measure rather than as a curative one. As one of the leading experts in pulmonary disorders at the time, Doctor James Clark, wrote in a book published that year:

> When [...] suppuration has actually taken place in the substance of the tubercles, my opinion is, that little or no benefit is to be expected from a change of climate in the cure of the disease; and, further, that by the great and numerous inconveniences and discomforts of so long a journey, the fatal termination of it is more frequently accelerated than protracted. That is very frequently the case in the very advanced stages of the disease, such as I have frequently met with on the Continent shortly after their arrival from England.[57]

Judging from his symptoms, it was clear that Keats was one such case, and that there was little hope of his ever coming back to England alive.

At first Keats was reluctant to leave: he felt it was hopeless, and hated the thought of dying in a foreign country, away from the people who loved him and cared for him.[58] In the end, however, encouraged by all of his friends, he agreed, and began making preparations for the voyage.

Among the more common destinations for pulmonary invalids were the south of France and the Italian cities of Pisa, Rome and Naples. The initial plan must have been for Keats to voyage or journey to Rome, where he was to spend a year under the personal care of Doctor Clark himself, who had settled there and "promise[d] to befriend [him] in any way".[59] Born in Cullen in Scotland, Doctor Clark had returned to Britain that summer to marry Barbara "Minnie" Stephen in Edinburgh on 30th August.[60] Keats was supposed to be introduced to Clark in London, but the meeting never took place.[61] It is believed that the intermediary may have been Doctor Darling, himself a Scot, or Taylor's fellow publishers Thomas and George Underwood, who had just published Clark's *Medical Notes*.[62] It is also possible that Keats's publishers had contacted Clark on their own initiative.[63]

As Taylor and Hessey started getting information about the journey, Keats received a kind letter from Percy Bysshe Shelley and his wife Mary, inviting him to take up residence with them in Pisa for the winter.[64] He gave this proposal serious consideration, and asked Taylor to look into "a Passage to Leghorn by Sea". "Will you join that to your enquiries," he added, "and, if you can, give a peep at the Birth, if the Vessel is in our river?"[65] Two days later he wrote to Shelley: "If I do not take advantage of your invitation it will be prevented by a circumstance I have very much at heart to prophesy—"[66] It was not death, however, nor the lack of available vessels, that in the end induced him to decline the Shelleys' offer, but a simple change of plan.[67]

"My present intention," he announced to his sister Fanny a few weeks later, "is to stay some time at Naples and then to proceed to Rome where I shall find several friends or at least several acquaintances."[68] Adding an extra leg to an already arduous trip seems odd and counter-intuitive. The usual way of reaching Rome from England would have been by travelling through France to Genoa and from there by vessel or hired carriage to Rome – a well-trodden route. Shelley's invitation would have made this itinerary even more appealing, offering free accommodation and congenial company in Pisa for the winter. What prompted the choice of a longer passage and a stopover in Naples – that "paradise inhabited by devils", as the saying went?

The recent *carbonari* insurrection of 1st–6th July 1820 had turned the city from a popular tourist attraction to a dangerous destination. The autocratic King Ferdinand I of the Two Sicilies, "Re Nasone" ("King Big-Snout"), had just about managed to hang on to his throne – which had been restored to him from the French only a few years before, in 1815 – by offering his subjects a constitution along the lines of the Spanish one of 1812 and by transferring his powers to his son Francis, Duke of Calabria, who posed as a more liberal-minded ruler. The anti-Bourbon movement had found expression in the ineffectual Neapolitan parliament – elected at the end of August and operative from 1st October 1820 – which was dominated by a moderate faction of senior officials and military officers, for the most part former supporters of Joachim Murat. The revolutionary wing of the *carboneria*, which had infiltrated the lower ranks of the army and represented the interests of the lower middle classes and of the rural masses, had only a few seats in the Neapolitan parliament, and was now very restless. There was widespread fear that this insurrectionary element would become even more radicalized and give rise to a full-scale revolt – which is what had happened in Palermo in mid-June 1820, when the revolutionaries had demanded a constitution, parliamentary representation and the restoration of a separate Kingdom of Sicily under Bourbon rule. The Neapolitan government was forced to send, at the end of August, a detachment of 6,500 troops to Sicily to stem the uprising, and was able to re-establish the monarchic rule on the island only in late November, after various diplomatic attempts and bloody clashes.

Worried that the flame of rebellion could spread to Naples, Ferdinand sought military help from the Austrians – his natural allies, since his late consort Maria Carolina, the de-facto ruler of his kingdoms for many years, was the daughter of Maria Theresa of Habsburg – arguing that a revolt in his kingdom could spark similar insurrections elsewhere and endanger peace in the whole of Europe. But an Austrian military intervention in Naples, which was opposed by Britain and France, could itself tip the balance of power on the Continent and lead to all-out war. The situation was tense, the streets teeming with soldiers – the capital of the Kingdom of the Two Sicilies was a powder keg waiting to be ignited. A dispatch published in the September issue of *The Examiner* warned of the Austrians' pending invasion:

BRUSSELS, SEPT. 12.—Various accounts from Germany, received by the Mail of this day, agree in stating the following intelligence:—That the Austrian troops have received orders to accelerate their march for Italy, and that their numbers have been further increased; that in consequence of an arrangement with his Holiness the Pope, a numerous Austrian army will enter the States of the Church: it will occupy the Principalities of Benevento and Ponte Corvo, which have been a prey to anarchy since some factious individuals have attempted to form them into Republics.[69]

Keats and his friends must have been well aware of the unstable political situation in Naples and the risk of sojourning there at that particular juncture. Yet the poet could not be expected to turn up in Rome before Doctor Clark had returned from Britain (whether or not his marriage had been followed by a honeymoon) and was given enough time to make arrangements for the poet's accommodation.

Also, Keats may have received medical advice that the voyage itself might have a restorative effect on him. "I [...] feel very impatient to get on board as the sea air is expected to be of great benefit to me," he wrote to his sister just before his departure.[70] More than anything else, he might have been spurred by financial considerations, since travelling on board a merchantman was much less expensive than journeying by land.[71] Strapped for cash as he was, he may have just gone for the cheaper option.

It is not to be supposed, however, that Keats and Severn were travelling blind to a foreign country in the midst of such a crisis. It would have been irresponsible of Keats's friends, unthinkable even, to plunge them into the simmering cauldron that was Naples – Italy's largest city – without any contact or support. Although only the slenderest evidence survives, it appears that similar arrangements had been made in that city as had been made in Rome. Keats had been introduced – either by his friend William Haslam, by Darling or by his publishers – to a local British doctor, "Milne, the pleasant Scot and accomplished physician of the Chiatamone", a well-known figure in the British expatriate community at Naples which gathered around Sir William Drummond, Sir William Gell and the Countess of Blessington.[72]

There is not much information available about Doctor Robert Miln's professional work, except a short article about 'The Expulsion of the Tape Worm' in the *Medico-Chirurgical Review* of October 1825, which styles him in a footnote as "Dr. Milne, resident physician at Naples", and a longer mention – also in a footnote – in a review of Doctor Harry William Carter's essay 'Remarks upon the Effects of a Warm Climate in Pulmonary Consumption, and some other Diseases', which appeared in the December 1820 issue of the same journal.[73] In the note, appended to a passage from Carter's work endorsing Naples as a suitable winter residence for the consumptive patient, the editor of the *Medico-Chirurgical Review*, the Scottish surgeon James Johnson, wrote: "It may not be improper to say that, in Dr. Miln, resident physician, at Naples, (a gentleman to whose professional character we can speak from personal knowledge) the English invalid will find a countryman, in whom he may place the fullest professional confidence." Being cited in the article alongside Doctor Carter and Doctor Clark, two experts of pulmonary diseases, and recommended by the editor of such a prestigious and authoritative journal was as good a reference as anyone could hope for.

Robert Miln had graduated from the Royal Medical Society of Edinburgh in 1814, with a dissertation on apoplexy.[74] A copy of his thesis, now in the Wellcome Library in London, bears an inscription to the Duchess of Devonshire dated Rome, 30th November 1817.[75] Earlier that year, perhaps before setting out for Italy for the first time, he had made an application to Sir Thomas Lawrence to be introduced to Antonio Canova in Rome. Lawrence's letter reads:

My dear Marquess,

I have been so much honor'd oblig'd and gratified by your kindness, that I feel any farther intrusion upon it to be almost ungrateful, Yet very powerful motives induce me to present to your notice the Bearer of this letter, Dr Robt Miln, a Young Physician respected by Men of Science in this Country and of great modesty and much private Worth.

Of his knowledge of Art I can say nothing; but his desire to be introduc'd to the great Artist of the Continent, is so rational, that I cannot deny him his request that I will venture this application.[76]

Securing Sir Thomas Lawrence's personal introduction to such an eminent personage as Canova was no small attainment.[77] It demonstrates how well connected and highly rated Miln was in the society of the time, and shows that as well as being a proficient physician he nurtured a sincere interest in the arts.

We don't know whether Doctor Miln was only supposed to offer medical assistance in Naples or also to escort Keats to Rome, but it is clear from William Haslam's letter of 4th December 1820 to Joseph Severn that he was to give his pronouncement on the condition of the poet's health: "Ere this reaches you I trust Doctor Milne will have confirmed the most sanguine hopes of his Friends in England and to you my Friend I hope he will have given what you stand much in need of—a confidence amounting to a faith."[78] We can understand Severn's dismay when, on their landing in Naples, he discovered that Miln was not there at that time, but in Rome.[79]

As he prepared for his voyage, Keats tried to "make a purse as long as [he could]". He tapped Abbey for money, but all he got from him was a cruel, mocking letter in reply. "It is therefore not in my power to lend you any thing," the guardian concluded, before adding a sweet envoy in the postscript: "When you are able to call I shall be glad to see you, as I should not like to see you want 'maintenance *for* the day'."[80] George Keats had written to John in June, saying that "[His] prospect of being able to send [him] 200£ very soon [was] pretty good", but these funds were conditional on the sale of a boat he had never even set eyes on – not the most promising of prospects.[81] Before Keats's departure for Italy one of his friends wrote to George, asking him "to send 200£ for the purpose of enabling his Brother to undertake the Journey—He replied that he could not then spare the Money but that it should be sent as soon as possible."[82] However, just at the time Keats was leaving Naples for Rome, George wrote another apologetic letter to his brother, saying, "I cannot yet find a purchaser for the Boat, and have received no intelligence of the man who offered the price I accepted [...]. I hope to be able to send you money soon untill I do I shall be fast approaching the blue devil temperament."[83]

Keats had no useful connections among wealthy aristocrats, and since none of his friends was in a position to lend or return money to him, or to raise any on his behalf, it was left to his publishers Taylor and Hessey to shoulder the financial burden of his voyage to Italy.[84] As mentioned before, even after the liquidation of Tom's inheritance and the payment of some old bills, Keats was still in debt by about £10.[85] He also owed more than £70 to his publishers, around £60 (excluding interest) to Charles Brown, £13 11s. to the local doctor and £30 or £40 to his tailor – so he was pretty much broke.[86] Taylor and Hessey gave him an additional £30 in cash, and for the £100 he owed them Keats assigned to them the copyright of *Lamia* and *Poems* for a term of twenty-eight years.[87] This was an act of pure generosity. As Taylor later wrote to Michael Drury: "Without the remotest Prospect of gaining any thing by this Speculation [...] we gave the Money as an Inducement to him to hope for better Things & to go on writing."[88]

Taylor and Hessey also gave the poet a letter of credit for £150, in the hope that the £200 promised by George would materialize before Keats started drawing money in Italy – which it didn't, causing great inconvenience to them.[89] Even though Keats was travelling on the cheap, a hundred and fifty pounds was not enough for a long sojourn in such expensive cities as Naples and Rome. In fact, by the time of Keats's death in February 1821, five months after his departure from England, most of the money had already been drawn and spent.

When it came to who might accompany Keats to Italy, there were further problems. If his purse had been deeper, he could have taken with him a doctor, as was customary for wealthier patients. But physicians, and their services, were very expensive: for such a trip, even a young doctor could charge up to £100 for each leg of the voyage.[90] Those were not the kind of fees Keats could afford, so the choice fell back on his friends. Charles Brown, as mentioned earlier, would have been the ideal travelling companion: he and Keats had lived together for a while, been on a walking tour of the north, collaborated on the writing of *Otho the Great* and even made plans to return to Scotland together in April that year. In short, they were quite close.

Brown, however, had problems of his own. Following an indelicate affair with his Irish maid Abigail O'Donohue, which had caused Keats and his friends all sorts of embarrassment, he had left his house – one half of Wentworth Place in Hampstead

– and, in May, let it for the summer, travelling up to Scotland on his own. During his absence Abigail had given birth to his illegitimate son, Carlino, while Keats – now without a home – had been forced to move from place to place as his health deteriorated, ending up in the care of Fanny Brawne and her mother, who were renting the other half of Wentworth Place from the Dilkes.[91]

Keats wrote to his friend at least twice in August 1820, and in at least one of his letters he asked Brown if he would join him on his voyage to Italy.[92] This correspondence has only survived through transcripts quoted by Brown in his planned 'Life of John Keats', which omitted several parts that the author was uncomfortable with, so it has to be taken with more than a pinch of salt.[93] The first letter, after two redacted passages, says: "I shall be obliged to set off in less than a month. Do not, my dear Brown, tease yourself about me. You must fill up your time as well as you can, and as happily."[94] The second begins with a cut, summarized by Brown in a note: "The commencement is a continuation of the secret in his former letter, ending with a request that I would accompany him to Italy." It then continues, in Keats's words: "I ought to be off at the end of this week, as the cold winds begin to blow towards evening;—but I will wait till I have your answer to this."[95]

Keats kept waiting for another month, but no reply came from Brown. Even supposing it is true that the letters were misdirected and that Brown only received them on 9th September in Dunkeld, as he later claimed, it's difficult to explain why he didn't write back at once from Dundee or was not in a hurry to return to London, but decided to come back from Scotland on a smack.[96] Despite his later protestations that on finding that Keats had left he planned to join his friend "very early in the spring" and was prepared to live in Italy with him, it is hard not to suspect that he was unwilling to accompany his friend to Rome – or at least reluctant to take on such a huge responsibility – because of his own commitments, strained finances and complicated circumstances at home.[97]

Brown's long silence left Keats and his friends in a quandary. It would have been dreadful for him to travel alone, in need as he was of constant care and assistance. For a while Keats must have considered leaving with Mrs Brawne, who was nursing him at the time. "Your brother [...] used often to wish she could go with him," his fiancée later wrote to his sister.[98] Propriety, however, made that proposition unsuitable, so nothing came of it. Fanny Brawne, in the mean time, insisted that Keats should not leave at all, but remain in England, where he could be looked after by his friends and, if the worst came to pass, die by her side. She almost managed to convince him, but "his kindness for [her]" and the interference of "those who should have been his friends" in the end persuaded him to follow medical advice and set out on that desperate voyage.[99]

Among Keats's other friends, his closest were Charles Wentworth Dilke, John Hamilton Reynolds, James Rice and William Haslam. Dilke's open disapproval of his engagement to Fanny Brawne meant that he and Keats didn't see much of each other during his last months in England. Dilke's main preoccupation remained his son: the year before, he and his wife had moved from Wentworth Place to Great Smith Street in order to be close to him after he had been accepted at Westminster School as a day pupil.[100] Reynolds was now "completely limed in the law", as Keats wrote to his brother George in March 1819; Rice was in poor health himself; John Taylor was too busy; his lifelong friend Haslam was very much occupied with his legal business, and his wife Mary had just given birth to their first daughter, Annette Augusta, so he could not be expected to leave everything behind and spend a long time abroad with Keats.[101] There was a real danger now that the poet would have to face the voyage on his own.

In the mean time, Taylor and Hessey had secured him a place on board the *Maria Crowther*, a trader bound for Naples, Palermo and Messina. According to the last advertisement run by the ship's agents in the *Public Ledger and Daily Advertiser* on 1st September 1820, the brig was about to sail very soon:[102]

> Wants only a few Packages, and will Sail immediately,
> For NAPLES, PALERMO, and MESSINA,
> With liberty to forward Goods from Naples to Messina, at the
> Ship's Expence for Freight only, and Shippers' Risk,
> THE new, fine, fast-sailing, Coppered Brig
> MARIA CROWTHER, A 1, Thomas Walsh Com-
> mander. Lying off the Tower. Burthen 130 tons. For
> Freight or Passage apply to R. and H. RICHARDSON,
> 3, Howford-buildings, Fenchurch-street;
> John's Coffee-house, Cornhill; and, in Exchange hours, or
> the Spanish, Portugal, and Italian Walks.

As was too often the case, ships' departures tended to be delayed until the hold was loaded to capacity and the lengthy customs-clearance checks were completed. Keats must have received confirmation that the ship was to set sail soon, because on the morning of 13th September he left Wentworth Place to get his passport, finalize the copyright assignment and "be ready to go by the Vessel".[103]

There are no descriptions of Keats's departure from Hampstead. We know that it was a fair, warm day, in the wake of more than two weeks of fine weather.[104] We also know that before the poet left he exchanged locks of hair with Fanny Brawne – who, on her part, lined his travelling cap with silk and gave him a pocketbook, a knife and a polished oval white cornelian.[105] It must have been a sad, subdued affair. Fanny Brawne commemorated the event in her copy of Hunt's *Literary Pocket-Book* with the simple words "Mr Keats left Hampstead".[106]

Later that day, around noon, Keats was with his publisher John Taylor at 93 Fleet Street when a messenger turned up with a hasty note from Haslam "beg[ging] by the bearer to be informed the name of the Vessel & of the Agents to the Vessel in which Mr Keats' Passage is taken.—Mr Taylor will be happy to hear," it went on, "that the motive for this enquiry is to secure a second passage *for* Keats' Friend Severn.—"[107]

Keats and his publisher were overjoyed. "Your Letter has given me the greatest Pleasure, and to Keats it is most cheering," Taylor answered at once, giving Haslam the details he requested and adding that "[they had] just now learnt that [the vessel would] not sail till Sunday Morning".[108] It was a narrow escape for Keats: the calamitous prospect of a solitary trip to Italy had been averted.

Joseph Severn was a good friend of Keats. They had known each other since at least autumn 1816, and they shared many interests, friends and acquaintances.[109] From time to time they "took a turn round the [British] Museum" or other art galleries, and discussed the merits of the various works on display.[110] Severn was a keen admirer of Keats's poetry.[111] Their relationship was uncomplicated and, above all, disinterested – which is what Keats liked and valued most in a friendship.

Yet, despite being a close friend, Severn was not on intimate terms with Keats. The poet had only heard about Severn's illegitimate son Henry, born in August 1819, through the gossipy tongue of Charles Brown, and by the time of their departure from England he had not yet disclosed to him his secret engagement to Fanny Brawne.[112] It is clear that Severn was a last resort. Keats's friends were worried he might not be suitable for the difficult task ahead. "He is scarcely the resolute, intelligent or cheerful companion which a long voyage and a sickly frame so anxiously call for," Reynolds wrote to Taylor a few days after the *Maria Crowther* departed. "I wish *you* yourself could have cast Fleet Street & Dull Care behind you, and have taken a trip with our ailing friend."[113] Fanny Brawne "never imagined it was possible for any thing to make [Severn] unhappy" and "never saw [him] for ten minutes serious".[114] Keats himself made an open reference to his friend's apparent lack of empathy in his first letter from Naples: "Severn now is a very good fellow but his nerves are too strong to be hurt by other peoples illnesses."[115]

Still, Severn was available and only too keen to leave for Rome. In December the previous year, he had been awarded a Royal Academy Gold Medal in historical painting, the first given in twelve years, for *The Cave of Despair*.[116] In Italy he would be able to further his studies and produce another painting that could be entered the following summer for a travelling fellowship from the Royal Academy, which would cover the cost of the journey to Rome (£80) as well as subsistence (£130 per year for three years). Apart from being an enriching experience and an opportunity to spend time with a friend he admired, this was an unmissable chance to advance his own artistic career.

Reminiscing more than fifty years later in his memoir 'My Tedious Life', Severn left a vivid account of what was for him a defining moment:

> [O]ne day a mutual [friend] William Haslam said to me "as nothing can save Keats but going to Italy why should you not try to go with him for otherwise he must go alone & we shall never hear anything of him if he dies—will you go["] I answered "I'll go" ["B]ut you'll be long getting ready[;] Keats is actually now preparing, when would you be ready?["] "[I]n three or four days" I replied & I will set about it this very moment.[117]

He then went to his father, who received the news with dismay and "reasoned with [him] in every way as to the rashness of this step". But, Severn recalls, "I had no ear to his reasons & as I had certainly the virtue of the donkey, obstinacy in the highest degree, so my plan went on preparing". He found, however, an ally in his mother, "who was ᵃⁿ Angel in her judgment as well as her affection": she "understood plainly that this ʷᵃˢ a turn in my poor fortune as an artist which might lead to fortune".[118]

So, a couple of days later, on 15th September 1820, he went to see Sir Thomas Lawrence in Russell Square. Lawrence, who had come back himself from a long sojourn in Rome on 30th March that year and been nominated on the same day as the new president of the Royal Academy, gave him two letters of introduction, one to Canova and the other to an "old German Artist who had done a large copy & an engraving from MichleAngelos Last Judgement" – the renowned painter, draughtsman and engraver Conrad Martin Metz.[119] Lawrence's letter to Canova has survived, and it is here reprinted for the first time:

Russell Square
Sept[ber] the 15th.
1820.

My Dear Marquess

I take the liberty to introduce to your Notice M[r] J. Severn the Bearer of this Note a Gentleman of private Worth and considerable Talent travelling to Rome for farther improvement and knowledge in his professional Pursuits. An historical Production by him has just gain'd him the Gold Medal of our Academy.

I intreat you to oblige My dear Marquess by allowing him the view of your noble Works; and [if] you can further assist him by ~~procuring~~ commanding admittance for him to the Roman Academy of St Luke and to the Venetian Academy, you will greatly add to the favor you do me.

With the most sincere Prayers for the continuance of your Health, and of all the blessings so justly due to Your Genius, and munificent Nature

I beg You to believe
My dear Marquess,
Ever Your Oblig'd and
most faithful & devoted S[vt]
Tho[s] Lawrence[120]

With this glowing endorsement in his pocket and £25 he had collected for a portrait he had done, Severn proceeded to make his final preparations for the voyage. In the mean time, Haslam had arranged for the care of his one-year-old son, Henry. A family called Roberts – "most honest and deserving people" – would be looking after him in Severn's absence.[121] Haslam would send them regular payments for his sustenance.

Everything was more or less ready when Severn went to his parents' home in the early hours of 17th September to take his final leave.[122] As Severn recollects in his memoir:

It was after midnight & I found my father sunk down with extream grief in his armchair—My mother & my sisters were preparing all my linen in my trunk and the time being near for my departure my eldest brother & I tried to lift up the trunk but twas beyond us & so I asked my Father ^{to help us}[—] he rose up in a fury, dashed my trunk to the ground & swore that I should not go but as I attempted to go & take leave of my youngest brother, my father stopp'd the door way & on my attempting to pass, in his insane rage ^{he} struck me a blow which fell me to the ground—my brother amazed at this indignity to me at once held back my raving Father—We all passed a dreadful moment even the neighbours who had come to wish me goodbye.[123]

Faced with the prospect of an arduous passage to Italy in the company of a dying man and shaken by his father's angry outburst, Severn "left the sad scene in silent grief" and made his way with his brother Thomas to the appointed place for his departure.

VOYAGE TO NAPLES

SUNDAY, 17TH SEPTEMBER 1820, was a cloudy day, a touch cold for the time of year.[1] Keats and a small group of friends comprising Haslam, Woodhouse and John Taylor left 93 Fleet Street early that morning to be shipside in good time for the embarkation.[2] The *Maria Crowther* was moored alongside one of the commercial wharves "on the southward bank of the Thames" opposite the Tower of London.[3] According to Severn's later recollections, Keats and his friends were the first to arrive there.[4]

The *Maria Crowther*, as we have seen, was advertised in the *Public Ledger and Daily Advertiser* as a "new, fine, fast-sailing, Coppered Brig" of 130 tons burden. The "new" was a little far-fetched, since by then she was already a well-travelled craft.[5] The scanty details provided by Henry C. Shelley in his 1906 book *Literary By-Paths in Old England*, which have been repeated by all Keats biographers, do not tell the full story of this famous trader, and are at least in part inaccurate.[6] "It has been stated," Shelley writes, "that the ship was ill adapted for the conveyance of passengers, and that such was quite literally the case may be inferred from the fact that she was only of 127 tons register."[7] That this was *not* the case can be proved by the fact that the *Maria Crowther* was always advertised "For Freight or Passage" on the London–Naples or London–Messina routes, and that she boasted "superior Accommodations for Passengers".[8] It should also be pointed out that most of the other brigs and schooners offering a passage to Italy were about the same size as the *Maria Crowther*, if not even smaller.[9]

According to Shelley, "The 'Maria Crowther' was built at Chester in 1810, and was primarily intended merely to trade between Cardiff and Liverpool. Probably the voyage to Naples was only a temporary departure from her usual route, for later she evidently returned to the St. George's Channel trade."[10] In actual fact, the brig had sailed across many seas and seen far more distant shores.

The *Chester Chronicle* of 25th January 1811 confirms that the *Maria Crowther* had "launched from Mr. Cortney's yard in Chester" the previous August. In December 1812 we find her at Liverpool, having just returned from Ireland, under Captain Kelly.[11] Less than three years later, in August 1815, she is at Dublin, having returned with a cargo of wines from Oporto, with Captain Watson in command.[12] During 1816 and 1817, still under the captaincy of Watson, she is recorded as plying the Liverpool–Dublin commercial route, while in August 1818 she is sighted on her way to Newfoundland.[13] On 7th February 1819, she arrives back in Liverpool from Lisbon, for the last time under the command of Captain Watson.[14] On 9th May 1820, she is docked at Gravesend, having been taken back from the Portuguese capital by Captain Thomas Walsh.[15] Her next voyage would be the one taking Keats and Severn to Naples.

Thomas Walsh was no doubt an experienced seafarer. It is difficult to give an accurate description of his early career, since there was more than one Captain Walsh active in those years, and naval bulletins tend to provide only the surname of a ship's master. If we exclude Captain Walsh of the *Kitty*, a brig operating on a similar route to that of the *Maria Crowther* at around the same time, but from the Clyde – who is identifiable with "Captain Nicholas Walsh of the Kitty of Glasgow" – and the skippers of local coasters, then some of the remaining mentions might well refer to our Thomas Walsh.[16]

We don't know if it was he who commanded the *Sir George Prevost* on her May 1813 voyage from Lisbon to Newfoundland – neither do we know if he was in charge of the *James & Ann* from Waterford to Cadiz in January and April 1815, or of the *Whim* from Gravesend to Amsterdam in September 1816.[17] But he is perhaps to be identified with the "T. Walsh" of the *Shamrock*, a ship that ran into trouble on her way from Waterford to Gibraltar, as reported by *Lloyd's List* of 8th April 1817:[18]

> The Shamrock, Walsh, from Wa-
> terford to Gibraltar, (with the
> Cargo of the Agnes, from Greenock,
> stranded in Tramore Bay in Decem-
> ber), grounded on Waterford Bar
> 2d instant, knocked off her Sheath-
> ing, and put back to repair.

If this was one of his first voyages as a master, Walsh was not daunted by the experience: the *Shamrock* went well beyond Gibraltar on that trip, all the way to Malta and back – perhaps more than once by the end of February 1818, when she is reported as having arrived in Liverpool "from Leghorn, with 40 tons brimstone 2 hhds tobacco for Blain and Sandar...80 tons valonia".[19]

At the time of Keats's departure, Walsh had not been long in charge of the *Maria Crowther*. His first two voyages as commander of the brig can be mapped out with a certain amount of detail. After departing from Liverpool, the *Maria Crowther* reached Genoa on 28th May 1819 and then went on to Leghorn and Smyrna, where she arrived on 16th July, returning to Liverpool on 6th November.[20] She then sailed for Lisbon on 17th February 1820 and, as we have seen, arrived back in Gravesend on 9th May.[21] Now, after a delay of more than two months from the first published sailing date, the *Maria Crowther* was about to set off for Naples, Palermo and Messina.[22]

"All being ready," Severn recollects of the morning of their departure, "we were soon under weigh."[23] High water that day was at 9.07 a.m. at London Bridge, not very far upriver from their wharf, so the ship must have cast off a short time after that.[24] Severn saw Thomas off at the dock, while Taylor, Woodhouse and Haslam sailed down the river to Gravesend with him and Keats.[25] Writing to his brother more than fifteen years later, Severn remembered the moment of parting: "I see you now in my minds eye, and the blue coat you had on, I can never forget you—how pale you look'd at the scene we had passed and how I trembled."[26]

Apart from Captain Walsh, his cat, his mate, the crew, Keats and his friends, there was another passenger on board, a lady called Mrs Elizabeth Pidgeon, also bound for Naples, who "looked and was the picture of health".[27] At about noon the *Maria Crowther* reached Gravesend. Keats decided not to go ashore, but to remain in his cabin and dine there with the captain, Mrs Pidgeon and Severn. A few hours later, at four o'clock, Keats's friends "left him [...] comfortably settled in his new Habitation with every prospect of having a pleasant Voyage".[28] Before taking his leave, Woodhouse slipped a sealed letter into Keats's hands, written the night before, in which he declared himself willing to offer his friend financial support in future, should he ever need it.[29] He also asked him if he could have a lock of his hair as a memento, and Keats let him cut one off on the spot.[30]

Severn tried to make the best of the situation. "This little Cabin with 6 beds and at first sight every inconvenience," he told Haslam in his upbeat report of the first day on board, "in one hour was more endeared to us—and to our every purpose—than the most stately Palace." After their friends had left, "the kind Mrs Pidgeon our Lady passenger did the honors of the tea table with the most unafected good nature". Keats "cracked jokes at tea and was quite the 'special fellew' of olden time". When tea was over, the two friends were so exhausted that they fell "into a sound sleep—and serenad[ed] [Mrs Pidgeon] with a snoring duett". Severn woke up more than once from his fitful dozing "with the oddest notions—the first time in a Shoe makers shop—the next down in [a] wine cellar pretty well half seas over". Then, when they "came to the last snore of [their] duett—[they] rubbed [their] eyes and said—'wee'll go to bed'". Mrs Pidgeon retired to the other side of the cabin, which was screened by a curtain, and they slept "most soundly".[31]

The following morning, Severn got up and looked at Keats, who was lying on the top berth opposite him.[32] His voice was hoarse, but in other respects he seemed well. After breakfast, Severn went ashore to Gravesend to make a few purchases for

Keats: fifty apples, two dozen biscuits and "some things from the Chymists" – including a "bottle of Opium—[which] he had determined on taking [...] the instant his recovery should stop".[33] Captain Walsh, in the mean time, tried "to buy a Goat for [Keats]—but was unsuccessful". Once they were back on the ship, they had dinner, and "Keats was full of his waggery—looked well—ate well—and was well".[34] Severn, on the other hand, "was very pale & wan", as he "was suffering at the time from liver complaint" – so much so that "a Lady visitor before [they] left enquired which was the dying man".[35]

At six, not long before they were due to sail, thanks to the good services of William Haslam, Severn received his passport, which had not been signed in time ahead of his departure from London. Soon after that, another passenger arrived, Miss Maria Cotterell, a "sweet girl of about 18" – embodying with Mrs Pidgeon "the quintessence of good nature and prettiness" – who was "labouring under the very same complaint as Keats" and was "a sad martyr to her illness".[36] As the *Maria Crowther* pushed away from Gravesend, Severn and Keats struck up a witty conversation with the girl. The arrival of the passport had taken a weight off Severn's mind and "unloosed all [his] prattle" – "and in a short time [with] Keats backing [him] with his golden jokes in support of [his] tinsel [they] reco[ver'd] Miss Cotterell—to laugh and be herself". After eating a plentiful meal of smoked beef and tongue from the captain's pantry, Severn drew a small caricature of himself for his sister Maria and then worked until midnight on a small watercolour, a moonlit scene of their ship viewed from the sea.[37] When he returned to the cabin, everyone had gone to rest, and Keats – who that day had been "not so well" – was now in a sound sleep.[38]

Some biographers have claimed that Elizabeth Pidgeon was Miss Cotterell's travelling companion, but the documentary evidence and various references in Severn's letters seem to point in the opposite direction. The two women are often mentioned as "one of the lady passengers" and "the other lady passenger", and their voyage is never linked in any way. In his late memoir,

Severn wrote: "There was [a] fellow passenger a Miss Cotterell & a Mrs Pidgeon so that we made a nice little party except that the young lady was also suffering from consumption & was on her way like ourselves to Naples."[39] The impression, reinforced by the fact that the two ladies joined the ship at different ports and applied for their passports more than two months apart from one another, is that Maria Cotterell was travelling on her own.[40] Moreover, if Mrs Pidgeon was Miss Cotterell's travelling companion, it would be difficult to justify why she would act as "a most consummate brute" and never "lend [her] the least aid", even when she saw her "stiffened like a corpse".[41]

The two women hailed from very different social backgrounds. When they enquired of Severn whether Haslam could forward their letters, Mrs Pidgeon asked if his friend could call on Mr Taylor, the keeper of the Half Moon tavern on Gracechurch Street; Miss Cotterell, on the other hand, requested that he apply to her father at No. 9 Richmond Terrace, Walworth.[42] This was a new, elegant development on the southern outskirts of the city, in what was at the time a desirable area favoured by the affluent middle classes. Although it is no longer there, Richmond Terrace is visible on London maps from about 1809.[43] There is no contemporary description of No. 9, but a letting advert for the property next door, published the previous year in the *Morning Chronicle*, may give an idea about the house, as well as its inhabitants.[44]

Genteel Leasehold Residence, Household Furniture and Effects, East-lane, Walworth.—By Mr. ADAMSON, on Monday, 27th instant, at eleven o'clock, on the Premises, No. 10, Richmond-terrace, Walworth, by direction of the Proprietor who is removing into the country, unless previously disposed of by Private Contract,

A Genteel DWELLING HOUSE, neatly finished and in perfect order, possessing every convenience for a small family, a garden amply stocked with fruit trees and shrubs. The house contains four bed rooms, dining room, breakfast room, two kitchens, pantry and cellaring; a lease will be granted for 14 years at a low rent.

At the same time will be sold the genteel HOUSEHOLD FURNITURE, piano-forte, eight-day clock, cellaret, window curtains, plate, linen, china and glass, books and numerous effects.

The house to be viewed till the sale, and the effects on the Saturday previous, when particulars and catalogues may be had on the premises; and of Mr. Adamson, 58, Fenchurch-street.

The word "genteel", which is used three times, perhaps best describes Miss Cotterell, her family environment and her social milieu. Maria was the daughter of Charles and Elizabeth Cotterell (née White) of Southampton.[45] She was born there sometime before 14th March 1801, when she was christened at All Saints' Church.[46] Maria grew up in a rather numerous family: she was preceded by Charles, born in 1793, who was now awaiting her in Naples, Eliza, Anne, Martha and William, and followed by George, John and Sidney, who died at birth in 1808 with her mother.[47] The following year, her father married again, to Marianne Jones, almost twenty years his junior, and there were more additions to the family before Maria's departure for Italy: Louisa Anne, Edwin, Emma, Walter and Louisa Augusta.[48]

Charles Cotterell is described as an "auctioneer" on his marriage licence of 1809 and in the 1811 *Cunningham's Street Directory* for Southampton, which gives his address as St Michael's Square and lists his wife Marianne ("Mrs Cotterell") as running a boarding school from the same location.[49] His work must have brought him to London, because we see him advertise from 1819 as an "Auctioneer and Appraiser" in the local papers.[50] Her father's lucrative profession and her stepmother's past occupation and family background help to explain why Maria had such a "very lady like" air about her.[51]

On Tuesday, 19th September, Severn woke up at daybreak to see a glorious sunrise in the east.[52] Miss Cotterell was rather ill, so he invited her to walk the deck with him at half-past six. Keats woke up at seven, looking much better. During breakfast, at around half-past eight, Severn began writing a letter to Haslam. They were about thirteen miles from Margate, off Dover Castle, when he was forced to stop. "The Sea & I have always been enemies," Severn wrote in his late memoir.[53] He "began to feel a waltzing on [his] stomach" while penning his note to Haslam, and was soon sick. "I was going it most soundly," Severn wrote two days later. "Miss Cotterell followed me—then Keats who did it in the most gentlemanly manner—and then the saucy Mrs Pidgeon who had been laughing at us—four faces bequeathing to the mighty deep their breakfasts." Miss Cotterell fainted, but was soon brought round. Severn was very ill, and had to lie down. Keats climbed onto his berth, and from there "he dictated surgically—like Esculapius of old in baso-relievo": thanks to him Miss Cotterell recovered.[54] Then they "had a cup of tea each and no more[,] went to bed and slept until it was time to go to bed". They could not get up again, and slept in their clothes all night. "Keats the King," Severn wrote, closing his report for the day, "not even looking pale—"

The following day was an eventful one. After a beautiful morning and breakfast on deck, the weather changed for the worse. "About 10 Keats said a storm was hatching," Severn wrote the next day.[55]

> He was right—the rain cam[e] on and we retired to our Cabin—it abated and once more we came on deck—at 2 Storm came on furiously—we retired to our beds—the rolling of the ship was death to us—towards 4 it increased and our situation was alarming—the trunks rolled across the Cabin—the water poured in from the skylight and we were tumbled from one side to the other of our beds.

Severn was very curious to see the storm, and, leaving Keats and the frightened ladies behind, went up on deck. He saw the ship surrounded by mountains of waves: "The watry horizon was like a Mountainous Country—but the ship's motion was beautifully to the sea—falling from one wave to the other in a very lovely manner—the sea each time crossing the deck and one side of the ship being level with the water." Realizing that all was fine, he went back to the cabin and reassured the others. "But when the dusk came," Severn later wrote,

> the sea began to rush in from the side of our Cabin from an opening in the planks—this ma[d]e us rather long-faced—for it came by pails-full—again I got out—and said to Keats— "here's pretty music for you"—with the greatest calmness he answerd me—only "Water parted from the sea".[56]

Severn staggered up again, as the storm grew in intensity. "The Captain & Mate soon came down," Severn wrote,

> for our things were squashing about in the dark—they struck a light and I succeeded in getting my desk of[f] the ground— with cloth's—books—&c—the Captain finding it could not be stopped—tacked about from our voyage—and the sea ceased to dash against the Cabin for we were sailing again[s]t wind and tide—but the horrible agitation continued in the ship lengthways—here were the pumps working—the sailes squalling the confused voises of the sailors—the things rattling about in every direction—and us poor devils pinn'd up in our beds like ghosts by day light—except Keats he was himself all the time—the ladies sufferd the most—but I was out of bed a dozen times to wait on them and tell them there was no danger.

The "surly rolling of the sea" – "worse than the storm", according to Severn – continued until the next morning, making it impossible for them to sleep or eat anything. They had started the day off the Brighton coast, but their ship had been pushed back by the storm along the Channel as far as Dungeness.[57]

The new morning was serene, and the four passengers sat down to an early breakfast on the deck of the ship at 6 a.m. "like a Quartett of Fighting Cocks", having eaten nothing since two o'clock the previous afternoon. As he started writing in a hurry his long diary letter to Haslam, recounting their first few days of sailing, Severn tried to remain positive.[58] Despite "a sleepless night and [...] a head full of care", he was better than he had been for years. In fact, they were all full of spirits. "Keats is without even complaining," Severn wrote to his friend, "and Miss Cotterell has a colour in her face—the sea has done his worst upon us."

But he was giving himself false hope: this was only the beginning of long weeks of "sad penance".[59] Severn's day-to-day account of their passage to Italy ends here, and we only know about the rest of their voyage through reported conversations, scrappy notes and distant reminiscences – some of them very fuzzy and at odds with each other. With this in mind, let's continue to follow the journey of the *Maria Crowther* to Naples.

We have no news of the ship and her passengers for the following week, except for two brief journal entries Severn jotted down for Friday 22nd and Saturday 23rd September, perhaps with the intention of revisiting and expanding them at a later date.[60]

Septr 22nd Friday	A Flat day—waiting for a wind in the Dundee Ness Roads—went on shore with the Captain—and found it a wide expanse of Gravel—2 houses in about 6 miles—and a solitary yard of furze—Keats appetite increasing—
Sept 23 Saturday	Still waiting for a wind—flat, very flat—Keats beat me hollow at the trencher

In his late memoir, Severn expanded his recollection of those days with an amusing anecdote:

[O]ur Captain permitted to land at Dungeness & ramble over the gravel, on the opposite side I was astonishd & delighted with the enormous waves, at least 10 feet high, rushing in upon the shore, the sight fixed me in wonder & abstraction, until a miserable exciseman appeared and demanded what I was doing, & my explanation only confirmed his suspicion that I was looking out for contraband, which let down all the high romance which the sublime waves had inspired.[61]

Their strolls along the shingle coast must have also taken them to the nearby village of New Romney, from where Severn's letter to Haslam was posted.

On Thursday, 28th September, as reported in a letter by Charles Brown to John Taylor, "after having been tossed about in the Channel for ten days", they landed at Portsmouth. "Having a day to spare," Brown continues,

they went to Bedhampton, a distance of 7 miles, to visit
M^r and Mrs Snook, who were here [in Chichester] yesterday
afternoon & gave me the following particulars. [...] On the
following morning (Friday) [Keats's] spirits were excellent.
He abuses the Captain, tho' he acknowledges him to be civil
& accommodating. He likes one of the Ladies, and has an
aversion for the other, whom he ridiculed with all the bustling
wit of a man in saucy health. He was so sick of the voyage,
that a word might have sent him back to London. [...] He
knew I was here (within ten miles) but did not dare to come,
lest the wind should change. [...] He sailed from Portsmouth
on Friday afternoon, with a fair wind, which has continued
ever since.[62]

On the following morning, Saturday, 30th September, as the
ship was becalmed off the Yarmouth coast, Keats's mood had
changed, and he vented all his gloom and frustration in a letter
to Charles Brown. "If my spirits seem too low," he wrote to
his friend,

you may in some degree impute it to our having been at sea a
fortmight without making any way. I was very disappointed
at not meeting you at bedhampton, and am very provoked
at the thought of you being at Chichester to day. I should
have delighted in setting off for London for the sensation
merely—for what should I do there? I could not leave my
lungs or stomach or other worse things behind me. I wish
to write on subjects that will not agitate me much—there
is one I must mention and have done with it. Even if my
body would recover of itself, this would prevent it—The
very thing which I want to live most for will be a great
occasion of my death. I cannot help it. Who can help it?
Were I in health it would make me ill, and how can I bear
it in my state? I dare say you will be able to guess on what
subject I am harping—you know what was my greatest pain
during the first part of my illness at your house. I wish for

death every day and night to deliver me from these pains, and then I wish death away, for death would destroy even those pains which are better than nothing. Land and Sea, weakness and decline are great seperators, but death is the great divorcer for ever.[63]

After asking Brown to put all his reservations to one side and be a friend to Miss Brawne, Keats continues:

I am in a state at present in which woman merely as woman can have no more power over me than stocks and stones, and yet the difference of my sensations with respect to Miss Brawne and my Sister is amazing. The one seems to absorb the other to a degree incredible. I seldom think of my Brother and Sister in america. The thought of leaving Miss Brawne is beyond every thing horrible—the sense of darkness coming over me—I eternally see her figure eternally vanishing. Some of the phrases she was in the habit of using during my last nursing at Wen[t]worth place ring in my ears—Is there another Life? Shall I awake and find all this a dream? There must be we cannot be created for this sort of suffering.[64]

Returning to earthly matters, Keats concludes: "We expect to put into Portland roads to night. The Captn the Crew and the Passengers are illtemper'd and weary."[65]

Keats appears to have found some respite from his illness, as well as his demons, when the ship landed on the Dorset coast to take fresh provisions on board. Long after the poet's death, Severn reminisced about this short stop in their voyage, giving rise to one of the most famous romantic myths about Keats and his poetry. In the February 1846 issue of the *Union Magazine*, he published the facsimile of a manuscript of the 'Bright Star' sonnet in his possession and appended to it the following letter:

SONNET BY THE LATE JOHN KEATS.

(TO THE EDITOR OF THE UNION MAGAZINE.)

21, JAMES STREET, *Jan.* 21*st*, 1846

SIR,

THROUGH the medium of the Union Magazine, I have the gratification to present the public with an unpublished MS. poem of Keats', (the last he ever wrote,) which I trust may be admired and well received, as the harbinger of many other unpublished works of the illustrious young poet, now editing by Mr. R. Monckton Milnes.

The present exquisite Sonnet was written under such interesting circumstances that I cannot forbear making them public. Keats and myself were beating about in the British Channel in the autumn of 1820, anxiously waiting for a wind to take us to Italy, which place, together with the sea-voyage, were deemed likely to preserve his life; for he was then in a state of consumption, which left but the single hope of an Italian sojourn to save him. The stormy British sea, after a fortnight, had exhausted him; and on our arrival off the Dorsetshire coast, having at last the charm of a fine and tranquil day, we landed to recruit.

The shores with the beautiful grottoes which opened to fine verdure and cottages, were the means of transporting Keats once more into the regions of poetry;—he showed me these things exultingly, as though they had been his birthright. The change in him was wonderful, and continued even after our return to the ship, when he took a volume (which he had a few days before given me) of Shakespeare's Poems, and in it he wrote me the subjoined Sonnet, which at the time I thought the most enchanting of all his efforts. Twenty-five years have passed away, and I have by degrees (in the love I bear to his memory) placed it in my mind as amongst the most enchanting poetry of the world.

After writing this Sonnet, Keats sank down into a melan-
choly state, and never wrote again, save one painful letter
on the same subject as the Sonnet—for the love so raptur-
ously sung in it was then hastening the poet's death: it was
a real and honourable love, which, but for the separation
occasioned by his direful illness, would have been blessed
in a happy and advantageous marriage. Alas! for Italy—he
only went there to die.

I remain, Sir,

Yours truly,

JOSEPH SEVERN[66]

Although some of the details in this letter are inaccurate, the
truthfulness of its substance should not be questioned. In his
letter of 19th September 1821 to Charles Brown, less than a year
from the events described, Severn wrote:

> [D]o you [know] the sonnet beggining – "Bright star—would I
> were stedfast as thou art"—he wrote this down in the ship—it
> is one of his most beautiful things—I will send it if you have it
> not—at present I have lent the book in which he wrote it—or
> I would send it.[67]

Severn was therefore aware at that time – or at least believed –
that the sonnet had been written down (not composed) on board
the *Maria Crowther*. Although it had been penned the previous
year, if not before, it was, in his view, the last piece of poetry
Keats had ever set down on paper.[68] And though it is true that
Keats wrote the sonnet on his copy of Shakespeare's poems,
on the blank page opposite *A Lover's Complaint*, the book is
likely to have been gifted to Severn some time later, perhaps in
January 1821, not handed to him "a few days before" on the
ship.[69] What led to the widespread belief that 'Bright Star' was
Keats's last poem was Milnes's biography of the poet (1848),
which elaborated on Severn's letter and skewed it in a romantic
direction:

He landed once more in England, on the Dorchester coast, after a weary fortnight spent in beating about the Channel: the bright beauty of the day and the scene revived for a moment the poet's drooping heart, and the inspiration remained on him for some time even after his return to the ship. It was then that he composed that Sonnet of solemn tenderness—

"Bright star! would I were stedfast as thou art," &c.

and wrote it out in a copy of Shakespeare's Poems he had given to Severn a few days before. I know of nothing written afterwards.[70]

When Severn revisited the episode in his late memoir, he may have relied both on his letter to the *Union Magazine* and on Milnes's biography for detail, and come to believe himself that "this sonnet was the very last poetical effort the poor fellow ever made". At any rate, there is no denying that Severn must have had the impression, when he landed with Keats on the coast of Dorset, that for a brief spell his friend had become "like his former self" and that the scenery had stirred in him a gush of poetic energy which, Severn thought, boded well for his possible recovery.[71]

After clearing the English Channel at the beginning of October, "the difficulties seem'd to decrease" and they "skipp'd the rest in 3 weeks". "Though quick", however, their voyage "was yet not well". "Close upon when I wrote you," Severn reported to Haslam on 22nd October, "Keats began to droop—and the many privations coming in the want of fair winds—nice provisions—airing of beds—and——made him impatient—this brings on fever—and at times he has been very bad."[72] Miss Cotterell was not faring much better. "I have sometimes thought her dead," Severn wrote after landing in Naples. "Full a dozen times I have recovered this Lady and put her to bed—sometimes she would faint 4 times in a day yet at intervals would seem quite well."[73]

As if the problems on board were not enough, the *Maria Crowther* got into trouble as she was sailing across the Bay of Biscay, "carried by a good wind" and going "up and down like a roundabout".[74] "Two Portugese Ships of War," Severn recounted a few weeks after the event,

> [...] brought us to [written "too"] with a shot—which passed close under our stern—this was not pleasant for us you will allow—nor was it decreased when they came up—for a more infernal set I never could imagine—after some trifling questions they allowed us to go on to our no small delight—our captain was afraid they would plunder the ship.[75]

Recalling the same incident decades later, Severn added some more detail and a bit of colour:

> A large Porteghese Man of War ^{a four decker} crossed our path & as our Captain did not ^{stop} a shot was fired to bring us too & passed our cabin windows whilst I was leaning looking over—Thro' the speaking trumpet it was demanded ^{in English} if we had met ^{with} any vessels & the Captain answered "that we had not" Soon after an English war brig stopped us & put the same question—The Captain answerd & described the big man of war & the brig instantly turned about in pursuit[.]
>
> We afterwards discovered that the Portughese was on the look out to intercept vessels going to the aid of Spain which was at that time in a state of Civil war with Don Carlos striving for the crown.[76]

Sometime after the Channel storm – which in later accounts Severn places in the Bay of Biscay and remembers as having lasted three days – "Keats took up Ld Byrons Don Juan accidentally as one of the books he had brought from England". "Singularly enough," Severn recollects, he opened on the description of the Storm, which is evidently taken from the Medusa frigate & which the taste of Byron tryes to make a jest of—Keats threw down the book & exclaimed, "this gives me the most horrid idea of human nature, that a man like Byron should have exhausted all the pleasures of the world so compleatly that there was nothing left for him but to laugh & gloat over the most solemn & heart rending scenes [written "since"] of human misery[—] this storm of his is one of the most diabolical attempts ever made upon our sympathies, and I have no doubt it will fascenate thousands into extreem obduracy of heart—the tendency of Byrons poetry is based on a paltry originality, that of being new by making solemn things gay & gay things solemn.["][77]

Byron had already raised Keats's hackles a few times before. "There is a great difference between us," the latter had written the previous year to his brother George in America. "He describes what he sees—I describe what I imagine—Mine is the hardest task."[78] This latest outburst against a more famous and successful rival poet – a poet, which was even worse, "really popular among women" – has the ring of truth about it and, as we will see, won't be Keats's last, if we are to believe Severn's later reminiscences.[79]

"Off Cape St Vincent", to everyone's relief, "[...] the sea became calm like oil," and on 16th October, in the early dawn, the *Maria Crowther* at last entered the milder waters of the Mediterranean.[80] Severn painted a watercolour of the Barbary Coast "lit up with the Suns first rays" and, later that day, one of the Malaga coast.[81] As they crossed the Strait of Gibraltar, Severn "perceived great changes [written "greats change"] in Keat[s] for the better—he seem'd recovering—at least looked like it—but in two days the blood came from his stomach [...] with fever at night and violent perspiration".[82]

It must have been dreadful for Severn to witness his friend's suffering while confined to a small cabin on the open sea. No help was to be had until they reached Naples, and he must have wondered many times whether Keats would make it alive. The crossing from Gibraltar to Naples took them six days.

After five weeks at sea and a "most horribly rough" passage, on 22nd October they at last reached the Bay of Naples, as reported by the *Giornale generale del commercio*.[83]

> INTERNO.
> *Bastimenti approdati nel Porto di Napoli.*
> a' 21 Ottobre.
> Brick Inglese Woods Capitano Roberto Barr da Gloschow in gni. 41 con manifatture, e Zuccheri per li Sign. Hardou Maingy et. Price.
> Da S. Lucido Paranzello Napolitano S. Maria di Portosalvo P. Domenico Gaglione in gni. 4 con fichi ed altro per diversi.
> Dall' Acciarolo Paranzello Napolitano la Madonna del Carmine P. Giuseppe d' Angelo in gni. 2 con fichi, ed altro per diversi.
> a 22 Ottobre.
> Da Terranova Brick Inglese Ceres Capitano Iohn Adey in giorni 26 con baccalari per i Sig. Bardon Maingi e Price.
> Da Amsterdam Brick Svedese nuova intenzione Capitano Nicolas Nicolaissens in giorni 48 con formaggio, ed altro per i Sigg. Forquet, e Giusso.
> Da Londra Brick Inglese Maria Crow Cap. Thomas Walsh in giorni 21 con mercanzie per il Sig. Giuseppe Ascione.

"Here we are thank God," exulted Severn from the deck of the ship the moment they arrived – and then hastened to add: "but in quarantine—*therefore accordingly*."[84] Despite Severn's obvious disappointment, this could not have come as a total surprise. Italian ports enforced quarantine on most inbound vessels, in particular those coming from abroad, as Captain Thomas Walsh must have known, having sailed to Genoa and Leghorn the year before.

The Neapolitan health authorities had issued a detailed set of quarantine directives for the ports of the kingdom earlier that year, which replaced less stringent regulations.[85] Incoming vessels were classified according to their country of origin, their cargo, the seas they had crossed and the ports at which they had called during their voyage. British trade vessels fell by default under the category of "*sospetti*" ("suspect"). This is not because, as Severn misremembered decades later, "the Typhus fever was in London": there had indeed been a typhus epidemic between 1816 and 1819 – whose epicentre was Ireland rather than England – but by the beginning of 1820 new cases had dwindled.[86] The real reason, as revealed by the heated discussions between the health authorities (Supremo Magistrato di Salute) and the Ministry of Internal Affairs (Ministero di Stato degli Affari Interni) of Naples at the beginning of that year, is that English ports had no preventive health measures in place against the spread of epidemics, in particular for vessels arriving from America and Spain, where there had been recent outbreaks of yellow fever.[87]

According to the *Regolamenti sanitarii*, "suspect" vessels would have to undergo a minimum quarantine period of twenty-one days and a maximum of forty. This applied to people, animals, birds and goods classified as "*suscettibili*" ("susceptible to contagion"), such as wool, cotton, fabrics, carpets, sponges, paper, books, animal skin, leather, candles, metals, tobacco, flowers, some fruits, and so on. The quarantine for the rest of the goods (classified as "*insuscettibili*", "non-contagious") tended to be a week shorter. The quarantine period could be extended or shortened according to a worsening of or an improvement in the conditions over the year. In January 1820, English vessels arriving in Naples with a cargo of goods "susceptible to contagion" were required to observe a twenty-eight-day quarantine, and their crew and passengers to isolate for twenty-one days. The Ministry of Internal Affairs, however, argued that, since the yellow-fever epidemic in Spain and the plague in Africa had now abated, and since the Leghorn port authorities had reduced the quarantine period for British ships from ten to five days, Naples should follow suit. Also, the long quarantine delays created all sorts of problems and extra expenses, to the tune of 1,000 piastre per vessel, and the British complained that this was affecting trade and warned that merchants may choose to boycott the measures.[88]

The conditions must have improved over the course of 1820, since by the time the *Maria Crowther* reached the Bay of Naples the mandatory period of isolation for people landing at that port had been reduced to ten days.[89] Keats and his fellow passengers should have considered themselves very lucky to have escaped the torment of a much longer quarantine.[90]

As it was, those ten additional days on board the ship were almost enough to kill the poet. In his late memoir Severn remembers that as a happy period – "We passed the 14 days quarantine with delight & regretted the finale for each day had a new feature" – and fills it with romanticized detail:

The aspect from the Bay of Naples was sublime, on the right was the range of Appenines with Sorrento to the left the splendid city of Naples, terrassed up & up with gardens & vineyards, in the centre Vesuvius with its clouds of smoke opening & extending all along the horison, the clouds edged with golden light, then the lovely deep blue sea making the foreground, all this was an inchantment with the people surrounding our ship with their guittars & songs & no end of delicious fruits in great abundance grapes peaches watermelons & plums [...] The charming novelty was so great & striking of this magic scene that it is after ½ a century still vividly before my eyes as tho' it was present.[91]

But Severn's own contemporary assessment of their time of confinement was quite different, and on getting ashore he wrote to Haslam at once, complaining about "the loathsome misery of Quarantine—foul weather and foul air for the whole 10 days kept us to the small Cabin—surrounded by about 2000 ships in a wretched Mole not sufficient for half the number".[92] The "foul weather [...] for the whole 10 days" and the "2000 ships" were a great exaggeration, because the weather in Naples had not been too bad in late October, and the real number of crafts must have been much lower, but I suppose we can excuse Severn for his rant after such a long and wearying journey.[93]

On her arrival at the port, the *Maria Crowther* would have been met by health officials. They would have spoken to Captain Walsh, assessed the situation and appointed one or more guards to ensure no one would break the quarantine. The officials would then inspect the ship and her cargo, and a doctor would examine the passengers. If he thought they were unwell or showing suspicious symptoms, they would have to strip naked – women too, as far as propriety would allow. Food and water were put on an empty boat towed by another vessel, and left shipside. No contact with the ship could be made before dawn or after sunset. Any helper or other person allowed to speak to those under quarantine, the *contumacisti*, must do so at a distance and windward, well in sight of the guards. Quarantined people could not bathe or swim by their ship, and if they wanted to post a letter, this would have to be placed in a wire basket at the end of a long pole held by a guard, who would then unseal it and unfold it using long scissors and expose it to the fumes of wet straw or sulphur until well fumigated.[94]

In short, quarantine was no fun – all the more so if illness forced you to remain in a small cabin most of the time. And what made matters worse, in Keats's case, was that two consumptives had to share the same space. "[T]he lady passenger though in the same state as Keats," Severn wrote once he got ashore,

> yet differing in constitution required almost every thing the opposite to him—for instance if the cabin windows were not open she would faint and remain entirely insensible 5 or 6 hours together—if the windows were open poor Keats would be taken with a cough (a violent one—caught from this cause) and sometimes spitting of blood.[95]

"[T]he knowlege of her complaint," the poet wrote while still on board the *Maria Crowther*,

> the flushings in her face, all her bad symptoms have preyed upon me—they would have done so had I been in good health. [...] I remember poor Rice wore me in the same way in the isle of wight—I shall feel a load off me when the Lady vanishes out of my sight.[96]

Severn had much to worry about during quarantine, and only managed to write a hasty note to Haslam on the day they arrived in Naples, cut short by the sudden appearance of the courier. Keats also wrote just one letter, addressed to Mrs Brawne but in reality meant for her daughter,[97] which he started at the same time as Severn but appears to have dispatched two days later – unless he got the date wrong, something not unusual for him. His tone is very melancholy – by then he seems to have already lapsed into his "posthumous" mood.

> Give my Love to Fanny and tell her, if I were well there is enough in this Port of Naples to fill a quire of Paper—but it looks like a dream—every man who can row his boat and walk and talk seems a different being from myself—I do not feel in the world. [...] It is impossible to describe exactly in what state of health I am—at this moment I am suffering from indigestion very much, which makes such stuff of this Letter. I would always wish you to think me a little worse than I really am; not being of a sanguine disposition I am likely to succeed. If I do not recover your regret will be softened[,] if I do your pleasure will be doubled—I dare not fix my Mind upon Fanny, I have not dared to think of her. [...] O what an account I could give you of the Bay of Naples if I could once more feel myself a Citizen of this world—I feel a Spirit in my Brain would lay it forth pleasantly—O what a misery it is to have an intellect in splints![98]

And then, after his farewells, he added in a heart-breaking postscript: "Good bye Fanny! god bless you." These were the last words his fiancée would ever receive from him.

The tediousness of the quarantine was mitigated by the attentions and frequent visits of Charles Cotterell, Maria's brother – an ex-warrant officer of the Royal Navy. After three years of active service as a purser, he had moved to Naples and set up in business, working as a shipping agent, merchant, private banker and winemaker.[99] By all accounts he was a very active and generous man. He was grateful to Keats and Severn for looking after his sister during the crossing, and repaid them with gifts, assistance and, once they got ashore, warm hospitality. "[H]e supplied us with every delicacy in fruit, fish & fowl that Naples could produce," Severn wrote in his memoir. "As we had been attentive to his sister, so he went unbounded in his attentions to us."[100] And the day after their release from quarantine he wrote to Haslam: "[He] has shown unusually humane treatment to Keats—unasked."[101]

Cotterell also brought good humour and, on occasion, acted as an interpreter:

> The Italian boatmen who came about us when we were per-forming Quarantine in the bay of Naples, used to laugh at our Cabin boy, who was a favorite of us all—on one occasion an Englishman Mr Cotterell who was very kind to us, was ask[ed] by Keats the reason, the boatmen said that the boy laughd like a beggar.—Keats indignantly said "tell him he laughs like a damn'd fool"—Mr Cotterell could not put this into Italian as they have nothing equivalent to our damn—At which discovery Keats exclaimed, "No, they are not worth a damn."[102]

Cotterell was not the only one showering attentions on the poet and the other passengers. "The Captain has behaved with great kindness to us all," Severn wrote two days after getting off the ship, "but more particularly Keats—every thing that could be got or done—was at his service without asking—he is a good-natured man to his own injury—strange for a Captain—I wont say so much for his ship," he added, remembering the discom-forts they had suffered over the previous weeks, "it's a black hole—5 sleeping in one Cabin—the one you saw—the only one—"[103]

As if their inconvenience were not enough, a curious incident made the last days they spent on board the *Maria Crowther* even more of an ordeal. Around that time, a

number of men-of-war from the British fleet stationed in
the Mediterranean had been called to Naples, and were now
cruising the bay. They were the *Rochfort*, an 80-gun ship of the
line (2,082 tons burden) commanded by Admiral Sir Graham
Moore, the *Liffey* (50 guns, fourth-rate, Captain Sir Henry
Duncan), the *Active* (46 guns, frigate, Captain Sir James A.
Gordon), the *Revolutionaire* (or *Révolutionnaire*, 46 guns,
frigate, Captain Fleetwood Pellew), the *Spey* (26 guns, sloop,
Captain John Donaldson Boswall) and the tender *Express*
(schooner, Captain Barnes).[104] Their presence, coupled with
the assumption of an imminent Austrian invasion, caused
great alarm to the Neapolitan government, and gave rise to
a host of conspiratorial stories.[105] The official British position
was one of strict non-interference: their fleet was there for
the purpose of observation, and would engage only if driven
from neutrality by hostile aggression. But it was believed in
many quarters that the king, while feigning acceptance of the
new constitution, was planning an escape.[106] And there was
some truth in this: before the middle of September that year,
King Ferdinand had applied to the British envoy in Naples,
Sir William à Court, suggesting a possible retreat on board
an English man-of-war.[107] Worse than that, once the British
warships began to assemble in the Gulf of Naples, he tried
to engineer clandestine meetings with Sir William:

The King endeavoured yesterday [29th October 1820] to
obtain written answers to a string of questions relating to his
"departure;" but they were put aside as needless considera-
tions at this time. He then desired a personal conference in a
secret mode with the British Minister, but this was declined
peremptorily.

N.B. The proposition was to go from the Prince of Denmark's
in another carriage with an officer, who would drive round
to a *private* door of the palace; and then a priest would meet
Sir W. A'court and conduct him by a *private staircase* to one
of the King's apartments.[108]

In the mean time, rumours grew that Sir William, under orders from his government, was trying to persuade the royal family to go on board one of the ships of the British squadron – not just to offer them safety, but for a more sinister motive: once removed from the city, the king might be induced to issue a declaration reneging on the constitution and denouncing his people as being in a state of rebellion.[109] Others even went so far as to claim that the British and French fleets were there to prevent the Russians from taking possession of Sicily – which seemed to be Emperor Alexander's covert intention.[110]

As is often the case, the truth was, perhaps, much more simple and mundane. After the July revolution, the British community in Naples, fearing reprisals from the *carbonari* for their nation's alliance with the autocratic powers of Europe, were preparing to leave the city at the first opportunity. A squadron of British warships was expected in the Bay of Naples as early as mid-August. By then the British envoy had already "packed up his plate and books, and many of his pictures". Two weeks later his wife, Lady à Court, had "called on Lady Colchester to mention her own intention of proceeding to England, *the danger being such in Naples*, that the garrison had been kept under arms for several nights [that] week in apprehension of an insurrection". Since the British squadron wouldn't have been able to play any crucial military role in Naples, whether the Austrians were to invade or not, its main task – declared or otherwise – was to "aw[e] the resident authorities [...] into a guarantee for the safety of the British merchants and their property" – or, in more general terms, "to protect her British interests".[111]

In the middle of all the royal shenanigans, the international intrigues and the local threats and uncertainties, an officer of the British Fleet – whom Severn in his late memoirs calls "Lieutenant Sullivan" – offered a short comic interlude.[112] He was roaming the bay in his boat with ten of his men when he spotted the *Maria Crowther*. Either he didn't notice the yellow jack or he forgot that British traders had to undergo quarantine on their arrival in Naples, like most other foreign vessels, including warships.[113] So he went over, enquired about the passengers – which was the gallant thing to do – and made the mistake of boarding the brig. As a result, he and his ten sailors were forced to perform the quarantine with the people on board the *Maria Crowther*, and could not leave the ship until their period of isolation was over.[114] "The 10 Sailors & their chief," Severn wrote in his memoir, "was a continued source of fun to the people coming about, indeed the accident attracted hundreds to come & ridicule them—Mr Cotterell translated the jokes & made continued roars of laughter."[115]

If the episode was entertaining for those who watched, it must have been less so for those on board the *Maria Crowther*. The presence of eleven additional people would have made the already crowded and difficult conditions even worse. Keats must have been on edge all the time, ready to lash out.

Feeling poorly and exhausted, anxious about what he was leaving behind, dejected about his future, the poet longed for peace more than anything else – and the last thing he wanted was bad or boisterous company. "In the Ship when we were performing Quarantine," Severn wrote to John Taylor in January 1822,

it was proposed that the Sailors should sing us some songs to kill the time—2 or 3 sung—coarsely and brutally enough—but I was astonished at the effect on Keats—he started up—and said—"O! God! I doubt the immortality of my Soul—this grossness takes away my belief—I fall into a brute even to hear it—why do I live if these are my fellow creatures"?—[116]

More than twenty years later, perhaps referring to the same incident, Severn recollected:

When we were in the dull Quarantine with the other passengers (who were two English Ladies) the captain requested the sailors on deck to continue singing just to amuse us—I confess I did not understand or listen sufficiently to be aware of the kind of thing they were singing, but my surprise was great

when on a sudden Keats rose with a rather frantic look &
exclaimed that ["]nothing could teach him the extent of
mans depravity, that it must be part of demon existance, that
it would be difficult for these sailors in any way to rise up to
the level of brutes beasts." I soon found that Keats had pain-
fully understood they were sin[g]ing abominable songs when
they knew the Ladies below in the cabin were listening—this
he added is only another tho more sincere spec[i]men of the
unmanly depravity which Byron so publicly assumes to feel or
tries to make others feel—'tis all the same system of a crampd
& wilfull nature the one by a preverted education—the other
by no education at all.[117]

At long last, the quarantine came to an end: Lieutenant Sullivan
and his men could return to their ship, the *Maria Crowther*
was granted pratique and the passengers were allowed to go
ashore, forty-four days after their departure from London. It was
31st October, the day of John Keats's twenty-fifth birthday.

NAPLES

"A PULMONARY INVALID had better avoid Naples at any time," wrote Henry Matthews in 1818, "but certainly during the winter, unless he wish to illustrate the proverb, '*Vedi Napoli e po' mori*'."[1] The irony of this famous adage, still very common in Italy, would not have escaped Keats if he had happened to hear it.

After exchanging their passports with a *biglietto di polizia*, the passengers were allowed to disembark.[2] Their baggage was subjected to the usual examination by the custom-house officers, and they could then proceed to their lodgings. In his late memoir, Severn remembers the anticlimactic feeling he experienced on setting foot ashore:

> When the quarantine was done we were all in great regret & more so as on landing the fine city, [most] beautiful from the sea, lost all its charms, the dirt the noise, the smells, every thing seemd offensive except the glorious October atmosphere, all light & joy for the Vintage was going on every where with its songs and joy, the whole city seemd in motion, the men were running with their baskets of grapes, bawling [&] screaming with delight, not one but all & altogether & the City was well in harmony with all the noise for it had a smell of one great kitchen, cooking was going on in every street & all out of doors, at every corner was a barelegged neapolitan devouring macaroni & roaring for more, mariners in their red capes were hawking fish at the tip top of their voices & beggars were every were playing guitars & howling ballads—the whole occupation of this populous city seemd to be done in the streets, & never ceased for it went on all night so that we could not sleep for the continued row.[3]

Keats and Severn's hotel was Villa di Londra on Strada S. Lucia, just a short walk from the royal palace and not too far from the docks. Between the late nineteenth and early twentieth century that area underwent great transformation, and large portions of land were reclaimed from the sea and built over, blocking the view of the bay, but in those days Strada S. Lucia was right on the coast and, together with the adjacent Chiatamone and Chiaia, was one of the city's fashionable hotspots and a popular promenade. In the summer, it was a bustling place, and Neapolitans flocked there at all times to eat oysters and other shellfish or macaroni in the street.[4]

Although it must have been quieter during the rest of the year, it remained the area of choice for foreign travellers, and was favoured in particular by consumptives and invalids for its cleaner air and beautiful setting. It was also the site of a famous sulphur spring that was used in the treatment of several ailments.[5] People could take sulphur baths and drink *acqua suffregna* – that is, water impregnated with hydrogen sulphide – which was believed to have a curative effect.[6] Further down the road – towards the Chiatamone, near Castel dell'Ovo and the royal pleasure house – there was an ancient source of *acqua ferrata*, another beverage with miraculous properties for the ailing and the valetudinarian.[7]

"The situation of this inn," wrote a guest of Villa di Londra in October 1819, "is remarkably fine; our rooms faced the beautiful Bay; on the left was the lovely village of Portici, and above it Mount Vesuvius, proudly looking down from its fiery top on Naples; on the right, Procida, Ischia, and Capri."[8] The building in which the hotel was housed, the Palazzo d'Alessandro alla Calata di S. Lucia, had a long and distinguished history. In Parrino's 1725 guide for foreigners in Naples, it is described as a "*bel Palaggio*", a fine palace, in which

> Prince Castiglione of Aquino lived for a long time, and which, after the advent of the Duke of Anjou, having been embellished by the prince with precious furnishings, became the residence

of the Viceroy of the Kingdom, the Duke of Escalona; it belonged to President Amendola, and now belongs to his heir and successor, Duke d'Alessandro of Pescolanciano.[9]

The palace appears to have been erected at the end of the sixteenth or the beginning of the seventeenth century, when Strada S. Lucia was widened by Viceroy Enrique de Guzmán and many aristocratic residences and monumental fountains and stairs were built to adorn the littoral and replace the old fishermen's huts.[10] The building became the property of the D'Alessandros through the marriage of Isabella, daughter of President Amendola, to Fabio, jun. 1st Duke of Pescolanciano, in January 1653. It remained in the family for over 150 years, until it was sold by Nicola Maria II to Giovanni de Majo in 1820, as he attempted to clear the debts contracted by his father Pasquale Maria.[11]

The palace was never inhabited by the D'Alessandros, who preferred to rent it out from time to time to a series of wealthy and illustrious tenants, and was the scene of glittering banquets and parties which attracted not only the Neapolitan beau monde, but the highest echelons of European aristocracy. Towards the end of the eighteenth century, the building hosted a small inn, the Aquila Nera, run by a man called Don Ambrogio, and it is there that the Venerable Marie Clotilde of France, the exiled Queen of Sardinia, died on 7th March 1802, as testified by a commemorative stone plaque erected on its façade in 1939.[12]

A few years later, from before 1810, another inn operated from the same address at No. 82 Strada S. Lucia: the Albergo delle Quattro Nazioni.[13] In one of its rooms, the renowned court oculist Professor Michel Duchelard performed cataract operations in public.[14] The inn was still active under that name in June 1814, when it is mentioned in an advert for a light carriage made in Vienna that was being sold by the coachman Giovanino for 800 ducats.[15] Sometime after that, before March 1817, the Villa di Londra opened on the same site.[16] It is listed by Mariana Starke in her influential 1820 *Travels on the Continent* among the best hotels in Naples, and often quoted in other contemporary travel guides.[17]

According to Ewa Kawamura, it remained open only for a short period: from the 1830s pulmonary invalids preferred to lodge in Chiaia and Chiatamone, since those areas were regarded as more salubrious than S. Lucia.[18] The Villa di Londra is still mentioned in Gabriele Quattromani's 1827 *Itinerario delle Due Sicilie* and Mariana Starke's 1828 *Travels in Europe*.[19] After that, it seems to have closed or fallen into disregard.[20] It was replaced at the same address from around 1845 by another first-rate hotel, the Villa di Russia, which continued in several incarnations well into the twentieth century.[21] Today the building contains a mixture of offices and flats, and all its past glories have been forgotten. When I went there in the summer of 2019, I told the three caretakers in the porter's lodge that John Keats, a very famous English poet, had stayed there in November 1820, in a hotel called Villa di Londra. They said there had been an inn there, yes, a long time ago, but that wasn't the name: there was a plaque outside, if I wanted to check. I returned twenty minutes later and showed them a photo of the edifice from one of Keats's biographies. They looked at me, and then at each other, with a mixture of bewilderment and suspicion.

The first guest who left a record of his stay at Villa di Londra is Jacques Augustin Galiffe, who arrived in Naples in March 1817. His experience wasn't the most enjoyable, and the Swiss appears to have been altogether oblivious to the Neapolitans' wicked sense of humour:

> We alighted at the hotel *La Villa di Londra*, at *Santa Lucia*, where a very miserable room, containing two beds and looking to a narrow back-lane, was assigned to us, for which we were charged two dollars a day [around 20 carlins, or 7*s*. 6*d*.]: and the next morning our dislike of these quarters was increased by finding a scorpion in the window-curtain, notwithstanding our host's assertion that the reptile was harmless in winter.[22]

Scorpions apart, this was a bit of a rip-off, and Galiffe and his friend were soon able to move to "a neat though small lodging on the *Largo di Castello* [...] comprising a drawing-room, two bed-rooms, and an ante-chamber, on a first floor,—for thirty ducats, or twenty-five piasters (about five pounds ten shillings sterling) a month."[23]

Revd William Berrian, who stayed at Villa di Londra in April 1818, thought it was an "excellent hotel", where he found "comfortable apartments".[24] Another Anglican priest, Revd Thomas Pennington, was a happy resident there between October 1819 and February 1820.[25] Not so satisfied, however, was Count Martinengo, who turned up at Villa di Londra with his wife and his entourage a week after Pennington left, after a gruelling journey from Rome.

We arrived in Naples towards evensong, entering from Capo di Chino, and traversed the whole city from end to end with the intention of taking up lodgings on the coast [...].

Along the seafront – that is, in Chiaia – we found no available rooms at Magatti's, our intended destination, and we heard that all hotels were completely full and booked up. We therefore went to the Villa di Londra at S. Lucia. There were no available rooms there except for "Apartment <u>zero</u>", which consisted of three gloomy and ill-furnished rooms. Yet it was so late by then that we had to take it, since we didn't know where to turn to – moreover, the postilions were not prepared to keep wandering about.[26]

A few days later the count was able to exchange "Apartment zero" for No. 6, perhaps one with a view of the bay, for which he had to pay fifty rather than forty carlins. When he checked out of the hotel on the evening of 16th March 1820, his grumpy comment was that "if, for any quirk of fate, they were to come back to that city, they would never return to that hotel, and they would warn all their friends and acquaintances against lodging there".[27]

I suppose it is impossible to make everyone happy, and customer satisfaction – then as today – depends on the age, personality, mood and expectations of the individual guest. For Keats and Severn, after the hardships of the previous weeks, Villa di Londra must have seemed a haven of comfort. "[N]ow we are breathing in a large room," Severn wrote to Haslam the day after getting off the *Maria Crowther*,

> with Vesuvius in our view—Keats has become calm—and thinks favorably of this place—for we are meeting with much kind treatment on every side—more particularly from an English Gentleman here (brother to Miss Cotterell one of our Lady passengers)—who has shown unusually humane treatment to Keats—unasked—these—with very good accommodations at our Inn (Villa da Londra) have kept him up through dinner—but on the other hand—Dr Milne is at Rome (wither Keats is proposing to go)—the weather is now cold—wet and foggy—and we find ourselves on the wrong side—for his hope[d]-for recovery—[28]

Earlier in the letter, Severn had made a painful confession to his friend:

> I am horror struck at his sufferings on this voyage,—all that could be fatal to him in air and diet—with the want {of} medicine—and conveniences he has weather'd—if I may call his poor shattered frame—and broken heart—weathering it.—For myself I have stood it firmly until this Mor^g when in a moment my spirits dropt—at the sight of his suffering—a plentiful shower of tears (which he did not see) has relieved me somewhat—but what he has passed still unnerves me.

Keats was still alive, but the long voyage had taken its toll on his body and mind. That morning, 1st November, revived a little by the fresh air, he wrote his famous letter to Charles Brown, which he hoped would "relieve the load of WRETCHEDNESS which pressed upon [him]". He told his friend that the thought of not seeing his beloved any more would hasten him to the grave – that he should have had her when he was in health, and that he could not bear to leave her.

Oh, God! God! God! Every thing I have in my trunks that reminds me of her goes through me like a spear. The silk lining she put in my travelling cap scalds my head. My imagination is horribly vivid about her—I see her—I hear her. There is nothing in the world of sufficient interest to divert me from her a moment. This was the case when I was in England; I cannot recollect, without shuddering, the time that I was prisoner at Hunt's, and used to keep my eyes fixed on Hampstead all day. Then there was a good hope of seeing her again—Now!—O that I could be buried near where she lives! I am afraid to write to her—to receive a letter from her—to see her hand writing would break my heart—even to hear of her any how, to see her name written would be more than I can bear. My dear Brown, what am I to do? Where can I look for consolation or ease? If I had any chance of recovery, this passion would kill me. Indeed through the whole of my illness, both at your house and at Kentish Town, this fever has never ceased wearing me out. When you write to me, which you will do immediately, write to Rome (poste restante)—if she is well and happy, put a mark thus + ,—if—Remember me to all. I will endeavour to bear my miseries patiently. A person in my state of health should not have such miseries to bear. Write a short note to my sister, saying you have heard from me. Severn is very well. If I were in better health I should urge your coming to Rome. I fear there is no one can give me any comfort. Is there any news of George? O, that something fortunate had ever happened to me or my brothers!—then I might hope,—but despair is forced upon me as a habit. My dear Brown, for my sake, be her advocate for ever. I cannot say a word about Naples; I do not feel at all concerned in the thousand novelties around me. I am afraid to write to her. I should like her to know that I do not forget her. Oh, Brown, I have coals of fire in my breast. It surprises [written "surprised"] me that the human heart is capable of containing and bearing so much misery. Was I born for this end? God bless her, and her mother, and my sister, and George, and his wife, and you, and all!

Your ever affectionate friend,

John Keats[29]

That evening he confided to Severn his big secret – his love for Fanny Brawne and their engagement. "Keats went to bed much recover'd," Severn wrote the following morning, 2nd November, continuing his letter to Haslam.

I took every means to remove from him a heavy greif that may tend more than any thing to be fatal—he told me much—very much—and I dont know wether it was more painful for me or himself—but it had the effect of much relieving him—he went very calm to bed—Poor fellow!—he is still sleeping at ½ past nine—if I can but cure his mind I will bring him back to England—*well*—but I fear it never can be done in this world—the grand scenery here effects him a little—but he is too infirm to enjoy it—and but for intervals of something like ease he must soon end it———[30]

He then concluded:

[H]e requests you will tell Mrs Brawn what I think of him—for he is too bad to judge of himself—this Mor^g he is still very much better—we are in good spirits and I may say hopefull fellows—at least I may say as much for Keats—he made an Italian Pun today—the rain is coming down in torrents—

Going for a walk or a ride in that weather would have been out of the question. "When it rains hard at Naples, Galiffe wrote, "the streets are inundated by so broad a torrent, that it is absolutely impossible to cross them on foot" – or, as Théophile Gautier puts it, they are transformed "into so many torrents, and sweep away dogs and even donkeys into the sewers".[31] The damp climate would have added to Keats's sense of frustration: he must have wondered many times why he had taken the trouble to come all the way from England to face the rigours of the Italian autumn and winter seasons.

Turmoil was simmering both inside and outside the walls of the hotel Villa di Londra – and not just in the bowels of Mount Vesuvius, which had erupted earlier that year and continued to be very agitated. The radical *carbonari* were becoming more and more restless. The constitutional parliament had not delivered the results they were hoping for. As the Austrians' preparations for an invasion intensified in the north of Italy, the locals' focus switched to the bleak reality of having to assemble, in the shortest time possible and with very limited financial resources, a credible force for the defence of the kingdom.

The July insurrection, which had been initiated by the lower ranks of the infantry and the provincial "legions" of *carbonari*, had found in General Guglielmo Pepe, a hot-headed Calabrian imbued with grand liberal ideas, an unlikely figurehead. The revolutionaries' first choice as a leader would have been the older and more charismatic Michele Carrascosa, another general who had served under Joachim Murat, but they had been unable to lure him into joining their cause, and he remained suspicious of the sect's ultimate political aims.

Once the insurgents had entered Naples and the king had sworn to the constitution, Guglielmo Pepe was appointed Commander-in-Chief of the constitutional army, while the more cautious and reactionary Carrascosa was made minister of war. Just before the revolution, the kingdom's army counted around 2,000 officers, 27,000 infantry and 2,000 cavalry troops.[32] Of these, about 4,500 belonged to the police and other corps not engaged in active service, so the effective available forces amounted to just over 26,000 soldiers – not enough to confront a well-drilled Austrian army almost three times the size.[33]

Pepe engaged in a feverish effort to reorganize the constitutional army and bolster its numbers. In September, decrees were issued for raising a militia of 90,000 soldiers and a further 100,000 legionaries, most of them enlisted from radical *carbonari* lodges ("*vendite*") scattered across the provinces.[34] The force was to be divided into four military divisions – three active plus a reserve contingent of infantry and cavalry.[35] In the mean time, the *carboneria* itself, until then divided into various provincial sections, merged into a single entity and gave itself a governing body, called the "General Assembly", composed of representatives from the local *vendite*. This had its headquarters in a large building in Naples, and had its own laws, finance, magistrates and a supreme leader called "President". The General Assembly was so powerful that the constitutional government often resorted to it in order to recall those who had been discharged from military service, arrest deserters, collect taxes or enlist troops.[36] The *carboneria* expanded to include most of the soldiers and almost every citizen among its supporters, and even admitted women into its ranks, who were called "*giardiniere*" ("gardeners"). In Naples alone there were ninety-five *vendite*, one of them comprising 28,000 members.[37]

The minister of war, who was closer to the royal family and their interests, became very worried about the latest developments. In particular, he feared that the rising influence of the *carboneria* among his troops – where military *vendite* had been organized which held secret nightly meetings – would dent discipline and lead to open insubordination towards the higher-ranked officers. Carrascosa did everything in his power to ostracize Pepe's army expansion programme and rearmament drive, stoking further suspicion and hostility among the ranks of the *carbonari*.

The situation became even more tense and difficult after 1st October 1820, when with the inauguration of the constitutional parliament Guglielmo Pepe relinquished the command of the armed forces, as he had promised to do after his entrance in Naples. Now a private citizen, Pepe was seen by his radical supporters as an unrecognized hero of the revolution and a victim of envy and political back-stabbing. On the other hand, the royalists – the so-called *calderari*, who were a strong presence among the King's Guard – suspected that Pepe's real plan was to put himself at the head of a republican government with the help of the provincial troops, and hatched a plot to arrest him together with the most influential *carbonari*, which wasn't pursued because of lack of support from the British fleet in the bay.[38] In order to keep him on side and ensure public order, in mid-October Pepe was appointed inspector general of all the militia, legionaries and national guard, a huge job that, in the words of Lord Colchester, was "looked upon by many persons with great jealousy".[39]

Seeing the swelling number of radicalized and armed people in the kingdom, the minister of war warned that the situation was now out of control, and offered his resignation to Francis, Duke of Calabria, the prince regent (vicar general). When this was turned down and he was invited to carry on with his job, he refused to budge, and it was only thanks to the intercession of the king himself that he agreed to return to his post. Carrascosa's frictions with Pepe, however, continued to escalate, while in secret he began making arrangements to reinforce the gates of the royal palace and strengthen Castel Nuovo as a possible temporary stronghold for the king and his family, in case of all-out insurrection. At the same time, he remonstrated with parliament about the growing lack of discipline in the army, and demanded that the *carboneria* be outlawed among soldiers. The response was that the only remedy was to give all the troops the same colours: the red, blue and black of the *carboneria*.[40]

The number of desertions continued to grow, with 899 soldiers abandoning their posts during the first nine days of October, and 3,000 more reported as having gone off with their arms into the mountains on the ninth of that month.[41] Mutinies and clashes were an everyday occurrence, and the army was riven by rivalries, favouritism, factiousness, disengagement, discontent, snitching and careerism, as well as shortage of weapons and financial fragility.

The tensions between the troops and within the militias were mirrored in civil society. "Robberies take place nightly in the streets, shops and private houses," Lord Colchester wrote in his diary on 18th October, adding that the minister of justice, who had written to the parliament the week before to alert them to the "alarming increase of robberies", thought "the evil [was] enhanced by the shelter which the offenders took under their denomination of members of patriotic societies".[42]

It was against this backdrop that the powers of the Holy Alliance – Austria, Prussia and Russia – met from 20th October 1820 in Troppau, Silesia, to decide what course to take in order to suppress the Neapolitan revolution and restore King Ferdinand to his throne. The atmosphere in Naples was more strained than ever and full of expectation. On 23rd October, Florestano Pepe – Guglielmo's brother, who had served as the commander of the Neapolitan troops in Sicily previously, but had just been recalled and replaced by General Pietro Colletta – gave a rousing speech to parliament:

We think we are reposing upon a bed of roses, whilst we are on a bed of thorns, and on the summit of a volcano which is about to overwhelm us. Our destiny has, perhaps, been decided at Vienna; their disastrous measures are, perhaps, about to be enforced against us; and what are we doing? [...] The Fortresses [... are] destitute of *material*, the National Guards [are] undisciplined, no troops [are] dispatched to protect the Frontiers, no plan de guerre traced out, and the ardor of the Nation [is] daily abating. With respect to myself, I protest, that on the first signal of War I will abandon this august Assembly, I will run to meet the Enemy, and defend the National Liberty to Death.[43]

His parliamentarian colleague Michelangelo Castagna followed this speech with the proposal "that the troops should be placed upon a war footing without delay, and the command of the

Army given to 'the Quiroga of the Nation, Lieutenant-General WILLIAM PEPE'",[44] while the president of the Neapolitan parliament, Matteo Angelo Galdi, declared that "the rightfulness of their cause, the restraint of the great powers of Europe, the martial attitude of the Two Sicilies' nation, combined with 52,000 troops of the line and a 150,000 militia ready for deployment, should have chased away any hint of fear".[45]

A letter from Naples, dated 29th October, sounded a more sobering and ominous note:

> From the tenor, as well as from the contents of the Speech of Mr. Pepe, in the National Parliament, [...] it is to be inferred that the Kingdom of Naples is likely to become the scene of further bloodshed, not from the height to which party feeling may be carried by the People, but by the approach of a large Austrian force.

"The most recent accounts from Vienna," said another letter of the same date, also from the capital,

> breathe nothing but hostility against Naples, and July next is even named as the ultimate period when an Austrian force will be in occupation of the Neapolitan territory. The army, which is already distributed along the Po, is stated to amount to 70,000 men, and a second of 80,000 men is to be formed on the Adige, to serve as a reserve when the first advances.[46]

The Neapolitan papers put on a brave face, feigning composure:

> In the midst of the excitement which animates every region of our kingdom, we are enjoying the utmost peacefulness. Our armed force is almost at full strength: for the great part, its ranks are composed of battle-hardened veterans who are eager to show off their abilities in the glory of the battlefield.

We are waiting for confirmation of the rumour, which was spread a few days ago, that the Austrians are withdrawing their armies: we are not afraid of war – although we'd rather not engage in one.[47]

The report of an Austrian retreat was unfounded: perhaps, as suggested by the last sentence in this extract, it was just wishful thinking.

Although the local papers, "not [being] allowed to give any details", made no mention of this, Naples "was almost every day a prey to the greatest disorders".[48] The last day of October, the day Keats and Severn took up lodgings at Villa di Londra, was no exception. On that evening, in nearby Chiaia, Pasquale Fannino, "a captain affiliated with the infantry of the National Guard of Naples, in the company of some armed individuals [...] had the effrontery to seize from the hands of the police a man who was under arrest". The news only emerged ten days later, when Fannino was taken to the criminal court in order to be charged for his offences and dismissed from the military. "This prompt and exemplary measure, made officially public in the *Giornale Costituzionale*," wrote the author of the article, "will further persuade any malevolent foreigner that the Neapolitan Nation makes the greatest effort to prevent that a single disturbance should go unpunished, and to preserve the glory of the National Guard in all its unsullied purity."[49]

But this was empty talk: the reality was quite different. The 2nd of November was an even more eventful day, as reported on the front page of the *Oesterreichischer Beobachter* sixteen days later, and soon relayed by other Italian and international newspapers:

According to the latest accounts of 3rd inst. from Naples, it appears that the anarchy that has been simmering in that city is about to explode. On 2nd, two *carbonari* were arrested – one of them, belonging to the lowest rabble, for refusing to pay his taxes and hurling insults at the public authorities; the other, an officer and an adjutant, for an attempt on the life of the minister of war, General Carrascosa. Armed bands of *carbonari* then gathered in front of Castel Sant'Elmo, where their companions were detained, with the aim of setting them free and subsequently storming the Vicaria (one of the public jails) and releasing the criminals who are held there. Although the troops were able to foil this plan, there were great fears about its consequences.

On the evening of the same day, numerous throngs of *carbonari* turned up in front of the royal palace with the intention of giving offence to the royal family. But the cavalry of the King's Guard dispersed the insurgents and, blocking their way, stopped them from attacking the Vicaria: many guns were soon mounted there, as well as in front of the royal palace. Though the mutiny had been quelled for the time being, there were strong apprehensions about the following nights, and it was ordered that 3,000 men from the National Guard should be on armed duty each night. It was also resolved that anyone who refused to join the National Guard would be detained at Castel Sant'Elmo.

This may be Austrian propaganda, of course, but the account is quite circumstantial, and there was no official rebuttal by the constitutional papers.[50] It is true that Carrascosa doesn't mention this attempt on his life in his memoir, but a letter of 4th November from the prince regent to Pepe, who was inspector general of the National Guard at the time, seems to corroborate the events: "I was delighted to learn from your report of yesterday that during the previous night [2nd November] the public peace was not broken at all."[51]

A separate incident was reported by Lord Colchester in his diary on 4th November:

A day or two ago, the police arrested a Marchese Rossi, whom they found in a low pot-house, armed with pistols and a stiletto. He being a Carbonaro, his lodge immediately assembled, and their Grand Master, a cook of the Duca di Sangro, with sixteen others, rescued him, but are themselves now prisoners in the Vicaria. The lodge having decreed that the house of the commissary of police who arrested Rossi shall be pulled down, it has been protected since Thursday night [2nd November] by a guard of 200 men patrolling the streets. General Pepé was actively employed in making the arrest. A strong force also bivouacked in the Villa Reale.

As these disturbances raged outside, not far from Villa di Londra, the two English travellers were still recovering from quarantine in the quiet and comfort of their room. "Keats was but so so," Severn recalled of their days in Naples, "& scarcely strong enough to go about, but yet he pick'd up for awhile with the excitement for there was the revolution of 1820 still going [on] & every one talking about it—He was persuaded to go to a grand review," he added, as the memory of that rare day of enjoyment reawakened in his mind.[52] The parade in question was on Saturday, 4th November. There had been another one, even more imposing, a few days before, on Sunday, 29th October, which had been reported in several national and international newspapers, but recent events must have persuaded Pepe, Carrascosa and the prince regent to make a further show of force, and send a signal both to the international powers, in particular the Austrians, and the local radical *carbonari*.[53]

The *Giornale Costituzionale del Regno delle Due Sicilie* of 4th November published the following announcement:

This morning, H.R.H. the Duke of Calabria, the Vicar General, has passed in review in the Field [of Mars] the third active division of the army – if a corps of thirteen thousand men can be called a "division". Alongside the third, six battalions of the second division were gathered in the Field, as well as eight squadrons of cavalry, thirty guns and a reserve artillery park. It had been a long time since we last saw such a numerous and orderly gathering of troops, dressed in such fine uniforms – and, we may add, displaying in most of the soldiers and of the officers that martial demeanour which is the revealing sign of those veterans who served, not without distinction, in Spain, in Germany and in the farthest north, and who even during the ill-fated campaign of the last Italian war achieved no little glory, though faced with an enemy infinitely superior in number. H.R.H. rode in front of the two lines and the reserve one, and all the troops were made to parade before him, after which they returned to their quarters.[54]

Another local paper shared in the enthusiasm and praised the warlike appearance of the soldiers:

Are the Austrians going to attack us? This is the question that occupies the minds of all our troops, among whom circulate various alarming rumours. This state of alarm, however, is of no small advantage to us, since our government is setting up defensive measures in all expeditiousness. On Saturday 4th instant, a division of our armed forces made a beautiful display of itself in a drill at the Field of Mars. All good Neapolitans were extremely delighted at the spectacle – the choiceness of the soldiers, the noble demeanour with which they advanced and their altogether martial outfit.[55]

Severn was impressed by the parade, but Keats seemed underwhelmed. "[T]he King [was] in command," Severn wrote in his late memoir, "& it appeard to me that the Neapolitan soldiers were fine looking men tho without any military air—Keats pronounced upon them that they were not fighting men & that they would never stand."[56] In another, earlier account of the review, Severn recalled: "I was struck with their fine appearance but Keats said—'Its all nothing, the've not stamina, they'll all run away.'—As this was at the moment when they had settld the Revolution of 20, it show'd great discrimination—"[57]

The Field of Mars (Campo di Marte), a large ground used for military manoeuvres, was also a popular destination for day outings and even the site of occasional cricket matches.[58] It was located to the north-east of the city, in open countryside, in an area now occupied by Capodichino International Airport. Since Keats was, according to Severn's testimony, weak and in poor health most of the time during his stay in Naples, after coughing blood while at sea a couple of weeks before, and since they left for Rome soon after 7th November, it is possible that 4th November was the only day when the poet was able to go out, enjoy some of the city's amenities and experience any social interaction.

Perhaps we can connect his presence at the parade with the famous story related by the Scottish writer Charles Macfarlane in his *Reminiscences of a Literary Life*:

Late in the autumn of 1820, when he arrived at Naples, or rather at the commencement of the winter of that year, he was driving with my friend Charles Cottrell from the Bourbon Museum, up the beautiful open road which leads up to Capo di Monte and the Ponte Rossi. On the way, in front of a villa or cottage, he was struck and moved by the sight of some rose-trees in full bearing. Thinking to gratify the invalid, Cottrell, a *ci-devant* officer in the British Navy, jumped out of the carriage, spoke to somebody about the house or garden, and was back in a trice with a bouquet of roses.

"How late in the year! What an exquisite climate!" said the Poet; but on putting them to his nose, he threw the flowers down on the opposite seat, and exclaimed: "Humbugs! They have no scent! What is a rose without its fragrance? I hate and abhor all humbug, whether in a flower or in a man or woman!" And having worked himself strongly up in the anti-humbug humour, he cast the bouquet out on the road. I suppose that the flowers were China roses, which have little odour at any time, and hardly any at the approach of winter.

Returning from that drive, he had intense enjoyment in halting close to the Capuan Gate, and in watching a group of *lazzaroni* or labouring men, as, at a stall with fire and cauldron by the roadside in the open air, they were disposing of an incredible quantity of macaroni, introducing it in long, unbroken strings into their capacious mouths, without the intermediary of anything but their hands. "I like this," said he; "these hearty fellows scorn the humbug of knives and forks. Fingers were invented first. Give them some *carlini* that they may eat more! Glorious sight! How they take it in!"[59]

Macfarlane wrote this towards the end of his life, when lame, almost blind and without a farthing in his pocket he had been admitted as a poor brother of the Charterhouse on the nomination of the Archbishop of Canterbury. He was bitter about life and felt short-changed by the world of letters, which he thought he had enriched with over thirty published works and a number of articles and essays, now all forgotten. "Literature no longer affords me the ample income I derived from it during more than a quarter of a century," he moaned in the preface to his book of reminiscences. Yet he was by no means an old man at the time: he was only fifty-seven – and, if we are to believe him, "[his] memory [was] unimpaired" and he thought that he could "report with tolerable accuracy".[60] And in truth his recollections, full of memorable anecdotes and often told with a novelist's gusto, are at times very colourful and detailed. The trouble is that it is difficult to distinguish between fact and fiction in his memoirs, and whereas some of his literary portraits seem authentic – such as the one of Thomas James Mathias, the author of the satirical poem *The Pursuits of Literature*, whom he appears to have known very well in Naples, where they lived in the same building in Pizzofalcone – others appear to be imaginary lives rather than actual snapshots of biography.[61] Take for example his chapter on Percy Bysshe Shelley, which opens the collection and precedes the shorter piece on John Keats.[62] In it we see a nineteen-year-old Macfarlane meeting

Shelley at the Bourbon Museum and striking up an unlikely friendship with him.[63] They talk about the statues, converse about the eternal feminine, meet Gabriele Rossetti – whom they both think a pedant and a bore – then Macfarlane takes his new friend upstairs, and there, "being well acquainted with all the librarians", he shows Shelley a number of rare books and some manuscripts. The museum is about to close, and they leave together. The young Scot is due to dine with Gioachino Rossini and the painter Giacomo Micheroux at a villa in Capodimonte, so he bids a reluctant goodbye to his new friend – but, as luck would have it, he bumps into Shelley the next morning in the Via Toledo, where he is introduced to him by a common acquaintance, Doctor John Roskilly. It was "a cheering, glorious day under the unclouded sky and warm sun of Naples", and on the spur of the moment, Macfarlane and Shelley hire a coach and two and fly off to visit Pompeii, which they enter from the Street of Tombs – "as people should always do" – "not by the barracks of the Roman soldiers".[64] They stay there for hours, and "in the scarcely injured house, called *La Casa di Pansa*, [partake] of an excellent refection, with fruit and good wine of the vintage of Gragnano, on the shelving hills near Castellamare, all furnished by the provident care of the two old *ciceroni*, who were already [Macfarlane's] old friends". On the way back they stop near an unspecified ancient Norman castle and walk to the shore, where they remain in meditative, melancholy silence until sunset – and where, Macfarlane is confident, Shelley "*thought* [...] those thrilling verses [...] called 'Stanzas, written in dejection, near Naples'". That is not enough: before making their way back to the city, they pull up in Torre Annunziata, where Macfarlane gives Shelley a quick tour of one of the macaroni manufactories, then they rattle over the lava-buried city of Herculaneum, see a short column of fire projected from the uppermost crater of Mount Vesuvius and return in a cheerful mood to Naples, where Macfarlane is introduced to Shelley's wife Mary.[65]

Their budding friendship, however, was not destined to bloom, since Shelley, Macfarlane informs us, left Naples for Rome a day or two later. "I did not see him again till late in the year 1820," he writes,

and then I saw but little of him, for he was staying at Pisa with Lord Byron, Leigh Hunt, Captain Medwin, and one or two others, and I was only passing through Pisa on my way to Florence. I saw him no more, though I was very near meeting him at Leghorn in 1822, and just before his boat was capsized in the Gulf of Spezzia. But in the interval I had heard a great deal of him and of his generous doings, from Keats, Severn the painter, Bopp the sculptor, and others.

There is always a lot of name-dropping, local colour and specific knowledge in Macfarlane's book of memoirs – as in the rest of his works – which makes his account very persuasive. He knows everybody: everyone is a "friend", a "dear friend" or an "old friend" of his. He seems to have the ability to be always at the right place at the right moment: he is ubiquitous, omnipresent, a kind of Forrest Gump or Zelig *avant la lettre* – time and distance never appear to be a problem for him. Yet he is never mentioned in the letters, journals or memoirs of his contemporaries. In fact, the more one reads of his work, the more one analyses the chronology and the context of the events he relates, the easier it is to demonstrate that he was not just an unreliable narrator, but a consummate fabricator.[66]

Something that Macfarlane perhaps could not have foreseen when he was writing his chapter on Shelley is that today we are able to compare his account with other sources. According to Mary Shelley's journal, she and her husband visited Pompeii twice during their stay in Naples: first on 22nd December 1818 and then on 25th February 1819, three days before setting off for Rome.[67] Shelley left a very detailed description of their first visit in his letter of 26th January 1819 to Thomas Love Peacock.[68] The poet was accompanied there by his wife Mary. They "entered the town from the side towards the sea" – that is, from the Quadriportico dei Teatri, or the barracks of the

Roman soldiers, as it was also known – Pompeii's southern entrance.[69] They first saw the Large Theatre and the Odeon, strolled through the ancient streets, visited the temples of Aesculapius and Isis – then, through "labyrinths of walls and columns", they came to the Forum and stopped under the colonnade of the portico of the Temple of Jupiter, where they "pulled out [their] oranges, and figs, and bread, and medlars— sorry fare [...]—and rested to eat." From there they made their way back through the consular road, exiting Pompeii from the north-eastern gate of the city – which Shelley was supposed to have entered earlier that morning in the company of his new young friend – and saw the famous Street of Tombs. There were no *ciceroni* that day, no Gragnano wine, no visit to a Norman castle, no macaroni – and, of course, no Charles Macfarlane.

The Shelleys' second trip to Pompeii did indeed take place only a few days before they left Naples for Rome, as Macfarlane recounts in his memoir, but it was a cursory visit at the end of a three-day excursion to Paestum. Mary's journal entries for those days read:

> Teusday 23 [February 1819]—
> A ~~rayni~~ rainy day—set off for Paestum—sleep at Salerno
> Wednesday 24th
> Go to Paestum—Stopt at a river five miles from Paestum & obliged to walk—A dull day but a fine evening untill senset when it begins to rain again—
> Thursday 25
> Return to Naples—Visit Pompeii on our road—finish Sismondi
> Friday 26th
> Visit the Studii—
> Saturday 27th
> Pack—
> Sunday 28th
> Leave Naples at 2 o'clock—

Again the Shelleys were travelling together, and again they would have entered Pompeii from its southern entrance as they returned to Naples on the road from Salerno.

Perhaps Macfarlane met the Shelleys or had a glimpse of them at the Bourbon Museum (the "Studii") on the Friday before their departure, and heard that they had just returned from Pompeii. Had he known that they had visited Paestum, he might have spun a much longer tale, as he later did in one of his published books, where he reminisced about a long pedestrian trip to the ruins of that city during the Easter holidays of 1822 in the company of an English friend.[70]

As to Macfarlane's passing visit late in the autumn of the following year, we know that although it is true that Captain Medwin was at the Shelleys' from around 22nd October 1820 – it is a well-attested fact that Byron moved to Pisa only in early November 1821 and that Leigh Hunt could not honour his friends' invitation to join them in Italy until July 1822, after an eight-month voyage from London.[71]

Macfarlane professed to have had no other aim in mind, in jotting down his reminiscences, than to "amuse [his] solitude".[72] His book remained unpublished during his lifetime, and it was salvaged from destruction and oblivion by pure accident. The romantic halo surrounding the rediscovery of the manuscript and the alleged disinterestedness with which it was written fooled many critics, and contributed to lending credence and authority to the literary myths it created. It is clear, however, that Macfarlane was not a simple fantasist, but the author of a crafty web of half-truths and deceptions, which he hoped would help him, after his death, achieve the fame his contemporaries had denied him in life.

Did Macfarlane ever meet John Keats? It is very unlikely. In his affectionate portrait of the poet he calls him "John" and declares that "He was one of the most cheery and plucky little fellows I ever knew", but it is difficult to see how he could have got to know Keats during his short stay in Naples. Most of the information in the first half of his piece appears to be derived from

Monckton Milnes's biography of the poet, published in 1848. However, the second part of his account, quoted above, despite having the ring of a second-hand after-dinner anecdote, should not be altogether dismissed, and warrants closer inspection.

Macfarlane does not appear in it as one of the characters, and his grasp of the timeline of Keats's stay in Naples is rather tenuous, suggesting that he heard about it only sometime after the event. Who could have told him the story? The most obvious candidates are Cotterell and Severn – the only two people who had any reason to be with Keats on that day. But although Macfarlane calls Charles Cotterell "[his] friend", his description of him as a "*ci-devant* officer in the British Navy" indicates that he wasn't very well acquainted with him and his activities, and that perhaps he only knew him by sight or through the circle of Sir William Drummond and Thomas James Mathias.[73] On the other hand, it is quite possible that the source for the story may have been "[his] dear friend Joseph Severn".[74] The painter only spent a week or so in Naples on that occasion, but returned to the city in the summer of 1822, when he was a guest of Charles Cotterell in Naples and of a "very kind Gentleman" in Sorrento.[75] Since we know that during that visit he spent some time at the Bourbon Museum, a favourite haunt of Macfarlane, he would have had ample opportunity to talk to him and reminisce about his friend, who had died the previous year.[76]

We're drifting, of course, into the realm of pure conjecture, but what makes this episode interesting is that it is consistent with the chronology of Keats's sojourn in Naples and gives a plausible portrayal of his state of mind. The coach drive to Capodimonte and the ruins of the Roman aqueduct at Ponti Rossi was one of the touristic highlights of the city, and Keats's passion for flowers is well documented.[77] The 4th of November was a clear, mild day.[78] The poet seemed to revive a little that morning, and it is possible that Cotterell, wishing to express his gratitude towards him and Severn, offered to be their *cicerone* and took them on a tour of some of the city's most celebrated attractions. After passing under the arches of the Ponti Rossi bridge, they would have met crowds of people going to see the review at the Field of Mars, either through the shorter but very steep Calata Capodichino or the magnificent Strada Nuova del Campo a little further down the road, which was longer, but gentler and more comfortable for someone in Keats's condition.[79] Cotterell, an ex-military man, would have been keen to show his friends the parade, while the poet, who hated anything soldierly and martial, perhaps only agreed to go there on the spur of the moment, out of courtesy towards his guide.[80]

Although it is true that the words Macfarlane puts in the poet's mouth as they stopped near Porta Capuana on their return to the city sound more phoney than the "humbug" they are supposed to revile, and although it is unlikely that Keats would have asked his friend to throw carlins at the macaroni-eating *lazzaroni* – quoting Swift, for good measure, to illustrate his point – this remains a fascinating anecdote that, even if imaginary in part, offers a chink of light and good cheer in the bleak expanse of Keats's final months.[81]

"We went that evening to San Carlo," Severn recalled of the day of the review.[82] Dinner followed by the opera – both no doubt offered by Charles Cotterell as a further token of his gratefulness – was the perfect way to crown a day of entertainment. The San Carlo, which had been rebuilt a few years before after being destroyed by fire, was no ordinary theatre: it was a world-renowned architectural marvel and the heart of Neapolitan society.[83] In the words of Sir William Gell, it was "the splendid coffee house of the Kingdom & the place where visits [were] made" – it "swallow[ed] up every thing."[84] Tickets were coveted by tourists and Neapolitans alike, and since seats were numbered and habitués abounded, Cotterell must have gone to some trouble to secure admission for Keats and Severn that night.[85]

The programme for 4th November 1820 included Rossini's opera semiseria in two acts *Torvaldo e Dorliska* and the historical ballet in five acts *Otranto liberata* by Salvatore Taglioni.[86] After its premiere at the Teatro Valle in Rome on 26th December 1815, *Torvaldo e Dorliska* had further productions, in 1818, at the Teatro San Moisè in Venice and at La Scala in Milan, where the legendary tenor Giovanni Battista Rubini took the male title role. The opera made its debut at the San Carlo on 26th September 1820, enjoying a run of fifteen performances.[87] Its cast boasted some of the most celebrated singers of the day: the Spanish prima donna Isabella Colbran (Dorliska) – who married Gioachino Rossini in March 1822 – Andrea Nozzari (Torvaldo) and Filippo Galli (Duca d'Ordow).[88] Among the audience that day, as well as several local dignitaries and, no doubt, many of the officers from the British squadron, were members of the royal family.[89] This meant it was a gala night, and a "prodigious number of wax lights" were lit, turning the interior of the theatre into a coruscating feast of gaudiness.[90]

"[W]e [...] were both struck with the scenery," Severn wrote in his 1845 account of that evening,

> particularly with two sentinels admirably done & which Keats praised as the finest painting he ever saw—At the close of the first act, our amazement cannot be described, nor Keats['s] emotion when he discove[r]d that they were real Sentinel{s} but placed in the midst of scene where no Englishman could expect or indure such a thing.—Our surprise over, Keats exclaimd—"We'll go instantly to Rome, for as I know my end approaches, I could not die calmly, were I to kno{w} that my bones were to remain amongst a people with such miserable politicks—"[91]

We know, of course, why the soldiers were there – the presence of members of the royal family would have prompted a stepping-up of security – and we can't accuse the authorities of being too cautious and vigilant, because less than three weeks later a group of rioters stormed the theatre, looking for trouble, as reported by the *Messaggere Tirolese* of 8th December 1820:

> Two days ago [22nd November], there was the dress rehearsal for a ballet at the Teatro di San Carlo. The doors were shut,

and entrance was strictly forbidden to everyone. The relevant authorities were presiding over the rehearsal, when a band of ill-intentioned people, about 50 in number, demanded admittance. Since their request to be let in was rejected, they knocked down the doors and rushed into the stalls area and onto the stage, and as a result of this disturbance the rehearsal was suspended. It should be added that, having penetrated by force into the theatre's coffee shop, which was then closed and unattended by its manager, they drank their fill of Malaga and Rosolio without paying anything. Everyone expects these people to be handed out an exemplary punishment. In the mean time, the public has applauded the severe measures taken by the government yesterday morning and yesterday evening in relation to the above-mentioned theatre.[92]

After all the excitement and the fatigue of the previous day, Keats must have spent the Sunday in the quiet of his hotel room, recovering his strength ahead of the daunting journey to Rome. It may well have been on that day, 5th November, that Severn saw the king pass through the streets of Naples, as he recalled in his late memoir:

I stood up one day & waited 20 minutes to see the King & when he came I was dismayd for he [had the] face of a goat & I said to myself "if ever I might have to do with legislation I'd make a law that sovereigns should be good looking people at least"—the sight of this King Ferdinand with his goat countenance, let down my loyalty 50 degrees—he was true to his countenance for

The next day the King ~~escaped~~ stole away having taken the most solemn oath to the constitution his first step was to break it the moment the Popes absolution arrived[.] & Naples found itself betrayd, for a moment there was a silence in Naples in the atonishment that the King was fled & they were betrayd.[93]

Here "the next day" is not to be read in a literal sense – or it could be an error caused by chronological compression, not uncommon in Severn – because King Ferdinand only left Naples on 13th December 1820 in order to join the representatives of Austria, Russia and Prussia at the Congress of Laibach (Ljubljana), but it is clear that the image of goat-faced Re Nasone and his much-publicized "escape" on board the British warship HMS *Vengeur* left a deep mark in Severn's memory.[94]

That Sunday, Keats and Severn would also have heard – and perhaps seen – a salvo of loud explosions in the bay. At 1 p.m. the British fleet fired a 19-gun salute in commemoration of the Gunpowder Plot, and at 1.30 p.m. an 11-gun salute was discharged from the *Liffey* on the visit of the English consul, followed by a 13-gun salute on Lord Ruthven leaving the ship.[95] The unaware locals must have heard all those booming noises with a touch of concern.

The following days were used by Keats and Severn to make preparations for their journey to Rome. No doubt Charles Cotterell – an industrious, hospitable, extremely active man – would have helped them with every aspect of the trip, from giving them advice on the best means of transport, to choosing the *vetturino*, to haggling with him over the fare and getting all their paperwork in order.[96] As well as his experience in the shipment of goods and his useful contacts at the British legation, he could provide the moral support the two young travellers needed so much in the chaotic and rather hostile environment of Naples.[97] Although he would have had no time to introduce them to his local network of friends and acquaintances, he would have been able to offer guidance and entertainment to his English guests. And Cotterell was no dry merchant or dour ex-military man: as well as being a generous, lavish host who loved a party and a glass or two of good wine, he had strong literary inclinations, as testified by Madden's recollections, which place him right at the heart of the British expatriate community of early-1820s Naples, one that included antiquarians, linguists and literati:

Those persons are not likely to forget Dr. Quin who remember Naples and its society in the time of Sir William Drummond, Sir William Gell, the Honorable Keppel Craven, Sir Frederick Faulkner, the Margravine of Anspach, the well-known Abbé Campbell, the Blessingtons, Sir Richard Acton and his lady; Dr. Watson, the celebrated linguist; Ramsay, the Scotch merchant, with his elegant tastes and classic lore; Cottrell, the wine merchant, of Fallernian celebrity, renowned for his *lachrymachristi*, and his efforts to rival Francis, and to render Horace into better English than all previous translators; Reilly, the true Hibernian; Dr. Milne, the skillful Scot, and accomplished gentleman of the Chiatamone; old Walker, of the Largo Castello, the expatriated Manchester reformer, who, in the good old times of William Pitt and George III., was tried for sedition, and narrowly escaped the fate of his reforming brethren, Muir and Palmer; and, though last, not least deserving of remembrance and of honorable mention in the list of worthies from foreign lands who figured in Neapolitan society some thirty years ago, the venerable commandant of the Castello d'Ovo, General Wade [...]. Maurice Quill should have lived in Naples in those days, and Lever should have recorded all the extraordinary scenes and ridiculous occurrences.[98]

Cotterell's translation efforts do not appear to have survived, but someone with those interests – who loved Horace and hoped to rival the greatest Latin translators of the past – must have made very good company for Keats and Severn.

On Monday, 6th November, Keats and Severn had their passports signed at the British legation in Naples. The endorsement, translated from the French, reads:

Seen at the Brit[h] Leg[n] in Naples on 6. Nov. 1820.
    Permission granted to travel to England
    by authority of the Minister.
                        A. DOUGLAS
                        Secr. of Leg[n].

"Why Keats wished his passport viséed for England, I am unable to understand," writes Amy Lowell in her biography of the poet. "Was it a necessary formality in case he wanted to go home by a different route?"[99] This is a very good question, and the only plausible answer is that Keats's intention, at that point, must have been to try to weather the winter in Rome and then make a desperate journey back to England and die there, among his friends and loved ones, tended by his fiancée.

On the following day, Severn and Keats obtained a visa to enter the Papal States – which, translated from the Italian, reads:

Seen at the Pap[l] Consulate General
   permission granted to enter His
   Holiness's States within twelve ds
Naples 7th Novr 1820
         The Consul General
      DOM[co] ALBERTAZZI

As well as having their passports signed by the British legation and the Papal States' consulate, any British travellers wishing to proceed from Naples to Rome were required to obtain a certificate of good conduct from the local police, to avoid being questioned or detained at the first Neapolitan checkpoint. Severn and Keats applied for their permits on 7th November from the Office of Public Security.[100] These certificates, which have escaped previous researchers, are a standard confirmation that the applicant "is not accused of any crime" and that "there is no claim against him in relation to any civil proceeding according to the police registers". They do not provide any new information, but confirm that Keats's intended final destination was indeed his yearned-for motherland, "Inghilterra" – and that he was desperate to return there to die.

INTERLUDE

BEFORE WE LEAVE NAPOLI "LA GENTILE" and accompany the two young travellers on their way to the Eternal City – and Keats on his final journey on earth – it is worth taking a short pause. We have analysed all the verified facts and events since Keats and Severn's departure from England. We have discussed some of the things they *may* have said or done. Now perhaps is the time to dispel the myths surrounding the last chapter of Keats's life and talk about what we are confident did *not* happen.

Many readers will be surprised that no reference is made in these pages to some of the incidents and picturesque detail that can be found in all other Keats biographies. The reason is quite simple: they are not supported by any actual evidence, and are derived in most part, as mentioned in the preface, from one source: Chapters III and IV of William Sharp's *Life and Letters of Joseph Severn*.[1] These fifty-odd pages, written more than a century ago, have shaped our general perception of the poet's time in Italy and propagated a host of falsehoods and half-truths that live on to this day.

Since we have already had a taste of imaginary biography in the previous chapter, there is no need to go into too much detail now. It may be useful, however, to take a cursory look at Sharp's methods, as well as what might have been his motivations in writing a fraudulent account of Keats's final months.[2] As we have seen, Charles Macfarlane made his stories more compelling by peppering them with credible detail and verifiable fact, sometimes experienced at first hand. William Sharp went one step further: in some cases he reproduced the original documents with no alterations or very few changes, often providing facsimiles; in others, he invented new, alternative versions of existing material;

in others still, he mixed and blended together *real* memoirs and letters from various periods, adding detail, smoothing out the chronology, inserting explanations and embellishing language ad hoc. The result of all his interpolations is not a gripping cut-up narrative worthy of William S. Burroughs or Alan Burns, but a crude pastiche, as might be expected from a writer who tries to mimic the language of someone who lived seventy years earlier. However, since some of the chapters from one of Severn's memoirs are supposed to be missing – including those that chronicle the passage to Italy and the journey from Naples to Rome – and since his letters and papers remained unavailable to scholars for consultation until the 1970s, Sharp's version of events – in which he filled the gaps and mashed up the material as best suited his purpose – went unchallenged for a long time, and was accepted and appropriated wholesale by Keats biographers.[3]

Severn emerges from Sharp's book as a voluble, cheerful, carefree young man, the devoted and self-sacrificing friend of John Keats. It is of course an idealized portrait, devoid of any psychological nuance, as anyone who reads the whole body of his letters and memoirs can confirm. Polished by Sharp, Severn's writing, which tends to be factual, concise and undescriptive, becomes garrulous and florid, and is interspersed with priceless anecdotes and a general sense of entertainment and adventure. As for Keats himself, who in Severn's letters and memoirs tends to remain in the background of his friend's speaking voice, he often takes centre stage in Sharp's narrative: we see him as a happy-go-lucky, witty, exuberant John-a-dreams – closer to the preposterous portrayal of him given by Anthony Burgess in *ABBA ABBA* than to the real-life irritable, moody, gloomy, bitter poet we know from his last letters.

In *The Life and Letters of Joseph Severn*, we are always given – whenever the narrative allows – an insight into Keats's mind and feelings, because its author was well aware that the main interest for his readers was not the painter's own life, but the halcyon days of his friendship with Keats – their voyage to Italy, their short stay in Naples and their final months in Rome, which created an eternal bond between them – and, above all, any accompanying new biographical revelation about the poet. And, to be sure, Sharp was not ungenerous in providing quotable snippets, which have found their way into all modern biographies of Keats.

When the *Maria Crowther* passes the Straits, we learn that "Keats was deeply impressed" with the great beauty of the scene. "Behind us," Severn says in Sharp's account,

> lay the mass of Gibraltar, now all glowing like a vast topaz; around us a wide expanse of ocean, calm and yet full of life and motion with the favouring westerly breeze; beyond us, a sunlit waste of dancing shimmering wavelets; and, seeming close to starboard, so translucent was that fine air, the African coast, here golden, and there blue as a sapphire, stretching away into a pearly haze. Keats lay entranced, and with a look of serene abstraction upon his worn face; while I, glad of the easy motion and the genial warmth, sat near and made a sketch in water-colours.[4]

Later on, when they enter the Bay of Naples, words seems to fail Severn, but Sharp is only too happy to oblige:

> It would be difficult to depict in words the first sight of this Paradise as it appears from the sea. The white houses were lit up with the rising sun, which had just began to touch them, and being tier above tier upon the hill-slopes, they had a lovely appearance, with so much green verdure and the many vineyards and olive grounds about them. Vesuvius had an immense line of smoke-clouds built up, which every now and then opened and changed with the sun's golden light, edging and composing all kinds of groups and shapes in lengths and masses for miles. Then the mountains of Sorrento to the right seemed like lapis lazuli and gold; the sea between being of a very deep blue such as we had not seen elsewhere, and so rich and beautiful that it gave great splendour to all the objects on

shore. So lovely was the ever-changing scene that we were not so bitterly chagrined as we would otherwise have been when we were informed that we were placed in quarantine for ten days, owing to the fact that there was then an epidemic of typhus in London, and it was feared that we might have brought the contagion. Keats was simply entranced with the unsurpassable beauty of the panorama, and looked longingly at the splendid city of Naples and her terraced gardens and vineyards, upon the long range of the Apennines, with majestic Vesuvius emitting strange writhing columns of smoke, golden at their sunlit fringes, and upon the azure foreground covered with ships and all manner of white-sailed small craft. It was a relief to me that he was so taken out of himself, for he was often so distraught, with so sad a look in his eyes, with, moreover, sometimes, a starved, haunting expression that bewildered me. Yet at that time I never fully understood how terrible were his mental sufferings, for so excruciating was the grief that was eating away his life that he could speak of it to no one. He was profoundly depressed the day we went ashore at Naples, though he had been so eager to leave the ship and explore the beautiful city; indeed, I was more alarmed on his behalf that night than even during that wretched three days' storm in the Bay of Biscay.[5]

During the early days of quarantine, Severn tells us, in Sharp's account:

It was a delight to hear him talk of the classic scenes he seemed to know so well; he made it all live again, that old antique world when the Greek galleys and Tyrhenian sloops brought northward strange tales of what was happening in Hellas and the mysterious East. He could even be gay before Miss Cotterell, for he seemed to breathe an inspiration from the lovely environment. There was constant entertainment, too, in the people surrounding our ship, as they passed by playing upon their guitars and singing songs, or came alongside to barter with us.

Our schooner was anchored near the Castell' d'Uovo, and was soon, and constantly afterwards, surrounded by scores of Neapolitan boats with gorgeous heaps of autumnal fruits—grapes, peaches, figs, melons, and many other kinds I had never before seen, all in such abundance that it seemed as though we had arrived at the Enchanted Island—an illusion heightened by the endless array of picturesque skiffs and shallops, with sweet stirring music coming from many of them, the tinkling of the guitars mingling with happy laughter and innumerable shouts, cries, and exclamations of all kinds. Perhaps the novelty alone was an irresistible charm, and made our haven seem, to me at least, as though it were the shore of Paradise.[6]

"It must, indeed," Sharp interjects at this point, "as Severn says elsewhere, have been a delightful experience for the young artist who had seen so little that was beautiful; and had Keats only been able to enjoy it aright, the time would have passed happily indeed."

Indeed. These few examples suffice to show how distant Sharp's accounts are in language, tone, style and mood from their original counterparts. And as if the embellishments, the factual inaccuracies and the descriptive fripperies were not enough, Sharp invents some gratuitous details out of thin air. The day after the theatre outing, Keats is supposed to have "received a letter from Shelley, then in Pisa, urging him to come northward, and be the guest of him and his wife; a most generous letter, and the second he had received from that fine poet and noble man". This is all very circumstantial, but we know it is an outright lie, since Shelley wrote to Marianne Hunt on 29th October 1820, when Keats and Severn were still undergoing quarantine:

Where is Keats now? I am anxiously expecting him in Italy where I shall take care to bestow every possible attention on him. I consider his a most valuable life, & I am deeply interested in his safety. I intend to be the physician both of his body & his soul, to keep the one warm & to teach {the} other Greek & Spanish. I am aware indeed in part {tha}t I am nourishing a rival who will far surpass {me} and this is an additional motive & will be an added pleasure.

[…] An old friend & fellow townsman of mine Captain Medwin is on a visit to us at present, & we anxiously expect Keats, to whom I would write if I knew where to address.[7]

If Keats never received Shelley's second letter from Pisa, then how can we believe what follows in Severn's spurious memoir?

But our plans were already fixed, and all our arrangements made for an immediate departure for Rome. Before we left Naples Mr. Cotterell would have a farewell dinner-party for us. Poor Keats made a special effort and was very entertaining; and he did not appear to suffer much. All the time we were at the Hotel d'Inghilterra he read 'Clarissa Harlowe,' in nine volumes I remember, and finished it just before our departure.[8]

These and dozens more creative additions demonstrate not only that Sharp was editing authentic documents and combining disparate material in a cavalier way in order to enhance the narration and spice up his story, but that there was an underlying fraudulent intention to bamboozle his readers – as well as literary critics and biographers with a short attention span and a penchant for the romantic.

But who was William Sharp, and what prompted him to falsify the historical record in such an unwarranted way? Literary forgers – both famous ones such as Chatterton, Ireland and Macpherson, and lesser-known operators such as the Sharps and Macfarlanes of this world – are a very fascinating subject. Their motives may appear inscrutable at times, but can often be explained by examining their lives.

In the words of William F. Halloran, the editor of a recent edition of his letters, William Sharp was an "obscure and complex man".[9] He was born in Paisley, near Glasgow, in September 1855. His father David, a partner in an old-established mercantile house, had married the eldest daughter of the Swedish vice consul at Glasgow, Katherine Brooks. William, the first of five children, was a boy with a keen sense of adventure "who loved swimming and fishing and climbing", according to his wife Elizabeth, who wrote his biography.[10] As a child he grew up listening to the stories and songs of his nurse Barbara, a Highland woman, developing a passion for old Celtic sagas and the exploits of ancient knights and warriors. In his boyhood, he spent long summers on the shores of the Clyde or one of the sea lochs, or on the Isle of Arran, sailing with his father along the coast of the Western Highlands and the Inner Hebrides, and falling in love with the rugged nature that surrounded him.

After completing his studies at the Glasgow Academy in 1871, Sharp went on to study literature at Glasgow University, but he found the shackles of student life too oppressive. In the summer of 1872, he went roaming for weeks with a band of Gypsies without telling his parents. He returned to his classes in the autumn, but soon dropped out and was apprenticed to a Glasgow law office. Meanwhile, intent on becoming a writer one day, William remained a voracious reader of "literature, philosophy, poetry, mysticism, occultism, magic, mythology, folk-lore".[11]

Following his father's death in August 1876, Sharp – always of delicate health as a boy, and later as a young man – experienced a physical breakdown, and his family shipped him off to Australia in the hope he would recover.[12] Having tried without success to find a job there, he returned to Scotland the following summer. His mood was one of gloom and depression. He wrote in his diary: "I feel another self within me now more than ever; it is as if I were possessed by a spirit who must speak out... I am in no hurry to rush into print; I do not wish to write publicly until I can do so properly."[13] Yet in the spring of 1878 Sharp moved to London, resolving to start a literary career.

He worked for a while for a bank, but then, by sheer determination – by penning several articles and poems, and getting them published in papers and magazines, by sending letters to

authors asking for advice and finding ways to be introduced to
famous writers – he managed to establish himself in the competi-
tive world of contemporary letters and devote himself full-time
to writing. He became acquainted with Dante Gabriel Rossetti
and his sister Christina, Algernon Swinburne, Mrs Craik and
many other prominent literary figures, receiving encouragement
from them.[14] "I was quite taken aback by the extent of Rossetti's
praise," Sharp wrote in January 1881 in a letter to his cousin
Elizabeth, who was later to be his wife, recounting a night spent
at the painter's house.

> He said he did not say much in his letter because writing so
> often looks "gushing" but he considered I was able to take a
> foremost place among the younger poets of the day—and that
> many signs in my writings pointed to a first-class poet—that
> the opening of 'The Dead Bridegroom' was worthy of Keats.[15]

He never published this poem, but he would remember being
compared to Keats by one of his literary heroes for the rest of
his life.

During the 1880s, Sharp became a well-known literary figure
in his own right. In the year of Rossetti's death he published
his first book, a full-length tribute to the artist's life and works,
which was followed in quick succession, between 1882 and 1884,
by three collections of original poetry.[16] In 1883 he made con-
tact, on the pretext of a Keatsian fragment he had come across
in one of Rossetti's drawings, with Harry Buxton Forman,
the famous editor of the works of Shelley and Keats, who had
published, in 1878, the *Letters of John Keats to Fanny Brawne*.
It is around this time that Sharp appears to have become infatu-
ated with literary biography, and fascinated in particular with
the dichotomy between real life and projected, romanticized
image. He once wrote:

> A group of intimate letters, written with no foreseen or
> suspected secondary intention, will probably give us more

insight into the inner nature of a man than any number of hypothetical pros and cons on the part of a biographer, or than reams of autobiography... I know Keats for instance far better through his letters than by even the ablest and most intimate memoirs that have been written of him: the real man is revealed in them and is brought near to us till we seem to hear his voice and clasp his hand.[17]

The 1880s were very busy years for Sharp. Apart from the already-mentioned books, he edited three poetic anthologies, wrote a number of articles and reviews, married his cousin, his childhood sweetheart Elizabeth, and published another collection of poems, two novels, three tales for boys and, between 1887 and 1889, the biographies of Percy Bysshe Shelley, Heinrich Heine and Robert Browning. In the mean time, following a chance meeting in Surrey between Sharp and the watercolour artist Walter Severn in late June 1884, the former had been asked by the painter to write a biography of his father. He had obtained access, as he wrote in a letter to Edward Dowden, to "[a] great mass of material [...] with much of interest relating to Keats & others, including Shelley".[18] "I am engaged," Sharp continued in the same letter,

> spider-like, in absorbing it before I spin it out again in book-form—a book bound to be widely interesting to all lovers of literature on a/c of its bearings on the revered names of two of our great poets of this century, besides "many other attractions" as theatrical slang has it. I have not had time to examine it except very superficially, yet: but I have made one or two most important "finds".

This material – letters, memoirs and other unpublished manuscripts written by or related to Joseph Severn – would form the basis, several years later, of his biography of Keats's friend.

Despite his frantic literary activity and the commercial success it generated – one of his last books, the *Life of Robert Browning*, was "going splendidly", with "already 10,000 copies disposed of" – William Sharp, who fancied himself as the spearhead of a "Romantic revival", was frustrated with the reception of his original work, which didn't bring him the acclaim he craved.[19] Like many other authors before and after him, he was bitter at the lack of acknowledgement of his writing. He thought of himself as an unappreciated genius: "In the past I prefer to be, however humbly, in the company of Shakespeare, Milton, Blake, Wordsworth, Shelley, and Keats,—and in the present with Tennyson, Browning, and Rossetti—than with the Wycherleys and Congreves, the Rochesters and Sedleys, or the luscious-and-lust poeticules and the Swinburnes."[20] In a letter of 13th July 1889 to Louise Chandler Moulton, he complained that his latest novel, *Children of Tomorrow*, had been, "on the whole, badly received by the press". "Nothing I have ever done," he continued,

> seems to have aroused so much enthusiasm. But quite apart from praise and blame, I am vain enough to believe that with all its faults & demerits it is not altogether a book of "today". I have written it as an artist—and someday, if not now, it will gain its measure of recognition.[21]

Plagued by recurrent bouts of ill health, dissatisfied with the London literary establishment, "sick of pot-boiling" and of living in an "abominable climate", Sharp embraced the lifestyle of a "Bohemian", beginning an itinerant life which saw him travel to Paris, cross the Atlantic for a tour of Canada and the United States and, after a few months at home and a short stay in Heidelberg, arrive in Rome with his wife in December 1890, hoping to settle there for good.[22] According to his wife Elizabeth, that "Winter in Rome was one long delight to the emancipated writer. It amply fulfilled even his optimistic anticipation. He revelled in the sunshine and the beauty; he was in perfect health; his imagination was quickened and worked with great activity."[23] Sharp explored the capital, visited the Campagna Romana, Tivoli, Ardea, the Sabine valleys and the Alban Hills, and fell in love with a young married woman, Edith Wingate Rinder, who was the inspiration for a collection of free-verse poems Sharp wrote and published in Italy, *Sospiri di Roma*. No doubt influenced by the poetry of Walt Whitman, this is perhaps Sharp's best book.[24]

This idyll of creativity, blessed by warmer climes and a liberated existence, was not destined to last long, however. Towards the end of March 1891, Sharp was already on his way back to Britain. On his return to England, he had to face again the "thorns of life", and was soon busy at work on his biography of Severn. This was a challenging and ambitious project, which required a great amount of dedication and mental energy. According to the original plan, the biography was to be issued in two bulky volumes, but Messrs Sampson Low, Marston & Company, as he wrote in a letter to Horace Scudder, got cold feet ahead of publication due to the cost of the illustrations and "questions of outlay", and asked the author to recast the whole thing in one volume at the very last minute. "This involved a complete reconstruction of the book," Sharp explained in the same letter,

> and, as I have found to my cost, a complete reconstruction of *that* reconstruction. In accomplishing this I not only removed over 500 MS. pages of unnecessary though often most entertaining matter, but have practically done away with the record of Severn's life during close on 20 years, the period which he himself thought, and in his experience undoubtedly was, the most interesting of all.[25]

It was a hard grind – and, no doubt, dispiriting work: despite the frenzied speed at which he toiled, Sharp found it difficult to organize and condense such a huge amount of material in the time he had been given. In mid-July, he travelled with his wife to Whitby, on the Yorkshire coast, where he buried himself in work for the next four weeks. On 13th August he wrote in his diary: "Wrote 25 pp. digest of Severn's novel and worked at other things. Later I wrote the concluding pages, finishing the book at 2 A.M. I can hardly believe that this long delayed task is now accomplished. But *at last* 'Severn' is done!"[26] It is interesting to see that Sharp called his biography a "novel" – although he had used the more orthodox "memoir" in a letter he had written from Whitby.[27] Perhaps he thought that the only way for him to survive the drudgery of his task was to liven up the narrative with a little fictional zest.

After two more weeks of dull, draining revision work, he delivered the manuscript to his publishers and, towards the end of August, left with his wife for the south of Germany, in search of milder weather, and as an antidote for mental exhaustion and the onset of depression. Sharp reached Stuttgart at the beginning of September, where he was to collaborate with the American writer Blanche Willis Howard on a romantic epistolary novel, *A Fellowe and His Wife*, published the following year to good acclaim. The book marked the first step of Sharp's transformation into a writer of popular romances, which he would achieve in full under the pen name of Fiona Macleod. Despite the success of *The Life and Letters of Joseph Severn*, Sharp would never write a page of literary biography again: instead, he went on to live an imaginary life until the end of his days.[28]

For William Sharp, Fiona Macleod was not a simple pen name: it became a kind of alter ego, a female *Doppelgänger*. Since his very early writings – for example, his 1880 poem *Motherhood*, centred on the act of giving birth – Sharp had tried to penetrate the feelings and thought processes of women. Now he became more and more convinced that his "other self", the feminine half of his personality he had repressed since his childhood, was trying to be liberated, to "speak out".[29] As his wife Elizabeth later wrote:

Once again, he saw visions and dreamed dreams; the psychic subjective side of his dual nature predominated. He was in an acutely creative condition; and, moreover he was passing from one phase of literary work to another, deeper, more intimate, more permanent. So far, he had found no adequate method for the expression of his "second self".[30]

Following the success of *A Fellowe and His Wife* – in which he had assumed a female persona, writing the Countess von Jaromar's letters – Sharp decided to publish a new book, the novel *Pharais, A Romance of the Isles*, under the guise of an Edinburgh-based Scottish author called Fiona Macleod – who, in her introductory dedication to "E.W.R." (Edith Wingate Rinder), portrays herself as a latter-day Keats:

The most nature-wrought of the English poets hoped he was not too late in transmuting into his own verse something of the beautiful mythology of Greece. But while Keats spun from the inexhaustible loom of genius, and I am but an obscure chronicler of obscure things, is it too presumptuous of me to hope that here, and mayhap elsewhere, I, the latest comer among older and worthier celebrants and co-enthusiasts, likewise may do something, howsoever little, to win a further measure of heed for, and more intimate sympathy with, that old charm and stellar beauty of Celtic thought and imagination, now, alas, like so many other lovely things, growing more and more remote, discoverable seldom in books, and elusive amid the sayings and oral legends and fragmentary songs of a passing race?[31]

Pharais was a hit with the critics and the reading public, and brought in a fair amount of money. This persuaded its author to divide himself into two separate characters. William Sharp – the ubiquitous literato, the journeyman of the written word, the unsuccessful middle-of-the-road author – continued his work as an editor and reviewer, becoming more and more interested in occultism, paganism and the Celtic revival. In 1892, using a number of pen names, he wrote the five stories and two poems that appeared in the first and only number of the *Pagan*

Review, which was lambasted by the critics. Two years later he brought out a collection of poems, *Vistas* – which he later described, in a dedication added to its American edition, as "vistas into the inner life of the human soul, psychic episodes" – a book that sank without trace.[32] In 1896 he published *Lyra Celtica: An Anthology of Representative Celtic Poetry* and edited Macpherson's *Poems of Ossian*. In his long introductory note to this volume, Sharp goes into some detail about the controversy surrounding the poems' authenticity, stating all the most recent, well-informed critical opinions about it. Although he agreed that it could not be denied that Macpherson's *Ossian* was "not a translation of either ancient or mediæval legendary sagas", he disputed the then-current thinking that it was "no more than a gigantic fraud", claiming that Macpherson based his poetry on a fragmentary substratum of authentic oral Celtic lore. If that weren't the case, Sharp argued, Macpherson "would be one of the few poetic creators of the first rank".[33] In what sounds like a justification of his own creative fabrications and double literary life, Sharp claimed that "no single work in our literature has had so wide-reaching, so potent, and so enduring an influence".[34]

Alongside his run-of-the-mill existence in London, William Sharp enjoyed the high-flying life of a successful author through the West Scotland novels and tales of Fiona Macleod. In order to keep her real identity hidden and protect himself from the mounting rumours that he may be behind her writings, William Sharp gave Fiona Macleod a biography and a personality. The daughter (or at other times the wife) of a rich Scot, she was a shy, reserved, well-educated, well-travelled woman steeped in Celtic history and culture, and something of a recluse – although she often slipped off on a yachting cruise to the Western Isles. Ever the indefatigable self-promoter, William Sharp used every opportunity to advance the works of Fiona Macleod. At times he acted as her agent, defending her rights against the notorious greed of publishers. He claimed that she was his cousin, and hinted to a few friends that he was on intimate terms with her. He went further: he began writing letters under her name, which were sent to his sister Mary in Edinburgh, who would copy them in a female handwriting and post them on.[35] And whenever her true identity was brought into question, Fiona would react with deep indignation, complaining about those who accused her of being "a greater fraud than Macpherson of Ossianic fame" and expressing her determination "to safeguard her privacy" more than ever.[36]

As demonstrated today by the "Elena Ferrante" phenomenon, the mystery surrounding the authorship of a literary work can be an effective marketing tool. William Sharp realized this very soon and, happy to bask in vicarious glory, capitalized on the publicity generated by the "Fiona Macleod" controversy to further his financial interests and his ideas of a Celtic and Romantic revival. He carried on with his charade for over a decade – suffering one or two mental breakdowns in the process, as the efforts of maintaining a double existence took their toll – until his premature death in Sicily in 1905, at the age of fifty. In a strange twist of fate, Sharp accomplished what Keats had been planning to do when writing *The Cap and Bells*: to publish and be successful under a woman's name.

It appears that towards the end of his life William Sharp came to believe that Fiona Macleod was a real, separate person inhabiting his body. Whether it was self-delusion or some form of split-personality disorder or ambiguous gender identity we cannot know, but the critical consensus is that, of the two writers Sharp nurtured inside him, Fiona was by far the better one.

In his introductory note to *The Poems of Ossian*, written a hundred years after the death of James Macpherson, Sharp argued that the question of his authorship "must remain in abeyance, if for no other reason than the fact that the time wherein verification was possible is now past".[37] Perhaps Sharp was hoping to play a long game of "catch me if you can", and thought that if enough time passed, his forgeries, falsifications and mystifications would become unchallengeable, truer than reality – more iconic, more memorable – like the stories narrated by ancient historiographers, like the characters of a Shakespeare play, like the stuff of myth and legend.

Only five years after his death, William Sharp's game was up when his widow, Elizabeth, published her memoir and revealed to the world what a few friends knew and many people already suspected: the true identity of the elusive Scottish–Celtic writer. It took much longer, a hundred years, until the publication of Joseph Severn's original letters and memoirs by Grant F. Scott, to expose Sharp's cavalier editorial practices, as well as his creative additions to the canonical biographies of Keats and Severn, which find currency to this day. William Sharp's own life and works are now a mere footnote in the history of nineteenth-century English literature, yet his story is both a cautionary tale and a stark reminder, for future researchers, of the dangerous allure of Romantic biography, where truth and fiction, event and invention, fact and imagination are entangled with the life of their creator – making it difficult, almost impossible, to extricate one from the other.

JOURNEY TO ROME

IN KEATS'S TIME, the distance of the journey from Naples to Rome was about 152 miles, or 245 km – similar to that between London and Cardiff, or between Newcastle and Glasgow.[1] Today, the same trip can be made in less than two hours by car via the Autostrada del Sole, which shortens the ride by more than 10 miles – and if you feel like following Keats and Severn's original route, it will take you about four hours, but only because of traffic and speed restrictions. By train it's much faster: you can get from Napoli Centrale to Roma Termini in little over an hour. Many people commute between the two cities for work. Young Romans who fancy drinking a *real* espresso after a night out will drive to Naples in the early hours, while their Neapolitan counterparts will be zooming in the opposite direction to grab a cornetto on the outskirts of Rome at the break of dawn. The two cities are close today, very close.

Not so in 1820: Rome and Naples were then separated by a political, cultural and geographical chasm which was much wider than the distance measured by the twenty-odd stages between them. Although it was a well-travelled commercial and touristic track, inns were scarce and expensive, roads ill kept, food and accommodation inadequate, and corruption widespread among customs and police officials. Stories abounded – some of them true – of murderous attacks along the way by gangs of merciless robbers. As a result, what could have been a pleasant excursion through picturesque towns and the Italian countryside turned into a gruelling, dangerous trip fraught with inconvenience and unknowns.

No doubt the journey seemed even more arduous and hazardous to foreign travellers, since they had little knowledge of the places and people they met on the way and could not speak or understand their language. When it comes to this part of the itinerary, their accounts – at times suffused by a sense of adventure and discovery, at others pervaded by nostalgia for a long-lost past – tend to be coloured by fear, prejudice, misunderstanding and incomprehension.

There were two possible routes at the time from Naples to Rome, about the same in length.[2] After reaching Terracina, in the Papal States, from the capital of the Kingdom of the Two Sicilies, one followed the ancient Via Latina, the other the old trail of the Appian Way through the Pontine Marshes. The first passed through the Volscian towns of Piperno (today's Priverno) and Sermoneta, and then over the hills surrounding Velletri and Marino, along the edge of Lake Albano, before descending into the Campagna Romana and rejoining the Appian Way before the Lateran Gate (Porta San Giovanni). This route had been all but abandoned by travellers by the mid-1780s, after the completion of a system of canals which led to the partial reclamation of the Pontine Marshes and the building of a straight road over them from Tre Ponti, near Cisterna, to Terracina.[3] Vallardi's 1815 *Itinerario italiano* says: "Normally this road is not much frequented: we describe it only to gratify the curiosity of the antiquary and the naturalist."[4] There were no inns worthy of the name along this route, and although the path wound its way through a delightful scenery of wooded hills and valleys scattered with overgrown Roman ruins à la Ann Radcliffe, the traveller would have found the journey much colder and damper, and been troubled by the niggling fear of mountain bandits and lurking Spalatros.[5] Also, the roads were poor – even more so in autumn and winter. Writing in 1819, Antonio Nibby said that although it was possible to reach Velletri by coach, to get from there to Cori, a town about halfway to Sermoneta, one had to ride on a horse for a stretch of over ten miles, since the track was so bad and looked as though it had not been mended for many years.[6] Of all the contemporary travel accounts, not one describes the journey from Terracina to Rome through the Via

Latina. Someone in Keats's condition would never even have contemplated such a taxing itinerary.

As mentioned, the second route passed through the Pontine Marshes and continued for most of the way along the course of the ancient Via Appia. This was the journey of choice of almost every traveller, and it offered foreign tourists many points of attraction. Since it was busier, it was also better served and maintained, and in parts it was guarded by soldiers, who could also be hired, if not for added protection, at least as a deterrent against the assaults of real or imaginary banditti.

There were modes of transport tailored to every purse and requirement. Anyone who wanted to reach Rome in the fastest and safest way, if not the most pleasant, would have jumped on the government courier, a special mail coach that ran every other day, cost over 300 carlins (around £6) per passenger and had the added benefit of being escorted all the way by two or three armed dragoons. Assuming a smooth change of post-horses and no breakdowns or other accidents, the entire journey could be performed in around thirty-six hours without any overnight stay. This utilitarian method, though well suited to businessmen and doctors on a flying visit to Rome, was expensive, very fatiguing and didn't permit much sightseeing along the way.

People who were eager "to get on" and make a quick job of their trip, like the crusty Englishman in Washington Irving's celebrated tale 'The Inn at Terracina', could travel by post-horses in their own coach or a rented carriage, a method called "*cambiatura*". This was also rather expensive, because besides any hiring costs there was a fee for each post-horse that was replaced and for the occasional draught horse (or donkey) added on steep slopes, a charge to secure an escort of armed soldiers, barrier tolls on each passenger, tips for the postilion and the groom, living expenses for food and overnight stays, as well as potential customs duties, bribes for douane officers and soldiers, and all sorts of little extras based on the number of passengers, the size of the coach, the weight of the trunks, and so on.[7] More than one tourist wondered why Italy needed robbers if they were able to fleece foreigners in such a systematic way. This mode of transport, however, was about a third cheaper than the government courier, and allowed travellers to complete their journey in two to five days, breaking it according to their wishes and needs. In order to minimize the risk of being attacked by brigands, whenever possible coaches tended to travel in small convoys. Most travellers divided their trip into four legs, spending the first night at Sant'Agata (or Mola di Gaeta), arriving well before sunset at Terracina, rushing across the Pontine Marshes the following morning, reaching Velletri in the evening and entering Rome the next day between midday and early afternoon. But there were no fixed rules, and of course anything could happen along the road – a problem with the coach springs, a wheel flying off, a strange encounter, an impassable swollen river or an overzealous customs officer – causing delays that had a knock-on effect on the original schedule.

By far the most popular and cheapest way of getting around in Italy was to engage the services of a *vetturino*. "The *vettura*," wrote Theodore Dwight in 1821, "is the common conveyance of Italians; and, as it stops every night and travels very leisurely all day, affords every desirable opportunity for seeing the road. Besides, the expense is not half so great as with the corriere."[8] The same mules or horses were used for the entire journey, so the *vetturino* had to proceed at a walking pace and make frequent stops to rest them. There were also strict rules regulating the speed of *vetture*, since the authorities did not want them to undermine the post-house system. As a result, they left at a very early hour in the morning, spent a long time on the road and stopped late in the evening, before dusk, only to start again the following day at first light.

The *vettura* was more or less the equivalent of a hackney carriage. Before setting off, the passengers entered into an agreement with the *vetturino*, who undertook to drive them in his own carriage and in some cases, in order to avoid later disputes, signed a piece of paper confirming the main terms:

the fare – inclusive of breakfast, dinner, supper and overnight accommodation – the duration of the journey and the tip, which would be paid at the end of the trip if the customers were happy with the service provided. "To bind the bargain," Dwight explains, "the coachman gives a ducat, which, by common law, is to be retained if he fails in performing the contract; or, if the traveller gives up his journey, must be returned doubled."[9] The problem was – as we can read from many contemporary accounts – that some unscrupulous *vetturini* had a tendency to renege on the negotiated terms, in particular when there was no written agreement, or subcontracted the journey to another coachman along the way, or resorted to all sorts of little tricks in order to save a bit of money. As a consequence, travellers found, to their disappointment, that

> they were generally taken, not to the inns where they could be best accommodated, but where the prices were most reasonable. The sleeping rooms, therefore, had the fault which indeed is common in some degree to most houses of entertainment on the Italian roads; they were disgustingly filthy, and the food set before them [...] ill-dressed.[10]

Most of the time, however, things went according to plan, and since frequent travellers – in particular English ones – had their own trusted *vetturino*, we can be sure that Charles Cotterell would have spared no expense and chosen a caring and trustworthy coachman for the delicate task of taking Keats and Severn to Rome.[11]

Despite being a slow, boring mode of transport, the *vettura*, besides being very cheap, had several added benefits.[12] The main attraction was that it was flexible: it allowed its passengers to travel at their leisure, have a good look around, take small detours and make as many stops as they wished either to rest or for their own convenience, without being forced on at the frantic pace of *cambiatura* coaches. This was the ideal conveyance for tourists with time on their hands, people who were not just eager to hurry to their destinations, but wanted to get a feel of the land, enjoy the experience and derive some pleasure from the trip. It was also the perfect way to get around for someone like Keats, who, being in very poor health, could not be jolted about, had special dietary requirements and needed frequent breaks and privacy.

Another great advantage was that it made the journey less risky. "A *vetturino*," explains the anonymous author of *Travels in Southern Italy*,

> [...] travels only by day, and as his interest depends on the safety of his passengers, he generally contrives to travel in company with others of the same description, and thus they form, when united, a party sufficiently strong for mutual protection. [...] Besides, there is not the same expectation of booty from persons travelling in this cheap way, as from persons posting.[13]

In addition to this, just like an experienced cab driver, a *vetturino* would know his way about. As well as being acquainted with every bend and pothole on the route, he would have a host of useful contacts along the road, including innkeepers and customs officers. He could also act as a *cicerone*, pointing out all the major sights and amenities. In short, he would be able to provide the kind of personalized service that a passenger could not expect from a postilion.

In order to keep the costs of sustenance and accommodation to a minimum, passengers travelling in a *vettura* aimed to get from Naples to Rome in four or five days. There is every indication that Keats and Severn completed their journey on the seventh or eighth day from their departure. This was a little unusual, although Severn, travelling back to Naples a year and a half later in the company of Maria Erskine and her two young daughters, spent six long summer days on the road.[14] Considering Keats's parlous state of health and the limited amount of daylight available to them in which to travel at that time of the year, we must assume that the *vetturino* divided the journey into manageable legs, going at a slower rate during the first four days among steep tracks and treacherous terrain, accelerating over the Pontine Marshes, as everyone else did – since the road was good, flat and straight, and the air was thought to be insalubrious – and then slowing down again among the sharp hills and winding roads of Velletri and Genzano, before entering Rome at a reasonable hour. Taking it easy and advancing with caution during the first stages of the trip would also allow Keats, who was always fearful of a relapse even when he was feeling a little better, to hurry back to Naples if he found the journey too demanding, or in case of an emergency – since we shouldn't forget how difficult it must have been for the young poet, who was still recovering from a debilitating crossing, to venture on such a long and fatiguing carriage ride.[15] As Severn wrote a few weeks later in Rome, bewailing the fact that Keats's frame had "most surely broken down" under the effort, "journies to [written "too"] and about Italy are not for an Invalid".[16]

Many of those who travelled between Naples and Rome left detailed descriptions of their trips. For some of them, this was one of the highlights of their sojourn in Italy, and their pages are filled with colour, commentary and thrilling incident. Severn, on the other hand, all but glossed over the days spent with Keats on the road. Since he had other, more pressing things on his mind, we can't blame him for that. However, we can still try to piece together the movements of the two young travellers on their way to Rome.

All we have to go by, if we discard Sharp's novelistic interpolations, are a few lines from a letter Severn wrote to his sister three days before Keats's death – "The journey from Rome to Naples is beautiful—the vineyards extending down for miles and miles in vallies and over hills—these are formed with Vines—festooned from tree to tree in every direction" – and a short passage from his late memoir, which suggests the trip was rather leisurely and uneventful:

the journey was pleasant in such a season & as the carriage went slow enough I got down & walked nearly the whole way & delighted Keats by gathering the wild flowers[.]

There was nothing very remarkable until we got into the Campagna of Rome when a large crimson cloak attracted my attention & on my approaching it I found a Cardinal engaged in shooting small birds.[17]

Based on the few unquestionable facts in our possession, we can assume that Keats and Severn, after reclaiming their passports on the 7th, left Naples early in the morning of either 8th or 9th November.[18] They would have covered around 25 miles on their first day, stopping at Capua for the night. Considering that this stretch was regarded by some as "infernal", this was good progress.[19] On their second day on the road, they would have travelled the 19 miles to Sant'Agata, spending the night there.[20] On the third day they would have crossed the Garigliano on a bridge of boats, a complicated affair, reaching the inn at Mola di Gaeta after another 18-mile journey. If they left on the 8th, then in all probability Keats and Severn spent a second night in one of these towns, as there were no other inns available until Terracina, which was about 22 miles from Mola.[21] Since there is nothing in Severn's laconic accounts that suggests adverse weather, accidents or problems on the road, it is likely that they departed from Naples on 9th November, or that they stopped an extra day at Mola di Gaeta, a pleasant town with a comfortable inn, so that Keats could recover from fatigue ahead of a longer leg, or to wait until they could travel through the most dangerous part of the route in the company of other carriages. Leaving Itri and Fondi behind, on 12th November they reached the border of the Papal States, the Torre dell'Epitaffio, as recorded by the visa on Keats's passport. They then pushed on to nearby Terracina, where they would have spent the night. The following morning, they would have traversed the Pontine Marshes, then passed Cisterna and reached Velletri in the evening. The next day, 14th November, they would have covered the hilly stretch to Albano, and lodged there overnight, leaving at dawn to make their way across the Campagna Romana. There, in the morning, they saw the cardinal shooting at small birds, just before entering Rome by the Lateran Gate. Later that day, 15th November 1820, Keats drew some cash from the Roman banker Torlonia, before or after turning up at Doctor Clark's in Piazza di Spagna.[22]

Now that we have an outline of Keats and Severn's itinerary, we can start adding details and filling in the gaps, as we accompany them on their way to Rome, through the descriptions given by contemporary travellers and guidebooks. Many artists made the same journey, in one direction or the opposite, at around the same time, and produced sketches and drawings along the way – among them J.M.W. Turner. For those who want to have a visual idea of what our two young travellers may have seen en route to Rome, I recommend Luigi Rossini's series of engravings *Viaggio pittoresco da Roma a Napoli*, which includes pictures of all the stages and the main sights between the two cities, drawn from nature.[23] The journey can also be followed on Google Street View for most of the itinerary: it is surprising how much is still there and how many things have not changed, such as the Roman relics, the buildings of Italy's ancient town centres – at least those not ravaged by war – and the profile of the mountains on the horizon.

Setting off from Villa di Londra, Keats and Severn's *vettura* clattered its way towards the turnpike out of Naples. If they followed, as is most probable, the same route as Count Martinengo's carriage, which departed from the same hotel, after clearing the S. Lucia quayside and the Strada del Gigante they would have traversed the Piazza del Real Palazzo, leaving the Royal Palace on their right and, on their left, the Basilica of San Francesco da Paola, still under construction at the time.[24] Proceeding up the Strada Toledo, they would have reached the Bourbon Museum and turned right into Largo delle Pigne. After covering the whole length of the majestic Strada Foria, going past the Botanical Gardens and the Real Albergo de' Poveri, they reached the toll barrier, where they showed their documents, and then took the broad road on which perhaps they had travelled a few days before to attend the military review.[25] When they reached Capodichino at the end of the Strada del Campo, they continued straight and were out of Naples.

Passing through the villages of Secondigliano and Melito, the *vettura* made its way north-west through cultivated fields and vines festooned from tree to tree, and about four miles down the road entered the monumental Arco dell'Annunziata, the gate of the city of Aversa, built in 1777. A Norman town founded in 1030, Aversa was renowned in those days for the Reali Case de' Matti, an institution established in 1813 by Joachim Murat, then king of Naples, which made use of enlightened methods, such as theatre and music, for the cure of mental illness. Keats's carriage didn't go past the hospital, but kept to the elegant main street, which continued straight until they emerged out of town.

Twelve miles further on they reached the first stage of their journey, the fortified town of Capua, surrounded by moated walls and strengthened by bastions that had been renovated by the king in recent times.[26] They entered the city through its southern gate, Porta Napoli, which is no longer in use, but can still be seen today. There they had their passports checked. Despite its venerable history and status as the capital of the Terra di Lavoro until 1818, Capua was somewhat run down at the time. James Fenimore Cooper, visiting in the late 1820s, called it "a mean dirty town".[27] Selina Martin, who spent a night there in June 1819, was even more blunt: "I like neither the appearance of the town nor the inn, both look dirty and miserable."[28] Another traveller, Louis Simond, concurred, describing the town as "an ugly dirty place, noisy beyond all bearing", where "people disput[ed] with the utmost violence about mere trifles, as if they were going to attempt each other's lives".[29] Theodore Dwight, in February 1821, was hounded by beggars through its muddy streets and inside one of its churches.[30] Most of the *vetturini* stopped there just long enough to rest the horses and grab some food and wine, which were deemed so "execrable" by some of their clients "as would have been no snare to the rudest Carthaginian".[31]

The reference is to the so-called "*otia Hannibalis*". According to a story narrated by Livy, Hannibal led his invading army to Capua, then the second most important city of the Italian peninsula, to encamp for the winter.[32] His hardy soldiers, accustomed to the rigours of military life, gave themselves up to the enjoyments of Capua's luxuries and lost all their discipline and vigour, which resulted in the Carthaginians' ultimate defeat by the Romans. The modern Capua, which did not share in the glories of its ancient counterpart, was often the butt of learned jokes. "The only specimen we had of Capuan luxury," quipped Cooper, "was a guitar at supper."[33]

The site of the old Roman city was less than three miles away, and could be reached on foot or by a short horse-and-buggy drive from the modern town. Many travellers took advantage of the stop to visit the "wreck of a noble amphitheatre [...] ornamented all round with Doric columns" and transformed into "a corn field", passing through a "country [...] enlivened with vineyards and groves of olives, oranges, and fig-trees; [...] strewed about in all directions [...] [with] rich marbles and fragments of pillars, indicative of former magnificence".[34]

Leaving their inn early in the morning, Keats and Severn exited Capua from the gate at the north-western end of the town, the Porta di Capua, and crossed the old Roman bridge over the murky waters of the Volturno, which wound its way below. As the road began to ascend, "the sea opened [...] to the left, and the Appenines skirted the plains to the right", revealing a "perpetual succession of pleasing prospects, where the soft beauties of cultivation were mingled with the wildness and grandeur of mountain scenery", and offering, "far behind, [...] a last sight of Ischia and Vesuvius".[35]

The approach to the next post, Sparanise, presented no remarkable features. "If it wasn't for its station-house," wrote Michele Tenore in 1824, "one would be hard-tasked to find it on the map."[36] The track continued to rise among swathes of fields on the left and fertile hills on the right, passing through the villages of Francolise and Cascano, until it reached the hamlet of Sant'Agata, about six hours' journey by *vettura* from Capua. "St. Agata," wrote Lady Morgan in 1820, "is a solitary inn, the true *locanda* of the middle ages, with few of its windows sashed, and its open corridor running round a court containing little sleeping-rooms, bare and rude as a hermit's cell."[37] Theodore Dwight, who was a guest there only a few months after Keats and Severn, left a detailed description of his stay:

> An hour after sun-set we arrived at St. Agata, and drove through a dark gate into the yard of the inn, which is very old, and built of whitish stone. The yard has the house on two sides, and the buildings connected with it complete the square. A spacious, but half furnished dining room, is on the second floor; and a gallery runs along the other wing, which looks into the yard, and gives access to a dozen or fifteen bed-chambers, the last of which are situated over the stable. The great gates were immediately shut and locked; and while we were waiting in the dining room, a large pan of coals was brought in and set upon the brick floor; for there was no fire-place to be seen. [...] We were all summoned to the long dinner-table, where our coachman sat down among us with an air of equality. A bottle of decent red wine, and a napkin, were placed for each person; and maccaroni soup, a boiled and fried dish, which I could not comprehend, boiled mutton, fennel, salad, oranges, and cheese, were served up, one at a time.[38]

Not so homely had been the reception accorded in 1817 to another traveller, Jacques Augustin Galiffe, the gruff Swiss who had found a scorpion in his room at Villa di Londra. He left an amusing record of his experience:

> We slept that night at *Sta. Agatha*, where we found the most impudent and insolent waiter that probably ever existed. The supper was the worst I had ever seen on a table, even in the wilds of Westphalia;—it was literally impossible either to eat

a morsel of any thing, or to swallow a drop of the wine. When we retired to the only room which the Count and I had been able to obtain for our joint lodging, I found that there was no cover to the dirty pillow on my bed; and having called up the waiter to supply this omission, the insufferable insolence of the man enraged me to such a degree, that our altercation ended by my literally kicking him out of the room. I soon perceived that this step was as imprudent as it was unworthy of me; for the fellow put his hands to all his pockets for a knife, with such fury, that had he found one I might have paid dearly for my fit of anger. Very fortunately he had none about him, and I succeeded in bolting him out of the room; after which we heard no more of him, nor did we see him in the morning, the account having been settled over night by the coachman.[39]

Although "scarcely more than a tavern", Sant'Agata stood "in the midst of the most enchanting scenery" – embellished by "beautiful oaks and leafy chestnuts" from which hung "long garlands of wild vine" – and was less than a mile away from the Roman ruins of Sessa, an ancient town founded by the Italic tribe of the Aurunci before the eighth century BC.[40] According to contemporary reports, it was a popular stop-off among antiquarians and "a frequented sleeping stage".[41]

Leaving Sant'Agata behind, the road began its gradual descent towards the Garigliano pass, with magnificent olive groves adorning the hills on the right, where the vines for Falernian wine had been grown in ancient times, and low-lying fields extending all the way to the sea on the left.[42] As the river came into view, the landscape became less luscious and more drab. Keats and Severn's *vettura* crossed the Garigliano, the Liris of antiquity, on a precarious bridge formed by ten boats and "passed through a gate defended by two old weather-beaten towers", bearing a long inscription by Quintus Iunius Severianus, decurion of Minturnae.[43] The remains of the ancient Roman city, once a large Ausonian settlement, could be seen beyond, scattered on the left-hand side of the road – among them an amphitheatre and a theatre – and were visited by travellers as the crossing and tolling procedures were being completed.

> The ruins stand on a plain a mile or two in extent, now unin-habited, though partly covered with young wheat. Several shapeless masses of masonry, in different places, show where massive buildings once stood; though they leave it entirely doubtful whether they were palaces or tombs. The principal ruin is that of an aqueduct, of which about an hundred arches remain, built of brick, and stretching above half a mile. They vary in height, according to the irregularity of the surface, the highest being probably fifty feet; and under one of these passes the road. The soil is much injured by the materials of edifices which have now disappeared, being overspread with bits of stone, bricks, and earthen stone.[44]

It must have been a scene of utter desolation and decay. Surveying the landscape as he glided past in his coach, Michele Tenore was struck by a melancholic sense of an irretrievable past: "These lands, which were once the pride and joy of the rulers of the world, are now covered by unwholesome marshes and inhabited by noxious reptiles."[45]

Keats and Severn continued to travel over a tract of low country between the sea and hills almost bare of vegetation, a monotonous landscape only broken by the occasional cluster of olive trees and glimpses of the Mediterranean. After a journey of about 18 miles, they reached their next destination, Mola di Gaeta.

The joint villages of Mola and Castellone (now both part of Formia) formed a flourishing town of about 5,000 inhabitants, built by the sea on the site of the ancient city of Formiæ. Its beau-tiful location, commanding a fine view of Gaeta's promontory and fortress across its bay and of Mount Vesuvius in the distance to the south, made it a popular stopping place for travellers and Grand Tourists. From there, people could walk, along the shoreline, the four miles to Gaeta – renowned for having been founded by Aeneas in honour of his wet-nurse Caieta, as recorded by Virgil in the seventh book of his *Aeneid* – or visit the many vestiges of antiquity scattered over the area, from the Castellone Tower to the ruins of an aqueduct and other ancient relics.

But what rendered Mola even more interesting to the traveller, as Thomas Pennington explains, was "that it was the favourite residence, or at least one of the residences of that ornament of literature, Cicero".[46] The locals had been quick to capitalize on this, and every ancient monument and mouldering piece of rubble in the neighbourhood had acquired, as if by magic, some association with the great Roman orator and statesman. Mola's most popular inn, the Albergo di Cicerone, about a mile from the town, in nearby Castellone, was no exception.[47] "The gardens and the orange-grounds of the Albergo," writes a contemporary guide, "lead down to the bay; where, close to the shore, are the ruins of Cicero's Formian Villa; and beneath the bright waters of the Mediterranean are clearly seen the foundations and substructures of this marine Villa in which Cicero delighted."[48]

There was more than one inn in Mola, but the overwhelming majority of travellers, in particular those from Britain, stayed at the Albergo di Cicerone, both for its comfort and for its reputation.[49] It is most likely that Keats and Severn stayed there too.

Among Severn's watercolours of his voyage to Italy there is one which has been labelled 'Unknown Bay'.[50] Because of its geographical features, the scene is reminiscent of a Mediterranean, Tyrrhenian coastline. Severn did not give it a title, but in fact it depicts one of the most iconic and portrayed bays in southern Italy: the Gulf of Gaeta.[51] The watercolour appears to have been painted from the hills overlooking the Albergo di Cicerone. Although the bay, in two hundreds years, has been ravaged almost beyond recognition by indiscriminate unauthorized development, its main landmarks – the medieval fortifications of the city of Gaeta jutting out into the sea, the profile of the hills on the horizon, Mount Orlando with the Tempio di San Francesco at its foot and the mausoleum of Lucius Munatius Plancus at its top – are still visible. Grant F. Scott, who rediscovered this and two other watercolours executed by Severn during his Italian journey with

Keats, which the painter pasted onto a single sheet of light-blue backing paper from his scrapbook, describes it as "[t]he most finished… most carefully drawn and delicately colored of the three sketches".[52] It is obvious that Severn had time to capture the landscape in some detail – which suggests that he and his friend did not just stop over at the inn for one night, arriving late in the evening and leaving early the following morning, but in all probability spent an extra day at the Albergo di Cicerone to rest before the long leg ahead, and had perhaps a chance to visit its surroundings, as well as some of Mola's celebrated antiquities. This reinforces the possibility that they left Naples on the 8th rather than 9th November 1820.

This "classic inn", according to Lady Morgan, was "the most beautifully situated in the world". Over its door, "Cicero [hung] as a sign, in a purple mantle, and pair of lemon-coloured pantaloons, surrounded by appropriate inscriptions".[53] Theodore Dwight was even more expansive:

The inn [...] is at the end of the town, and situated on a hill which slopes to the water. A balcony before the windows of the dining room, which is up two pair of stairs, looks down upon a terrace, and a garden, which descends to the margin of the bay, full of olive and orange trees, the latter loaded with fruit: so that it is like a beautiful prospect seen through a rose-bush. The island of Ponza, and the rest of the cluster among which we lay so long becalmed when coming on the coast, are on the horizon off the mouth of the harbour. On our left, the swelling cones of the barren Appennines rise from the bay; and on the right, a long beach sweeps boldly round in a semicircle to Gaeta [...]. There is something uncommonly beautiful in the scene [...].

Our spacious dining room, notwithstanding its half furnished and cheerless appearance, has its walls painted in fresco, with nymphs and cupids; and what is more substantially useful, the first fire-place I have seen in any Italian house, except for cooking.[54]

The impressive remains of what was believed to be Cicero's marine villa, the so-called "Formianum", could be visited by tourists, either alone or accompanied by modern-day *ciceroni*. "[M]any ruins," wrote the German dramatist August von Kotzebue, "[were] scattered round the garden, in which at first sight the Roman architecture was manifest. Arched passages and walls, and deep vaults, were every where overgrown and covered with shrubs."[55] It was an antiquarian's paradise.

And the town had other attractions, too: the women were renowned for their beauty, and there were coffee houses in which to enjoy a little social interaction and hear a guitar being strummed after dinner.

Of all the inns on the route from Naples to Rome, the Albergo di Cicerone is the one that received most positive comments. Many of the travellers who stayed there were so impressed that they left descriptions, drawings or paintings of the beautiful view – which is as breathtaking today as it was in Keats's time.[56]

The departure from Mola would have been at break of day, in order to pass the more dangerous parts of the road in broad daylight. The stage ahead was the longest and most arduous so far. The six or so miles of steep mountainous terrain to Itri were followed by an eight-mile stretch deep into banditti territory.[57] Then there was a series of lengthy customs and police controls, first at Fondi and then at the border checkpoints of the Kingdom of the Two Sicilies and the Papal States, before the final four miles of narrow, bumpy track to Terracina, which was notorious for "robberies and midnight murders".[58]

Leaving Mola, the road at first rose over a gentle slope and then became steeper, winding its way through charming scenery which offered beautiful views of the coast and was enriched by olive groves, orange and lemon trees and fragrant myrtle. About a mile from the inn, on the left, Keats and Severn passed the Cenotaph of Cicero, a monument which is supposed to mark the spot where the great statesman was killed by hired assassins sent after him by Mark Antony. At the end of a punishing uphill climb, in a valley between the sea and the imposing brows of the Aurunci Mountains, a small medieval village, with its castle and ruined walls, "was at last discovered [...] in the midst of hills, covered with vines and oranges, rich in the foliage of figs, and myrtles, and olives, and laurels".[59]

But the town of Itri "look[ed] well only at a distance": "[its] streets are narrow",

> its trailing length of hovels cling[s] in most disorderly irregularity to a ridge of rocks, the houses all doorless, and constructed of shapeless stones, without cement, giving them much more the look of dens than human habitations, and suggesting the first rude attempts at masonry after man had emerged from his caves in the earth.[60]

No one among the many travellers who passed through Itri around that time has a kind word to spare about the town or its residents. Tenore doesn't mince his words, and calls it a "dirty and most wretched gullet".[61] "With its grimy hovels and its ragged, fierce inhabitants," he adds, "it looks to me as if it's a place that deserves to be among the Bedouins in the depths of Africa rather than on the border of a civilized and fertile country." Louis Simond, trying to hide his disquiet, adopts a mocking tone: "The women and children scantily covered with filthy rags, and sitting out of doors, were very busy about each other's heads, looking for what is usually found there."[62] Lady Morgan, like many others before and after her, equates Itri and its people to its most illustrious native, the infamous Fra Diavolo, describing the village as "the palladium of brigandage", before launching into a tirade against what she pronounces to be the evident consequences of obscurantism and despotism: "want, vice, disease, bigotry, and assassination".[63] Sir Arthur Brooke Faulkner, writing more than a decade later, goes even further, in pages that exemplify the prejudice and paranoia of many contemporary visitors – and which today, at a time when poverty, "crime" and "malady" are not always pronounced in the same breath, make for uncomfortable reading:

Itri is no hypocrite; it looks exactly what it is—a nest of murderers, the very head-quarters of robbery and assassination: every human being you meet has Cain's mark legible on his brow. They eye you with a tiger ferocity, and are only kept in check by the vigilance and determination of a reconnoitring patrol ever at hand and in motion, and by their fears for the revelations of broad day, for it is only in open daylight that travellers now venture to pass this fearful road.

After culling some flowers in a field close to the village, I had no sooner regained the highway than I observed an eye fastened upon me with a steadfast gaze: it was the eye of the foulest-looking fiend I ever saw in human shape. He was labouring in a field by himself, and kept his eye on me without winking for a full minute. At last he turned round with a dogged air, and resumed his occupation. No one could doubt what was passing in his mind, but it was noon, and our party were numerous.

The rising brood of assassins, not more than two or three years old, may be seen crawling over the rocks of Itri without a rag to hide their mahogany pelts, or any body to look after them, more than if they were so many wild goats.[64]

Leaving Itri behind, the road wound its way downhill across rugged hills and barren rocks, "fit to be the abode of the heroes of Salvator [Rosa]".[65] Keats and Severn were entering "the true classic ground of brigandage", a region "well fitted for deeds of horror".[66] When they travelled without a military escort, carriages tried to advance in a convoy over this stretch, remaining as close as possible, or at least within sight of each other. To give travellers a sense of security, the path was punctuated by frequent sentry posts, less than a mile from one another, "glittering with arms piled around them".[67] As they approached Fondi, the landscape changed again. The road now ran across a gentle plain of lemon and orange orchards, olive groves and vines. It was "a scenery worthy of paradise", but not long ago, passing by that same spot, Lady Morgan had seen a gibbet hanging "with the limbs of some lately executed criminal, taint-ing gales that breathed odours of Arabia" – a grisly reminder that the threat of an attack from the robbers was very real.[68]

Seen through the lens of contemporary diarists and travel writers, Fondi looked just as squalid and poor as Itri. Lady Morgan describes it as "one of the chief towns of the brigands", inhabited by a "half-savage and wholly degraded population".[69] "The air of Fondi," she says, "is particularly insalubrious, from the stagnant waters of a great lake, which lies between the town and the sea."[70] "It grieved us not a little," writes Pennington, "to see the pallid countenances of the half-starved inhabitants of this wretched place [...]; the country for many miles round, indeed, seemed affected, and men, women, and children appeared in a dying state."[71]

Besides being unattractive to the eye and an unwhole-some place to stay, Fondi was the customs checkpoint of the Neapolitan state. As Faulkner put it, it was not a place "for a man of nerves peculiarly sensitive to the vexations of doganas, police-officers, and such like impediments to his republican ideas of free locomotion".[72] Unless one were willing to proffer a generous "*mancia*" or "tip" to the customs officials for checks to be waived, long detentions were inevitable. Those who as a matter of principle refused to grease the wheels of bureaucracy could expect their coach to be emptied and their trunks given a thorough examination. Even if the douaniers found nothing objectionable, which was rare, they knew how to throw every possible trivial obstacle in their way and delay their onward journey – and that of the unfortunate people stuck behind them in the queue. If someone were travelling too light, they became very suspicious. A passport bore an undecipherable foreign name. Another one was thought to be a forgery because it mentioned a place the officer had never heard of and did not believe existed: Utrecht. A fussy "jack-in-office", similar to that ridiculed by Horace when he stopped at Fundi on his way to Brundisium, refused to let a servant pass because she was not listed in her master's passport. In the mean time, the greedy harpies circled around their carriages gesturing and shouting in an incomprehensible language. As the travellers stood there dumbfounded or returned from the custom house after getting their declarations signed, they met the truculent looks of the locals or were surrounded by gaunt figures wrapped to the eyes in long mantles, nodding to the Neapolitan guards, and by swarms of professional beggars, most of them children, as if risen from the earth, "all filth, dirt, gesticulation, and pantomime", stretching their bony arms and screaming "*Carità, Cristiani*".[73]

There was nothing, however, that could not be resolved with a little backhander or a scattering of coins, and we can't blame the harried and mistrustful stranger for choosing this course of action and trying to quit Fondi as soon as possible rather than staying to examine its historical relics or visit its surroundings.

And it was wise to get on, because the obstacles were far from over. About five miles down the road, leaving on the right the brigand haven of Monticello, perched on the summit of a hill, travellers had to undergo another lengthy and vexatious passport and baggage inspection at the police checkpoint of Torre Portella, which marked the boundary of the Kingdom of the Two Sicilies.[74] A garrison of dragoons was stationed here, who could be deployed as an escort to carriages, for a fee regulated by tariff, as far as Terracina in one direction and Fondi in the other.

Less than two miles ahead was the Torre dell'Epitaffio (or "dei Confini"), the entrance to the Papal States. "The *Torre dei Confini*," writes Lady Morgan,

a castellated mass, guarding the frontier pass between the ocean and the mountains, and separating the Neapolitan territories from those of Rome, is one of those stations, where the traveller's patience and temper are tried to their utmost, by all those devices of fraud, extortion, and power, which obstruct the progress of the foreign visitors of Italy.[75]

It is here that Keats and Severn had their passports signed. Keats's visa reads, in translation:

> Seen at the Epitaffio on 12 Novr 1820
>   permission granted to enter the Pap^l States and to
>   be shown at the Police Direct[orate] in Terrac[ina]
>   [signed:]   IACOMINI
>   [countersigned:]   BC

Once inside the Papal territories, the road continued between a chain of desolate hills on the right and the swampy shores of Lake Fondi on the left. The stretch from Torre Portella to Terracina was the one where banditti assaults were more frequent. The geography of the place enabled the aggressors to make a hasty retreat into the mountains after their attacks, and its vicinity to the frontiers of Rome and Naples allowed them to take refuge in one territory when pursued by the forces of the other. There were sentries along the road within hailing distance of each other, but the pope's soldiers were powerless or too frightened in the face of large bands of brigands intent on striking. Many even suspected that some of the guards were colluding with the robbers, their pay being so low.

Before traversing this region in either direction, worried travellers exchanged thrilling tales about the exploits of the legendary banditti of the past – the infamous Fra Diavolo or the fearless Peppe Mastrilli, whose skull was exposed in an iron cage above one of the gates at Terracina – or whispered the names of the most egregious villains of the day: Vardarelli, Massaroni, Gasbarrone – some of them killed, some captured, others still out there, lying in wait for unsuspecting victims... The assault on the coach of the jeweller Baldini earlier that year, his abduction and his lucky escape from the kidnappers were still fresh in people's minds.[76] In October there had been news that "the banditti of Terracina [had] broken off their treaty with the Pope, and [were] gone back into the mountains".[77] The escorts pointed with sadistic pleasure at the spot where so-and-so was attacked the previous week or a sentinel was killed only a few hours ago – and with each retelling, the accounts grew more gruesome and sensational.

The coachmen, in the mean time, shrugged their shoulders. Dwight's *vetturino* reassured his passengers "that he had travelled [that] road thirty years without seeing a single robber".[78] Some travellers calmed themselves with the idea that multitudes made the same journey each day and accidents were rare: since so many came out unscathed, the risk was very small. Others felt safe in the conviction that "bandits often figure more on paper".[79] I wonder if Keats was scared or amused by all this, or if he was too ill to take any interest in such stories or in the dramatic scenery around him.

A couple of miles from Torre dell'Epitaffio, steep, craggy hills buttress the sea. A narrow path winds its way at their base, bordering the Mediterranean. Dwight's narrative of this stage of the journey shows how the lurid hues of Gothic fiction could at times colour the imagination of foreign visitors to Italy, magnifying the contours of reality.

The waves were rolling up and breaking so near us, as sometimes to make our horses start and almost to wet us with spray. This was the place of danger; and though few of my companions seemed to be afraid, all of them had some anxiety in their countenances, when they found themselves on the spot which had been, for many years, in the undisputed possession of a band of robbers, and where they had committed so many acts of violence and barbarity. The dragoons pointed towards the summit of the mountain, to remind us of the people by whom it was inhabited, and spurred on as if they were really apprehensive of danger. Conversation was suddenly at an end, as our horses and mules got into a round trot, almost for the first time since we had left Naples, and we rode on in silence for two or three miles, looking at every large rock as we passed it, to see if there were not some moving thing behind. We met a small party of men loitering by the road side, dressed in old cloaks made of reddish cloth, with one end thrown over the shoulder. They greeted us as we passed, and we hastened on towards Terracina without seeing a single habitation, or meeting another living being.

At length a turn in the road, which wound round a little point in the mountain, still on the sea-shore, brought us in sight of a strong gate, under which we were to pass. It leaned against a rock, which had here been cut down forty feet, and was supported on the other side by a tower rising from the water. We were now in safety, and congratulated ourselves on our good fortune, as we passed through the gate and came in sight of Terracina.[80]

Relief was the reaction of most travellers on reaching Porta Napoletana. A former papal residence, Terracina – the "splendidus Anxur" of Martial – was a lovely town of around 5,500 inhabitants with inns, coffee houses, a high-steepled cathedral, picturesque scenery, ancient relics and other attractions for those who were not in a rush to get on, but wanted to stay. Above all, it felt safe. The day Keats and Severn arrived there was a Sunday. The streets would have been filled with locals in their best clothes and permeated with a festive atmosphere. The tolling of the bells would have cheered the travellers after the desolate, inhospitable places they had traversed.

After entering the gate of Terracina, Keats and Severn would have gone to the nearby custom house to have their luggage examined and their passports signed by a police officer stationed there, ahead of the next day's early departure.[81] They were then free to take up their lodgings, dine and rest for the night.

It is almost certain that the inn where they stayed was the Albergo Reale, since it is the one mentioned by all other travellers stopping at Terracina around that time, and since there weren't any other known alternatives for foreigners. The hotel has since been immortalized by Washington Irving, who used it as the setting for his series of stories 'The Italian Banditti', in which a group of travellers while away their time telling each other scary tales of murderous robbers, and boasts a long history and an impressive roster of illustrious guests, which includes the king of Naples, Joachim Murat.[82] The Albergo (or Locanda) Reale was founded towards the end of the eighteenth century as part of an ambitious development, the so-called "Borgo Pio", commissioned by Pope Pius VI, who had also overseen the reorganization of his states' postal route and the construction of the new road across the Pontine Marshes.[83] An imposing building with a porch opening onto the Appian Way, under which carriages could park, was built opposite the post-house.[84] The eastern wing, by far the largest, housed the custom house, while the western part had been turned into a smart modern hotel. The Albergo Reale was laid out in three storeys, with the kitchens and an "enormous" dining room on the ground floor and ten guest rooms on each of the two floors above, named after cities.[85] Its windows looked out over the sea on one side and, on the other, onto the overhanging rock of Mount Sant'Angelo, with its Temple of Jupiter Anxur at the top. Its beds were large and square, measuring six feet each side.[86] "The bedsteads," Dwight writes from Terracina, while talking of his experience of Italian inns so far, "are of iron, and have boards in the place of sacking; but they are made very soft, with a sack of straw and a fine feather bed, and we have been [...] supplied with clean and fresh linen."[87]

Louis Simond, describing the Albergo Reale in 1818, says that "although well-looking outside [...] our pontifical inn this evening was certainly worse than such inns usually are. But the view over the sea, dashing against its massy walls under our window, was in the true Radcliffe style of the picturesque."[88] Soon after that, however, the hotel must have undergone some renovation, and perhaps even a management change, because Lady Morgan describes it as "a new and spacious building" and Pennington calls it "an admirable inn, large, commodious, and comfortable in every sense of the word".[89] The Albergo Reale, which Stendhal had pronounced an "*auberge magnifique*" in 1817, later fell on less glorious days.[90] Charles Colville Frankland, who stayed at the hotel in May 1828, declared: "This inn is remarkable throughout Europe, for the badness of its accommodation and the impertinence of its people; and, in truth, I think it richly deserves its reputation."[91] James Cobbett, writing at around the same time, is even more blunt: "There is but one inn [in Terracina] that is any way tolerable. [...] But the '*auberge magnifique*' is a great dirty place, and the keepers of it are not attentive. They are as lazy and careless a set as I have ever met with."[92] Many travellers, in particular those coming from the cheaper provinces of the Neapolitan kingdom, also complained that it was overpriced.

Early the following day, 13th November, after the mists of the nearby plains had cleared, Keats and Severn were back on their journey. The next stretch was through the dreaded Pontine Marshes, the Pomptinæ Paludes of antiquity. The region had been reclaimed, at least in part, through a system of drainage canals ordered by Pope Pius VI, which was begun in 1777 and more or less completed by 1793.

This had been a sorry stretch of land since prehistoric times. The first attempts at draining the bogs had been made by the Latins, using a network of underground tunnels and wells. Centuries later, the Romans were able to reclaim a large tract of fields for cultivation. The ancient Appian Way, built between the fourth and the third century BC, went straight across the marshes, and many towns are reported to have flourished in the area during the age of the Empire: the names of some of them are quoted in the Bible and in ancient Roman sources. Horace travelled through the Pontine Marshes on his journey to Brundisium, and in his *Satires* complains of the dreadful water giving him bellyache, and nasty mosquitoes and frogs keeping him awake at night.[93] During the Middle Ages the region was again covered by swamps. Later on, a number of popes, from Martin V to Leo X, who approved a plan devised by Leonardo da Vinci, an expert on fluid mechanics, from Sixtus V to Urban VIII, made further attempts to reclaim the marshland, but they all came to nothing. In the late eighteenth century, Pius VI was able to improve the area through a series of major infrastructural projects, which included the closure of unauthorized fish farms, one of the main causes of waterlogging and a great obstacle to the works; the clearing of large swathes of the plain; the building of a new highway from Tre Ponti to Terracina along the trail of the ancient Via Appia; the opening of a large navigable waterway to carry the excess waters – the so-called Linea Pia – running alongside the road for most of its length; the construction of four new post-houses; and the creation of a network of larger and smaller drainage canals to lighten the load on the Linea Pia and take the waters away from the plains to the sea. Thousands of labourers were employed on this monumental task. Pius VI oversaw the project and often visited the sites in person, staying at his residence in Terracina, Palazzo Braschi, during that time. After the death of Pope Pius, this great feat of civil engineering fell into disrepair, and the marshes spread again over large portions of the plain. It was only during the years of the Fascist regime that the whole of the Agro Pontino – thanks to the latest advances in technology, and also to some of Leonardo's original ideas – was reclaimed as agricultural land.

In Keats's time the swamps of old had been replaced by vast open fields crossed by canals. Many travellers were surprised by the look of the Marshes. "They are really a fine piece of country," Cobbett observed, "[...] very different from what I had imagined, from the many accounts I have listened to of this deadly spot. Here is fine high grass contending with the strongest weeds."[94] "[They] appeared to me to differ but little from many parts of Cambridgeshire," wrote Matthews.[95] Others described them as a better, more picturesque version of the Dutch plains.

The new highway, which extended for over twenty miles, was "hard, wide, and smooth, and scarcely deviate[d] from a right line".[96] "The road is excellent," pronounced Cobbett, "[...] as straight as an arrow, and with rows of poplar trees on each side of it."[97] Theodore Dwight, who followed the same route less than three months after Keats and Severn, describes the landscape around him on leaving Terracina.

We entered upon a large plain very early this morning, the first part of which was well cultivated, and had some cottages upon it. As we proceeded, however, we found ourselves among vast, neglected fields; wet low grounds, overgrown with thick bushes like willows, and standing ponds, full to the brim. [...] The mountains had retired to a great distance on the right, and not a habitation was to be seen on the whole plain beyond us. The rising sun, which had not yet reached us, shone on villages perched on the lower peaks of the mountains; and the road, which still continued broad and flat, stretched out before us for many miles. It is lined with rows of trees, and by canals filled with water from neighbouring ponds.[98]

In those days, it was believed that the air of the Marshes was pernicious, causing illness and death to those who were long exposed to it. It was not known, at the time, that the disease we today call "malaria" – which then indicated both the "bad air" and the malignant fever provoked by the infection – resulted from the bite of mosquitoes carrying noxious micro-organisms. People were advised, as a precaution, to go through the Pontine Marshes during the day, after the mists had lifted and before the dew began to fall, and on a full stomach – or, if travelling by night, to make sure none of the passengers succumbed to the humid, soporific atmosphere and fell asleep.[99] People were also urged not to drink water or cross the Marshes at the height of the summer season, when the air was deemed more pestilential.[100] Smoking was also considered a good remedy to counteract the effects of bad vapours.[101] Of course, many disregarded the advice and still lived to recount their experiences. One sure method of steering clear of trouble, or at least of limiting the risks linked to exposure to "the unhealthy exhalations of these moist, low grounds", was to traverse the Marshes as fast as possible – and this was followed without exception by every traveller, also because the smooth surface and the good condition of the road allowed it.[102] By riding post it took around five hours to clear the Marshes, allowing no breaks along the way – by *vetturino*, much longer.[103]

Leaving from Terracina, the next four posts were Ponte Maggiore, Mesa, Bocca di Fiume (also known as "Posta del Fico") and Torre de' Tre Ponti, between five and six miles apart from each other. The post-houses were little more than places where to change or rest the horses: there were no real facilities to stay overnight, and food was hard to come by and disgusting, according to all testimonies.[104] They were more like road shelters than proper inns – and, though impressive from the outside, they were pretty run down. The unlucky few who had the thankless job of keeping them going, and were compelled to remain in the same station for two years, seemed to have the look of malaria about them. Diarists and travel writers describe them as pale, sallow, sickly, cadaverous, ill-smelling – with the shadow of death hovering over their head. They had been "sent there to die the worst of deaths,—by a slow poison".[105]

Except for a few scattered fields of corn, the majority of the reclaimed land was used for grazing. "Multitudes of horses, droves of black hogs, and herds of buffaloes" and grey horned cattle ranged about, with or without a keeper.[106] "The number of birds is incredible," writes Simond. "They rose up in clouds, and obscured the air—water-fowl busily swam about the canal, while hawks hovering over, chose their prey;—large game, such as wild boars and deers, are also very plentiful, but we did not see any."[107] Cobbett was struck by the curious look of the herdsmen:

> The cattle are guarded by men who, at the hazard of their lives, have to remain on the marshes at all seasons of the year. They are dressed, after the manner of this part of Italy, in jackets and breeches of coarse linen; they wear a hat with a very peaked crown; a sort of stockings made of the same material as the upper garments; on the feet a sort of sandal (called *ciocia*), which is an oblong piece of leather, with the hair left on, the hairy side being worn outwards. [...] These herdsmen are all mounted on horseback, wearing a spur on one heel, and carrying a long pole to drive the cattle with; and they have dogs to assist them. There is something romantic

in their appearance: to see one of them couching his pole like a lance, and gallopping off at full speed, you might take him for a knight errant, if you did not happen to see the stray cow or colt that he was in pursuit of.[108]

Along the road there were frequent patrols of mounted or foot soldiers of the Papal army, stationed in little pyramidal huts "made of straw or haulm", who provided support to passengers and put their minds at rest over the possible danger of banditti.[109] This was a very safe and rather boring stage of the journey to Rome, but strangers, always on the lookout for "the slightest adventure, [or] even an alarm that could form a romantic incident in [their] narrative", saw robbers and assassins everywhere.[110] When she stopped at Forum Appii, between Bocca di Fiume and Torre de' Tre Ponti, a halting place on the Appian Way at the time of Horace, Lady Morgan saw a drove of wild colts being corralled. "Their herdsman," she notes in her travel diary, "[was] more wild than the cattle, and in better times a bandit. In these stations," she adds, "the very postilions have something lawless and ferocious in their looks: [...] they are out of the pale of humanity."[111] The warm reception of the locals was often mistaken by the untrusting foreigner. "The natives of Treponti," says Faulkner,

> live like aborigines, hutted over the marsh in a sort of *mapalia* or sheds. [...] When we entered, they were amusing themselves at cards over their wine, of which with a most generous hospitality they pressed us to partake. There could be no reasonable question that every man of them was a professional assassin, and yet did they appear in no respect more ferocious than other people, or their conscience less at ease.[112]

"Few persons are met with in this desert," writes William Brockedon, "and some of these are dressed so like Pinelli's brigands, that they startle the traveller, until he has learned that they are the pontifical police—the Sbirri."[113]

Nothing, however, is more amusing than the mishap James Fenimore Cooper experienced as he was about to get out of the Marshes:

> I was reading, when [A—] drew my attention to a group of three men in the road, who were evidently awaiting our arrival. I did not believe that three banditti would dare to attack five men,—and such, including the postilions, was our force,—and felt no uneasiness until I heard an exclamation of alarm from A—. These men had actually stopped the carriage, and one of them poked the end of a pistol (as she fancied) within a foot of her face. As the three men were all armed, I looked about me; but the pistol proved to be a wild duck, and the summons to "deliver," an invitation to buy. I believe the rogues saw the alarm they had created, for they withdrew laughing when I declined the duck.[114]

Severn's view was not immune to prejudice. Soon after enthusing about the beauty of the journey from Naples to Rome, he writes: "O how I wish the Inglish had this country what a fine account they would turn it to—It is thrown away upon these idle beasts of Italians—they crawl about like moving logs—they never [put] their arms in the sleeves of their great coats."[115] I wonder if his friend had strong opinions about Italy and its dwellers too.

The last post-house on the Marshes was Torre de' Tre Ponti (or Tor Tre Ponti) – the ancient Tripontium – which in the late eighteenth century was identified by some as Tres Tabernæ, a station on the old Appian Way mentioned in the Bible.[116] The name derived from a medieval tower and an ancient three-arched Roman bridge nearby, the so-called "Ponte di Traiano" – begun by Emperor Nerva and completed by his adopted son and successor Trajan – which spanned the Ninfa canal at the point at which it divided, branching into the Linea Pia and the Sisto canal.[117] In the vicinity of the post-house, Pope Pius VI had ordered the construction of a Capuchin monastery, as well as a church consecrated to St Paul the Apostle, who according to Acts 28:15 met some friends at Forum Appii and Tres Tabernæ on his way to Rome. Despite all their religious zeal, the poor Capuchin Fathers were devastated by malaria, and soon abandoned the site. By the time of Keats and Severn's passage, the post-house, the church and the monastery – which in Napoleonic times had been turned into a garrison – had fallen into a state of disrepair.

Emerging from the Pontine Marshes, the road continued on a featureless plain for several miles, until it came to a forest of old oaks and other trees, which had been cleared on both sides of the path to deprive ill-intentioned people of any hiding place where they might lurk. Keats and Severn entered the village of Cisterna through a small gate surmounted by a cage containing the skull of a local robber – a reminder that this was another hotspot of banditism, and until recent times the haunt of the notorious brigand Barbone, "of whom a hundred romantic tales [were] still told".[118]

After leaving Cisterna and crossing the little river Astura, the track ascended to Velletri over an almost unbroken rise, climbing to an elevation of over 1,000 feet in the space of eight miles. "It is an odious uphill road," commented Tenore, "because it combines an excessively steep gradient with dismal paving."[119] To avoid discomfort, the passengers of a *vettura* took every opportunity, if the weather was fine, to proceed on foot alongside, behind or ahead of their carriage – in particular over a steep rise or descent, as recommended by old and modern travel guides.[120] I doubt, however, that Keats would have been able to walk all the way up to Velletri at the end of such a long and fatiguing stage. His underlying weakness, compounded by the inevitable nausea caused by the bumps and jolts of the ride, would have made this last leg an excruciating one.[121]

At last they reached the southern gate of Velletri, Porta Napoletana, engraved with the letters "S.P.Q.R.", a memento of the former glories of this once powerful city – the Velester of the Volsci, the Velitræ of the Romans, home to the *gens*

Octavia, who gave the world the Emperor Augustus. Keats and Severn would have arrived close to sunset, and would not have had the energy, the inclination or even enough daylight to take a look around. Their main preoccupation would have been to take up lodgings as soon as possible, and rest ahead of the next day's journey. Since Velletri was, for most travellers, the first overnight stop en route to Naples and the last on the way to Rome, it offered a number of inns, catering for different tastes and pockets. Most foreigners stayed at Palazzo Ginnetti, which had been converted into L'Albergo Reale, "an immense palace, which bore many traces of its former grandeur".[122] "It might make an excellent palace," complained Thomas Pennington, who stayed there the first night after leaving Rome, "but it makes a wretched inn, and is a miserable specimen of fallen greatness." He adds:

There are eighteen windows in front, and one of the most beautiful staircases in Italy, leading to a noble corridor, but the corridor and apartments are full of *broken statues*, and you can scarcely find a whole one in the house; there are, however, some good busts. You have from hence a fine and extensive view of the country, which, indeed, was all that we had, for we got scarcely any refreshment or attendance in this *palace of an inn*, and if we had not the gnats and frogs which so much annoyed the poet in his night's lodging, as the coldness of the night was a security against the first, and the local situation of the place against the second, yet were we kept from sleep in our *wretched magnificent apartments* from other causes; and the wind beating against the tottering hinges of the old and decayed window-shutters of the Palazzo, put us in mind of the descriptions one has read of a night passed in an old baronial castle (from the howling of the wind and other incidental causes) said to be haunted; added to this, we had the constant noise of a cascade belonging to the house, so that passing the night unrefreshed with sleep, we were glad to mount our carriage in good time, to resume our journey.[123]

This stately old pile "belong[ed] to a prince who ha[d] let the whole to serve as an inn, with the exception of two rooms, which he himself inhabited".[124] Cold, dreary and creaking as the palace might have been, its spacious rooms would still have guaranteed a very comfortable night to most wearied travellers – including Keats and Severn, if they spent their night there.

The following morning, 14th November, they were on the road again. Rome was now within a day's journey – it must have been a heartening thought for them. The twenty-five miles to the city could be done in just over five hours by post, but it took more than double that time to cover that stretch by *vettura*.[125] Even a very early departure from Velletri – which would have been a great strain after the previous day's forty-mile trip – would mean arriving in Rome after dusk. Keats and Severn could not inconvenience Doctor Clark by turning up too late at his door. For that reason, and also because of Keats's delicate condition, they were forced to make one more overnight stay before reaching their destination.

Leaving Velletri from the north gate, Porta Romana, their *vettura* turned southwards onto a "rather nasty" road winding its way downhill through frequent hairpin bends.[126] The stretch between Velletri and Albano was the most charming and picturesque, in particular around Genzano – an uninterrupted hill-and-dale landscape with beautiful views and "a very respectable sprinkling of villas, vineyards, and cornfields, presenting a remarkable contrast to the dreary monotony" of the Pontine Marshes.[127] Here the country was covered in olive groves and vineyards – no longer festooned to trees, but planted *a filare*, "trained in the neatest manner, and most closely to the ground [...] in rows five or six feet apart".[128]

At the end of the steep descent, the road emerged onto a magnificent terrace overlooking the Tyrrhenian Sea from Terracina to Ostia.[129] Then, turning westward, it ascended again, passing by the imposing ruins of Castle San Gennaro, leaving Civita Lavinia – the ancient Lanuvium of the Romans – to the left and climbing three more miles to the "delightful village" of Genzano, which at an elevation of around 1,400 feet would be the highest point reached by Keats and Severn on their journey to Rome.[130]

Genzano offered a welcome change and "a novel sight" with its "wide streets, laid out with regularity".[131] Since the ancient medieval *borgo*, huddled around Palazzo Sforza-Cesarini, is some distance from the postal route, travellers admired the broad elm-lined avenues and the beautiful linear geometries of the new town, with its elegant system of sloping triangular intersections. Genzano was renowned for its salubrious air and its June flower festival, the Infiorata, which attracted thousands of visitors each year from the neighbouring areas and from the capital. It was also famed for its delicious wines, which many travellers were eager to taste. Alexandre Dumas, who stopped at Genzano on his way back from Naples, was among them.[132] And then, for those with energy and time to spare, there was a breathtaking view of Lake Nemi – the "*speculum Dianæ*" ("Mirror of Diana") of antiquity, with its hallowed wooded slopes and the Alban Mount (Monte Cavo) rising in the distance – from a terrace up in the old town, and the opportunity to visit the nearby *casino* designed and once occupied by the painter Carlo Maratta and his beautiful daughter, the poet Faustina Maratti, who survived a kidnapping attempt by the son of the Prince of Genzano. We don't know if Keats and Severn, like other travellers before and after them, were able to enjoy any of this, but I'd like to think that it was then that Severn found the first inspiration for one of his best and most enduring works, *The Vintage at Gensano in Italy*.

Genzano to Albano is a delightful two-mile walk today, thanks to modern viaducts and the monumental 1854 Ariccia Bridge, rebuilt after being destroyed by Allied bombs in 1944. In Keats's time, this was the most arduous and dangerous stretch of the whole journey. The post-road didn't follow the path of the ancient Appian Way, which bypassed Ariccia by descending into the valley underneath its citadel before reascending towards Albano. The old Via Appia was too narrow, winding and broken for riding post. Towards the end of the eighteenth century, many of its blocks of peperino had been uprooted and used to pave the new Strada Corriera. This was in turn steep, slippery and tortuous, and accidents along the way were commonplace. The young Genzanese doctor Gregorio Giannini, a local *improvisatore*, even addressed a poem to the pontifical treasurer general, Cardinal Antonio Tosti, begging him to pull a few strings, in particular those of the papal purse, to get a new road built between the two towns:

Beginning from Albano you descend,
But then a little way before you gain
Ariccia, there's a slope that takes you up,
And after that you go down to the plain;
To reach Genzano then you'd need a winch
To haul you up the hillside inch by inch.

Here there's a crag, a gaping scar, a cliff,
There a ravine, a chasm, an abyss,
Now comes a ridge, an arduous slope to climb,
And then a gorge, an edge, a precipice;
A rivulet, embankments, scattered blocks –
And rubble, slime and mud, and jagged rocks.

It's pitiful to see the wretched horses
Who drag the carts and carriages this way,
Plodding so patiently up these steep paths,
Urged onward by the cruel whip all day:
Some nights I ask why they don't shed their load
And leave the mail coach standing in the road.

The journey's one I've often made on foot
(A choice we poets are obliged to make).
And if you haven't tried, you won't believe
The effort and the energy it takes.
I'll only say, if that's enough for you,
I sometimes felt like spitting blood – it's true.

The things I've seen! The coaches and barouches
That cross in front of carts and then go smash
Into oncoming phaetons and caleches –
A slam, a bam, a mighty crush, a crash.
Horses and mules and donkeys all around
Lie in a tangle, writhing on the ground.

Muleteers, carters, coachmen, all dead-drunk,
Come staggering to see, then go berserk,
Scurrying here and there, set for a brawl,
With frightful curses like an infidel Turk;
The howls, the oaths, the blasphemies could, I swear,
Provoke a tempest in the offended air.

In recent months, Your Eminence, you'd have seen
Young dandies and blue-blooded escorts there –
Spruced up, with spotless breeches, trim and tight:
They come out riding mares to take the air.
The jolly scene would have aroused your mirth –
It was the finest spectacle on earth.

One slips, another stumbles, and a third
Loses his saddle that's not fully strapped,
And yet another breaks his shinbone as
The horse collapses on him and he's trapped;
But the young ladies, though they may be hurt,
Are not afraid of lifting up their skirt!

A little love, served with a little wine,
And they're as easily plucked as pickled pears;
Ribs may be broken, but they'll still stand up,
And there's not one who bothers what she wears!
Not many broken bones: these girls are tougher,
And fear has been the worst they've had to suffer.

What else? Some days ago a Monsignor
On his way home to Naples had bad luck;
Down in Galloro, where the road's not wide,
His horses pressed together and got stuck;
Unable to get through the bottleneck,
They overturned the carriage. What a wreck![133]

A nasty accident, but Monsignor
Had all his limbs intact; at any rate,
Thank Heaven above, no serious harm was done,
Except the shattering of certain plates
Meant for a special dinner with his friends
Back home in Naples, when his journey ends.

Those plates! They must have cost… I wouldn't know,
But I am told that they were very rare;
In fact, our local antiquarians
And mineralogists went running there
To grub around, collecting all the scraps
To decorate their studios, perhaps.

Disaster's always waiting on that road –
If not today, tomorrow, Eminence;
And there are many who won't come or go
Because they're so afraid of such events:
For this alone Genzano lost all hope
Of welcoming his Holiness the Pope.

In Porto d'Anzio you've done so much;
In Terracina, Tivoli… What the hell!
The whole world knows your wondrous works in Rome;
Doesn't Your Eminence think it would be well
To think of our poor folk who slip and fall
And give us a new post-road after all?

You see, an awful lot of accidents
Will be prevented when the road gets done;
A public work of such utility
Brings solid benefit to everyone;
Trade might return and flourish unconfined
Where now it's partly lame and badly blind.

In any case, I leave it up to you:
Your Eminence is provident enough...
Do it, and I can promise you a sonnet,
A madrigal, an ode, or some such stuff;
If it's not on, that's all the same to me,
I always have a cure for poverty.

Indeed, for me I'd almost say it's better
That our old road remain a serious threat,
Where people break their heads, their legs, their neck:
Just think of all the patients that I get.
But now you're weary of my eloquence,
Enough! I'll take my leave, Your Eminence.[134]

[tr. ANTHONY MORTIMER]

And when Giannini said, earlier in the poem, that part of the
road was so bad "it [was] a miracle to come out unscathed", it
was not too hyperbolic, as Severn almost had the misfortune
of finding out for himself only a few months later:

June 25 [1821] Thanks to God I have escaped a dreadful
accident which might have cost me my life—Yesterday
Sunday all the English Artists and others proposed and set
off to see a Grand Festival about 20 Miles from Rome [the
Infiorata at Genzano]—they went in a open Carriage and
in returning the Coachman drove too near the hedge and
they were all precipitated down 9 or 10 feet of hedge—one
has his Collar Bone broken and all the others are very much
hurt—none dangerously—Now I was to have been one of

this party—but my picture must be gone on with and the
Model could not come to me any other day than Sunday
so that I declined going—or I should have been disabled or
perhaps killed—This poor fellow will be obliged to be in
bed for 3 Weeks—The only Englishman unhurt set to [writ-
ten "too"] and horsewhip'd the Coachman so terribly that
they brought him in the Coach groaning—The Coachman
was drunk.[135]

Leaving Genzano at the intersection of the Olmata and two
other elm-lined avenues, Keats and Severn's *vettura* began
to wind its way downhill. In the vale below, they came to the
Fontanaccio, "a fountain of limpid, pure water originating
from the hills above".[136] Since it was a warm day, it is possible
that Keats and Severn stopped to drink from the cool stream.[137]
The post-road then climbed to the Sanctuary of Santa Maria di
Galloro, a seventeenth-century church surrounded by woodland
and commanding a delightful panorama of the Tyrrhenian
coast, before descending to the bottom of a valley and ascend-
ing again to Ariccia. After entering the ancient town through
Porta Napoletana, Keats and Severn's carriage skirted Bernini's
Palazzo Chigi and Piazza di Corte, and then rattled down its
narrow thoroughfare, coming out at the end of it through Porta
Romana.[138] Here the road became steep and tortuous again
as it descended into Vallericcia, the ample vale below the city,
"towards which the old walls of the town presented a high and
inaccessible precipice of masonry".[139] The *vettura* then entered
the so-called "Galleria", a picturesque track canopied by tall
trees and ascending a gentle slope towards Albano, their final
destination for the day. On their left, they passed a group of
Roman ruins and the sixteenth-century church and monastery
of Santa Maria della Stella; on their right, the imposing mass of
the reputed Tomb of the Horatii and Curiatii, with its crumbling
conical towers rising above a solid square base.[140] The Strada
Corriera soon emerged into a long, broad avenue, Via del Corso,
the main street of Albano.

Albano's rich history blends with that of Rome, stretching back into mythical times. The modern town was described by many contemporary guides and diarists as the "Hampstead of Rome". Despite its vicinity to the malarial Campagna Romana, its air was considered salubrious, making it the summer retreat of choice for wealthy Romans. If we look at the 1819 land-registry maps and records of the territories of Genzano and Ariccia and compare them with Albano's, we can see that "vineyards", "olive groves", "arable land" and "cane fields" abound in the former two, whereas "lodging houses", "holiday houses" and "holiday villas" are very common in the latter. Many of these *case di villeggiatura* were owned by famous earls and marquises. One of them belonged to the exiled Prince Louis Bonaparte, the younger brother of Napoleon and a former king of Holland.[141] The most palatial of these residences was Villa Doria-Pamphilj, situated at the north end of Via del Corso, near Porta Romana. Its vast grounds, which included what are believed to be the ruins of Pompey the Great's country villa, extended over an area similar in size to that of the entire town.

Being so close to Rome, Albano was not a common overnight stay for travellers going to or coming back from Naples. As a result, there were only two inns. The first was the large post-house on Via della Posta, off the Corso, at the southern end of the town centre.[142] The other, only two doors down from Palazzo Doria-Pamphilj and looking out onto its grounds from the back windows, was a smaller inn bearing the same name as the one in which Keats and Severn had stayed in Naples, Villa di Londra.[143] As its name suggested, it was favoured by tourists, in particular English ones, who disdained the discomfort of Italian post-house inns. Mariana Starke, in her 1824 *Information and Directions for Travellers on the Continent*, writes: "The best Inn at Albano, namely, *La Villa di Londra*, furnishes good dinners, and tolerable beds, at reasonable prices."[144]

The inn was known among the locals as the "Locanda di Emiliano", from the name of its host, no doubt a renowned figure in the community. Born in 1758, Emiliano was the son of the architect Pietrantonio Giorni, author of *View of the City of Albano*, and had started his career in hostel management as the innkeeper of the local post-house, where he ran the trattoria between 1799 and 1807.[145] He set up on his own soon after, since the hotel Villa di Londra was already well established by the beginning of the 1810s, when it welcomed, during the summer, famous guests such as Antonio Canova and Juliette Récamier.[146] The inn was located on the site occupied today by the building at No. 4 Corso Giacomo Matteotti, whose north façade looks onto Piazza Giuseppe Mazzini, the location of Palazzo Doria-Pamphilj, which was damaged by the Allied bombing of 1st February 1944 and demolished in 1951.[147]

Thanks to a survey commissioned in November 1850 by one of Emiliano's grandsons, the grammarian and historian Revd Francesco Giorni, we are able to reconstruct a detailed layout of the building.[148] The rooms in the basement were occupied by the kitchen and the cellars. The main entrance, opening up onto the Corso, was on the ground floor. The three upper floors housed rooms for travellers, summer residents and Emiliano's family. The piano nobile – reserved for the most prestigious guests – was composed of six intercommunicating rooms, with a large dining room at the front, lit up by three windows, and a canopied balcony at the back, looking out onto a most picturesque rural landscape with Roman ruins and a view of the sea on the horizon.[149]

Albano became very busy in the summer, when all those who could afford to would leave the stifling heat of a low-lying city such as Rome, reputed to be malarial, and seek relief among the refreshing breezes of the Alban Hills.[150] Villa di Londra, in the words of Tenore, was "really rather a good inn, which add[ed] to the many amenities of Albano." "Several wealthy foreigners," he wrote, "during the summertime leave Rome and take up residence there."[151] Turning up at the inn without a booking during high season could lead to disappointment, as testified by the German poet Wilhelm Müller:

So the three of us, along with our servant and the luggage, set off on our journey on the day we had agreed. Our plan was to wait in Albano for the person who was staying behind – and as soon as he had joined us, we would go to Genzano together [to take up lodgings for the summer]. On a cool evening four days after the festival of St Peter [29th June], we left via the Porta San Giovanni. We did not arrive in Albano until nightfall. We discovered that the hotel Villa di Londra, where we usually stayed, was fully occupied. They suggested we go to the Post-House, which is a little higher up, not far from the market square. There we soon agreed on a price for the rooms and beds we needed – which was achieved all the quicker when the *cameriere* realized that we were not entirely unacquainted with Italian ways.[152]

[tr. SANDER BERG]

It's unlikely that Keats and Severn would have found the inn busy in the middle of November and been forced to stay at the post-house for the night. We can't tell whether they had the time or the inclination to visit any of the celebrated sights of Albano – which included its lake, several Roman ruins and even a small museum – but we can be sure that they spent a very pleasant and quiet evening at the Villa di Londra inn, in preparation for their arrival in Rome.[153]

The 15th of November was another warm day.[154] Keats and Severn would have left their hotel early in the morning, trying to cross the Campagna as fast as possible to avoid the deadly exhalations that were believed to be brought forth by the heat of noon. There were only about fifteen miles to the Lateran Gate: Rome must have felt very near now. From the nearby Porta Romana, and for a long time after clearing it, they would have been able to see in the distance – if the day was clear and there was enough light – the vague profile of St Peter's cupola.

Many travellers have recounted their feelings on first seeing the capital and the barren flatland that encircled it. Lady Morgan called the boundless desert of the Campagna "the grave of graves". "It is one of the finest views of picturesque desolation which even Italy presents," she said.[155] Most of the observers were left stunned by the spectacle. "It is hard for the traveller," commented Tenore, "to shake off the surprise caused by this wilderness, which seems to lead to the ruins of Babylon, of Numantia or of Palmyra, rather than to a magnificent capital."[156] Dwight and his travelling companion were left speechless: "The sight was new and unexpected to my friend as well as to myself. What his thoughts were I do not know; he instantly ceased talking, and looked steadfastly before him a long time in perfect silence."[157] One of the best descriptions of the approach to Rome from Albano has been left by James Fenimore Cooper:

I was too impatient to await the slow movement of the *vetturino*, and hurried on alone, afoot, as soon as my breakfast was swallowed. Passing through a gateway, I soon found myself at a point whence I overlooked much of the surrounding scenery.[158] Such a moment can occur but once in a whole life.

The road ran down a long declivity, in a straight line, until it reached the plain, when it proceeded more diagonally, winding towards its destination. But that plain! Far and near it was a waste, treeless, almost shrubless, and with few buildings beside ruins. Long broken lines of arches, the remains of aqueducts, were visible in the distance; and here and there a tower rendered the solitude more eloquent, by irresistibly provoking a comparison between the days when they were built and tenanted, and the present hour. At the foot of the mountain, though the road diverged, there was a lane of smaller ruins that followed the line of the descent for miles in an air line.[159] This line of ruins was broken at intervals, but there were still miles of it to be distinctly traced, and to show the continuity that had once existed from Albano to the very walls of Rome. This was the Appian Way; and the ruins were those of the tombs that once lined its sides,—the "stop traveller" of antiquity. These tombs were on a scale proportioned to the grandeur of the seat of empire, and they altogether threw those of Pompeii into the shade; although the latter, as a matter of course, are in much the best preservation. There were several near Albano, circular crumbling towers, large enough to form small habitations for the living: a change of destiny, as I afterwards discovered, that has actually befallen several of them nearer the city.

Rome itself lay near the confines of the western view. The distance (fourteen or fifteen miles), and the even surface of the country, rendered the town indistinct, but it still appeared regal and like a capital. Domes rose up above the plane of roofs in all directions; and that of St. Peter's, though less imposing than fancy had portrayed it, was comparatively grand and towering. It looked like the Invalides seen from Neuilly, the distinctness of the details and the gilding apart. Although I could discern nothing at that distance that denoted ruins, the place had not altogether the air of other towns. The deserted appearance of the surrounding country, the broken arches of the aqueducts, and perhaps the recollections, threw around it a character of sublime solitude. The town had not, in itself, an appearance of being deserted, but the environs caused it to seem cut off from the rest of the world.

The carriages soon came rolling down the hill, and we proceeded in company, absolutely silent and contemplative from an indescribable rush of sensations. The distance across the waste appeared to be nothing, and objects rose fast on every side to heighten the feeling of awe. Here was a small temple, insignificant in size and material, but evidently Roman; there, another line of aqueducts; and yonder, a tomb worthy to be a palace. We passed beneath one line of aqueduct, and drew near the walls—the ancient unquestionable walls of Rome herself![160]

That morning, as their *vettura* proceeded at a slow pace towards their destination, Keats and Severn would have had a chance to take in that same surreal landscape, those same spectral ruins, and the young dying poet must have felt, with his sick eagle's gaze, like others before and after him, a keen contrast between the grandeur of ancient Rome and the rude wasting of old time.

As we have seen, Severn wrote in his late memoir that nothing very remarkable happened to him and Keats during their journey from Naples until they reached the Campagna Romana, when he saw the large crimson cloak of a cardinal. As he approached, he discovered that he was engaged in shooting small birds.

> He had an owl tied losely to a stick & a small looking glass was annexed to move about with the owl, the light of which attracted numerous birds & the whole merit of this sport was not to shoot the owl—Two Footmen in Carpet livery kept loading the fowling pieces of the Cardinal & it was astonishing the great number of birds he killed.[161]

This was written fifty-three years after that strange meeting. That large crimson spot in the bleak expanse of the Campagna must have left a very vivid impression if it blotted out anything else that happened or was seen during the entire journey to Rome. What Severn is describing is a traditional technique for shooting skylarks.[162] The end of October and the first half of November are the time when skylarks halt in the Campagna Romana during their autumn migration towards the south. The skylark is by and large a terrestrial bird. Camouflaged in its light-brown plumage, it spends its life in open country where the vegetation is not too thick or high and the soil not too wet, foraging for plants and insects. That morning was not only warm but sunny too, if the looking glass could be used alongside the owl to lure the birds.

Although Severn's description makes it sound as if shooting the skylarks was child's play, it is something that requires a certain skill, and it is clear that the high prelate was not just an occasional sportsman but a consummate hunter. But who was this cardinal, and why was he there that morning?

Since hunting was an aristocratic pastime and many ecclesiastical dignitaries hailed from noble stock, there are several possible candidates, but there is one wearer of the purple robe, in particular, who was famous for his passion for shooting birds: Cardinal Annibale della Genga.

Born into a patrician family from the Marches in 1760, Della Genga studied theology at the Collegio Campana in Osimo and the Collegio Piceno in Rome. He then entered the Pontificia Accademia dei nobili ecclesiastici, to be trained in the diplomatic service, and was ordained to the priesthood in 1783. His religious education did not prevent him from developing very early on a strong interest in hunting, which he nurtured throughout his youth and adulthood. His pleasant looks and manners, his solemn figure and dignified demeanour, as well as his eloquence and erudition, ensured his rapid ascent through the ranks of the Catholic Church. After being appointed titular archbishop of Tyre, in 1794 he was dispatched to Germany to serve as papal nuncio to the Electorates of Cologne, Mainz and Trier, a challenging mission that saw him at the heart of the wrangling between Austria and the France of Napoleon, then at war with each other. It was during that time that he began to show signs of the illness that would plague him for the rest of his life.[163] Despite rumours about his private conduct and his love of worldly pursuits, his religious position was one of absolute moral rigour. "He is," wrote Stendhal in the *New Monthly Magazine*,

> like the Count d'Artois in France, a reformed man of pleasure, and, like most other converts, possesses, or affects to possess, a greater rigidity of manners than if he had never strayed from the golden path of propriety. [...] His time while at Munich was divided between the pleasures of the chase, gallantry and ecclesiastical affairs. If public rumour is to be believed, he left behind him in that city three children, who are still alive.[164]

At the end of 1801, following some disagreements with other powerful prelates close to the pope, Della Genga renounced his nunciature and returned to Rome. Towards the middle of 1806 he was sent on another mission, this time to Bavaria. As he set off on his way back to Italy at the beginning of 1808, he learnt about the French occupation of Rome, and in the autumn of that year entered the Abbey of Monticelli, near Genga, his family's ancestral pontifical fief. He lived there for a few years, as a kind of prisoner of state, finding comfort in music, literature and, of course, the joys of the chase. An embittered man, he believed his career to be over. His thoughts soon turned to death, and he made plans for his own sepulchre to be built inside the abbey, even writing its inscription.

But by a sudden twist of fate, after the restoration of the Papal States in 1814, he was recalled to Rome, and was sent on a mission to France by Pope Pius VII. Two years later, he was elevated to Cardinal of Santa Maria in Trastevere, and later appointed archpriest of Santa Maria Maggiore and titular of the Diocese of Senigallia, which he had to renounce due to his poor health. On 12th May 1820, as his condition seemed to improve, he was created vicar general of the Diocese of Rome, one of the highest ecclesiastical positions in the Catholic Church. "His health, however," wrote Della Genga's first biographer, Alexis-François Artaud de Montor, "could not be wholly restored." After St Louis's Day, 25th August 1820, "he was prescribed the Acqua Santa Baths, near St John Lateran".[165]

This small thermal resort, which had been renovated and reopened only two years before,[166] was located about three miles from the Lateran Gate, off the road from Albano to Rome, on what is now called Via dell'Acqua Santa. Close to Rome and surrounded by vast fields, it was a convenient, peaceful retreat used by Church dignitaries seeking to recover their health and wishing to remain in touch with the affairs of the capital. "While he lived in Rome," wrote the Church historian Gaetano Moroni,

[Della Genga] made frequent use of the Acqua Santa Baths in the building of that name, and he was rarely seen in the Papal Chapel. This, however, did not prevent him from applying himself with unstinting zeal to the performance of his duties, especially in his delicate and important role as Vicar of Rome.[167]

And, true to this description, Della Genga was unrelenting in his pursuit of any breach of religious observance. In the years between 1820 and 1822, he published twenty-five 'Edicts' relating to liturgical, doctrinal and moral matters. These included precise rules of behaviour – which, if flouted, were sanctioned by imprisonment, fines and corporal punishment.[168]

We know that Della Genga was still at the Acqua Santa Baths on 15th November 1820 because his 'Invito sagro' ("Holy Summons") of 11th November was endorsed by his deputy, Antonio Argenti, and because the *Diario di Roma* of 18th November published the following report:

The solemn public rites for the late Card. Vicar Lorenzo Litta of ever blessed and commendable memory were celebrated last Thursday, 16th instant, by the venerable College of Most Revd Priests of our Dominant Church in the ancient Chiesa di San Salvatore alle Coppelle, above whose main door, on the outside wall, was affixed the following inscription:

Lavrentio. Littae
S. R. E. Cardinali
PII. VII. P. O. M.
In. Vrbe. Sacrorum. Vicario.
Parochorum. Collegium
Ivsta. Persolvit

Mons. Vicegerent Candido Maria Frattini, Archbishop of Philippi, celebrated the Holy Requiem Mass, accompanied by funeral chants and assisted by the very same Order of Curates, the Examiners of the Most Revd Clergy, the Superior of the Priests of the Mission, as well as the whole Civil and Criminal Curia of the Vicariate. [...] Had he not been prevented by health problems, the Most Emt and Revd Card. Vicar [Della Genga], the current incumbent, would have given the honour of his respectable presence, adding to the pomp of the above-mentioned funeral service.[169]

Della Genga's health did recover in part over the following years, and, by another twist of fate, at the death of Pius VII in August 1823 the conservative faction of the conclave – the so-called "*zelanti*" – elected him as the new pope, under the name of Leo XII.

Della Genga was as intransigent as a pope as he had been as a cardinal. His harsh measures and restrictive edicts – one of them, dated 10th July 1826, setting out for the first time detailed rules for hunting in the Papal territories – made him unpopular with the Roman populace.[170] He was one of the favourite targets of Giuseppe Gioachino Belli and the subject of several lampoons, including the following pasquinade:

> The pope's a hunter, and our towns are turned
> Into so many forests every day;
> His ministers are like a pack of hounds –
> His subjects are his prey.[171]

Whenever he had a relapse, Della Genga returned to the Acqua Santa resort. "The blessed memory of Pope Leo XII," wrote Filippo Maria Gerardi in his historical notes on the Baths, "to the unquestionable benefit of his health, did not fail to sojourn there almost every year[... a]s recorded by a marble plaque now lost." His private residence in the vicinity of the Baths became known as the "Casino del Papa", the Pope's Lodge.[172]

Annibale della Genga kept pursuing his passion for the chase until the end of his days. The French writer François-René de Chateaubriand, then serving as ambassador to the Holy See for the king of France, went to see him on two separate occasions, a short time before his death in February 1829, and left the following cameo portraits of the pope:

> His Holiness received me in private audience – public audiences no longer being held and costing too much. Leo XII is a very tall prince, who looks both serene and sad, and who dresses in a simple white cassock. He eschews all pomp and occupies a spartan room with very little furniture. He barely eats – and lives, with his cat, on a bit of *polenta*. He knows he is gravely ill, and sees himself wither away with a resignation suffused with Christian joy.[173]

> Leo XII is a hard worker; he sleeps little and barely eats at all. The only pleasure from his youth he still indulges is hunting, an exercise necessary to his health – which, I might add, appears to be improving. He will on occasion fire a few shots with his fowling-piece in the vast enclosure of the Vatican Gardens. The *zelanti* find it difficult to excuse this innocent distraction.[174]

> [tr. SANDER BERG]

Unaware of having had a chance audience with a future pope, Keats and Severn pushed on towards the walls of Rome and, about an hour later, reached the Lateran Gate. After the usual customs checks, they proceeded through the streets of the capital and "were soon struck with the Stupendous Coloseum". "[B]ut the essential sight in Rome," Severn continued in his late memoir, "was D^r (Sir) James Clark ^himself," the young Scottish doctor who would give his long-awaited verdict on Keats's chances of survival.[175] So we leave our two travellers on that warm, sunny day as their carriage rattles over the *sanpietrini* pavement of the Eternal City and they advance at a slow pace towards the end of their journey, half in hope, half in dread of what the future held for them.

My Chest of Books divide among my friends. In case of my death this scrap of Paper may be serviceable in your possession.

All my estate real and personal consists in the hopes of the sale of books publish'd or unpublish'd. Now I wish Brown and you to be the first paid Creditors — the rest is eu multebus — but in case it should shower pay my Taylor the few pounds I owe him.

1a. Keats's undated 'Testament', enclosed in his letter of 14th August 1820 to John Taylor (see p. 12 and p. 268, note 13)

1b, 1c. Keats's passport (recto, verso)

2a. 'The *Maria Crowther*, Sailing Brig',
watercolour by Joseph Severn (see p. 45)

2b. 'Handfast Point, Dorsetshire / Studland Bay',
watercolour drawing by Joseph Severn (see p. 286, note 65)

2c. 'Ceuta / Coast of Barbary',
watercolour by Joseph Severn (see p. 288, note 81)

Bright Star, would I were stedfast as thou art—
Not in lone splendor hung aloft the night
And watching, with eternal lids apart,
Like nature's patient sleepless Eremite,
The moving waters at their priestlike task
Of pure ablution round earth's human shores,
Or gazing on the new soft-fallen masque
Of snow upon the mountains and the moors.
No—yet still stedfast, still unchangeable,
Pillow'd upon my fair love's ripening breast,
To feel for ever its soft swell and fall,
Awake for ever in a sweet unrest,
Still, still to hear her tender-taken breath,
And so live ever—or else swoon to death.

Chas Brown writes sending a letter from Severn
from Rome, Sept 19th 1821, "published by me in
Atheneum 23 aug. 1879, " He wrote this down in
the ship — it is one of his most beautiful things. I will
send it." This was therefore Keats' last poem, &
it ends with the word Death.

3. The 'Bright Star' sonnet, written down by
Keats in *The Poetical Works of William Shakspeare*
on the blank page opposite *A Lover's Complaint*,
while on board the *Maria Crowther*

4a. 'Unknown Bay', watercolour by Joseph Severn (see pp. 135–36)

4b. The Gulf of Gaeta seen from the hills overlooking Formia,
with the mausoleum of Lucius Munatius Plancus visible atop
Mount Orlando, in a 1955 postcard (see pp. 135–36)

4c. Villa Patrizi, the eighteenth-century palazzo that housed the
Albergo di Cicerone (see p. 135), in a painting by Pasquale Mattej, c.1850.
In the background, the promontory of Gaeta

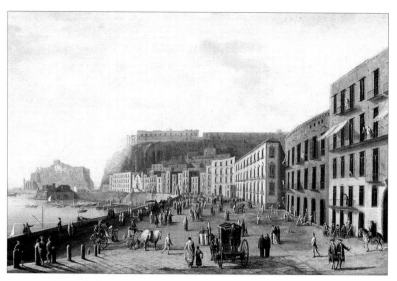

5a. Strada S. Lucia in Naples, in a painting by Pietro Fabris, *c.*1770.
Palazzo d'Alessandro, the building which housed the Hotel
Villa di Londra in the 1820s, is the fourth from the right

5b. The courtyard of Palazzo d'Alessandro,
which is also visible on the 1828 map of Naples on p. IX

III. DIPARTIMENTO

REGISTRO 17
Num. 4709

OGGETTO

Certificato per passa-
port o

CONNOTATI

Patria *Suddito Inglese*

Età *28 anni*

Condizione *Gentiluomo*

Statura *2°*

Viso *°*

Capelli *castro*

MARCHE VISIBILI

Sottoscrizione del Latore

Consiglio di Pubblica Sicurezza

FERDINANDO I.

PER LA GRAZIA DI DIO

E PER LA COSTITUZIONE DELLA MONARCHIA

RE DEL REGNO DELLE DUE SICILIE

DI GERUSALEMME ec.

INFANTE DI SPAGNA, DUCA DI PARMA, PIACENZA, CASTRO, ec. ec.
GRAN PRINCIPE EREDITARIO DI TOSCANA. ec. ec. ec.

Il Sig Giovanni Keats

non è accusat o di alcun delitto; nè esiste contro di ess o
alcun reclamo per causa civile, per quanto risulta da' registri
di Polizia.

Vale il presente certificato accio poss a ottenere il passa-
porto, che dimanda — per *Inghilterra*

Rilasciato sul *suo passaporto* —

Dato in Napoli 7, *7bre 1820,*

L' Uffiziale del 3.° Dipartimento

Registato num. *6709,*

6a. Keats's certificate of good conduct from the Neapolitan police

6b. Joseph Severn in 1822 (left); 6c. William Sharp in 1894 (right)

7a. The Appian Way at Terracina (looking towards Naples), with the town's gate and the porch of the Albergo Reale visible in the background

7b. The road through the Pontine Marshes (looking towards Naples)

8a. View of the Campagna Romana from the Appian Way

8b. View of the Claudian Aqueduct from the Appian Way,
near the Acqua Santa Baths

8c. Pope Leo XII (Annibale della Genga) soon after his election
to the pontificate in 1823 (left); 8d. Doctor James Clark in 1865 (right)

9a. Anna Angeletti's petition to the local magistrate for the removal of
John Keats from her house or the reimbursement of all costs and damages
in case of his death (left); 9b. Draft of the governor of Rome
Tommaso Bernetti's letter to the Sacra Consulta (right)

9c. The first page of Doctor Domenico Morichini's letter
to the Secretary of the Sacra Consulta

Wolfa Sept 1873

My Tedious Life

Joseph Severn

As my life has been a hull blank without the least interest except its length of 80 years & as I am now in these mountains passing a tedious time a blank — still don't know how to fill up; it occurs to me to take this blank waste of my long life & make some of it just as a cook takes a tasteless article of food & flavours spices, — it into something palatable, so will I try & be spices, picant & palatable against all this in my actual progress of life I could never dispel the dulness; yet now in trying to live it over again with my pen I may be more careful of the gaps & not stumble over the hillocks of my past existence — I may laugh at my follies & feel shame at my vanities & altho I could not do it myself for myself, yet some lucky wight born with a genius like may thro' me turn it to account by seeing what I have so ill done or not done & turn away from it & look at the back of my looking glass

I am an Hoxtontonian that is in 1793 I was born in Hoxton a village a little north of London & call'd, my father made some noise in the world for he was a Musician & he took a liking to me beyond his other five children as I was his eldest & most companionable & could soonest laugh at his jokes & stare at his rubbishing old pictures which he was always picking up when other people dropped 'em — Yet this drew out of me or put into me a turn for painting evinced when I was an urchin

4.16.4.

10. First page of the manuscript of Joseph Severn's
1873 memoir 'My Tedious Life'

11. Charles Edward Cotterell after 1860

12a. Keats's gravestone in 1832

12b. The gravestones of John Keats and Joseph Severn today

ROME

THIS IS THE SADDEST CHAPTER IN OUR STORY. Many biographers gloss over the harrowing details of Keats's physical pain and mental deterioration during the last three months of his life, but it is essential to give an honest record of his final days if we want to appreciate him in full as a human being rather than just as a poet.

When Keats turned up at James Clark's home in Piazza di Spagna, the doctor was a little surprised.[1] "{I w}as writing to some friends at Naples ab{out him}," he wrote twelve days later, on 27th November 1820, "{a}t the moment he unexpectedly made h{is appear}ance here."[2] This suggests that he had not heard from the travellers ahead of their journey from Naples, and that he was awaiting news of the poet's arrival in Rome. Clark's letter came to us through a partial transcript made by Keats's publisher, James Augustus Hessey. We don't know for sure who the recipient was, but since the letter is part of a collection that included the copy of another extract, as well as an original letter to a medical man called "Gray", it is fair to assume that the November letter was also addressed to the same person, identified by Amy Lowell with the pharmacologist Samuel Frederick Gray, author of the influential treatise *A Supplement to the Pharmacopœias* and co-editor of the *London Medical Repository*.[3] Whether this identification is correct or not, it is clear that there is a tone of familiarity between Clark and the recipient of the letter, who appears to be acting as an intermediary between the doctor in Rome and Keats's publishers:

Keats arrived here about a week ago & I have got him into comfortable lodgings. I can hardly yet give you a decided opinion of his case but will in my next. The chief part of his disease, as far as I can yet see seems seated in his Stomach. I have some suspicion of disease of the heart and it may be of the lungs, but of this say nothing to his friends as in my next I shall be able to give you something more satisfactory[.] His mental exertions and application have I think been the sources of his complaints—If I can put his mind at ease I think he'll do well—get Mʳ Taylor or some of his friends to write him. I'm afraid the Idea of his expenses operates on his mind and some plan must be adopted to remove this if possible. The truth is, having come abroad for the purpose of restoring his health, every thing must be done to favor the ch{ange} of climate—I mean that he shall buy or hire {by the} month a horse to ride out whenever the w{eather perm}its & so forth—After all his expences will {be very lit}tle, and he's too noble an animal to be allowed to sink without some sacrifice being made to save him. I wish I were rich enough his living here should cost him nothing. He has a friend with him who seems very attentive to him but between you & I is not the best suited for his companion, but I suppose poor fellow he had no choice. I fear much there is something operating on his mind—at least so it appears to me—he either feels that he is now living at the expence of some one else or something of that kind. If my opinion be correct we may throw medicine to the dogs. Let every thing be done to relieve his mind from any Idea of that kind as far as possible—I feel very much interested in him and believe me will do every thing in my power to be of serv{ice} to him. I am glad to find the Edinburgh Rev{iewe}rs have been just towards him. He seems much pl{eased} with Rome and prefers it greatly to Na{ples.}⁴

By Clark's own recommendation, "the consumptive patient may pass the winter at Rome fully as well as at any other part of Italy, and perhaps better. The best residence," he wrote in a book he published that year, "is somewhere about the Piazza di Spagna, which is well sheltered, and has the advantage of being close to the Pincian Mount, which affords the best protected and most delightful walk at Rome."[5]

The "comfortable lodgings" Clark had secured for Keats were just opposite his own house, "so that he might be near his patient at all hours", at No. 26 Piazza di Spagna, on the second floor of the house on the right-hand side of the Spanish Steps, which was then known as "Casina rossa" for its deep-red colour.[6] The building, dating back to the late Renaissance, was remodelled in the 1720s, at the time of the construction of the Scalinata di Trinità dei Monti, when it received its new façades.[7] It is now the home of the Keats-Shelley Memorial House, and has become one of the most famous and photographed buildings in Rome.

The landlord of 26/27 Piazza di Spagna is given as "Alessandro Angeletti, son of the late Pietro" in the city land registry for the year 1818.[8] Alessandro appears to have been a Roman etcher of plates for prints, and may have been related to the Neoclassical artist Pietro Angeletti, professor of painting at the Accademia di San Luca.[9] The upper floors of the house had already been operating for years as boarding accommodation, under the management of Alessandro's wife, the Venetian Anna Kafur (Italianized Cafurri, Caffurri, Cafurro, Caffuro). Her family hailed from Corfu, an island under the rule of the Serenissima until 1815, and she was forty-three at the time of Keats's arrival in Rome.

One of the previous lodgers, the English antiquarian and philanthropist Robert Finch, who had stayed in the house on several occasions, left a vivid description of the landlady.[10] "Signor Vasi," he wrote in his 1815 diary,

> who has a magazine of books and engravings here, [...] directed me to his niece, Signora Angeletti, with whom I have fix'd my abode. It is No. 26, Piazza di Spagna at the corner of the steps leading up to the church of Santa Trinita del Monte, and I pay 19s. a week for four rooms, elegantly furnish'd. The neatness, which distinguishes every thing about

the Signora, is truly charming; and is rare in this country. Her husband has been for some years in Portugal, and has quite neglected her. She is a lively, smart, handsome little woman, and has two nice daughters, who scarcely appear younger than their mother. She has much taste for the fine arts, & draws and engraves.[11]

According to Church census records, Anna was widowed sometime in 1820.[12] One of her two daughters, Lucrezia, had married the year before, at the age of twenty-one, and left home, while the other, Virginia, who was five years younger, married in 1820 and continued to live in the house with her husband Nicola Palmieri and their infant son Giulio Tito.[13] Anna resided in the back rooms of the building with her young daughter's family and a serving woman, Maria Domenica Merigioli. An elderly English gentleman, Thomas Gibson, with a French valet called Jean Montbrun, occupied the front rooms on the first floor. Keats and Severn moved into the two rooms just above him, which had recently been vacated by an English doctor, Richard Clark, and which communicated with Anna's own quarters. The front door of their apartment, on the left of the second-floor landing, led into a small dark hall, and from there into a bright sitting room looking out onto the piazza, where Severn made his bed. Keats's room, opening from it to the right, was on the corner of the building, with a view of the Scalinata, the Barcaccia fountain and Piazza di Spagna from its two windows. Through a door at its back, this led to a small boxroom overlooking the Steps, which Severn used for his painting. On the third floor lived a twenty-five-year-old Irishman, James O'Hara, with his young servant Achille Baldini, and a twenty-seven-year-old army officer, Giuseppe d'Alià, with his own unnamed manservant.

The rooms were neat, comfortable and well furnished, but rather small and expensive – around £4 16s. per month in English money excluding dinner, which was another 4s.[14] As we have seen from Doctor James Clark's letter, Keats seemed very pleased with Rome, at least on the outside. His real feelings, however, can be glimpsed from his letter of 30th November 1820 to Charles Brown, the last he ever wrote.

'Tis the most difficult thing in the world ~~for~~ ^{to} me to write a letter. My stomach continues so bad, that I feel it worse on opening any book,—yet I am much better than I was in Quarantine. Then I am afraid to encounter the proing and conning of any thing interesting to me in England. I have an habitual feeling of my real life having past, and that I am leading a posthumous existence. […] I am so weak (in mind) that I cannot bear the sight of any hand writing of a friend I love so much as I do you. Yet I ride the little horse,—and, at my worst, even in Quarantine, summoned up more puns, in a sort of desperation, in one week than in any year of my life. There is one thought enough to kill me—I have been well, healthy, alert &c. walking with her—and now—the knowledge of contrast, feeling for light and shade, all that information (primitive sense) necessary for a poem are great enemies to the recovery of the stomach. There, you rogue, I put you to the torture,—but you must bring your philosophy to bear—as I do mine, really—or how should I be able to live? Dr Clarke is very attentive to me; he says, there is very little the matter with my lungs, but my stomach, he says, is very bad. […] Remember me to all friends, and tell x x x x I should not have left London without taking leave of him, but from being so low in body and mind. Write to George as soon as you receive this, and tell him how I am, as far as you can guess;—and also a note to my sister—who walks about my imagination like a ghost—she is so like Tom. I can scarcely bid you good bye even in a letter. I always made an awkward bow.

God bless you!

John Keats[15]

It is a disconsolate, heart-rending letter. Keats's emphasis, it should be noted, is on the disease of his mind, as opposed to that of his body. He says he's feeling much better than in the recent past, and appears ready to silence his inner fears and make an effort to fight his illness, but he is almost unwilling to entertain any hope. He quotes the doctor's opinion as if attempting to persuade himself to believe him, and asks his friend to make up his own mind about the state of his health.

The tragic thing is that the poet did feel better after his arrival in Rome. "Keats rallied wonderfully," Severn wrote in his late memoir, and Doctor Clark himself, when he first saw him, was of the opinion that something could be done to help him recover.[16] The mild weather, combined with the opportunity of spending time outdoors and seeing people, must have had an invigorating effect on the poet and filled him with cautious optimism, despite his money worries and stomach troubles.[17]

By an unfortunate trick of fate, a letter from Severn to Haslam covering all the events leading up to Keats's relapse on 10th December 1820 has not survived.[18] All we have to fill the blank of this period is fragmentary information from later letters and memoirs.

As we have seen before, the first thing Keats and Severn did on their arrival in Rome on 15th November was to visit Torlonia's bank. In order to avoid incurring heavy banking charges by taking out small sums each time, Keats drew £120 of the £150 Taylor and Hessey had made available through their letter of credit and deposited it in the bank in Roman money (552 scudi), withdrawing 92 scudi in cash on the day.[19] That enabled them to pay for their lodgings and buy a few things. "When we first came here," Severn wrote to Brown on 14th February 1821, "[Keats] purchased a copy of Alfieri,—but put it down at the second page,—

> "Misera me! sollievo a me non resta
> Altro che il pianto,—ed il pianto è delitto"[20]

He went back to that incident in 'My Tedious Life':

The return of apparent health brought ^{with} it the return of his gay spirits & even fun, he once more showd his charming wit & humour which was no doubt his natural characteristic for his wit was never satirical or spitefull & his humour was the pleasantry of imitation which he sometimes showd up before the persons themselves. In this there was no vanity or pretension[.]

He even talkd on the subject of Poetry & explained a new subject "Sabrina" from Miltons sketch, but he was not able to write. We talked over the Italian poets & he bought an Alfiere—in reading it he marked

Here Severn's memory failed him, and he left a blank in the manuscript, but concluded, after a short gap:

On Tasso my great favorite, he said that he anticipated that "he should be^come a greater Poet if he were allowd to live" but he shook his head and bewailed his cruel fate that he was about to be cut off before he had completed any thing.[21]

A few months after the death of his friend, Severn wrote to Charles Brown:

I recollect a point—which may be know[n] to you—perhaps—Keats mentioned to me many times in our voyage—his desire to write the story of Sabrina and to have connected it with some point in the English history and character—he would sometimes brood over it with immense enthusiasm—and recite the story from Miltons Comus in a manner that I will remember to the end of my days—[22]

And early the following year he reiterated, in a letter to John Taylor:

Did you know it was Keats intention to make a long Poem about the story of Sabrina—he mentioned this many times to me—it would have been a most beautiful subject for him—he intended Sabrina to be modelled on Spencers

Una—or its principle [written "principal"] to have been moral beauty.[23]

According to British legend, King Locrinus deserted his wife Gwendolen for a former lover, Estrildis, and had a child with her called Sabrina ("Hafren" in Welsh).[24] The enraged Gwendolen gathered an army and killed Locrinus, then drowned Sabrina and Estrildis, and ordered that the river be named after the young princess – who appears in Milton's poem as a gentle water nymph. Since Hafren is what is known in English as the River Severn, Keats may have intended to write the poem as a tribute to his friend in the event of his recovery. We cannot exclude a self-gratulatory motive behind Severn's insistence in recounting this story.

On 23rd November, Keats withdrew 100 more scudi, leaving a balance of 360 scudi in their account. As well as for lodging and sustenance, the money was used to rent a horse (£6, about 28 scudi a month) and a piano (7 scudi a month) a few days later.[25] In his late memoir, Severn recalls his outings with Keats and another invalid on the Pincian Mount.

[A] gentlemanlike young man Leif.t Elton had joined us & so we made a trio on the Pincio—Elton who was a handsome man attracted the glances of the Princes[s] Pauline Napoleons sister & Keats was very severe in his satire on this famous Coquette but he thought she was only imitating the empresses of Rome as her illustrious brother was the Emperours, but she soon came to an end with her excesses[.]

There was a pretty fountain in a corner of the Pincio & Keats remarked "that it was a corner watering out of revenge for watering in a corner"[.] In the middle of January he was able to go out on Hores-back always in the company of Leif.t Elton who was a victim to consumption like Keats—But he was alone & he often explained to me that [his] first sym[p]toms of decline were caused by his bolting his food at his mess—he survived Keats nearly a year.[26]

Very little is known about Elton. His identification with Lieutenant Isaac Marmaduke Elton has so far been rather tenuous, and based on a process of exclusion rather than direct proof or circumstantial evidence. A letter written on 7th March 1914 by William Gordon Perrin of the Admiralty to Louis Arthur Holman, an American artist, writer on art, seller of prints and Keats enthusiast, stated that the poet's friend "would appear to be Lieutenant Isaac Marmaduke Elton of the Royal Engineers (Seniority 1 July 1812). This officer [...] died in Switzerland on the 24th May 1823." This cautious, twice-removed opinion was accepted by Rollins and all other subsequent scholars and biographers as a fact. Other Lieutenant Eltons were discarded because their profiles didn't quite fit, or their picture was "*not good looking at all*".[27]

It can now be confirmed that the identification was in fact correct. An obituary published in the *Morning Post* of 20th June 1823 reports:

> *DIED*—On the 24th of May, at Coire [Chur], in Switzerland, on his way from Rome to Gaiss [Gais], to which place he was proceeding for the improvement of his health, Lieutenant Elton, of the Royal Engineers.[28]

Elton was made second lieutenant on 14th December 1811 and was promoted to the rank of first lieutenant on 1st July 1812.[29] He served as an engineer officer in Wellington's army in the Iberian Peninsula between July 1813 and June 1814, and was engaged in the Battle of Orthez.[30] He then took part in the Campaign in the Netherlands in 1815 and fought at the Battle of Waterloo.[31] He would have had many colourful stories to tell his new acquaintances in Rome.

It is unlikely that Keats, Severn and Elton wandered off farther than the nearby Pincio or visited any Roman monuments. It would have been against the recommendations of Doctor Clark, who wrote in his *Medical Notes*:

Many of the streets in Rome [...] are damp and chilly, and the alternation between these shaded streets, and situations exposed to the sun is often very great. On this account the open carriages, so much in use at Rome, are very dangerous to the delicate, and close carriages should be alone used during the winter. Neither must the invalid pass his time among the ruins of the ancient city, nor the churches of the modern,—both of which are frequently damp and always cold,—until the season is so far advanced as to make them safe for him.[32]

In addition to walks and horseback-riding, music also provided much-needed distraction and relief to the ailing poet. "[H]e expressed a strong desire," Severn recalled in his late memoir,

that I would hire a piano forte & play to him for he was passionately fond of musick—D.r Clark procured me many volumes of Music & it was a solace to the painful hours Keats had to pass—there was a volume of Haydns Symphonies & this music was his delight and he would say "This Haydn is like a child, for there is no knowing what he will do next."[33]

Apart from his own health and his dwindling finances, Keats worried about his friend's career prospects. He was aware that the young painter, instead of spending his time looking after him, should be getting on with a painting he could submit to the Royal Academy for a travelling fellowship. As Severn later recalled,

To be in Rome with Keats was in itself an event independant of Rome for at last there seemd a chance of his being saved & then his rising up in so famed a place would secure his recovery—But the good Doctor also thought of me & at once made known to John Gibson the great sculptor & poor dear Keats insisted on my going straight [written "strait"] [to] his study—On my arrival I found a great man just entering, this was Lord Colchester & so I thought it prudent to retire but Gibson caught me by the arm & insisted on my intering with

My Lord—During the visit & sights of his works he showd me
the same attention as he did to Lord Colchester [...]. [T]his
sole act opened to me a new world[.]

On my return Keats was delighted with this ^{1st} treat as he
called it to humanity & discussed the plans he devised for my
sojourn & to begin he would have me make a beginning even
of a sketch, [...] & as Keats suggested I might have offended
the pride of the Academy [by winning the Gold Medal] &
that it required a greater amount of prudence than I possessed
to clutch at the pension.[34]

The poet related to his friend an incident at a dinner he had
attended in London, where, in Severn's absence, one of the guests
had poured scorn on the winner of the Gold Medal, saying that
"the work was very inferior but the artist being an old fellow
& his attempts for the prize frequent the Council had given it
out of pity & not for any merit". In disgust at such a mean lie,
Keats had defended his friend and had "r[isen] from the table &
abruptly left the party". He now warned his friend that he "had
to contend with these Artistic enemies & must find a way of
upsetting them before [he] could succeed".[35] Severn thought that
the slanderer was the Royal Academician William Hilton, when
in fact it appears to have been Hilton's close friend and brother-
in-law Peter De Wint.[36] In later life, the painter still remembered
his friend's outrage at the unfairness of those comments.

He became much excited at this villiany & would place himself
in my position—Altho' small of stature yet on these occassions
of acts of meaness, he seemd to rise up to a larger stature &
it formed a marvellous contrast to his charming manner when
he was tranquil[.]

However I proceeded to make the sketch of [the] death
of Alcibiades & Keats continued to be anguished on my
account for I well knew that I must produce another picture
in competition for the pension & [...] it was a great consola-
tion to Keats to see that I was building up the composition.[37]

Keats's keen sense of injustice also found expression in another famous incident from this period, which displays a mischievous, rebellious streak in his character.

'Twas a joy to me to see Keats improve from day to day, the winter being very fine he walked every day & was even like himself but our drawback was in the very bad dinners, so that Keats said to me "Severn I have found ^{out} a way of having good dinners" but he would not tell me how—When the Porter came with ^{the} Basket Keats opend it & seeing it was the same horrid mess as usual he opend the window & quietly & deliberately emptied out on the steps each plate, this done he closed the basket & pointed to the Porter to take it away—Sure enough this was a masterpiece more eloquent than words as in half an hour we got an excellent dinner, & so on every day.[38]

But the relative calm that Keats and Severn had enjoyed since their arrival in Rome was destined to be shattered soon. On 10th December, as Severn recalled in his late memoir,

[Keats] had a most alarming attack, a spitting of blood in such quantity that he declared it to be the forerunner of his death—D.ʳ Clark was taken by surprise, as he had formed a favorable opinion of his patient & encouraged ^{me} in thinking that Keats would recover—But now I saw that the Doctor had no longer hopes.[39]

Writing to Charles Brown a few days after the event, he began:

I fear our poor Keats is at his worst—a most unlooked for relapse has confined him to his bed—with every chance against him: it has been so sudden upon what I almost thought convalescence—and without any seeming cause that I cannot calculate on the next change. I dread it, for his suffering is so great, so continued, and his fortitude so completely gone, that any further change must make him delirious.[40]

Here Severn was forced to break off his letter, and was only able to continue a few days later, at four o'clock in the morning.[41]

> Not a moment can I be from him—I sit by his bed and read all day—and at night I humour him in all his wanderings. he has just fallen asleep—the first for 8 nights, and now from mere exhaustion. I hope he will not wake until I have written this, for I am anxious beyond measure to have you know this worse and worse state—yet I dare not let him see I think it dangerous.—I had seen him wake on the morning of this attack, and to all appearance he was going on merrily and had unusual good spirits—when in an instant a Cough seized him, and he vomited near two Cup-fuls of blood.—In a moment I got Dr Clarke, who saw the manner of it, and immediately took away about 8 ounces of blood from the Arm—it was black and thick in the extreme. Keats was much alarmed and dejected—O what an awful day I had with him!—he rush'd out of bed and said "this day shall be my last"—and but for me most certainly it would. At the risk of losing his confidence I took every destroying mean from his reach, nor let him be from my sight one minute.

The "destroying mean" Severn refers to is the bottle of opiate they had purchased at the beginning of their voyage.[42] As Keats had surmised, this was not a temporary relapse. Continuing his night-time letter, Severn wrote:

> The blood broke forth again in like quantity the next morning—and the doctor thought it expedient to take away the like quantity of blood—this was in the same dismal state, and must have been from the horrible state of despair he was in—but I was so fortunate as to talk him into a little calmness, and with some English newspapers he became quite patient under the necessary arrangements[.]

This is the 9th day, and no change for the better—five times the blood has come up in coughing, in large quantities generally in the morning—and nearly the whole time his saliva has been mixed with it—but this is the lesser evil when compared with his Stomach—not a single thing will digest—the torture he suffers all and every night—and best part of the day—is dreadful in the extreme—the distended stomach keeps him in perpetual hunger or craving—and this is augmented by the little nourishment he takes to keep down the blood—Then his mind is worse than all—despair in every shape—his imagination and memory present every image in horror, so strong that morning and night I tremble for his Intellect. The recollection of England—of his "good friend Brown"—and his happy few weeks in Mrs Brawn's Care—his Sister and brother—O he will mourn over every circumstance to me whilst I cool his burning forehead—until I tremble through every vein in concealing my tears from his staring glassy eyes.—How he can be Keats again from all this I have little hope—but I may see it too gloomy since each coming night I sit up adds its dismal contents to my mind.

Dr Clarke will not say so much—although there is no bounds to his attention, yet with little success—"can he administer to a mind diseased"—yet all that can be done most kindly he does—whilst his Lady, like himself in refined feeling, prepares and cooks all that poor Keats takes—for in this wilderness of a place (for an Invalid) there was no alternative. Yesterday Dr Clarke went all over Rome for a certain kind of fish, and got it—but just as I received it from M^rs C delicately prepared, Keats was taken by the spitting of blood and is now gone back all the 9 days.—this was occasioned by disobeying the Doctors commands.—Keats is required to be kept as low as possible to check the blood—so that he is weak and gloomy—Every day he raves that he will die from hunger—and I was obliged to give him more than allowed—You cannot think how dreadful this is for me—the Doctor on the one hand tells me I shall kill him to give him more than he allows—and Keats raves for more till I am in complete tremble for him. But I have talked him over now.—We have the best opinion of D^r C's skill—he seems to understand the case, and comes over 4 & 5 times a day—he left word at 12 this morning to call any time in case of danger[.]

I heard Keats say how he should like Mrs Brawn and Mrs Dilk to visit his sister at Walthamstow—will you say this for me—and to Mr Taylor that Keats was about to write favorably on the very time of his relapse—For myself I am keeping up beyond my most sanguine expectations—8 Nights I have been up, and in the days never a moment away from my patient but to run over to the Doctor—but I will confess my spirits have been sometimes quite pulled down—for these wretched Romans have no Idea of comfort—here I am obliged to wash up—cook—& read to Keats all day—added to this I have had no letters yet from my family—this is a damp to me for I never knew how dear they were to me—I think of my Mother & I think of Keats for they are something the same in this tormenting Indigestion—But if Keats recovers—and then letters bring good news—why I shall take upon myself to be myself again. [...] [I]t was my custom to walk until Keats awoke—we did breakfast about 9 o'Clock—My head begins to sally round so much that I cannot recollect—I will write to Mr Taylor on the next change in my friend, and to the Kind Mrs Brawn when I have any good news. Will you remember me to this lady—little did I dream on THIS when I saw her last in London. Will you, my dear Brown, write to me—for a letter to Keats now would almost kill him—give Haslam this sad news.—I am quite exhausted—farewell—I wish you were here my dear Brown.[43]

Over the following days there were no improvements in the patient. Severn kept his promise of sending regular accounts to the poet's friends. On 24th December, Christmas Eve, late into the night, he began writing the following letter to Keats's publisher, John Taylor, which has come down to us in rather damaged condition:[44]

My dear Sir

Keats has changed somewhat for the worse—at least his mind
has much—very very much—and this leaves his state much
the same—and quite as hopeless—yet the blood has ceased to
come—his digestion is better—and but for a cough he must be
improving—that is as far as respects his body.—but the fatal
prospect of Consumption hangs before his "mind's eye["]—
and turns every thing to despair and wretchedne{ss—he} will
not bear the idea of living much less strive {to live}—I se{em
to} lose his confidence by trying to give him this hope{—he}
will not he{a}r that his future prospects are favorable—he
says {tha}t the continued stretch of his imagination has killed
him—and were he to recover he could not write another
line—then his {go}od fr{ie}nds in England—he only cherishes
the idea of what they have {done} and this he turns to a load
of care for the future—the {hig}h hopes of his—his certain
success—his experience[—]h{e shakes his} head at it ~~all~~ and
bids it farewell.—The remembrance {of} his brothers death—
I cannot keep [written "kept"] it from him—all his own
sym[p]toms he re[c]ollects in him and this with every cough
and pain—the many troubles—persecutions—and I may say
cruelties he has borne now weigh heavy on him—if he dies I
am witness that he dies of a broken heart and spirit.—would
that his enemies could see this martyrdom of the most noble-
feeling and brightest genius to be found in existence—I only
wish this for their punishment.—he is now only a wreck of
his former self—the knawing weight upon his mind—with
the intire loss of bodily strength and appearence;—push him
to malevolence—suspicion—and impatience—yet every one
is struck with him and interested about him—I am aston-
ished [written "astonisted"] and delighted at the respect paid
him—but even this—I mean the general utmost endeavour he
receives—his dreadful state of mind turns to {per}secuti{on
and some}times even murder—he is now under the {impres-
sion that poison} was administered to him by an individual
at London—. All that fortitude and as it were—brav{ery} of

mind against bodily suffering are away from him—and the want of some kind hope to feed his voracious imagination leaves him to the wreck of ideas without purpose—imagination without philosophy—yet this night he said to me "I think a malignant being must have power over us—over whom the Almighty has little or no influence—yet you know Severn I cannot believe in your book—the Bible—but I feel the horrible want of some faith—some hope—something to rest on now—there [written "their"] must be such a book—and I know that is it—but I can't believe it—I am destined to every tor{ment i}n this world—even to this little comfort on my death bed {...}" [two words missing]—O! my dear Sir you cannot imagine what {I} sometimes feel—I have read to him incessantly—until no more book{s} could be had—for they must be new to him—and above a{ll} the book he has set his mind upon all through this last {week} is no{t} to be had—the works of Jeremy Taylor—his des{ire to ha}ve these read to him is very great—and yet not to be {had—is not} this hard—the other books he wished me write down are not in Rome—they were Madam Dacier's Plato and the Pilgrims Progress—I have read to him Don Quixote at his request and some of Miss Edgeworths Novels—but there are no Books in Rome—we sometimes get some English papers[.][45]

Now observe my dear Sir I dont for a moment push my little but honest Religious faith upon poor Keats—except as far as my feelings go—but these I try to keep from him—I fall into his views sometimes to quiet him and tincture them with a somewhat of mine, but his many changes both body and mind render my charge most affecting and even dangerous—for I cannot leave him without some one with him that he likes[46]—This is the third week—and I have not left him more than two hours—he has not been out of bed the whole time—he says this alone is enough to kill him was he in health—and then seeing no face but min{e around} him he {will} say it makes him worse to think how I should be occupied and how I am[—] sometimes I succeed in persuading him that he will recover and go back with me to England.—I do lament a thousand times that he ever left England—not from want of medical aid or even friends—for nothing can be superior to the kindness of Dr Clark &c—but the journey of 2000 Miles was too much for his state—even when he left England— […]

Dr Clark gives very little hope of him—he says he may {rec}over from {th}is by some change in his mind—but he will {m}ost certainly die (at some not distant period) of Consumption—{n}o disorganisation exists at present—but a total derangement {of} the digestive powers—they have nearly lost their functions […]

For myself my dear Sir—I still keep up nearly as we{ll} as I did—altho' I have not got any person to relieve me—{Keats} makes me carefull of myself—he is my doctor—a change {of sc}ene [written "scence"] might make me better—but I can do without it.—It is 6 oclock in the Mor^g I have been writing all night—this is my 5th Letter—Keats has just awoken—I must leave of[f] and boil my kettle—he hears me writing and inquires—"Tell Taylor I shall soon be in a second Edition—in sheets—and cold press"—he desired me tell you some time since—that he would have written you—but felt he could not say anything—it gave him pain—We have received 5 Letters—3 to Keats—2 to myself—he read one from Mr Hessy and another [from] Mr Brown—but the third one he could not read and was effected most bitterly—he says—"no more letters for him—even good news will not lift him up—he is too far gone"—but he does not [know] I think this—nor does he know D^r Cs opinion—but his own knowledge of Anatomy is unfortunate—farewell my dear Sir—Jos^h Severn.[47]

The painter then added a long postscript promising to write to Haslam and Mrs Brawne, telling Taylor that he still hoped Keats would get better, despite his not taking any food, and expressing his worries about money and the great cost of nursing an invalid in such an expensive city as Rome. He had just finished pouring out his financial concerns when something unexpected happened, making that ill-fated Christmas Day even more gloomy, and he hastened to add a cross-written coda to his letter:

4 oclock   This moment the doctor sends {me wor}d that my Landlady has reported to the Police that Keats is dying of a Consumption—now this has [made] me vent some curses against her—the words dying and Consumption has rather dampt my spirits—the laws are very severe—I do not know the extent of them—should poor Keats die—everything in his room is condemned to be burned even to paper on the walls[—] the Italians are so alarmed at Consumption that the expences are enormous after a death—for examinations—and precautions to contagion—Fools. I can hardly contain myself—O! I will be revenged on this old Cat—for putting the notion in my head of my friends dying—and of Consumption—but stop I know the Doctor half thinks so—but will not say it—he has brought an Italian Physician here who thinks Keats has a malformed chest—should he die the law will demand him to be opened.—I have got some books—Scots Monastery and some travels—he seems inclined to hear me read all this evening—Keats has just said that it is his last request that no mention be made of him in any manner publically—in Reviews Magazines or Newspapers—that no Engraving be taken from any Picture of him—Once more—farewell———[48]

Severn might have been surprised and outraged at his landlady's reaction, but consumption had long been regarded as a contagious illness in Italy. If he had read Smollett's *Humphry Clinker* (1771), he would have come across Matthew Bramble's tirade on infectious diseases.[49] Henry Matthews had also cautioned pulmonary invalids intending to travel to Italy that it might be difficult for them to get lodgings if the exact nature of their illness were known, and that they might have to pay a higher price on that account – "for consumption is here considered to be contagious, and in case of death, the whole of the furniture in the occupation of the deceased is burnt, and his rooms are fumigated and white-washed".[50] Doctor Clark must have been aware himself of all this. He was later to write in one of his books:

> The contagious nature of consumption has been believed by some authors of high authority, at the head of whom may be placed Morgagni, and altogether disbelieved by others. In the south of Europe the general opinion is in favour of contagion, in the north of Europe against it. [...] The view which I take [...] leads me entirely to disbelieve that consumption can be communicated by contagion.[51]

It is very odd that Clark didn't give Severn and his friend any advance warning of what would happen if it transpired that Keats was a pulmonary invalid, but we cannot accuse Anna Angeletti – who had just been widowed and had two young married daughters to worry about, as well as an infant grandson living in the house – of overreacting.

The Venetian landlady had, in fact, very early on set the wheels of the law in motion against her lodger. Soon after the poet's relapse, she had lodged a complaint with the local magistrate, Marchese Stanislao del Drago, the Presidente Regionario di Polizia, a kind of Justice of the Peace dealing with public grievances in Campo Marzo, one of the 14 *rioni* into which the city of Rome was divided. Angeletti's letter has survived, and it is here published for the first time:

> Your Excellency,
>   The petitioner Anna Angeletti, who lives in Piazza di Spagna No. 26, declares that Mr John Keats, a consumptive who is nearing the end of his life, is a guest at her house, and therefore implores Your Worship to find the means of getting him removed from my house, or, should he die, to make sure I'll be reimbursed of all costs and damages. In the hope of appropriate measures and help from Your Worship = = = = = = =

> To His Excellency the Marchese Del Drago
> from Anna Angeletti, Piazza di Spagna No. 26[52]

The landlady's petition has no date, but Del Drago reported it to the Roman Police Directorate on 18th December. Keats's name was entered in the police register (under the letter X, since his name had been misread "Xeats"), and Angeletti's request, accompanied by Del Drago's covering letter, was passed on to the governor of Rome Tommaso Bernetti, acting as chief of police, who forwarded the two documents to the Sacra Consulta, the police branch who dealt with sanitary matters.[53] His letter reads:

Rome   19 Dec. 1820
From the Directorate-General of the Police
Section 7   No. 14329

1291

The undersigned, Governor Director-General of the Police, herewith transmits to Your Most Rev. and Hon. Excellency a petition by Anna Angeletti. Mr John Xeats, a foreigner, has been lodging in her house, and since she says that he is now close to death from consumption, she begs that, should he die, she will not be held liable to the costs and damages that would result from it.

I would therefore be grateful if the Sacra Consulta, as the body which is specifically responsible for any matters of Health, would let me, the undersigned, know which measures should be taken in this case. I am, Most Rev.
and Hon. Excellency, with the highest
and most obsequious esteem,
Your most humble and
obedient servant,
T. Bernetti Gov[54]

As soon as the case was entered in the registers of the Sacra Consulta, its secretary wrote to Doctor Morichini for advice. Since Morichini was a prominent figure in the Rome of his time and his involvement in Keats's story has until now been unknown, he deserves a few words of introduction.[55]

Domenico Morichini was born on 23rd September 1773 in Civita d'Antino, a small commune in the Abruzzi, to Anselmo, a farmer and small merchant, and Domitilla Moratti. A very precocious and talented student, he was destined by his family to an ecclesiastical career from a very early age. After three years at a seminary in nearby Sora, however, it was clear that he did not have a religious calling, so he continued his classical and scientific studies in another local boarding school, completing his courses at the age of fifteen.

Having joined his father's brother, the priest Carlo Antonio Morichini, in Rome, Domenico immersed himself in the study of medicine, and by 1793 he had obtained a degree in Philosophy and Medicine from La Sapienza University, a gold medal in Obstetrics, an honorary surgeon's licence and a medical one. After a short stint as a doctor's apprentice, he became a junior doctor at the Arcispedale di Santo Spirito in Saxia, Europe's oldest hospital. There he spent several years, dividing his time between clinical activity and research, almost working himself to death – indeed, on one occasion he was given the last rites, before making a full recovery. It was during this time that he wrote one of his first works: 'Medico-Chemical Reflections on Pulmonary Consumption, Its Symptoms and the Nature of Expectorations during the Course of the Disease'.[56]

After an unsuccessful attempt at the age of twenty-two, in 1797 he was awarded a teaching post at La Sapienza's department of Chemistry, which he held for over thirty years, until his retirement in February 1833 due to health reasons.

Although he was offered, in 1802, the post of head physician at the S. Spirito Hospital, he decided to pursue his academic career and research activities, combining them with medical practice in order to support his growing young family, after his marriage to Cecilia Calidi in 1804.

Morichini was a selfless and compassionate doctor. In an 1806 letter to Monsignor Nicola Riganti, he wrote:

[O]ur regulations against consumptives prove to be odiously harsh to the humane duties of a physician – and I can easily demonstrate that this is the case. How many times have we seen a poor, honest family that has spent all its available means to alleviate in any way the sufferings and the inconvenience of a father, a mother or a son affected by this lingering and revolting disease lose at the same time the dear object of their cares, their whole sustenance and their indispensable furniture, without any hope of being compensated for it? To all this, add the fact that, while the corpse of the deceased still hasn't been removed, the greedy landlord arrives with all the force of the law and demands that the floors, the walls, the ceilings and the doors be refurbished – nay, that the entire house be rebuilt from its foundations! So judge for yourself if it is reasonable or not that our humanity takes exception at such excessive, unjust and, what is more, unnecessary measures!

And what shall I say of the cruel task imposed on physicians to denounce the poor wretches who suffer from pulmonary consumption to the police magistrates – not to provide some comfort or consolation, but to initiate a procedure against them that makes their affliction more bitter, that plunges them into the bleakest despair and that resembles more a death sentence than a salutary, beneficial measure? No doubt those officers who come to give a rundown of all the objects that must be consigned to the flames and that evoke in advance in the invalid's mind the scene of his death and of his family's destitution cannot but unnerve his languishing spirit and trouble his quiet, at a time when he is approaching his death and should therefore be shown more regard. Indeed, this cannot but hasten his demise. Although a doctor cannot always restore the health of his patients, his duty is always to comfort them, and even if they are about to fall into their graves, he must adorn them with flowers and make them look as attractive as possible. Moreover, there is or must be a deeper bond between a physician and his patient – one of friendship and absolute trust. It is impossible to arouse and sustain courage in the invalid – a condition which is essential for the positive outcome of any disease – if he doesn't receive words full of hope and tokens of friendly care from his doctor. Now, how can a doctor reconcile these duties with the obligation to reveal so openly and in such a revolting manner that he despairs for the life of his patient?[57]

Morichini's research – in particular in the field of chemistry – brought him to the attention of the international scientific community. As well as being the first to identify fluorine in human teeth and the magnetic properties of UV radiation, he hypothesized the presence, in addition to heat, of electrical and magnetic "fluids" in light rays. He conducted detailed chemical tests on a number of mineral waters, including those of the Acqua Santa Baths, which he made the subject of a short essay published in 1818. His scientific writings on the most diverse and eclectic subjects, collected after his death in 1836, fill up two large volumes and run to a thousand pages.[58]

Alongside his scientific and academic interests, Morichini continued to practise medicine all his life, as a doctor, as a surgeon and as an advisor. He was chief physician of Pius VII and Pius VIII, and conducted the autopsy on the latter's body, proving that the cause of death was not herpes but heart failure. In 1819 he was asked to provide a medical opinion on the declining health of Napoleon, at the time exiled at St Helena. He was the personal doctor to Sir Humphry Davy and treated the poet Giacomo Leopardi as well as other famous people, such as the Hereditary Prince of Denmark.[59] And although he was the doctor of choice of many rich personages, he did not disdain to call on poor households, offering them medical help and often paying for the prescriptions himself.

As we have seen, Morichini also acted as the Sacra Consulta's special advisor. He was called on to pronounce his opinion on a variety of issues, but his surgical and clinical experience of pulmonary diseases as a junior doctor at S. Spirito made him an expert in that field. In 1816 he was asked by the Roman authorities to provide a list of regulations to prevent the spread of contagious diseases, in particular consumption.[60] As his first biographer, Iandelli, later wrote:

> One could say that the sanitary police was born with him, because the principles of preventative public health were in part unknown and in part misguided or unimplemented. He was the first who, thanks to his intelligence and hard work, was able to devise many schemes and put others into effect. To this end, he was in constant correspondence with the health authorities. He drew up rules for the location and layout of cemeteries and graves; he was a member and later the president of the general council for vaccination.[61]

True to his original ideals, Morichini tried to make the Roman laws against consumptives less draconian, and, whenever possible, to soften the existing measures, in order to avoid additional misery for the invalid and those around him. In Keats's case, as soon as he received the communication from the Sacra Consulta about Angeletti's petition, he decided to pay a visit to Doctor Clark and see if any arrangements could be made to resolve the unpleasant situation. Having received all the necessary assurances, Morichini wrote back to the Sacra Consulta on 9th January 1821.

> Most Rev. Exc.y
> I have spoken with the English doctor Clark, who is looking after Mr John Keats, affected with consumption, about the cautionary procedures that must be followed in his patient's room, and the measures that are usually taken in Rome in relation to the belongings of consumptives and the furniture in the room they live in. He will correspond with me on this matter, and I will report to the Sacra Consulta, so that the Supreme Tribunal may be kept informed about everything. The landlady will have all the furniture in the room replaced, except the linen, which is purified by washing. The walls and

the floor will be scraped and whitewashed again. Woollen fabrics and cotton coverings will be taken to S. Giacinto. Wood items broken down to make fire. And Doctor Clark himself will respond and be responsible for all this.

This much I have felt obliged to report in discharge of my duties, and with great esteem and respect I am,

Most Rev. and Hon. Exc.,

Your most humble and obedient servant,

Domenico Morichini[62]

Clark's pledge to underwrite all costs and damages was enough to satisfy the Sacra Consulta and Signora Angeletti, and Keats was allowed to spend his final days in his lodgings in Piazza di Spagna.

By this time, Severn had an inkling of Clark's misgivings about the poet's chances of survival. These are revealed in a letter written by the doctor to his contact in London at the beginning of the new year:

In my last I said a few words about poor Keats. Since that date he has had another attack of bleeding from the lungs which has weakened him greatly, and he is now in a most deplorable state—His stomach is ruined and the state of his mind is the worst possible for one in his condition, and will undoubtedly hurry on an event that I fear is not far distant and even in the best frame of mind would not probably be long protracted. His digestive organs are sadly deranged and his lungs are also diseased—either of these would be a great evil, but to have both under the state of mind which he unfortunately is in must soon kill him. I fear he has long been governed by his imagination & feelings {&} now has little power & less inclination to ende{avou}r to keep them under. I feel much interested i{n the} poor fellow indeed—it is most distressing to {see a} mind like his (what it might have been) in th{e de}plorable state in which it is. His friend Mr Sev{ern is} most attentive to him. Were Christianity of no us{e b}ut to give tranquillity to the sick bed it were the greatest blessing on earth[.] I am sorry indeed, and much disappointed in having to communicate such sad accounts of poor K. When I first saw him I thought something might ~~have been~~ be done, but now I fear the prospect is a hopeless one—[63]

Many critics and biographers have criticized Clark because he misdiagnosed Keats's tubercular illness for some disease of the stomach, and considered the poet's past imaginative and emotional exertions, as well as his current state of mind, contributing factors in his pulmonary condition. They have accused him of blatant incompetence and even lack of intelligence, of having inflicted unnecessary suffering on his patient by keeping him on such a scant diet, drawing large quantities of his blood and refusing to give him laudanum to lessen his pain. These accusations are rather absurd: it is like condemning the ancient philosophers for believing that the Earth was flat.

Viral transmission of tuberculosis was only demonstrated in the late 1860s, and the bacillus responsible for the disease was identified as late as 1882. It took a few more decades to find an effective cure for the infection. In Keats's time, in the absence of physical tests, doctors could only rely on the external appearance of the patient, auscultation and stool examination for their diagnoses. And only an autopsy could reveal whether the lungs had been affected and the patient had died of consumption. Doctor Clark's methods were not unsound or haphazard, but backed by study, observation, analysis, experience, scientific consensus and a set of suppositions that made him the leading pulmonary expert of his generation and a respected authority for several decades to come.

According to his theory, consumption was not a localized disease that could be ascribed to a specific cause, i.e. the tubercles formed in the lungs, as advanced in 1819 by the French pathologist René Laennec. Clark believed that "consumption [...] [was] only a secondary affection, the consequence of a pre-existing constitutional disorder—the necessary condition which determines the production of tubercles". In other words, he was of the opinion that the tubercles were not the cause, but the result of an underlying condition or constitution. This could be occasioned by a hereditary predisposition or "a peculiar morbid condition of the general system" that could be acquired at any period in life, which he called "tuberculous cachexia" and which he thought "g[ave] rise to the deposition of tuberculous matter, on the application of certain exciting causes, which have no such effect on a healthy system". He was also convinced that the disorder of the digestive organs "[was] capable [...] of generating this constitution, and of leading ultimately to tuberculous cachexia" – hence his insistence on a strict, controlled diet for his patients.[64] That excessive mental strain, intense emotion, a despondent mood, constant worries, a strong disappointment or a thwarted passion could rupture a blood vessel or aggravate a consumptive condition was a common, accepted notion which was not questioned even by Keats or any of his friends. As to bloodletting, it was advocated by most medical practitioners of the time as a means to remove pulmonary congestion, prevent haemorrhage and reduce the inflammation of the lungs.[65] Clark was not against the use of opiates, either, but warned:

Narcotic medicines of the mildest kind should be tried before having recourse to opium, which, although one of the most valuable medicines in the treatment of consumption, should be used sparingly, and deferred, if possible, till a late period of the disease, in order that the patient may obtain the more benefit from it when its aid is most required. One of the common errors [...] is, in my opinion, a too early and too prodigal use of opiates in large doses [...]; indeed it is always desirable to begin with the smallest doses, because, as the disease advances, it is generally necessary to increase the quantity, for in the last stages it often becomes the chief solace of the patient amidst his multiplied sufferings.[66]

This is the basis on which doctors still act today, and I am sure Clark did not deny Keats a dose of laudanum when he most needed relief. To accuse Doctor Clark of being insensitive, careless or amateurish is to fail to understand how science works, and that experimental trial and error are essential in its development. It is unfortunate that Keats, together with many millions like him, found himself on the wrong side of scientific progress and could not benefit from later discoveries. Of course, Keats could have been saved if he had been born today, but without serious, honest, humane, self-denying scientists such as James Clark none of the terrible diseases that have afflicted and still afflict our world could be cured.

Severn was not a skilled bearer of bad tidings, and when he had to face the task of writing the long-postponed letter to Mrs Brawne on 11th January, at one in the morning, knowing how desperate she and her daughter were to receive a positive report of the poet's health, he was forced to take a narrative angle that wavered between self-delusion and disingenuousness.[67]

My dear Madam

I said that "the first good news I had should be for the kind Mrs Brawn."[68] I am thankful & delighted to make good my promise—to be at all able to do it—for among all the horrors hovering over poor Keats this was the most dreadful[:] that I could see no possible way and but a fallacious hope for his recovery. But now thank God I have a real one. I most certainly think I shall bring him back to England—at least my anxiety for his recovery and comfort make me think this—for half the cause of his danger has arisen from the loss of England—from the dread of never seeing it more. O this hung upon him like a torture—never may I behold the like again even in my direst enemy—Little did I think what a task of affliction & danger I had undertaken—for I only thought of the beautiful mind of Keats, my attachment to him—and his convalescence.

But I will tell you dear Madam the singular reason I have for hoping his recovery—In the first fortnight of this attack his memory presented to him every thing that was dear & delightful—even to the minutiæ—and with it all the persecution & I may say villainy practised upon him—his exquisite sensibility for every one save his poor self—all his own means & comfort expended upon others—almost in vain—These he would contrast with his present suffering—and say that all was brought on by them—and he was right. Now he has changed to calmness & quietude, as singular as productive of good, for his mind was certainly killing him. He has now given up all thoughts hopes or even wish for recovery—his mind is in a state of peace from the final leave he has taken of this world and all its future hopes. this has been an immense weight for him to rise from[—]He remains quiet & submissive under his heavy fate[.]

Now if any thing will recover him it is this absence of himself. I have perceived for the last 3 days symptoms of recovery—Dr Clarke even thinks so—Nature again revives in him—I mean where art was used before—Yesterday he permitted me to carry him from his bed room to our sitting room—to put him clean things on, and to talk about my Painting to him—This is my good news—Don't think it otherwise my dear Madam, for I have been in such a state of anxiety & discomfiture in this barbarous place that the least hope of my friends recovery is a heaven to me[.]

For Three weeks I have never left him—I have sat up at night—I have read to him nearly all day & even in the night—I light the fire, make his breakfast & sometimes am obliged to cook—make his bed and even sweep the room. I can have these things done, but never at the time when they ought & must be done—so that you will see my alternative—What enrages me most is making a fire[—]I blow—blow—for an hour—the smoke comes fuming out—my kettle falls over on the burning sticks—no stove—Keats calling me to be with him—the fire catching my hands & the door bell ringing—all these to one quite unused and not [at] all capable—with the want of every proper material come not a little galling—

He then narrated with pride how, at the risk of incurring additional sanitizing costs after the poet's death, he had managed to sneak Keats into the sitting room without the landlady or anyone else noticing it – a move that he felt was essential for his friend's "health & spirits". After praising Dr Clark and his wife for all their kindness and care and asking Mrs Brawne to write to Taylor to explain that they had cashed a large part of his letter of credit on the advice of the bankers, to save trouble and expenses, Severn tried to end the letter on a high note:

[P]resent my respectful Compts to Miss B. who I hope & trust is quite well—now that I think of her my mind is carried to your happy Wentworth Place—O I would my unfortunate friend had never left it—for the hopeless disadvantage of this comfortless Italy—he has many many times talked over the few happy days at your House the only time when his mind was at ease. I hope still to see him with you again farewell my dear Madam—One more thing I must say—poor Keats cannot see any letters—at least he will not—they affect him so much and increase his danger—The two last I repented giving—he made me put them into his box unread. more of these when I write again—meanwhile any matter of moment had better come to me—I will be very happy to receive advice & remembra{nce} from you—Once more farewell

      Jo^s Severn

I have just looked at hi{m—he} is in a beautiful sleep—in look he is very much more him{self—}I have the greatest hopes of him—[69]

Mrs Brawne replied with a cordial, sanguine letter,[70] but her daughter didn't buy Severn's sugar-coated assurances. Writing to the poet's sister on the day she received Severn's letter, Fanny – who had been kept in the dark as to the gravity of Keats's condition – gave vent to all her repressed anguish:

> M[r] Severn says that for the first time he feels a hope, he thinks he shall bring him back to us. Surely, that is saying a great deal—and yet the reason he gives for that hope destroys it, [...] your brother [...] ha[s] resigned himself to die. [...] [M]y dear Girl, my dear Sister [...], forgive me if I have not sufficiently softened this wretched news.[71]

And in her next letter to Fanny Keats, written on 26th February, she added: "[F]aint as are the hopes M[r] Severn gives I dare not think they are well founded. All I do is to persuade myself, I shall never see him again—"[72]

Meanwhile, the question of the large sum cashed by Keats and Severn on their arrival in Rome had created great inconvenience and embarrassment. Taylor and Hessey, who had backed the £150 letter of credit on the assumption that they would receive money from the poet's brother in America, were taken aback when Torlonia presented a request for £120 to be paid out at once. This is not what had been agreed with Keats, and they asked the bankers to stop any further payments. News must have reached Severn when he called at Torlonia's on 26th December to cash another 100 scudi, or perhaps soon afterwards through Doctor Clark.[73] The prospect of not being able to access the remaining £30 and having to cope with the huge costs associated with his friend's funeral and the sanitization procedures plunged Severn into a state of sheer panic. As well as seeking Mrs Brawne's intercession, he asked Clark to write to Taylor through his contact in London and explain the situation, which the good doctor did without delay, on 13th January:[74]

I have not lost a Post, My dear Gray, in replying to your letter relative to p{oor Kea}ts as I am anxious to prevent any {fur}ther misunderstanding as {to} the Bill affair; I say misunderstanding becaus{e} it appears to me that there has been something of this kind either on Keats part or that of his friend Mr Severn. The truth I am sorry to inform you, is that Keats is at present so ill that he must know nothing of the matter, and therefore his particular motives from deviating from Mr Taylors instructions, or whether he quite understood these, cannot now be unde{r}stood, and perhaps it matters not much as things stand relative to the Bill.

The doctor then went on to reiterate that Severn claimed the money had been drawn in one large bill on the advice of the bankers, in order to incur less expense, and that the letter of credit should be honoured, and any remaining funds kept in escrow by the bank and remitted to the poet in due course, on Taylor's instructions. Above all, it was essential that Keats know nothing of the matter, "as it could answer no good purpose" and, the doctor added,

might add greatl{y} to his present sufferings to know that he ha{d done any} thing to displease gentlemen that had treated {him} so kindly. Write me therefore as soon as you have explained this matter to Mr Taylor and in {t}he meantime I will take {ca}re, if Keats is in want of any thing, that it shall be supplied.—Poor fellow he is now so ill as to be constantly confined to bed, his stomach is still in a very bad state, the affection of his lungs is increasing and the state of his mind is the most deplorable possible—under such melancholly circumstances amendment I fear is scarcely to be looked for, recovery almost out of the questions. His friend Mr Severn is most {atten}tive to him indeed scarcely {ever leaves} him. {His l}odgings are pretty comfortable & I do not beli{eve that he} would have a better chance of recovery any{where} else unless it were among friends who had the power {of} calming his mind—He has no religion—he has been {ro}bbed of that—& philosophy I fear is seldom su{fficient} to produce tranquillity of mind under suc{h sad circum}stances as he is placed [in]—his certainly is not suffic{ient}.—Pray when you write tell me if it was c{ons}umption his brother died of.

I have now my {d}e{ar Gr}ay explained to you the whole of th{is sad} affair & the melancholly situati{on of poor} Keats who in my opinion will ne{ver leav}e Rome.[75]

When they received this plain-worded account of Keats's state of health, Taylor and Hessey did not tarry before taking action and tried to raise funds among their friends in support of the dying poet. "Five of those who had seen poor Keats sufficiently to feel much interested for him" – Joseph Bonsor, John Percival, William Hilton, Peter De Wint and James Rice – promised to advance £10 each.[76] Lord Fitzwilliam sent Taylor a draft for £50.[77] Reynolds pledged to contribute the same amount, but nothing came of it.[78] "Another friend" – perhaps Richard Woodhouse – provided a letter of credit of £50 on a banker in Florence, to be drawn by Keats if he was well enough to find his way there in the summer.[79] At the same time, Taylor and Hessey mounted an attack against the poet's brother to recoup the money they had advanced, which had now been paid off.[80] On 17th February they sent a strong letter to George Keats warning him that they were about to draw on him for £150, informing him at the same time about the further £100 advanced by their friends and asking him if he would "empower [them] to return these Sums to those who have so generously contributed them".[81] George Keats declined to honour this request, and the draft was returned unpaid. Soon after hearing about the death of the poet, Taylor tried to "touch" Abbey, and received the following gem of a reply from Keats's erstwhile guardian:

Sir

I beg pardon for not replying to your favor of the 30th Ult respecting the late Mr Jno Keats—

I am obliged by your note but he having withdrawn himself from my controll and acted contrary to my advice, I cannot interfere with his affairs—

I am Sir

Your Mo Hble St

Richd Abbey[82]

Keats's publishers were only able to wrest back the £150 from George (via Abbey) four years later, and had to face some immediate financial pressures as a result of their generosity towards their author.[83] Severn, on his part, did receive the additional £100 in due course, but was forced to live in suspense for a while and rely, in the mean time, on the kind assistance of Doctor Clark.

Despite his protestations of resilience, his feelings of isolation and despair are evident as he appeals for money to one of Keats's closest friends, William Haslam, in his letter of 15th January, begun a little before midnight:

Poor Keats has just fallen asleep—I have watched him and read to him—to his very last wink—he has been saying to me "Severn I can see under your quiet look—immense twisting and contending—you dont know what you [written "your"] are reading—you are induring for me more than I'd have you—O! that my last hour was come—what is it puzzels you now—what is it happens"—I tell him that "nothing happens—nothing worries me beyond his seeing—that it has been the dull day"—getting from myself to his recovery—and then my painting—and then England.—and then—but they are all lies—my heart almost leaps to deny them—for I have the veriest load of care—that ever came upon these shoulders of mine—For Keats is sinking daily—he is dying of a consumption—of a confirmed consumption—perhaps

another three weeks may lose me him for ever—this alone would brake down the most gallant spirit—I had made sure of his recovry when I set out—I was selfish and thought of his value to me—and made a point of my future success depend on his candor to me—this is not all—I have prepared myself to bear this now—now that I must and should have seen it before—but Tolonia's—the bankers—have refused any more money—the bill is returned unaccepted—"no effects"—and I tomorrow must—aye *must*—pay the last solitary Crowns for this cursed lodging place—yet more—should our unfortunate friend dye—all the furniture will be burnt—beds— sheets—curtains and even the walls must be scraped—and these devils will come upon me for 100£ or 150£—the making good—but above all—this noble fellow lying on the bed—is dying in horror—no kind hope smoothing down his suffering—no philosophy—no religion to support him—yet with all the most knawing desire for it—yet without the possibility of receiving it.—It is not from any religious principles I feel this—but from the individual sufferings of his mind in this point—I would not care from what source—so he could understand his misfortunes—and glide into his lot—O! my dear Haslam this is my greatest care—a care that I pray to God may soon end—for he says in words that tear my very heartstrings—"miserable wretch I am—this last cheap comfort—which every rogue and fool have—is deny'd me in my last moments—why is this—O! I have serv'd every one with my utmost good—yet why is this—I cannot understand this"——and then his chattering teeth—if I do break down it will be under this—but I pray that some kind of comfort may come to his lot.—that some angel of goodness will lead him through this dark wilderness————————————
Now Haslam what do you think of my situation—for I know not what may come with tomorrow—I am hedg'd in every way that you can look at me—if I could leave Keats for a while every day I could soon raise money by my face painting—but he will not let me out of his sight—he cannot

bear the face of a stranger—he has made me go out—twice and leave him solus—I'd rather cut my tongue out than tell him—that money I must get—that would kill him at a word—I will not do any thing that may add to his misery—for I have tryed on every point to leave for a few hours in the day—but he wont unless he is left alone—this wont do—nor shall not for another minute whilst he is John Keats————————

Yet will I not bend down under these—I will not give myself a jot of credit—unless I stand firm—and will too—you'd be rejoiced to see how I am kept up—not a flinch yet—I read— cook—make the beds—and do all the menial offices—for no soul comes near Keats exc[e]pt the Doctor and myself—yet I do all this with a chearfull heart—for I thank God my little but honest religion—stays me up all through these tryals—I[']ll pray to God tonight that he may look down with mercy on my poor friend and myself.—I feel no dread of what more I am to bear but look to it with confidence———————— [...]

I have got a volume of Jeremy Taylors Works—which Keats—has heard me read to night—this is a treasure—and came when I thought {it} hopeless—{why} may not other good things come?—a{nd} even money—I will still keep myself up with the best hope[.]

Dr Clark is still the same altho' he has received notice about this bill—I have said to him—that if Keats is wanting in any possible thing now—that would give him ease—but would be out of his agreement—or at least fears the payment for—I will be answerable in any way he may think fit—but no he does his every thing—I lament a thousand times that Mr Taylor did not tell me about this money—that it was to be drawn in small bills—I could have stopt this—as it is I dont know what to do—unless money is coming through your means—altho' I know you cannot—but farewell—pray my dear fellow dont ask me for journals—every days would have been more or less like this[—]Not a word at my Fathers

Sincerely—ever—

Joseph Severn

This letter is for thine own eye and own heart—or as you see
fit[—]I wrote by last post to Mrs Brawn—I think she should
know these—but it will be a severe blow—see Brown too—
though I do you injustice to tell you—on Wednesday I write
to Mr *Hunt*[.]^{84}

The proofs ~~state~~ of Keats's present state—are expectoration
continually—of a fawn colour—sometimes streaked with
blood—his still wasting away—altho he takes as much food
as myself—a dry cough—night sweats—with great uneasi-
ness in his chest[—]D^r C is afraid the next change will be to
diarrhoea—Keats sees all this—his knowledge of anatomy
makes it tenfold worse at every change—every way he is
unfortunate—I cannot see him any way without something to
"dash the cup from his lip"—yet every one offers me aid on
his accou[n]t—but he cannot bear it—I must not leave him
night or day—I am quite well—thank God—once more good
bye—only one letter from you yet—I am in doubt wether you
shall have harrowing things like this—poor Keats cannot read
any letters—he has made me put 2 by unopened—they tear
him to pieces—he dare [not] look upon the outside of any
more—make this known—and should any communication
be required to make let it come to me—I will frame it to
his ear—he places the greatest confidence in me.^{85}

During one of those long, dreadful nights, something happened
to dispel, at least for a moment, the gloom and horror of the
situation, as Severn remembered many years later:

When watching Keats I used sometimes [to] fall asleep &
find we were in the dark—to remedy this one night I tried
the experiment of fixing a thread from the bottom of ~~one~~ a
lighted candle to the Wick of an unlighted one that the flame
may be conducted, all of which I did without telling Keats—
~~On his waking & finding~~ When he awoke & found the ~~flame~~
~~nearly done~~ 1st candle nearly out he was reluctant to wake me
& while doubting suddenly cried out, "Severn Severn heres a

little fairy lampliter actually has lit up the other candel"[—]
my experiment had succeeded & given him great and agre-
able surprise.—[86]

Days dragged on, and the poet's condition continued to dete-
riorate. His only real consolation during those lingering hours,
according to Severn, seemed to be a "polished oval white carnel-
ian, the gift of his widowing love, [which] he kept continually
in his hand, [...] the only thing left him in this world clearly
tangible".[87] But Keats knew what was still to come – pain and
delirium – and was well aware that no comfort was available to
him other than laudanum. Severn's next letter to John Taylor,
begun on 25th January, is stark and uncompromising in its
detail, and bereft of any hope:

My dear Sir
   Another week and less and less hope—I have still greater
cause to fear—that poor Keats is now upon his death bed—he
has shewn still worse symptoms every day—clay-like expecto-
ration—in large quantities—night sweats—a ghastly wasting-
away of his body and extremities—with the approaches to
a diarrhoea by laxity and griping of the bowels—his food
passing through him very quick and but little digested—Yet
from all this he ~~could~~ might get up if he could bear over that
intense feeling—and those unfortunate combinations and
passions of mind—from which no medicine in the world can
relieve him—nor any other means—for they are a part of
his nature—It now quite astonishes me that he has lived so
long without the almost essence of human-life—I mean that
sometimes calm of mind to keep the machinery of the body
going—this I am certain poor Keats never posses[s]ed or even
felt—he has described to me many parts of his life—of various
changes—but all moving to this restless ferment—no doubts
all the ~~sensations~~ emotions of his mind even to his happiest sensa-
tions—have brought him to this dreary point—from which I
pray God speedily to lift him up—his suffering now is beyond

description—and it increases with increasing acuteness of his memory and imagination—his nerves will not bear the only {easy} comfort from things that "smell of mortality"—and to any other source he has still greater horror—he cannot bear any books—the fact is he cannot bear any thing—his state is so irritable—is so every way unfortunate—that I begin to sink under the very seeing him—without the labor—without the want of rest and occupation—I shall be ill from this cause alone.—The hardest point between us is that cursed bottle of Opium—he had determined on taking this the instant his recovery should stop—he says to save him the extended misery of a long illness—in his own mind he saw this fatal prospect—the dismal nights—the impossibility of receiving any sort of comfort—and above all the wasting of his body and helplessness—these he had determined on escaping—and but for me—he would have swallowed this draught 3 Months since—in the ship—he says 3 wretched months I have kept him alive—and for it—no name—no treatment—no privations can be too bad for me—I cannot reason him out of this even on his own ground—but now I fall into his views on every point—before I made every sacrifice for his personal comfort in his own way—trying every manner to satisfy him—now I must do the same mentally—I even say he should have this bottle—but I have given it to Dr Clarke—the fact is I <u>dare</u> not trust myself with it—so anxious I was to satisfy him in every thing—

Poor fellow! he could not read your letter when it came—altho he opened it—I did not regret it for not a syllable had I let him know about the Bill—it would have killed him—I trembled when he looked at your name—but he wept mo{st} bitterly—and gave the Letter to me—Dr Clark has rec^d yours respecting the Bill—it is now quite right—you will have received my explanations about it—and I am once more at rest about it—

I have been taken ill in this last week—in 6 weeks I have not had 6 hours fresh air—and sometimes sitting up 3 nights

together—now I cannot sleep although I may—and the con-
sequence is a heaviness of mind—no power of thinking—but
at my altered appearence today Keats is much alarmed—he
has talked it over—and proposing having a nurse for no one
has come near him but the Doctor and myself—I hope this
will soon bring me round—but my anxiety would alone make
me ill—without the bodily fatigue I am under—every one is
astonished that I have kept up so long—

The Doctor has most certainly done all that could be
done—but he says Keats should never have left England—
the disorder had made too great a progress to receive benefit
from this Climate—he says nothing in [the] world could ever
cure him even when he left England—by this journey his
life has been shortened—and rendered more painful—yet it
will be a satisfaction to you as it is to me—that for delicate
climate nothing could exceed this in mildness—the fruit
trees have been long in blossom—perhaps every thing that
could be done for Keats has been—you will have seen my f^d
Haslam—I have been in great trouble about a most painfull
letter I wrote him—Say to him that I was in a dreadfull state
of mind—but could not wait sending—the post goes once a
week—Yours very truly

Joseph Severn

If I can get a nurse—I shall not leave Keats for more than an
hour in the day—merely to keep—up my health—

26th

The nurse has just been—but I am afraid she wont do—there
are so many little things that no one can do but myself—that
I think I will not leave poor Keats at all—I feel something
better this Mor^g—and have determined to keep on—without
any more going out—Keats is wanting to say something or
have something done every minute in the day—no one to do
these—he may become irritated—for I can assure his mind
is bordering on the insane—

11 oclock—The doctor has just been—nature cannot hold out another fortnight—he says—the mucus is collecting in such quantiti[e]s[—]the body & the extremity receive no nourishment—and above all poor Keats[']s mind is determined on being worse and worse—nearer and nearer his death—that he cannot possibly last but a short time—Keats is desiring his death with dreadfull earnestness—the idea of death seems his only comfort—the only prospect of ease—he talks of it with delight—it sooths his present torture—The strangeness of his mind every day surprisses us [or perhaps "me"]—no one feeling or one notion like any other being—[88]

But the agony and the long watches continued. On the night of 28th January, Severn drew one of the most iconic images of the poet, the pen-and-ink sketch known as 'Keats on His Deathbed'.[89] The gaunt, haggard face of the young man it portrays, surrounded and set off by a dark halo, has a supernatural aura about it. The poet's sparkling hazel eyes are closed – his features are lifeless. Keats has been reduced to a ghostly presence, a dim shadow of his former self.

When awake, however, the poet's mind was as alert as ever. As Severn recollected soon after his death:

It was wonderfull how deeply Keats felt beauty—I even think much of this gave him such pain on his death bed—it was not at all the fear of dying—but the leaving this World of Beauty so soon—before he had experience in it—or knew the purpose of his life—One Morning early in February (before his death) I was delighted to find the Spring had commenced here—and when the poor fellow awoke I told him of it—I told him I had seen some trees in blossom—this had a most dreadful effect on him—I had mistaken the point—he shed tears most bitterly—and said—"The spring was always inchantment to me—I could get away from suffering—in watching the growth of a little flower—it was real delight to me—it was part of my very soul—perhaps the only happiness I have had in the world—has been the silent growth of Flowers—Ah! why did you let me know this—why show me that this comfort is gone—that I shall never see the Spring again—I hoped to die before the spring came—O I would to God—that I were in my grave—<u>quiet and insensible to these ghastly hands</u>—<u>these knobbed knees</u>—The grave—with flowers on its top—send me to it now"—[90]

Among the many letters Severn received during this period was one from Charles Brown, dated 15th January, which is worth quoting in full.

My dear Severn

Your letter of 17th Decr arrived here last Thursday the 9th[—] I cannot dwell on the subject of it[—]Either I am shortly to receive more favorable accounts or to suffer the bitterest news. I feel—and I cannot help it—all your attentions to my unhappy Keats as if they were shown to myself,—yet how difficult I have found it to return you thanks—until this morning it has been utterly out of my power to write on so melancholy a story. He is present to me every where and at all times—he now seems sitting by my side and looking hard in my face,—though I have taken the opportunity of writing this in company,—for I scarcely believe I could do it alone. So much as I have loved him I never knew how closely he was wound about my heart. Mrs Brawne was greatly agitated when I told her of—and her daughter—I don't know how,—for I was not present,—yet she bears it with great firmness,—mournfully but without affectation,—I understand she says to her Mother, ["]I believe he must soon die, when you hear of his death, tell me immediately,—I am not a fool![″] Poor girl! she does not know how desolate her heart will be when she learns there is no hope, and how writched she will feel,—without being a [written "a a"] fool. The only hope I have rests on Dr Clarke not considering the case in so gloomy a light as you do,—for his kindness ask him to receive a stranger's thanks. But you and I well know poor Keat's desease is in the mind,—he is dying broken hearted. You know much of his grief, but do you know how George has treated him? I sit planning schemes of vengeance upon his head. Should his brother die exposure and infamy shall consign him to perpetual exile. I will have no mercy,—the world will cry aloud for the cause of their Keat's untimely death, and I will give it. O Severn nothing on my part could stop that cruel brother's hand. I have already written to him. Not a penny remitted yet?—I authorise you to open my letters to Keats,—if he is still alive, you may perhaps cull out something to cheer him,—if not it is no matter,—but take care you do not open a letter with *my* hand writing on the address which *contains another* hand writing,—there *is* such a letter, and you can avoid opening it by peeping inside. I hear your family are well but I suppose you are by this time satisfied on that score. Tak{e} care of your own health. While attending a sick bed [amended from "lad"], I know, by experience we can bear up for a long long [time],—but in the end we feel it severely[.]

God bless you

Yours sincerely

Chas Brown[91]

To this, Severn replied by return of post, on 8th February:

My dear Brown,

I have just got your letter of 15th January. The contrast of your quiet friendly Hampstead with this lonely place and our poor suffering Keats brings the tears into my eyes. I wish many, many times that he had never left you. His recovery must have been impossible whilst he was in England, and his excessive grief since has made it more so. In your care he seemed to me like an infant in its mother's arms; you would have smoothed down his pain by varieties; his death might have been eased by the presence of his many friends. But here, with one solitary friend, in a place savage for an invalid, he has one more pang added to his many;—for I have had the hardest task in keeping from him my painful situations. I have kept him alive by these means, week after week. He had refused all food; but I tried him every way. I left him no excuse. Often I have prepared his meals six times a day, and kept from him the trouble I had in doing it. I have not been able to leave him,—that is, I have not dared to do it, but when he slept. Had he come here alone, he would have plunged into the grave in secret;—we should never have known one syllable about him. This reflection alone repays me for all I have done. It is impossible to conceive what the sufferings of this poor fellow have been. Now—he is still alive, and calm;—if I say more, I shall say too much. Yet, at times, I have hoped he would recover,—but the doctor shook his head,—and, as for Keats, he would not hear that he was better. The thought of recovery is beyond every thing dreadful to him. We now dare not perceive any improvement; for the hope of death seems his only comfort. He talks of the quiet grave as the first rest he can ever have. I can believe and feel this most truly.

In the last week a great desire for books came across his mind. I got him all the books at hand; and, for three days, this charm lasted on him,—but now it has gone. Yet he is very calm. He is more and more reconciled to his horrible misfortunes.

14th February. Little or no change has taken place since the commencement of this,—except this beautiful one, that his mind is growing to great quietness and peace. I find this change has its rise from the encreasing weakness of his body; but it seems like a delightful sleep to me,—I have been beating about in the tempest of his mind so long. To-night he has talked very much to me, but so easily, that he, at last, fell into a pleasant sleep. This will bring on some change,—it cannot be worse,—it may be better. Among the many things he has requested of me to-night, this is the principal one,—that on his grave-stone shall be this,—

HERE LIES ONE WHOSE NAME WAS WRIT IN WATER.

You will understand this so well, that I need not say a word about it. But, is it not dreadful that he should, with all his misfortunes on his mind, and perhaps wrought up to their climax, end his life without one jot of human happiness?[92]

There are many possible inspirations for the gravestone inscription, but it is almost certain that Keats derived it from a passage in Beaumont and Fletcher's tragedy *Philaster* (Act v, Sc. 1):

> Your memory shall be as foul behind you,
> As you are, living; all your better deeds
> Shall be in water writ, but this in marble;
> No chronicle shall speak you, though your own,
> But for the shame of men.

We know that the poet owned the last three volumes of *The Dramatic Works of Ben Jonson, and Beaumont and Fletcher* (1811), which contain the plays written by the two "brother Poets": this set, no doubt one of his most prized possessions, is still preserved at Keats House. Volume 2, which includes *Philaster*, has an inscription from his brother George ("Geo. Keats to his affectionate Brother John"). In this edition, the expression "in water writ" (p. 63) is annotated, with Shakespeare's *Henry VIII* and a poem by Catullus quoted as possible sources. All this must have made those lines even more memorable and poignant to the poet, who on his deathbed appears to have been preoccupied, more than anything else, with thoughts of total oblivion and a lack of posthumous fame.

Continuing his letter, Severn then remembered the pang caused to his friend by the reading of two lines from Alfieri, which had stirred his dormant passions, and commented: "He was much affected at this passage; and now that I know so much more of his grief, I do not wonder at it."[93]

Brown's warning about the potential arrival of a letter from Fanny enclosed in an envelope addressed in his own handwriting had reached Severn too late:

Such a letter has come! I gave it to Keats, supposing it to be one of your's,—but it proved sadly otherwise;—the glance of that letter tore him to pieces,—the effects were on him for many days!—he did not read it—he could not—but requested me to place it in his coffin, together with a purse and a letter (unopened) of his sister's—since which time he has requested me *not* to place that letter in his coffin, but only his sister's purse and letter, with some hair. Here he found many causes of his illness in the exciting and thwarting of his passions, but I persuaded him to feel otherwise on this delicate point. In his most irritable state, he sees a friendless world, with every thing that his life presents, particularly the kindness of his friends, tending to his untimely death.

I have got an English nurse to come two hours every other day, so that I have quite recovered my health; but my nurse, after coming five times, has been taken ill to-day; this is a little unfortunate as Keats seemed to like her. Another and greater misfortune is the cursed rumpus betwixt the Neapolitans and the Austrians. We are daily fearing that the thievish Neapolitans will arrive and ransack Rome. They are on their way hither; and, from the grudge betwixt them and the Romans, we have little to hope for. Rome might be taken with a straw—it is only defended by its relics. At twelve last night they rumbled all their artillery by here to the Porta Santa Giovanna. The Pope was on his legs all night, trusting any thing rather than heaven. If the Austrians do not arrive in time, our P's and Q's are likely to be altered. The English are very numerous here. Farewell.[94]

There were indeed rumours around that time of a possible attack on Rome by the Neapolitans before the arrival of the Austrians, who were marching south. Lord Colchester wrote in his diary entry of 9th February: "The calculated time of [the Austrians] reaching the neighbourhood of Rome is the 25th inst. Much uneasiness among the inhabitants and some of the foreigners, who fear the prior arrival of the Neapolitans."[95] As the pope's right-hand man Cardinal Consalvi had confided to him, Rome was there for the taking:

> [T]he Neapolitan frontier [is] not twenty miles distant from Tivoli[:] nothing would be easier than for the Neapolitans to mount 3000 infantry behind 3000 cavalry, and occupy Rome in a few hours, and revolutionise the whole Roman state; so as to meet the Austrian army by opposing a revolutionised population of five millions in front of the Neapolitan territory.[96]

Most of the British living in Naples, hearing that "[a] general arrest of *all foreigners*, and placing them in a state of detention, like those formerly at Verdun, [was] also contemplated by the Carbonari", had followed Lord Colchester's example and repaired to Rome after the departure of the king for Laibach. But General Pepe – who fancied himself as a kind of dictator and hoped to take the reins of the Neapolitan kingdom – perhaps aware of the real strength of his army, dithered and failed to seize on the opportunity to attack. Despite the constant rumours and the threats, Rome and its population remained, for the time being, immune from the "epidemic [of] Carbonarism".[97]

Pushing away the thought of what was happening outside, Severn turned his mind again to the matters at hand within the close confines of their small apartment, and added in a postscript:

> In a little back-room I get chalking out a picture. This, with swallowing a little Italian every day, helps to keep me up. The Doctor was delighted with your kindness to Keats. He is a most worthy man; we must ever respect him for his unremitting kindness to Keats.
>
> P.S. The post does not go for another two hours. To my great astonishment, I found it half past three this morning when I had done writing. You see I cannot do any thing until

poor Keats is asleep. This morning he has waked very calm. I think he seems somewhat better. He has taken half a pint of fresh milk. The milk here is beautiful to all the senses—it is delicious—for three weeks he has lived on it, sometimes taking a pint and a half in a day.[98] ~~Your's~~

You astonish me about x x x x x x[99]

The Doctor has been; he thinks Keats worse. He says the expectoration is the most dreadful he ever saw. Keats's inward grief must have been beyond limit. His lungs are in a dreadful state. His stomach has lost all its power. Keats himself says he has fretted to death—from the first little drop of blood he knew he must die—he says no common chance of living was for him.

Keats's growing peacefulness, whether caused by the extreme debilitation of his body or induced by opiates, afforded Severn some respite. When Keats was asleep, he was able to receive daily visits from the architectural student Lewis Vulliamy, have "a pipe and pot" with Antonio Canova, meet Lord Colchester and Sir William Drummond, who commissioned him to paint a picture, and go out for dinners and walks.[100] During the very last stages of Keats's illness, Severn finished a long letter to his sister Maria which he had started writing on 21st January. The painter talks about his projects, his aspirations and his feelings of homesickness. His "dying friend" remains very much in the background, and after a short mention in a passage dated 11th February, when Severn picked up his letter again after a three-week hiatus, he says "no more [...] on a subject so sad" and goes on to talk about himself, giving colourful descriptions of his life in Rome, cracking the odd joke and speaking with confidence of his bright prospects as a student and artist in Italy. It is clear that Severn, who had parted from his father on very bad terms, is trying to paint a rosier picture than his situation would warrant at such a moment, and show that he is leading a good life and not wasting all of his time by the side of a dying friend. Finishing his letter on 20th February, Severn reminisced about his long voyage, the amusing incidents, the awe-inspiring storms, the beauty of the British and African coasts, the delightful journey from Naples to Rome – and those happy memories, in sharp contrast with the horror of his situation, brought back the palpable image of death into his mind: "[T]he young Lady who sailed with us is now poor creature dying in the same way as Keats—poor Keats cannot last but a few days more[.] I am not quite reconciled to his state—yet I fear I shall feel the miss of him—"[101]

That same day it became evident that his friend's end was near. Recollecting those final moments two weeks later, he wrote, in a letter to John Taylor:

> Four days previous to his death—the change in him was so great that I passed each moment in dread—not knowing what the next would have—he was calm and firm at its approaches—to a most astonishing degree—he told [me] not to tremble for he did not think that he should be convulsed— he said—"did you ever see any one die"[—]no—"well then I pity you poor Severn—what trouble and danger you have got into for me—now you must be firm for it will not last long—I shall soon be laid in the quiet grave—thank God for the quiet grave—O! I can feel the cold earth upon me—the daisies growing over me—O for this quiet—it will be my first"—when the morning light came and still found him alive—O how bitterly he grieved—I cannot bear his cries—
>
> Each day he would look up in the doctors face to discover how long he should live—he would say—"how long will this posthumous life of mine last"—that look was more than we could ever bear—the extreme brightness of his eyes—with his poor pallid face—were not earthly—[102]

Severn was performing the offices of a good friend both by the bedside and away from the sickroom. As he recollected in his late memoir:

At times during his last days he made me go to see the place where he was to be buried & he expressed pleasure at my description of the locality, of the Pyramid [of Cestius], of the grass and the many flowers particularly violets, the flock of goats & sheep & the young shepherd all intensely interested him & he assured me that he already seemd to feel the flowers growing over him.[103]

The graveyard was indeed an idyllic place. Percy Bysshe Shelley, who was later to be buried there, not far from his three-year-old son William, left the following description when he visited the grounds in late 1818:

The English bur[y]ing place is a green slope near the walls, under the pyramidal tomb of Cestius, & is I think the most beautiful & solemn cemetery I ever beheld. To see the sun shining on its bright grass fresh when we visited it with the autumnal dews, & hear the whispering of the wind among the leaves of the trees which have overgrown the tomb of Cestius, & the soil [amended from "coil"] which is stirring in the sunwarm earth & to mark the tombs mostly of women & young people who were buried there, one might, if one were to die, desire the sleep they seem to sleep. Such is the human mind & so it peoples with its wishes vacancy & oblivion.[104]

No doubt this is how Keats felt, too, in the final days of his life. What he didn't know, perhaps, is that the English burial ground was the subject of much religious and political wrangling at the time. Protestants – English and German for the most part – were regarded as heretics and met with displeasure in the Papal States. Their rites were banned in public, and their religious gatherings disapproved of. As Selina Martin, who was in Rome at that time, remembers: "The Roman government [has] taken umbrage at the conduct of the English, in so openly having a fixed place of worship: from which, if they [do not] desist 'the storm [will] burst upon their heads'."[105] According to the precepts of the Roman Church, non-Catholics could not be laid to rest in churches or hallowed ground. For more than a century they had been buried in the open countryside, in a plot of common land used for pasture just inside the ancient Aurelian city walls near Porta San Paolo. Protestant funerals were frowned upon, and in order to avoid any trouble with the locals, they were conducted at night or around daybreak, unless a special dispensation had been granted.

Much to the annoyance of the Protestant community in Rome, the burial grounds had no enclosure, and this led to the gravestones often being damaged or defaced. The local Protestants "[raised] a liberal subscription, which they lodged in the hands of Torlonia, [...] to have the place [...] enclosed by a wall, railing, or sunken fence: but their repeated applications [...], under different pretexts, met with a decided negative".[106] The controversy dragged on for some time. In the end, the Pontifical government agreed to make some concessions. In 1822, burials were suspended in the "old cemetery", the area by the tomb of Caius Cestius, about half a hectare in size, because it was thought that the graves and the surrounding trees spoilt the view of the pyramid. A larger sector (the "new cemetery") was created from the open fields to the west, and the more ancient part enclosed by a moat.[107] Keats's stone remained exposed to the elements – unshaded, overgrown with grass in a corner of the old cemetery near the ditch, apart from the other graves. Friends and well-wishers renovated it from time to time, adorning it with myrtles and laurels, giving it a stone pedestal and restoring the faded inscription.[108] Threatened by various town-planning proposals and developments, the whole site risked being obliterated between the early 1870s and the end of the First World War, when it was declared an "area of national interest", and was saved only thanks to the intercession of Queen Victoria and Kaiser Wilhelm II, as well as the efforts of diplomats.[109] Indeed, it is very fortunate that Keats's grave still stands today, and that one of the most treasured and revered shrines of literary pilgrimage has not disappeared.

The bleakness of the poet's final hours is well captured by Severn in his letters. On 22nd February, the day before his friend's death, Severn wrote to Haslam:

O! how anxious I am to hear from you—none of yours has come—but in answer to mine from Naples—I have nothing to break this dreadful solitude—but Letters—day after day—night after night—here I am by our poor dying friend—my spirits—my intelects and my health are breaking down—I can get no one to change me—no one will relieve me—they all run away—and even if they did not poor Keats could not do without me—I prepare every thing he eats—

Last night I thought he was going—I could hear the Phlegm in his throat—he bade me lift him up in the bed—or he would die with pain—I watchd him all night—at every cough I expected he would suffocate—death is very fast approaching for this Mor^g by the pale daylight—the change in him frightend me—he has sunk in the last three days to a most ghast[l]y look—I have these three nights sat [written "set"] up with him from the apprehension of his dying—Dr Clark has prepared me for it—but I shall be but little able to bear it—even this my horrible situation I cannot bear to cease by the loss of him— [...]

I have at times written a favorable letter to my sister—you will see this is best—for I hope that staying by my poor friend to close his eyes in death—will not add to my other unlucky hits—for I am still quite prevented from painting—and what the consequence may be—Poor Keats keeps me by him—and shadows out the form of one solitary friend—he opens his eyes in great horror and doubt—but when they fall upon me—they close gently and open and close until he falls into another sleep—The very thought of this keep[s] me by him until he dies—and why did I say I was loos[i]ng my time—the advantages I have gained by knowing John Keats—would to gain any other way have doubled and trebled the time—they could not have gain'd—I wont try to write any more—the want of sleep has almost taken away the power—The Post is going so I would try—Think of me my dear Haslam as doing well and happy—as far as——will allow—

Farewell—God bless you

Sincerly

J Severn

I will write by next post to Bro{wn}—a 2nd letter has just come from him—[110]

And it is to Brown that Severn communicated the bitter news a few days later:

He is gone—he died with the most perfect ease—he seemed to go to sleep. On the 23rd, about 4, the approaches of death came on. "Severn—I—lift me up—I am dying—I shall die easy—don't be frightened—be firm, and thank God it has come!" I lifted him up in my arms. The phlegm seemed boiling in his throat, and increased until 11, when he gradually sunk into death—so quiet—that I still thought he slept. I cannot say now—I am broken down from four nights' watching, and no sleep since, and my poor Keats gone. Three days since, the body was opened; the lungs were completely gone. The Doctors could not conceive by what means he had lived these two months. I followed his poor body to the grave on Monday, with many English. They take such care of me here—that I must, else, have gone into a fever. I am better now—but still quite disabled.

The Police have been. The furniture, the walls, the floor, every thing must be destroyed by order of the law. But this is well looked to by D^r C.

The letters I put into the coffin with my own hand.

I must leave off.

J. S.

This ~~comes~~ goes by the first post. Some of my kind friends would have written else. I will try to write you every thing next post; or the Doctor will.

They had a mask—and hand and foot done—
I cannot get on——[111]

Severn revisited his friend's last moments in a letter he wrote to John Taylor eleven days after the poet's death:

These four nights I watch him—each night expecting his death—on the fifth day the doctor prepared me for it—23rd at 4 oclock afternoon—The poor fellow bade me lift him up in bed—he breathed with great difficulty—and seemd to lose the power of coughing up the phlegm—an immense sweat came over him so that my breath felt cold to him—"dont breath on me—it comes like Ice"—he clasped my hand very fast as I held him in my arms—the mucus was boiling within him—it gurgled in his throat—this increased—but yet he seem'd without pain—his eyes look'd upon me with extrem[e] sensibility but without pain—at 11 he died in my arms—The English nurse had been with me all this {time—} this was something to me—but I was very bad—n{o} sleep that night—The next day the doctor had me over to his house—I was still the same—these kind people did every thing to comfort me—I must have sunk under it all—but for them—[112]

Saturday, 24th February, must have been a surreal day for Severn. His only friend was gone: he was shaken and grieving. He was forced to make Keats's death "known to the brutes [t]here" – his landlady and the police. As the mask-maker was taking casts of the poet's face, hand and foot, and he was being comforted by the Clarks in their house across the piazza, the streets were ringing with festive noise: it was the first day of Carnival. Nothing could have been more discordant to his feelings than the motley processions of masquerading locals dancing, playing and singing under his window.

On the following day, the grim practicalities of the autopsy were performed, as Severn reported to Taylor in his letter of 6th March:

On Sunday [...] Dr Clark and Dr Luby with an Italian Surgeon—opened the body—they thought it the worst possible Consumption—the lungs were intirely destroyed—the cells were quite gone—but Doctor Clark will write you on this head—This was another night without sleep to me—I felt worse and worse—[113]

"On the third day Monday 26th," Severn writes in the same letter, "the funeral beasts came." According to a note written in about 1850 by Ambrose Poynter, one of the few who attended the funeral, the mourners "started before daylight, a necessary precaution on a Protestant demonstration, [...] and arrived just at daybreak at the foot of the Pyramid of Caius Cestius".[114] Severn recalls that

[M]any English requested to follow him—those who did so were Dr Clark & Dr Luby[,] Messrs Ewing—Westmacott—Henderson—Pointer—and the Revd Mr Wolf who read the funeral service—he was buried very near to the monument of Caius Cestus—a few yards from Dr Bell and an infant of Mr Shelly's.—The good hearted Doctor made the men put turfs of daisies upon the grave—he said—"this would be poor Keats's wish—could he know it"—[115]

But Keats would never know it. He had drunk life's hemlock to the lees. He had left the world unseen, unheard by those who loved him most. He had become deaf to poetry, fame and beauty – to the echoes from the past and the discordant noise of posterity. His journey was now complete. His figure and his name – like that of others before and after him – had left only a gentle ripple in the water.

His music, however, lived on.

POSTHUMOUS JOURNEYS

EVERY END IS A NEW BEGINNING – every arrival a new departure. Even after our deaths, the shadows cast by our lives continue to affect the journeys of the people we leave behind.

Keats's tragic, premature end had a profound effect on the lives of his immediate circle, as well as on the course of world literature. Before we look at the vicissitudes of Keats's fame and the posthumous paths of some of the characters that appear in this story, I shall address an imponderable question: what would have happened if the poet had not died so young, but lived to a ripe old age – or at least been granted the ten years he had invoked in 'Sleep and Poetry', to "overwhelm [him]self in poesy"?

Keats's closest friends reacted to his death with grief and deep regret. Fanny Brawne thought that he had been "murdered [...] by the mere malignity of the world", sent to a "wretched country to die" by "ignorant and unfeeling" doctors.[1] She believed that "[a]ll his friends ha[d] forgotten him" at once, after "[getting] over the first shock". Above all, she was bitter because "had he returned [she] should have been his wife and he would have lived with [her and her mother]".[2] We cannot doubt that Keats would have tied the knot with Fanny and raised a family with her, either in England or abroad, if he had come back from Italy and recovered his health. It is impossible to say what shape this married life would have taken, what joys and tragedies might have been in store for the young couple, but we know that he had no intention of embracing a humdrum, respectable middle-class lifestyle: "[G]od forbid we should what people call, *settle*—turn into a pond, a stagnant Lethe—a vile crescent, row or buildings," he had told his fiancée a year before his departure. "Better be imprudent moveables than prudent fixtures—"[3]

After the death of the poet and a long period of mourning and trauma, Fanny endured two more tragic bereavements.[4] Her only brother, Samuel, died of consumption in the spring of 1828 at the age of twenty-three. In November of the following year her beloved mother passed away after suffering severe burns when her dress was set alight by a candle at the door of her home. Fanny then moved out of Wentworth Place, and in June 1833 married Louis Lindo (later "Lindon"), a Sephardic Jew of Spanish extraction, who was twelve years her junior. Within a year, the couple moved to Düsseldorf, where the first of three children was born. The Lindons resided in various cities on the Continent until 1859, when they returned to London. After a quiet married life, Mrs Frances Lindon – as Fanny called herself in later life – died on 4th December 1865, at the age of sixty-five, seven years before her husband. The couple rest in the same grave in Brompton Cemetery. The controversy surrounding Fanny Brawne's character – vilified when Keats's letters to her first appeared in print in 1878, and then vindicated by the publication of her own letters to Fanny Keats in 1937 – was a matter for posterity, and it still rages on.

Towards the end of his 'Life of John Keats', Charles Brown inveighed against the malevolence of the poet's detractors and the "credulity, carelessness and caprice" of the reading public, which he thought had dragged his friend to an early grave. "After twenty years," he wrote,

with all the charity of which my nature is capable, my belief continues to be that he was destroyed by hirelings, under the imposing name of Reviewers. Consumption, it may be urged, was in the family [...]; therefore, his fate was inevitable. Perhaps it was so; perhaps not. The brother who died was very tall and very narrow chested; our Keats was short, with well-proportioned limbs, and with a chest remarkably well-formed for strength. At the most, it comes to this: if an hereditary predisposition existed, that predisposition might not have been called into action, except by an outrageous denial of his now acknowledged claim to be ranked as a poet of

England. Month after month, an accumulation of ridicule and scoffs against his character and person, did worse than tear food from the mouth of a starving wretch, for it tore honour from the poet's brow. Could he have been less sensitive, could he have been less independent, could he have truckled to his self-constituted judges, could he have flattered the taste of the public, and pandered to their will and pleasure—in fact, could he have ceased to be John Keats, he might have existed at this moment, happy as one of the inferior animals of the creation.[5]

Would Keats have continued to write poetry if he had survived his illness? Would he have been deterred by hostile critics, or dissuaded by doctors and friends who feared for his health? Would he have "glided about the world like a ghost, sighing a melancholy tone in the ear of here and there a friend, but never sending forth his voice to greet the multitude", and witholding his great unpublished poem from the press, as fancifully imagined by Nathaniel Hawthorne? Again, it is impossible to say. When he was on his deathbed, the poet affirmed in desperation that "were he to recover he could not write another line", but it is doubtful whether he could ever have relinquished his own self, abandoned his ambitions, stifled his questioning mind or annihilated his imagination.[6] He could not cease to be John Keats.

Severn could never quite come to terms with the cruelty and injustice of his friend's destiny. "It was [...] to me a painfull riddle why he should die," he wrote in his earlier memoir.

Had he [arrived] a season sooner in Italy he might have been saved, for not only from many subsequent ^successfull^ Cases of consumption I have seen effected by the Italian climate, but also the soceity I have described would have helpd his convalescen[c]e & insured his future career & happiness by driving from his mind those images of despair & hatred which usurpd for awhile a mind that was never intended for them—[7]

He returned to this unsolved conundrum in a later memoir:

Ah how different might have been the fate of Keats, how stable his life, how brilliant & endearing his fame <u>even to himself</u>, which he never was [...][—]how different, if by some fair chance he had visited America & there produced his first volumes—with this charming hypothesis I can almost imagine him living now, & sitting beside me with his American fame achieving his English fame like an exotic, & he himself mature and even <u>philosophical</u>, laughing at the present work of science, which is reforming the world with steam instead of Poetry.

That he should be living now even in my imagination (for I certainly have calld up the possibility) in as much as I never could understand his strange & contradictory death, from health & strength & that fine compactness of person which we receive as a sign of longevity, & that elastic mind, exalting in youthfull feelings, cheerful, gay, generous, & living as it were onward on its own resources; I cannot imagine when I look back thro' forty years of worldly changes, to behold his dear image again in my "mind's eye" here in Rome, I cannot find the reason why in one sole year he should have been cut off "with all his imperfections on his head" & having only to look back on a world to him of <u>oblivion</u>.[8]

This is perhaps the most poignant conjecture, and the one that brings us closer to "what might have been". If, by a stroke of good fortune or an act of selfishness, Keats had not stayed in England to care for his dying brother Tom, but had travelled to America with George and his wife or boarded an Indiaman as a ship's surgeon – or Tom had left for Italy as he intended to do – he might have escaped tubercular infection and lived to see the age of train travel and electrical telegraphy, the coronation of Queen Victoria, the writings of Dickens and Thackeray.[9] He would have travelled the world, expanded his mind. Perhaps he would have reached international fame during his lifetime. His own works would have run into many volumes. We would have photographs of him today.

But that wasn't to be: he was destined to die young and remain unfulfilled, incomplete. W.B. Yeats, who often raged against old age in his poetry, feeling decrepit before his time, left us an endearing image of Keats, comparing him to a school-boy "With face and nose pressed to a sweet-shop window", who had sunk into his grave with "His senses and his heart unsat-isfied".[10] T.S. Eliot, who was always ambivalent about Keats and nurtured a love-hate relationship with his shadow, once stated that "the generation after 1830 preferred to form itself upon a decadence, though a decadence of genius: Wordsworth; and upon an immaturity, though an immaturity of genius: Keats and Shelley" – and that, as a result, "the development of English literature was retarded".[11] Leaving aside the question whether Eliot is right about the evolution of nineteenth-century English poetry, can we call Keats "immature", and can we blame him for failing to perfect his art in the short time he was granted by fate?

This leads us to some other interesting but unanswerable questions: in which direction would Keats's poetry have evolved? Would he have focused on poetry or on drama, which was his most recent ambition? Would he have turned to writing fiction, non-fiction, literary criticism, like some of his contemporaries? This also brings back to my mind the vivid memory of a conversation I had almost a quarter of a century ago with a rabid anti-Keatsian. He dismissed Keats altogether, both as a poet and as a person. He thought he was feeble, mannered, juvenile, and his poetry flawed. Even if there were any quality in his writing, which he very much doubted, he was convinced that he had already peaked by the time of his death. "If he had lived longer," he said, "he would have turned into a conservative old fogey like Wordsworth, adding nothing else to world literature." The assurance with which my friend delivered this verdict made me smile then and still makes me smile today. To affirm that Keats would have produced works of very little significance if he had been given another ten or twenty years to live, if not more, is rather absurd – not only because it fails to recognize the promise, if not the greatness, of Keats's poetry, but because it disregards the visceral intensity, imaginative unpredictability and audacious rule-breaking of his letters, and what manner of man and intellectual he was. How many of the authors we still read today would be remembered if only the works they wrote before the age of twenty-four were to be considered?[12] Barring perhaps a handful of young prodigies like Pushkin, Lermontov, Rimbaud and Leopardi, I can't think of any – at least not in the English language. Even a prolific and precocious author such as Yeats would be known only for a couple of early collections, *The Wanderings of Oisin* and *Crossways*, perhaps not enough to secure his lasting fame: it would take him another two decades and many more published collections of poetry to reach his mature phase with *The Wild Swans at Coole*. The truth is that the development of every poet is different, and in most cases it is a long and arduous process – "nothing but continual uphill Journeying".[13] Keats only began writing in earnest in late 1816, and it is remarkable how much he accomplished during his short period of poetical activity. In the end, we cannot condemn Keats if his journey of development, his constant "moulting", was cut off by premature death, and I agree with Charles Brown, who was his close friend and knew him well, when he says: "[H]e was, from the first day he became a poet, in progressive improvement. To this his poems bear witness. How high, had he not been destroyed by [...] disease, his genius might have soared, is a thought that at once exalts and depresses me."[14]

Fame, as everyone knows, is fickle. Keats was aware of this too, and warned any aspirant against the dangers of trying too hard:

Fame, like a wayward girl, will still be coy
   To those who woo her with too slavish knees,
But makes surrender to some thoughtless boy,
   And dotes the more upon a heart at ease...
She is a Gypsy will not speak to those
   Who have not learnt to be content without her;
A jilt whose ear was never whispered close,
   Who thinks they scandal her who talk about her...
A very Gypsy is she, Nilus-born,
   Sister-in-law to jealous Potiphar.
Ye lovesick bards, repay her scorn for scorn!
   Ye artists lovelorn, madmen that ye are,
Make your best bow to her and bid adieu –
Then, if she likes it, she will follow you![15]

Fame did follow Keats in the end, but only after a long and tortuous posthumous journey. Ignoring the dying poet's instructions, Taylor and Hessey were prompt in notifying English newspapers of his death, and kept advertising his latest books. The London *Sun* published the following obituary on 22nd March 1821:

JOHN KEATS, ESQ.—The admirers of poetry will regret to hear that this gentleman died at Rome, on the 23d ult., at the age of twenty-five. His work, entitled ENDYMION, displays strong proofs of imagination, impregnated with knowledge and genuine poetical spirit. This work induced Messrs. TAYLOR and HESSEY to bring forward a Volume of his Miscellaneous Poems, the chief of which are entitled LAMIA, ISABELLA, THE EVE OF ST. AGNES, and a fragment entitled HYPERION.—MR. KEATS possessed great descriptive powers, which are so strongly manifested in the fragment of HYPERION, that there is additional cause for lamenting that the ingenious author did not live to conclude it.

This and other notices, which appeared around the same time in various dailies, weeklies and magazines, were of course as much intended for "admirers of poetry" as for the man of law.[16] Taylor was keen to make the poet's death "sufficiently notorious" not so much to sell more copies of his books as "to satisfy the Law", so that he could make a legal attempt to recoup the £150 of the cashed letter of credit from George Keats or Richard Abbey.[17] This may seem heartless and cynical, but considering how generous Taylor and Hessey were in promoting and supporting uncommercial poets such as Keats and John Clare, they can be forgiven for trying to reduce their losses.

As we have seen, Keats had requested that his gravestone bear a simple inscription, with no name and no dates.[18] Taylor believed that the poet's dying wish should be respected, but Charles Brown thought he knew better, having been so intimate with Keats, and oblivious to the fact that sometimes less is more insisted on adding a ham-fisted, overdramatic commentary which destroyed the lapidary effect of the inscription and turned it into a mawkish, affected statement that smacked very much of Hunt.[19] Severn, who had ideas of his own, was caught in the middle of all this and tried to find a compromise, not wishing to offend Taylor or to alienate Brown, who had been such a generous friend to Keats and insisted on contributing half of the costs for the memorial.[20] In the end it was Charles Brown who had his way, and the result – the stone that was erected in late May 1823 and still stands today – has the following inscription:

This Grave
contains all that was Mortal,
of a
YOUNG ENGLISH POET,
Who,
on his Death Bed,
in the Bitterness of his Heart,
at the Malicious Power of his Enemies,
Desired
these Words to be engraven on his Tomb Stone
"Here lies One
Whose Name was writ in Water.
Feb 24th *1821*[21]

The verbose style, the cramped layout, the tone of self-pity, resentment, vindictiveness – in short, everything in this epitaph, which was supposed to be Keats's last pithy message to the world, was in poor taste. The carved Greek lyre with four broken strings seemed an apt representation of the discordant note hit by the expanded inscription.[22] The poet would have turned in his grave if he had seen it.

The epitaph soon became the subject of cruel mockery. "[W]hen the grave stone was placed with Keats's expressive line," Severn remembered decades later,

> then a host started up, not of admirers, but of scoffers & a silly joke was often repeated in my hearing[:] "Here lies one whose name was writ in water & his works in milk & water" & this I was condemned to hear for years repeated as tho' it had been a Pasquinade.[23]

The thought continued to vex Severn for a very long time. "As I am shortly to return to Rome," he wrote to Dilke on 3rd February 1859,

> one of my first acts must be to do away with poor Keats's gravestone, so disrespetfull & unjust to his memory as it is & distressing to my feelings—No doubt you are aware that it was written by Charles Brown & is one of his saddest mistakes[.] [...]
> When this unseemly stone was placed Keats memory was cherishd by a very few friends & perhaps his genius known to fewer: but now his fame is world-wide & his memory being cherishd by every feeling man this stone has become a downright anomaly—Being in such a beautifull & famous Roman locale, close to the Pyramid of Cajus Cestus, he should have a tomb with some characteristic decorum about it & at least a true inscription beyond ridicule—[24]

But the "anomaly" was never corrected, and remains for everyone to see.

The dispute about the gravestone was part of a larger-scale conflict among Keats's friends about who should be the keeper of his legacy and who should write a biography that might enhance the poet's reputation and promote his works. Just over a month after Keats's death, Taylor wrote to Severn: "I have been requested by several of our friends to write a short account of his Life, and for this purpose the most valuable of my Materials will be those communications which you are able to make me."[25] The publisher even advertised, in the first half of 1821, the imminent appearance of a book called *Memoirs and Remains of John Keats*.[26] Severn demurred, and replied in May that year: "I will make every communication to you—but not yet—I cannot stand it—only writing this has made me like a child.—"[27] The painter was not sure what to do. He wrote to Charles Brown in July: "M' Taylor has written me of his intention to write some remembrances of our Keats—this is a kind thought of his—& I reverence this good man—nothing can be more interesting than to have the beautiful character of Keats—described and apreciated."[28] Severn didn't want to offend Taylor, who was helping him secure a travelling pension using his influence with Hilton, but perhaps he wasn't convinced that the publisher had been close enough to the poet, or maybe he fancied himself as his only *real* friend, who had been next to him in his dying moments when everyone else had abandoned him.

Brown, on his part, was fuming. He had seen Taylor's advertisements and had been asked to cooperate, but he feared it would be a quick and dirty "bookseller's job".[29] He wrote to Severn, painting Taylor in the darkest colours and trying to persuade him to entrust all of his Keats material to him.

[H]e bears me no good will for claiming in return for MSS & information, a sight of his Memoir before it went to press. I confess I could not trust him entirely; now & then he is a mere bookseller,—somewhat vain of his talents, & consequently self willed; my anxiety for poor Keats' fame compelled me to make this request,—for, in my opinion,—Taylor neither comprehended him nor his poetry. I shall always be the first to acknowledge Taylor's kindness to Keats,—but towards me his conduct has been ungracious and even unmanly. Reynolds is the secret spring,—it is wished he should shine as the dear friend of poor Keats,—(at least I suspect so,)—when the fact is he was no dear friend to Keats, nor did Keats think him so.[30]

Severn decided to side with Brown, and sent him all his material.[31] At the same time, he kept Taylor in hopeful expectation, not wishing to disappoint him, and invented excuses for his procrastinations. "How goes the Memoir my dear Sir?" he wrote to him in January 1822. "[T]hough I should be the last to inquire since I have given you so little help—but I crave your pardon—for I cannot write—I cannot put my thinking to paper—"[32]

In another letter of August 1821 to Joseph Severn, Brown had continued to disparage Taylor, accusing him not only of dishonesty, but of cynical profiteering, and taking the high moral ground over the whole matter.

When I mentioned to you my fears about Mr. Taylor's memoir, I omitted to make known the original cause of those fears. It was this. Immediately on receipt of your letter announcing poor Keats's death, almost in the same newspapers where there was a notice of his death, even before Mrs. Brawne's family and myself had got our mourning, in those very newspapers was advertised "speedily will be published, a biographical memoir of the late John Keats, &c.," and I, among others, was applied to by Reynolds to collect with all haste, papers, letters, and so on, in order to assist Mr. Taylor. This indecent bustle over (as it were) the newly covered grave of my dear friend shocked me excessively. I told Mr. Taylor it looked as if his friends had been collecting information about his life in expectation of his death. This, indeed, was the fact. I believe I spoke warmly, and probably gave offence. [...] Mr. Taylor expected to be trusted implicitly, and takes dudgeon. Now, on such a point I know of none whom I could trust implicitly. He says no one understood Keats's character so well as himself; if so, I who knew him tolerably well, and others of his friends, greatly mistook him, judging from what has dropped from Mr. Taylor.[33]

Brown made it clear to Taylor that he would not cooperate with the project, and that he, Dilke and Hunt would not provide any material if the publisher didn't give him sight of the memoir before it went to press. The truth was perhaps that Brown, who had also heard that Charles Cowden Clarke was planning a biography of Keats, felt excluded and unappreciated: if there was anyone who had any right to say something about the poet, it was he himself – the intimate friend who had helped the struggling author on all fronts, who had lived and travelled and even co-authored a play with him.[34] And, possessive as he was about Keats, if he could not write his life – because he lacked most of the information prior to their first meeting in late summer 1817 and, perhaps, the necessary diplomatic skills for such a complex task – and was forced to join forces with Taylor or Clarke, he expected to have a say in it.[35]

From this hotbed of rivalry, jealousy and factiousness there was little hope that a fair appreciation of Keats's life and works could emerge any time soon. Sensing Brown's hostility and Severn's reluctance, Taylor's enthusiasm for the project cooled. The "short account" he had written, "by the writer's own desire[, ...] was never published, as he thought it would give pain to people then living".[36] Aware that all these squabbles were only detrimental to the memory and reputation of his dead friend, Brown decided that he would write the biography himself, and in 1829 communicated his intention to various friends. The trouble was that, as well as having burnt his bridges with Taylor and Reynolds, he was in fundamental disagreement with Dilke about George Keats's character and his financial dealings with his brother John, and didn't see eye to eye with Fanny Brawne – he could not therefore expect universal approval for his project.[37] The resulting 'Life of John Keats', begun after a long gestation in 1836 and completed in March 1841, was also never published. Despite being very short, incomplete and often redacted, it is an important document that gives us information about the poet that cannot be obtained elsewhere.

It was only with the appearance on the scene of Richard Monckton Milnes that the idea of a biography of John Keats gained new momentum.[38] When Severn first met Milnes in Rome in June 1832 as a young graduate and an aspiring poet travelling abroad, he presented him with a fragment of Keats's draft of *Lamia*, and no doubt regaled him with many stories and anecdotes about his dead friend, of whom he was painting a picture at the time.[39] That was enough to seal Milnes's fate.

Alongside his long activity as a politician, which he began in 1837 as a Conservative MP for Pontefract after returning from years of travel, Milnes launched into a successful career as a poet and writer. In the 1840s he had achieved such renown that he was thought of as a possible successor to Wordsworth as poet laureate.

Just before emigrating to New Zealand, Brown had tried, without success, to find a publisher for his brief biographical sketch. In the haste of his preparations for the voyage, in March 1841, without consulting any of the poet's friends, he asked Milnes if he would be willing to write a fuller life of Keats. Milnes agreed at once, and Brown sent him all the manuscripts in his possession, including his 'Memoir, with Literary Remains', which he expected to be published verbatim with editorial notes and comments.[40] This was of course impracticable, and few of Keats's friends would have consented to it, but since George Keats – the legatee of the poet's works – and Charles Brown died in the space of a few months, any objection to the use of the material disappeared.[41]

Milnes began to work in earnest on the biography only from around 1845. Over the following three years, he contacted most of Keats's friends, and was able to secure the assistance, among others, of Severn, Taylor, Charles Cowden Clarke, Benjamin

Haydon, Dilke, Haslam, Hunt, George Felton Mathew and even, after some wrangling, John Hamilton Reynolds, who intended "to write [his] own recollections of Keats".[42] Milnes hailed from an upper-class background, unlike Keats, but he had a poet's sensibility and showed a close affinity to his subject. Even if at times he veers towards romanticization, his enthusiasm, when he writes, is palpable. Despite being at times cavalier with dates and biographical details, and careless about the exact repro-duction of texts and quotations, his two-volume *Life, Letters and Literary Remains of John Keats*, first published in August 1848, is an excellent book by the standards of the time and a landmark in the re-evaluation of Keats's legacy.[43]

Keats's friends were unanimous in their praise, except Leigh Hunt, who took umbrage at some references to him in the poet's letters. Charles Cowden Clarke was among the most fervent admirers. When he received a copy of the biography, he wrote at once to Milnes:

> Although I have compassed but a few pages of your life of Keats, (for what delights me, I read at a ploughman's pace:—I chew, and chew; and go back, and ruminate) I cannot delay to send you the assurance that I am enchanted with the way in which you have performed your labour of love. It is a worthy tribute to his genius:—it is *all* I could have wished for his monumental fame.[44]

Milnes's own opinion of the book was not overenthusiastic. "I have published a Life and some remains of a remarkable young poet of the name of Keats, little known even in this country," he wrote to the German author Karl August Varnhagen von Ense soon after its publication. "It is the biography of a mere boy—he died at 24—, and therefore the literary interest is but small. [...] I cannot expect any reputation for the book, when the merits of the subject of it are so little known."[45]

Still, Milnes's biography had the effect of sparking a renewed interest in an obscure author who had once been derided and reviled. His 1854 edition of *The Poetical Works of John Keats*, published by Edward Moxon – to whom Taylor had sublicensed all the poet's writings for a mere fifty pounds in September 1845, reserving the right to issue new editions himself – was reprinted eleven times in the space of just over twenty years, and the *Life* was brought out in a revised version in 1867, incorporating new material while omitting the "Literary Remains", and reissued several times into the following century.[46] The time for Keats's poetry to be rediscovered and appreciated had come: a new sensibility had emerged which was attuned to his song and his imagination.

Milnes's greatest achievement was to arrange and connect the original material, take a step back and let the poems and letters speak for themselves. Keats's quirky, powerful, stirring voice spoke loud from beyond the grave, and readers fell in love with it. It is a pity that Milnes's biography also gave rise to some myths that were perpetuated and augmented by Sharp and other romantic biographers who came after him, but that perhaps facilitated, rather than hindered, Keats's long-deferred tryst with the wayward girl, Fame. It is due in large part to Milnes that Keats's name today is carved in stone "among the English poets".

The brig that had taken Keats and Severn to Italy, the *Maria Crowther*, sailed on to its own final destination. It left for Palermo a month after reaching the Bay of Naples, on 22nd November 1820, and returned to England at the beginning of the following March.[47] It continued to ply the Mediterranean waters for two more years under Thomas Walsh's command, then it became leaky, altered its routes, changed captains in quick succession, received a thorough repair in 1827 and was buried at sea a decade later, as reported in two separate articles in the *Carlisle Journal*:

Early in the morning of Tuesday last [7th November 1837], the brig Maria Crowther, Robert Dawes, master, when on her passage from Whitehaven for Dublin, laden with coals, ran on shore near Laxey, Isle of Man, where she remains in a very precarious state: crew saved.

The brig Maria Crowther, (says the *Manx Liberal* of Saturday,) stranded at Laxey, still remains in her perilous situation, but has had the greater part of her coals discharged, which were sold at a reduced price. Carpenters are now employed in repairing the damage so far that the vessel may be got off and taken to Whitehaven.—Since the above was written, we have received the unpleasant information, that owing to the in-shore wind which prevailed during the whole of Thursday week, with a heavy surf beating upon the rocks, the vessel has since partially broke up, and may be considered a total wreck.[48]

Thomas Walsh did not turn his back on the sea after relinquishing the command of the *Maria Crowther*, but became the master of a "fine new Brig", the *Naples Packet*, "A1 at Lloyd's, 150 tons", which also sailed between London and Sicily via Naples.[49] He was in charge of the vessel from the spring of 1824 until August 1833, when he handed over the command to a new captain and we lose all trace of him.[50]

Naples, by that time, had become again a popular tourist destination, welcoming travellers from all over Europe and from America, including famous writers, artists and antiquarians. After King Ferdinand's "desertion" in December 1820, the disgruntled *carbonari* made hasty preparations to meet the Austrians on the field of war. The clash between the two armies occurred at the Battle of Rieti, fought between 7th and 10th March 1821. What was supposed to be the moment of truth turned out to be an underwhelming encounter. The superior and better-organized Austrian forces had an easy task of defeating the troops of General Pepe and disbanding the rest of the Neapolitan army, under the command of General Carrascosa. Keats had been right when he had said that those soldiers "would never stand". Two weeks later, the Austrians escorted King Ferdinand into Naples and restored him to the throne. The Neapolitan parliament was shut down, the constitution revoked, and a great number of insurgents were executed or imprisoned. Pepe and

Carrascosa fled into exile, fought each other in a duel in 1823 and continued their skirmishes in the pages of their memoirs. Italy's first attempt at self-determination ended in failure: its citizens would have to wait four more decades before their lands would be free from foreign domination and their nation unified. For the time being, after all the commotion, nothing changed. "So you have been alarmed about the armies advancing," Severn wrote to his father in April 1821, "well you might be—for never was such warlike preparations—such valor in talk—such intrenchments—but I suppose you know it has all gone off with a pop—the Neapolitans are quite forgotten—it is all over—we are just the same here."[51]

While all this was happening – while Napoleon was dying on a remote island in the South Atlantic Ocean and the ponderous wheels of history whirred on – Maria Cotterell, the young lady who had travelled from London all the way to Naples with Keats, Severn and Mrs Pidgeon, was approaching the final stages of her own personal tragedy. She had weathered the rigid Neapolitan winter, survived the spring and reached the warm days of summer. But neither the mildness of the season, nor the help of the doctors, nor the attentions of her older sibling Charles could save her. She died in her brother's house on 15th July 1821.[52] She was only twenty years old.

After the loss of his sister, Charles Cotterell continued to live in Naples. Like Joseph Severn, he was blessed – or perhaps cursed – with a very long and active life. In Keats's biographies he only makes cursory footnote appearances, but I believe he deserves greater attention.

As we have seen before, Severn remained in touch with Cotterell after the death of the poet. In the summer of 1822 he was his guest in Naples, and they met again several times over the following years. Cotterell's intense commercial activities are recorded in the Neapolitan archives, but he also led a busy social life.[53] From references to him in the books and letters of some of his friends we know that he was a convivial fellow who enjoyed life, was a generous host and had literary interests.[54]

His bachelor life ended on 6th July 1831, when he married Elizabeth, daughter of Revd E.H. Warriner, rector of All Saints Church, Foots Cray, an ancient parish under the patronage of the Crown, which was presented to him by the Lord Chancellor in 1823.[55] Elizabeth had travelled to Italy with her parents in the spring of 1830, perhaps to treat some ailment.[56] After spending the summer on the island of Ischia, the Warriners went to Naples in September "partly to get medical advice, partly [...] to look for winter quarters". "Elisabeth," Revd Warriner wrote to his brother George, "is by dint of bathing & douching a little better & but a little."[57] It is there in Naples, no doubt, that she met Charles Cotterell and became engaged to him.

The couple had several children: Charles Edward, jun. (1834–77), Elizabeth Mariana (1835–36), George James (1837–77), Thomas Warriner (1840–1921) and Elizabeth Caroline Sophia (1842–76). James Minet, who had been a friend of the Warriner family since boyhood and a contemporary of Elizabeth, was a guest of the Cotterells during his long stays in the Neapolitan capital, and often mentions the hospitality and helpfulness of Charles and his wife.[58] "Pray tell Mrs Warriner," he wrote to his sisters in April 1835, "that I find her son-in-law to be a most worthy person. He has been most obliging to me in all respects."[59]

Cotterell's congeniality and generosity made him many friends among the English travellers who visited the city. One of them was Charles Dickens, who was in Naples in February 1845 and later corresponded, met and dined with Cotterell in London. From the three surviving letters to him from Dickens, we can gather that the celebrated author had been impressed by his new friend.[60] They talked about some manuscripts that Dickens was to help publish in London, about Bruce Castle School, prisons and systems of secondary punishment.[61] On saying goodbye to Cotterell in Naples, Dickens wrote: "Let me assure you that I would infinitely rather be a familiar star to you, than a distantly glorious one; and that I have had a sincere pleasure in our frank and unaffected intercourse. Mrs. Dickens and Miss Hogarth unite with me in best regards to Mrs. Cotterell."[62] Hearing that his friend was back in England, Dickens sent him a message at once, despite being busy finishing his Christmas novella *The Cricket on the Hearth*: "I hope you are not making a flying visit to England,—or at all events that you will be in London on Sunday Week the 23rd. when pray dine with me, unceremoniously, at Half Past Five o'Clock."[63] And when he learnt that he was still around a few months later, he wrote to him:

> I am really shocked to find you still in London. I took it into my head, and was quite satisfied (though I should be puzzled to say why) that you had gone to Italy long ago. You say "in a day or two". I hope that does not mean until after Saturday next, and that you will be able to dine here, that day, at 6. You would be interested, I think. I have two or three people coming, who are learned in Crime and Criminals (one of them the Governor of that Prison we saw, and whom I dare say you remember); [...] I hope you will be able to make this an Engagement between us.[64]

We don't know whether Cotterell was able to accept the invitation, but Dickens looked for him when he returned to Naples in November 1853. "Cottrel is no longer here," he wrote to his wife in surprise, "and is out of the partnership in the bank with Iggulden."[65] A few years before, in 1846, Cotterell had decided to sell his shares in the company to his partner and leave Naples.[66] The reason for this decision is not clear. It may be that the ageing banker had had enough of the frantic lifestyle he was leading in Naples, or that he wished to be closer to his sons, who were studying in England, or wanted to return to the sea or had been called back into service by the Royal Navy.[67] He was appointed paymaster and purser to HMS *Prince Regent* on 10th December 1847 and secretary to its commander, Commodore William F. Martin, in April 1851.[68] After serving on the *Neptune* and the *St Vincent*, he retired in July 1856, at the age of sixty-three.[69]

Another, more radical step was taken around that time: the whole family decided to emigrate to New Zealand. Before leaving his country for ever, in May 1857 Charles Cotterell was made co-trustee of the estate of Revd Warriner.[70] Charles and his seventeen-year-old son Thomas left England on 15th October 1857 and arrived in Nelson, then a small New Zealand settlement, on 10th February the following year.[71] The rest of the family joined them in September 1859, having sailed from England on the trader *Cresswell*.[72]

Charles Cotterell soon became a well-known figure in the local community. He was invited to important functions, such as receptions and dinners for the governor or the levee held, during his visit to Nelson in April 1869, by Prince Alfred, Duke of Edinburgh, to whom Cotterell was presented.[73] He was also involved in the cultural life of the small town, contributing to its 1861 Exhibition a number of fine paintings from his collection.[74] He remained proud of his military background until the end of his days, describing himself in his will as "retired Paymaster in Her Majestys Royal Navy" and being referred to in an obituary notice as "Charles Edward Cotterell, R.N."[75]

His children were notable figures in their own right. Their professional activities, their marriages, the births of their children and their deaths are all documented in the local papers of the time. Charles Edward, jun. became a prominent surgeon, accoucheur and lecturer, and George a famous entertainer and comic impressionist who toured New Zealand and Australia. Thomas worked as a surveyor in Nelson, Marlborough and the West Coast. He survived all of his siblings by more than four decades, and at the death of his mother in 1890 was named as sole executor and beneficiary, dying in 1921 without children.[76] The photos of all the members of the family, including two of Charles Cotterell, sen., and one of his wife, are preserved at the Nelson Provincial Museum and can be viewed online on their website. An old gentleman from a different era, the erstwhile banker, naval officer, jovial host, cracker of jokes and paterfamilias looks at us with a sullen, lifeless, almost uncomprehending expression, gloves in hand and top hat and glasses on the table next to him. Who knows if this man who shook hands with Keats, Severn, Dickens and Prince Alfred, among others, would ever have imagined that we would be staring back at him one hundred and fifty years on?

Charles Cotterell died in his country residence, "Crayfield",[77] on 11th March 1871, almost fifty years to the day after the death of the young ailing poet who had crossed paths with him in Naples, and is buried at Wakapuaka Cemetery, Nelson. His name and actions have only produced a gentle ripple and now are gone, but there may be documents he left behind, waiting to be rediscovered, that will help us fill some gaps in our story and create a more accurate picture of those long-forgotten events.

Joseph Severn's destiny was intertwined with that of John Keats both before and after the poet's death. His departure from England was a great gamble, but it paid off, and he always knew that his decision to accompany his friend to Rome was a defining moment in his life. "The death of Keats[,] altho he was unknown[,] & my devoted friendship," he wrote in 'Incidents of My Life', "had become a kind of pasport to the English hearts, & I soon found myself in the midst of [...] the most polished society[.] [...] This was a 'treasure trove' to me as a young Artist, invaluable, as it was my first acquaintance with my future patrons."[78]

Severn's career as an artist was, by and large, a successful one, although in later years he often had to suffer rejection and was hounded by creditors.[79] Menander's famous dictum – "he whom the gods love dies young" – did not apply to him.[80] Unlike his friend, he had to "undergo" a very long life and suffer the indignity of old age and decrepitude, with all their attendant evils.[81] He met with early recognition, was industrious and tenacious in his work, and a tireless self-promoter, had his fair share of joys and disappointments, and his life was often punctuated by tragedy, but also cheered by success. Although appreciated during his lifetime and gifted with undoubted talent, Fame did not follow him after his death. His art is now all but forgotten, and he is only remembered today as "Keats's friend".

The question for us now is: was he a good, disinterested friend, or did he exploit his position and profit from portraying himself as the selfless, devoted deathbed companion of John Keats? Opinions have ranged on this subject, from hagiographic portraits of the painter in Milnes, Sharp and later biographies to more recent critical reassessments, from which he emerges at times as an opportunist, in particular in his dealings with women and in his constant preoccupation with money. The truth is perhaps somewhere in the middle.

There is no doubt that when Severn left England he was motivated by artistic ambition and the chance of furthering his prospects, but we know that he halted all his activities – though short of money and under pressure to produce some work – to provide assistance to his friend during the last months of his life. It should not be forgotten that Keats was, at the time, an obscure poet, not a celebrated writer, so we cannot doubt that he was motivated by friendship. Reading the self-absorbed letters and diaries of some of the young artists who were in Rome at the time, it is to be wondered whether any of them would have done half of what Severn did.

It is true that after the poet's death he capitalized on his image as Keats's most loyal friend, but not, I think, in an opportunistic way: his profile increased alongside Keats's grow-ing reputation. And it is to be remembered that by promot-ing himself he was also publicizing the life and works of the poet. Someone like Keats – with no estate, a doubtful literary reputation at home and very few friends who had the energy, the connections or the will to keep his legacy alive – could not have been better served.

As we have seen, there were some flaws in Severn's character, which caused many of Keats's friends, before and after the poet's death, to dislike him or be wary of him. These foibles were also perceived by many of those who met the painter, and perhaps made it difficult for people to judge him with fairness and appreciate what was, in substance, a simple, decent, ami-able nature.

It is clear that he was vain, eccentric and self-centred, but these are traits we associate with most artists. It is also undeniable that he was feckless and chaotic in the management of his personal affairs, but so was Keats and, to a lesser extent, some of the poet's friends, including Brown. Many would have found his exuberance irksome, but that was part of his personality. In fact, there were others who liked Severn, and he was able to charm women, as well as build a large family and a number of lifelong friendships. Dilke wrote of him in 1826: "I always liked Severn, and shall like him the better as long as I live."[82] Faced with difficult situations, Severn often failed to display strength, and at times showed signs of rash, erratic behaviour, as when he smashed with his stick the crockery of poor Signora Angeletti, indignant at being presented a bill for some broken pieces of the set he had used – but then again, anyone can have a moment of temper or blind rage.[83] All things considered, he was a normal human being with the usual share of strengths and weaknesses.

As we have seen, Severn often claimed that he was a poor writer and that, being a painter, he found it hard to put words to paper. Truth or exaggeration?[84] His letters – with all their stylistic sloppiness – are terse, direct, spirited and even witty at times. He might have lacked discipline, which meant that, despite his friends' repeated requests, he was never able to keep a regular diary. This is a great shame, as his accounts are full of lacunae and scant on detail, and devoid of that kind of immediacy that only a diarist note can offer.

He was, however, an honest enough chronicler, on the whole – or at least he did not write with the deliberate intention of hoodwinking his readers or falsifying the historical record, as Sharp, Macfarlane and other biographers with novelistic ambitions did after him. If his memoirs are unreliable, it is only because he began writing them too late, after a very active and turbulent life. Succumbing to the usual slips caused by old age and its well-known tendency to repeat and embroider, his memory often failed him: people and events became blurred, the timeline compressed and the chronology muddled. His affection for Keats, however, never waned, and he remained a staunch advocate of the poet's legacy until his death in 1879. He now rests in the Protestant Cemetery of Rome, where he began, side by side with his friend, his own posthumous journey to eternity, six decades after their fateful voyage together to Italy.[85]

Acknowledgements

I would like to express my gratitude to the following people and organizations for their support during my research and the writing of this book:

Richard Davies; Anthony Mortimer; Sander Berg; Richard Stokes; Stephen Parkin; Mirco Gallenzi; Ettore d'Alessandro; Giovanni Pintori; Luca Caddia of the Keats-Shelley Memorial House; Ferdinando Salemme of the Archivio di Stato di Napoli; Mary Haegert and her colleagues at the Houghton Library, Harvard University; Adam Waterton and Mark Pomeroy of the Royal Academy in London; Stefano Pagliantini of the Biblioteca Civica di Bassano del Grappa; Giovanna Inverardi of the Biblioteca Queriniana, Brescia; Andrea Papini, Paola Ferraris, Filippo Vignato, Claudia Ambrosio, Maria Carmela De Marino and Luca Nicastro of the Archivio di Stato di Roma; Stephanie Coane of Eton College Library; Amelia Walker and her colleagues at the Wellcome Collection Library; Errin Hussey of the Henry Moore Institute; the National Archives; the Warwickshire County Record Office; the Derbyshire County Record Office; Vicky Green of the Southampton Central Library; Lesa Davies of the Isle of Wight Record Office; Archive New Zealand; the National Library of New Zealand; the Southwark Heritage Centre and Walworth Library; the Archivio del Banco di Napoli; the Archivio del Comune di Napoli; Jeanette Ware of the Nelson Provincial Museum; Jo Smith of Southampton Archives; Julie Sweeten of the State Library of New South Wales; Cambridge University Library; the Royal Medical Society; the Morgan Library & Museum; the Z. Smith Reynolds Library, Wake Forest University; the British

Museum; Ann-Marie Fitzsimmons of the UK Hydrographic Office; Barbara Orciuoli of the Archivio di Stato di Napoli; Rossella Celentano of the Museum and Historical Archive of Teatro San Carlo; Jo Jenkinson of Doncaster Archives; Giuseppe Ciprelli of the Archivio Storico Diocesano di Roma; Grant F. Scott; Andrea Milanese; Alberto Crielesi; and every researcher and writer whose work I have consulted in the preparation of this book.

Special thanks go to my editor, Alexander Middleton.

Sources

National Archives documents

ADM 6/195/398: Charles Edward Cotterell, Admiralty service record and correspondence regarding additional half pay

ADM 13/70/51, fos. 51–52: 'Charles Edward Cotterell, then aged 38, married Elizabeth Warriner on 5 Jul 1831 at Naples' (marriage recorded for potential Royal Navy widow's pension)

ADM 35/3400: HMS *Clio*, ship's pay book

ADM 35/3944: HMS *Thunder*, ship's pay book

ADM 37/6095: HMS *Liffey*, ship's muster

ADM 37/6282: HMS *Spey*, ship's muster

ADM 38/4515: HMS *Prince Regent*, ship's muster

ADM 51/3005: HMS *Active*, captain's log

ADM 51/3252: HMS *Liffey*, captain's log

ADM 51/3398: HMS *Revolutionaire*, captain's log

ADM 51/3417: HMS *Spey*, captain's log

ADM 52/4636: HMS *Thunder*, master's log

ADM 53/794: HMS *Liffey*, ship's log

ADM 196/74/774: Charles E. Cotterell, service record

FO 610/1: Entry Book of Passports, 26th June 1795 to 16th September 1822

PRO 30/9/3/34: Diaries of Charles Abbot, son of 1st Lord Colchester, while at Naples, including an account of the Austrian campaign there, February–March, 1821

Other works

ACE: *Un diario di viaggio di Giuseppe Acerbi: Roma–Napoli, 9 ottobre–12 novembre 1834*, ed. Emma Tedeschi (Mantua: L'Artistica, 1933)

AM: *Atlantic Monthly*, Vol. 68 (December 1891)

BATE: Walter Jackson Bate, *John Keats* (Harvard: Harvard University Press, 1979)

BER: Revd William Berrian, *Travels in France and Italy, in 1817 and 1818* (New York: T. and J. Swords, 1821)

BEW: *Life and Letters of William Bewick*, Vol. 2, ed. Thomas Landseer (London: Hurst and Blackett, 1871)

BLJ: *Byron's Letters and Journals*, Vol. 5, ed. Leslie A. Marchand (London: John Murray, 1976)

BMM: *Die Briefe Richard Monckton Milnes' ersten Barons Houghton an Varnhagen von Ense*, ed. Walther Fischer (Heidelberg: Carl Winters Universitätsbuchhandlung, 1922)

BNK: Joseph Severn, 'Biographical Notes on Keats' (October 1845 [?]), KC2, pp. 134–38

BROC: William Brockedon, *Traveller's Guide to Italy, or Road-Book from London to Naples* (Paris: Baudry, 1835)

CAR: Michele Carrascosa, *Mémoires historiques, politiques et militaires, sur la révolution du Royaume de Naples en 1820 et 1821* (London: Treuttel, Würtz, Treuttel fils, et Richter, 1823)

CARN: John Carne, *Letters from Switzerland and Italy* (London: Henry Colburn, 1834)

CASR: Carlo Brioschi, *Comentarj astronomici della specola reale di Napoli*, Vol. 1, Part II (Naples: Tipografia nella Pietà de' Turchini, 1824–26)

CDL4: *Pilgrim Edition of the Letters of Charles Dickens*, Vol. 4, *1844–1846*, ed. Kathleen Mary Tillotson (Oxford: Oxford University Press, 1977)

CDL6: *Pilgrim Edition of the Letters of Charles Dickens*, Vol. 6, *1850–1852*, ed. Graham Storey, Kathleen Mary Tillotson and Nina Burgis (Oxford: Oxford University Press, 1988)

CELF: *The Collected English Letters of Henry Fuseli*, ed. David H. Weinglass (Milwood, NY: Kraus, 1982)

CGCA: Catasto gregoriano, Comarca 110, 'Albano, sez. IV: Albano e Abbazia di San Pavolo'

CLA: Charles and Mary Cowden Clarke, *Recollections of Writers* (London: Sampson Low, Marston, Searle, & Rivington, 1878)

CLDR: *Collezione delle leggi e de' decreti reali del Regno delle Due Sicilie* (Naples: Tipografia del Ministero di Stato della Cancelleria Generale, 1820)

CLH: *The Correspondence of Leigh Hunt*, Vol. 1, ed. Thornton Leigh Hunt (London: Smith, Elder, 1862)

COBB: James P. Cobbett, *Journal of a Tour in Italy* (London: Mills, Jowett, and Mills, 1830)

COEN: Paolo Coen, 'Arte, cultura e mercato in una bottega romana del XVIII secolo: l'impresa calcografica di Giuseppe e Mariano Vasi fra continuità e rinnovamento', *Bollettino d'Arte*, No. 115 (2001), pp. 23–74.

COL: Pietro Colletta, *Storia del Reame di Napoli dal 1734 sino al 1825*, Vol. 2 (Capolago: Tipografia e Libreria Elvetica, 1834)

COM: *Commentari dell'Ateneo di Brescia per l'anno 1961* (Brescia: Fratelli Geroldi, 1961)

CONS: Charles Macfarlane, *Constantinople in 1828: A Residence of Sixteen Months in the Turkish Capital and Provinces* (London: Saunders and Otley, 1829)

CRI1: Alberto Crielesi, 'La Locanda di Emiliano a S. Rocco', in id., *Albano dimenticata* (Albano: Città di Albano Laziale, 2009)

CRI2: Alberto Crielesi, 'La famiglia Giorni ed Albano', in Francesco Giorni, *Storia di Albano* (Albano: Città di Albano Laziale, 2008)

DAV1: *The Collected Letters of Sir Humphry Davy*, Vol. 1, ed. Tim Fulford and Sharon Ruston (Oxford, New York: Oxford University Press, 2020)

DAV4: *The Collected Letters of Sir Humphry Davy*, Vol. 4, ed. Tim Fulford and Sharon Ruston, (Oxford, New York: Oxford University Press, 2020)

DCLC: *The Diary and Correspondence of Charles Abbot, Lord Colchester*, Vol. 3, ed. Charles Abbot, 2nd Baron Colchester (London: John Murray, 1861)

DDC: Diary of the Duke of Calabria, 'Promemorie, ovvero giornali contenenti la narrativa delle azioni del giorno, 1800–1830', Carte del re Francesco I, Archivio Borbone, Archivio di Stato di Napoli, 04401.00004

DGP1: Archivio di Stato di Roma, Direzione Generale di Polizia, Protocollo ordinario, index book No. 1717

DGP2: Archivio di Stato di Roma, Direzione Generale di Polizia, Protocollo ordinario, file register No. 48 (10th to 23rd December 1820, covering files 14000 to 14500)

DGP3: Archivio di Stato di Roma, Direzione Generale di Polizia, Titolo 7, Polizia Amministrativa, Sanità pubblica, 1820, posizione 14330, folder No. 2095

DIL: Charles Wentworth Dilke, *The Papers of a Critic*, Vol. 1 (London: John Murray, 1875)

DJM: *Diary of James Minet, 1807–1885: A Huguenot of the Fifth Generation*, ed. Susan Minet (Frome: Butler and Tanner, [1958?])

DOI: Henry Matthews, *The Diary of an Invalid* (London: John Murray, 1820)

DWI: Theodore Dwight, *A Journal of a Tour in Italy, in the Year 1821* (New York: Abraham Paul, 1824)

EB: Giancarlo Boeri, Pietro Crociani and Andrea Viotti, *L'esercito borbonico dal 1815 al 1830* (Rome: Edizione Ufficio Storico dello SME, 1995)

ECL1: Eton College Library, MS 608 02

ECL2: Eton College Library, MS 608 08

EI: James Fenimore Cooper, *Excursions in Italy*, Vol. 2 (London: Richard Bentley, 1838)

EMLR: *The European Magazine, and London Review*, Vol. 71 (May 1817)

ERA: *The Exhibition of the Royal Academy, M.DCCCXIX, The Fifty-First* (London: B. McMillan, 1819)

FAUL: Arthur Brooke Faulkner, *Letters to the Right Honourable Lord Brougham and Vaux; Presenting Rambling Details of a Tour through France, Switzerland, and Italy* (London: John Macrone, 1837)

FBB: Joanna Richardson, *Fanny Brawne: A Biography* (New York: Vanguard, 1952)

FBL: *Letters of Fanny Brawne to Fanny Keats [1820–1824]*, ed. Fred Edgcumbe (London: Oxford University Press, 1939)

FOR: Alice Ford, *John James Audubon: A Biography* (New York: Abbeville Press, 1988)

FRAN: Charles Colville Frankland, *Travels to and from Constantinople, in the Years 1827 and 1828*, Vol. 2 (London: Henry Colburn, 1829)

GAL: Jacques Augustin Galiffe, *Italy and Its Inhabitants*, Vol. 2 (London: John Murray, 1820)

GALI: *Galignani's Traveller's Guide through Italy* (Paris: Galignani, 1819)

GASP: Carlo Gasparri, 'Il Museo Torlonia: L'ultima collezione romana di sculture antiche', in *I marmi Torlonia* (Milan: Electa, 2020), catalogue of an exhibition held at Villa Caffarelli Capitoline Museums, Rome, 14th October 2020–29th June 2021

GCRDS: *Giornale Costituzionale del Regno delle Due Sicilie*

GGC: *Giornale generale del commercio*

GITT: Robert Gittings, *John Keats* (Harmondsworth: Penguin, 1979)

GMD: Sir Graham Moore: Diaries, University of Cambridge, MS Add.9303

GRDS: *Giornale del Regno delle Due Sicilie*

GREC: Nikolai Grech, *Письма с дороги по Германии, Швейцарии и Италии* ("Letters from a Journey through Germany, Switzerland and Italy"), Vol. 2 (St Petersburg: N. Grech, 1843)

GRI: Charles Macfarlane, *A Glance at Revolutionized Italy*, Vol. 1 (London: Smith, Elder, 1849)

GRJK: Nicholas Stanley-Price, *The Graves in Rome of John Keats and Percy Bysshe Shelley* (Rome: The Non-Catholic Cemetery in Rome, 2020)

GVI: Thomas Martyn, *Guide du voyageur en Italie*, Vol. 1 (Lausanne: Louis Luquiens, 1791)

GVSM: Giornale del viaggio da Venezia a Roma e a Napoli dei conti Silvio Martinengo ed Elisabetta Michel, Biblioteca Queriniana di Brescia, ms.M.III.28

HC: Tobias Smollett, *The Expedition of Humphry Clinker* (New York: Harper, 1836)

HERM: Victor-Joseph Étienne de Jouy, *L'Hermite en Italie, ou Observations sur les mœurs et les usages des Italiens au commencement du XIXe siecle*, Vol. 3 (Paris: Pillet Ainé, 1824)

HOL: James Holman, *The Narrative of a Journey, Undertaken in the Years 1819, 1820, & 1821* (London: F.C. and J. Rivington, 1822)

HPL: Artaud de Montor, *Histoire du Pape Léon XII*, Vol. 1 (Paris: Adrien Le Clere et C, 1843)

HT43: *A Handbook for Travellers in Central Italy* (London: John Murray, 1843)

HT53: *A Handbook for Travellers in Central Italy*, Part Two (London: John Murray, 1853)

IAN: Vittorio Iandelli, 'Biografia del cav. dott. Domenico Morichini professore di chimica nella università romana', *Giornale arcadico di scienze, lettere ed arti*, Vol. 73 (1837), pp. 248–70

IDTC5: Mariana Starke, *Information and Directions for Travellers on the Continent*, 5th Edn (London: John Murray, 1824)

IDTC6: Mariana Starke, *Information and Directions for Travellers on the Continent*, 6th Edn (London: John Murray, 1828)

IML: Joseph Severn, 'Incidents of My Life' (begun on 18th January 1857), Houghton Library, Harvard University, MS Keats 1434, Box 4: 493. A partial transcript of IML has been published in JSLM, pp. 577–606.

IPP: Antonio Menniti Ippolito, *Il Cimitero acattolico di Roma: La presenza protestante nella città del papa* (Rome: Viella, 2014)

IPRN1: Andrea de Jorio, *Indicazione del più rimarcabile in Napoli e contorni* (Naples: Tipografia Simoniana, 1819)

IPRN2: Andrea de Jorio, *Indicazione del più rimarcabile in Napoli e contorni*, New Edn (Naples: Fibreno, 1835)

ITA: Lady Morgan, *Italy*, Vol. 3 (London: Henry Colburn, 1821)

JCLA: James Clark, *Medical Notes on Climate, Diseases, Hospitals, and Medical Schools, in France, Italy, and Switzerland* (London: T. and G. Underwood, 1820)

JGD: *The John Goddard Collection*, catalogue of auction held at Dix Noonan Webb, London, 24th September 2015. Available at https://www.dnw.co.uk/media/auction_catalogues/Medals%20Goddard%2024%20Nov%2015.pdf

JOUS: M.J. Jousiffe, *A Road-Book for Travellers in Italy* (Brussels: Meline, Cans, 1840)

JSB: Sue Brown, *Joseph Severn, A Life: The Rewards of Friendship* (New York: Oxford University Press, 2009)

JSLM: *Joseph Severn: Letters and Memoirs*, ed. Grant F. Scott (Aldershot: Ashgate, 2005)

KC1: Hyder Edward Rollins, ed., *The Keats Circle*, 2nd Edn, Vol. 1 (Cambridge, MA: Harvard University Press, 1965)

KC2: Hyder Edward Rollins, ed., *The Keats Circle*, 2nd Edn, Vol. 2 (Cambridge, MA: Harvard University Press, 1965)

KNI: Cornelia Knight, *A Description of Latium, or La Campagna di Roma* (London: Longman, Hurst, Rees and Orme, 1805).

KOTZ: August von Kotzebue, *Travels through Italy, in the Years 1804 and 1805*, Vol. 1 (London: Richard Phillips, 1806)

KP: Edmund Blunden, *Keats's Publisher: A Memoir of John Taylor* (London: Jonathan Cape, 1936)

KSMB: *Bulletin and Review of the Keats-Shelley Memorial*, No. 2 (London: Macmillan, 1913)

LAM: *Lamia, Isabella, the Eve of St Agnes and Other Poems* (London: Taylor and Hessey, 1820)

LBP: Henry C. Shelley, *Literary By-Paths in Old England* (Boston: Little, Brown, 1906)

LEBR: Charles Macfarlane, *The Lives and Exploits of Banditti and Robbers in All Parts of the World*, Vol. 1 (London: Edward Bull, 1833)

LEO: Mario R. Storchi, *La vita di Giacomo Leopardi attraverso il suo epistolario integrale*, Vol. 6 (Napoli: Edizioni Manna, 2021)

LGG: Daniel Griffin, *Life of Gerald Griffin Esq.* (Edinburgh: Simpkin and Marshall, 1843)

LJK: *The Letters of John Keats*, ed. Maurice Buxton Forman (Oxford: Oxford University Press, 1935)

LLJS: William Sharp, *The Life and Letters of Joseph Severn* (London: Sampson Low, Marston & Company, 1892)

LLMM: Thomas Wemyss Reid, *The Life, Letters, and Friendships of Richard Monckton Milnes*, Vol. 1 (London, Paris and Melbourne: Cassell, 1890)

LLWS1: William F. Halloran, ed., *The Life and Letters of William Sharp and "Fiona Macleod"*, Vol. 1, *1855–1894* (Cambridge: Open Book Publishers, 2018)

LLWS2: William F. Halloran, ed., *The Life and Letters of William Sharp and "Fiona Macleod"*, Vol. 2, *1895–1899* (Cambridge: Open Book Publishers, 2020)

LNC: Augustus Phillimore, *The Last of Nelson's Captains* (London: Harrison, 1891)

LOW: Amy Lowell, *John Keats*, Vol. 2 (London: Jonathan Cape, 1925)

LRJC: J.L. Cherry, ed., *Life and Remains of John Clare* (London: Frederick Warne & Co.; Northampton: J. Taylor & Son, 1873)

LW: *Laurie and Whittle's New Sailing Directions for the Mediterranean Sea* (London: Robert Laurie and James Whittle, 1811)

MAAL1: Richard Robert Madden, *The Literary Life and Correspondence of the Countess of Blessington*, Vol. 1 (New York: Harper & Brothers, 1855)

MAEL2: Richard Robert Madden, *The Literary Life and Correspondence of the Countess of Blessington*, Vol. 2 (London: T.C. Newby, 1855)

MAM: Richard Robert Madden, *The Memoirs (Chiefly Autobiographical) from 1798 to 1886 of Richard Robert Madden* (London: Ward & Downey, 1891)

MAYN: *The Journal of John Mayne during a Tour on the Continent upon Its Reopening after the Fall of Napoleon, 1814*, ed. John Mayne Colles (London: John Lane, The Bodley Head, 1909)

MHC: Anonymous, *Mementoes, Historical and Classical, of a Tour through Part of France, Switzerland, and Italy, in the Years 1821 and 1822*, Vol. 2 (London: Baldwin, Cradock, and Joy, 1824)

MLP: Hyder Edward Rollins, ed., *More Letters and Poems of the Keats Circle* (Cambridge, MA: Harvard University Press, 1965)

MO: François-René de Chateaubriand, *Mémoires d'Outre-Tombe* (Paris: Librairie générale française, 1999)

MON: *Life, Letters and Literary Remains of John Keats*, Vol. 2, ed. Richard Monckton Milnes (London: Edward Moxon, 1848)

MOR: Domenico Morichini, *Notizie sopra le due acidule adoperate in Roma* (Rome: Francesco Bourliè, 1818)

MOT: Andrew Motion, *Keats* (London: Faber, 1998)

MRN: Alessandro Antonelli, *Memorie del Regno di Napoli* (Aquila: Tipografia Aternina, 1848)

MSJ: *The Journals of Mary Shelley, 1814–1844*, Vol. 1, *1814–1822*, ed. Diana Scott-Kilvert and Paula R. Feldman (Oxford: Oxford University Press, 1987)

MTL: Joseph Severn, 'My Tedious Life' (begun in September 1873), Houghton Library, Harvard University, MS Keats 4.16.4. A transcript of MTL has been published in JSLM, pp. 623–64.

MTU1: *A Memoir of Thomas Uwins, R.A.*, Vol. 1, ed. Sarah Uwins (née Kirby) (London: Longman, Brown, Green, Longmans, & Roberts, 1858)

MTU2: *A Memoir of Thomas Uwins, R.A.*, Vol. 2, ed. Sarah Uwins (née Kirby) (London: Longman, Brown, Green, Longmans, & Roberts, 1858)

MUN: Ion S. Munro, 'The British Academy of Arts in Rome', *Journal of the Royal Society of Arts*, Vol. 102, No. 4914 (11th December 1953)

MVI: Anonymous, *Manuel du voyageur en Italie* (Milan: Jean Pierre Giegler, 1818)

NC: *The Naval Chronicle for 1813*, Vol. 30 (London: Joyce Gold, 1813)

NLBS: *New Letters from Charles Brown to Joseph Severn*, ed. Grant F. Scott and Sue Brown (Boulder, CO: Romantic Circles, 2010). Rev. ed. 2024

NMM: *The New Monthly Magazine*, Vol. 11 (London: Henry Colburn, November 1824)

NNE: Anonymous, *Notes on Naples and Its Environs* (London: James Bohn, 1838; serialized in the *Metropolitan Magazine*, Vol. 20, September–December 1837)

OAKF: Joseph Severn, 'On the Adversities of Keats's Fame' (written before April 1863), Houghton Library, Harvard University, MS Keats 4.16.2. This short memoir is a preliminary draft of 'On the Vicissitudes of Keats's Fame', published in the *Atlantic Monthly*, Vol. 11, No. 66 (April 1863), pp. 401–7. A transcript of OAKF has been published in JSLM, pp. 607–22.

OSS: James Macpherson, *The Poems of Ossian*, ed. William Sharp (Edinburgh: Patrick Geddes, 1896)

PBSL: *The Letters of Percy Bysshe Shelley*, Vol. 2, *Shelley in Italy*, ed. Frederick L. Jones, (Oxford: Oxford University Press, 1964)

PCSR: Charles MacFarlane, *Popular Customs, Sports and Recollections of the South of Italy* (London: Charles Knight, 1846)

PEN: Revd Thomas Pennington, *A Journey into Various Parts of Europe*, Vol. 1 (London: G.B. Whittaker, 1825)

PEP1: Guglielmo Pepe, *Memorie del Generale Guglielmo Pepe intorno alla sua vita e ai recenti casi d'Italia*, Vol. 1 (Paris: Baudry, 1847)

PEP2: Guglielmo Pepe, *Memorie del Generale Guglielmo Pepe intorno alla sua vita e ai recenti casi d'Italia*, Vol. 2 (Paris: Baudry, 1847)

PLDA: *Public Ledger and Daily Advertiser* (London)

PMJ: *The Philosophical Magazine and Journal* (London: R. and A. Taylor)

PTFI: George Hume Weatherhead, *A Pedestrian Tour through France and Italy* (London: Simpkin and Marshall, 1834)

QUA: Gabriele Quattromani, *Itinerario delle Due Sicilie* (Napoli: Reale Tipografia della Guerra, 1827)

RAC1: *Raccolta degli scritti editi ed inediti del dott. Domenico Morichini*, Vol. 1 (Rome: Giovanni Resnati, 1852)

RAC2: *Raccolta degli scritti editi ed inediti del dott. Domenico Morichini*, Vol. 2 (Rome: Giovanni Resnati, 1852)

SOURCES

RBPP: William Sharp, *Romantic Ballads and Poems of Phantasy*, 2nd Edn (London: Walter Scott, 1889)

REM1: Joseph Forsyth, *Remarks on Antiquities, Arts, and Letters during an Excursion in Italy in the Years 1802 and 1803* (London: T. Cadell and W. Davies, 1813)

REM2: Joseph Forsyth, *Remarks on Antiquities, Arts, and Letters during an Excursion in Italy in the Years 1802 and 1803* (with a biographical note by Isaac Forsyth), 2nd Edn (London: John Murray, 1816)

RLL: Charles Macfarlane, *Reminiscences of a Literary Life* (New York: Charles Scribner's Sons, 1917)

ROE: Nicholas Roe, *John Keats: A New Life* (New Haven and London: Yale University Press, 2013)

ROL1: *The Letters of John Keats*, Vol. 1, ed. Hyder Edward Rollins (Cambridge: Cambridge University Press, 1958)

ROL2: *The Letters of John Keats*, Vol. 2, ed. Hyder Edward Rollins (Cambridge: Cambridge University Press, 1958)

RS: *Regolamenti sanitarii per lo Regno delle Due Sicilie sanzionati da Sua Maestà in conseguenza della legge de' 20. ottobre 1819* (Naples: Stamperia Cataneo e De Bonis, 1820)

SALM: Frank Salmon, '"Storming the Campo Vaccino": British Architects and the Antique Buildings of Rome', *Architectural History*, Vol. 38 (1995), pp. 146–175

SC1: Archivio di Stato di Roma, Sacra Consulta (Inventario No. 163), Sanità, Igiene generale, folder No. 26 (1820)

SCT: Amelia Lenormant, *Souvenirs et correspondance tirés des papiers de Madame Récamier*, Vol. 1 (Paris: J. Claye, 1860)

SEL1: Selina Martin, *Narrative of a Three Years' Residence in Italy, 1819–1822*, 1st Edn (London: John Murray, 1828)

SEL2: Selina Martin, *Narrative of a Three Years' Residence in Italy, 1819–1822*, 2nd Edn (Dublin: W.F. Wakeman, 1831)

SEV: 'Keats in Rome', with a mutilated list of the books Severn and Keats had with them in Rome, Houghton Library, Harvard University, MS Eng 1460

SHA: Elizabeth Sharp, *William Sharp (Fiona Macleod): A Memoir* (New York: Duffield, 1910)

SHER: Moyle Sherer, *Scenes and Impressions in Egypt and in Italy* (London: Longman, Hurst, Rees, Orme, Brown, and Green, 1825)

SIM: Louis Simond, *A Tour in Italy and Sicily* (London: Longman, Rees, Orme, Brown, and Green, 1828)

SOSC: Albert A. Gore, *The Story of Our Services under the Crown: A Historical Sketch of the Army Medical Staff* (London: Baillière, Tindall and Cox, 1879)

SPL: Artaud de Montor, *Storia del pontefice Leone XII*, Vol. 1 (Milan: Giovanni Resnati, 1843)

STIL: *The Letters of Charles Armitage Brown*, ed. Jack Stillinger (Cambridge, MA: Harvard University Press, 1966)

TC: Mariana Starke, *Travels on the Continent* (London: John Murray, 1820)

TD: Vere Foster, ed., *The Two Duchesses* (London: Blackie, 1898)

TE: Mariana Starke, *Travels in Europe between the Years 1824 and 1828*, Vol. 2 (Leghorn: Glaucus Masi, 1828)

TEN: Michele Tenore, *Viaggio per le diverse parti d'Italia, Svizzera, Francia, Inghilterra e Germania*, 2nd Edn, Vol. 1 (1832), an account of a journey through Italy and Europe made in 1824

TEUT8: Mariana Starke, *Travels in Europe for the Use of Travellers on the Continent*, 8th Edn (London: John Murray, 1833)

TEUT9: Mariana Starke, *Travels in Europe for the Use of Travellers on the Continent*, 9th Edn (Paris: A. and W. Galignani, 1836)

TI: Mariana Starke, *Travels in Italy, between the Years 1792 and 1798*, Vol. 2 (London: Richard Phillips, 1802)

TJIS: William Thomson, *Two Journeys through Italy and Switzerland* (London: John Macrone, 1835)

TPC: James Clark, *A Treatise on Pulmonary Consumption* (Philadelphia: Carey, Lea, and Blanchard, 1835)

TSC: Carlo Marinelli Roscioni, *Il teatro di San Carlo. La cronologia 1737–1987*, Vol. 1 (Napoli: Guida, 1987)

TSI: Anonymous, *Travels in Southern Italy* (Dublin: P.D. Hardy, 1825)

VADR: Antonio Nibby, *Viaggio antiquario ne' contorni di Roma*, Vol. 2 (Rome: Vincenzo Poggioli, 1819)

VAL: *Itinerario italiano* (Milan: Pietro e Giuseppe Vallardi, 1815)

VAS: Mariano Vasi, *Itinerario istruttivo da Roma a Napoli* (Rome: Vasi, 1819)

VDPR: Jørgen Birkedal Hartmann, *La vicenda di una dimora principesca romana* (Rome: Fratelli Palombi, 1967)

VG: Francesco Tiroli, *La vera guida per chi viaggia in Italia* (Rome: Paolo Giunchi, 1775)

VIS: Pier Paolo Visentin, 'Domenico Morichini: Medico e chimico romano del primo '800', *Atti e Memorie della Accademia di Storia dell'Arte Sanitaria*, No. 2, pp. 23–36

VPRN: Luigi Rossini, *Viaggio pittoresco da Roma a Napoli: colle principali vedute di ambedue le città, delle campagne, e dei paesi frapposti* (Rome: Presso l'autore, [1839])

WARD: Aileen Ward, *John Keats: The Making of a Poet*, Rev. Edn (New York: Farrar, Straus and Giroux, 1986)

Notes

PREFACE

1   The source of the quotation is Keats's letter of 30th November 1820 to Charles Brown, ROL2, p. 359.
2   ROE, p. 378; MOT, p. 537.
3   ROE, p. 378; WARD, p. 374.
4   ROE, p. 385.
5   Letter of 22nd October 1820 (dated 24th October by Keats) to Mrs Frances Brawne, ROL2, p. 349.
6   Letter of 30th November 1820, ROL2, pp. 359–60.
7   Keats's letter of 1st November 1820 to Charles Brown, ROL2, p. 352.
8   In MTL (fo. 20^r), Severn recalls: "At times in his suffering he still retained that elasticity ^{of} mind & spirit which was the characteristic of both the man & the poet", and in OAKF (JSLM, p. 611) he wrote: "[H]e retained that lively, undying spirit to the last. Nothing seemed to dim or diminish it, no suffering could disturb the vivacity of his large, sparkling hazle eyes, speculative & generous even in his last moments."

BEFORE THE DEPARTURE

1   Letter of 10th November 1819, ROL2, p. 227.
2   For the "battery" analogy, see Keats's letters to John Taylor (13th August 1820, ROL2, p. 315) and to Percy Bysshe Shelley (16th August 1820, ROL2, p. 322).
3   ROL2, p. 351. In a note to his transcript of this letter, Brown suggests that Keats may have intended to write "quit". Recent critics have proposed "quiff", a slang word for the sexual act.
4   Letter of 30th November 1820 to Charles Brown, ROL2, p. 360.
5   Letter of 6th August 1818 to Ann Wylie, ROL1, p. 358.
6   Letter of 31st May 1819 to Marianne Jeffery, ROL2, p. 113. Rollins mistakenly names the recipient of this letter as Marianne's sister Sarah.
7   Ibid.

8   John Taylor's letter of 19th February 1821 to Michael Drury, KC1, p. 217.

9   For the £700, see George Keats's letter of 10th April 1824 to Charles Wentworth Dilke, KC1, p. 278.

10 For his plan to combine medicine and law, see Keats's letter of 3rd May 1818 to John Hamilton Reynolds, ROL1, p. 277. For Edinburgh, see letter of 14th February 1819 to George and Georgiana Keats, ROL2, p. 70. For the apothecary position, see letter of 17th June 1819 to Fanny Keats, ROL2, p. 121. See also letter of June 1820 to Charles Brown, ROL2, p. 298. For Westminster, see letter of 14th February 1819 to George and Georgiana Keats, ROL2, p. 84. See also letter of 22nd September 1819 to Charles Brown: "I will write, on the liberal side of the question, for whoever will pay me. [...] I purpose living in town in a cheap lodging, and endeavouring, for a beginning, to get the theatricals of some paper" (ROL2, p. 176). For the idea of working as a tea broker, see letter of 20th December 1819 to Fanny Keats, ROL2, p. 237. For the idea of becoming a ship's surgeon, see letter of 31st May 1819 to Marianne Jeffery, ROL2, p. 113.

11 Letter of 9th April 1818 to John Hamilton Reynolds, ROL1, p. 268. See also his letter of 22nd December 1818 to Benjamin Haydon: "I have a little money which may enable me to study and travel three or four years—" (ROL1, p. 415), or his letter of 13th January 1820 to Georgiana Keats: "I wish I had money enough to do nothing but travel about for years—" (ROL2, p. 244).

12 The quotation is from Keats's letter of 5th August 1819 to Fanny Brawne, ROL2, p. 138. For the suggestion regarding emigration, see letter of August [?] 1820, ROL2, p. 312.

13 For the quotations "in nubibus" and "shower", see Keats's undated 'Testament' (plates, 1a), enclosed in his letter of 14th August 1820 to John Taylor, which ends: "My Chest of Books divide among my friends—" (ROL2, p. 319) – perhaps, if the iambic pentameter is intentional, the last line of poetry he ever wrote.

14 CLA, p. 140.

15 See John Barnard's essay 'First Fruits or "First Blights": A New Account of the Publishing History of Keats's *Poems* (1817)', *Romanticism*, Vol. 2, No. 2 (July 2006), p. 79. The actual print run of *Poems* is unknown.

16 EMLR, p. 435.

17 CLA, p. 140. See also Mathew's above-mentioned review of *Poems*: "This fragment ['Calidore'] is as pretty and as innocent as childishness can make it, save that it savours too much,—as

indeed do almost all these poems,—of the foppery and affectation of Leigh Hunt!" (pp. 435–36).

18 The full letter is printed in *The Athenæum*, 7th June 1873, p. 725.

19 See Charles E. Robinson, 'Percy Bysshe Shelley, Charles Ollier, and William Blackwood: The Contexts of Early Nineteenth-Century Publishing', in Kelvin Everest, ed., *Shelley Revalued: Essays from the Gregynog Conference* (Leicester: Leicester University Press, 1983), p. 188.

20 The quotation is from a letter, now lost, to his brother George in the spring of 1817, cited in a letter of 8th October 1817 to Benjamin Bailey (ROL1, p. 170).

21 Keats's total advance for *Endymion* was £100. See John Taylor's letter of 19th February 1821 to Michael Drury, KC1, p. 218.

22 Letter of 9th April 1818, ROL1, pp. 266–67.

23 Reproduced in Keats's *Complete Poems*, ed. John Barnard (London: Penguin, 2006), pp. 506–7.

24 Letter of 9th April 1818 to John Hamilton Reynolds, ROL1, p. 266.

25 Quoted from the first edition of *Endymion* (1818).

26 Letter of 9th April 1818 to John Hamilton Reynolds, ROL1, p. 266.

27 *Blackwood's*, Vol. 3, No. 14 (May 1818); Vol. 3, No. 17 (August 1818).

28 *The Quarterly Review*, Vol. 19, No. 37 (April 1818), pp. 204–8. For the September publication date, see Richard Woodhouse, 'Notes on the Critiques on *Endymion* in the *Quarterly Review* and *Blackwood's Edinburgh Magazine*' (October 1818), in KC1, p. 44.

29 Letter of 8th October 1818, ROL1, p. 374. The Scottish journalist John Scott (1784–1821), in a letter to the editor published in the *Morning Chronicle* of 3rd October 1818, while defending Keats's poem, had found in it "many, very many passages indicating haste and carelessness".

30 Letter of 14th October 1818 to George and Georgiana Keats, ROL1, p. 394.

31 For the loss of £130, see John's Taylor's letter of 19th February 1821 to Michael Drury, KC1, p. 218. This loss was reduced to £110 at the time of Keats's death (see Taylor and Hessey's letter of 17th February 1821 to George Keats, KC1, p. 215).

32 See *Don Juan* xi, lx.

33 Letter of 8th October 1818 to James Augustus Hessey, ROL1, p. 374.

34 Ibid.

35 Letter of 14th October 1818 to George and Georgiana Keats, ROL1, p. 394.

36 Letter of 16th August 1820 to Percy Bysshe Shelley, ROL2, p. 322. The quotation "little book of verses" is from the unpublished preface to *Endymion* (see note 23 above).

37 Letter of 22nd September 1819, ROL2, p. 167.

38 Letter of 21st September 1819, ROL2, p. 174. The word "It" at the beginning of this extract is written "I it". By "smokeable" Keats means "mockable".

39 Letter of 14th August 1819 to Benjamin Bailey, ROL2, p. 139. The reference is to the famous Shakespearean actor Edmund Kean (1787–1833).

40 Letter of 23rd August 1819 to John Taylor, ROL2, p. 144.

41 Letter of 10th May 1817 to Leigh Hunt, ROL1, p. 139 (for Hamlet's soliloquy, see *Hamlet*, Act III, Sc. 1, l. 78).

42 Ibid.

43 Lines 96–98.

44 Letter of 10th May 1817 to Leigh Hunt, ROL1, p. 139.

45 Letter of 30th November 1820, ROL2, p. 359.

46 The quotation "never wrote […]" is from Keats's letter of 9th April 1818 to John Hamilton Reynolds, ROL1, p. 267.

47 'Ode to a Nightingale': Vol. 4, No. 13 (July 1819); 'Ode on a Grecian Urn': Vol. 4, No. 14 (January 1820).

48 Letter of 13th January 1820 to Georgiana Keats, ROL2, p. 243. For Shelley's opinion of Keats's shorter poems included in LAM, see PBSL, pp. 244, 268.

49 *Hamlet*, Act II, Sc. 2, ll. 439–40. 'La Belle Dame sans Merci' appeared in *The Indicator* of 10th May 1820.

50 Letter of 16th August 1820, ROL2, p. 323. See also letter of 17th November 1819 to John Taylor: "I have come to a determination not to publish any thing I have now ready written; but for all that to publish a Poem before long and that I hope to make a fine one" (ROL2, p. 234). The collection in question was LAM.

51 Letter of 23rd August 1819, ROL2, p. 144.

52 Letter of 14th August 1819 to Benjamin Bailey, ROL2, p. 139.

53 Letter of 23rd August 1819 to John Taylor, ROL2, p. 143. Fanny Brawne later wrote: "Mr Brown calculated [Keats's] share [of the tragedy] would be about two hundred pounds" (letter of 23rd May 1821 to Fanny Keats, FBL, p. 26), having "stipulated for half the profits" (Charles Wentworth Dilke's letter of April [?] 1841 to Joseph Severn, KC2, p. 105).

54 Letter of 17th September 1819 to George and Georgiana Keats, ROL2, p. 185.

55 Ibid.

56 See Taylor and Hessey's letter of 17th February 1821 to George Keats: "The only chance for his life according to the opinion of his physician Dr Darling consisted in his immediate departure from this Country" (KC1, p. 214). George Darling (c.1782–1862) was John Taylor's personal physician. Among his other patients were William Hazlitt, John Clare, Benjamin Haydon and Sir Thomas Lawrence.

57 JCLA, p. 116.

58 See letter of 14th August 1820 to Charles Brown: "I have resolved to go to Italy, either by sea or land. Not that I have any great hopes of that,—for, I think, there is a core of disease in me not easy to pull out" (ROL2, p. 321).

59 For the plan to travel to Rome, see John Taylor's letter of 14th August 1820 to John Clare: "Keats, you know, broke a blood-vessel, and has been very ill. He is now recovering, and it is necessary for his getting through the winter that he should go to Italy. Rome is the place recommended" – quoted in LRJC, pp. 41–42.

For his plan to spend a year in Italy, see letter of 13th August 1820 to John Taylor, ROL2, p. 315. The quotation "promise[d] [...]" is from letter of 18th [?] August 1820 to Charles Brown, ROL2, p. 327.

60 Information from familysearch.org. The marriage ceremony was held at St Cuthbert's Church.

61 He was there on 17th August 1820, to be "admitted an Extra-Licentiate of the College of Physicians" – see William Munk, *The Roll of the Royal College of Physicians of London*, Vol. 3, 1801 to 1825, 2nd ed., p. 224 (London: The Royal College of Physicians, 1878).

62 The book was reviewed in the July 1820 issue of *The Edinburgh Medical and Surgical Journal*, Vol. 16 (April, July, October 1820), pp. 428–36.

63 In their letter of 17th February 1821 to George Keats, Taylor and Hessey wrote that Keats was in Rome "under the care of a very eminent English Physician to whom providentially we were able personally to recommend him" (KC1, p. 214). In his letter of 5th May 1848 to Richard Monckton Milnes, Severn wrote: "Keats had a letter of introduction to him [Doctor James Clark] [...] I cannot remember who from" (KC2, p. 232).

64 Letter of 27th July 1820, received by Keats on 12th August 1820, ROL2, pp. 310–11.

65 Letter of 14th August 1820, ROL2, p. 318.

66 Letter of 16th August 1820, ROL2, p. 322.

67 There were at least three brigs leaving for Genoa and Leghorn from London around the same time as the *Maria Crowther*: the *Albion* (PLDA, 25th August; 1st, 8th, 13th September 1820), the *Harmony* (PLDA, 22nd, 25th August; 1st, 5th, 12th, 15th September 1820) and the *Felicity* (PLDA, 22nd August; 5th, 8th September 1820).

68 Letter of 11th September 1820, ROL2, p. 332, which echoes Shelley's words to Keats in his letter of 27th July 1820: "[T]he sea air is particularly good for weak lungs" (PBSL, p. 221).

69 *The Examiner*, Vol. 13 (1820), reproduced in Yasuo Deguchi, ed., *The Examiner 1818–1822* (London: Pickering & Chatto, 1998), p. 610.

70 Letter of 11th September 1820, ROL2, p. 332.

71 See, for example, another contemporary account of a voyage from London to Naples on a trader: "Dr. Mortimer had recommended the long voyage, not only as much less fatiguing, and less expensive, but also as useful to Charles's health, there being many instances in which the sea has been found beneficial to persons inclined to consumption" (TSI, p. 9).

72 For Miln and the quotation "Milne, the pleasant Scot [...]", see MAM, p. 55 (see also MAEL2, p. 122). In MAAL1, p. 400, he is described by Madden, himself a doctor, as "Dr. Milne, the skillful Scot and accomplished gentleman of the Chiatamone". The Chiatamone is a street in the Borgo Santa Lucia. In Keats's time, it ran along the shoreline and, together with Chiaia and Strada S. Lucia, boasted some of the most luxurious hotels for foreigners.

For the poet, philosopher and scholar Sir William Drummond of Logiealmond (1769–1828), who served twice as envoy to the Court of Naples, see MAAL1, pp. 385–88. For the classical archaeologist, illustrator and socialite Sir William Gell (1777–1836), see MAAL1, pp. 322–84. The Irish novelist and literary hostess Marguerite Gardiner, Countess of Blessington (1789–1849) was a pivotal figure in the British expatriate community in Naples.

73 The tapeworm article appeared in *Medico-Chirurgical Review*, Vol. 3, No. 6 (1st October 1825), pp. 574–75. The review appeared in the same journal, Vol. 1, No. 3 (1st December 1820), pp. 396–99. The footnote is on p. 398. Carter's essay was originally published in *Medical Transactions, Published by the College of Physicians in London*, Vol. 6 (1820), pp. 54–91. "Miln, Dr. Res. Phys. Naples" is also listed as one of the *Medico-Chirurgical Review*'s subscribers in Vol. 1, No. 4 (1st March 1821), p. 798.

74 *Dissertatio medica inauguralis, de apoplexia sanguinea* (Edinburgh: J. Moir, 1814).

75 Wellcome Library, EPB/B/36842: "To Her Grace, / The Duchess of Devonshire, with every sentiment of respect, and with sincerest thanks for Her distinguished protection and friendship, from her faithful Servant, The Author. / Rome 30.ᵗʰ November / 1817—" Elizabeth, Duchess of Devonshire (1758–1824), a long-time friend of Sir Thomas Lawrence, had settled in Rome in January 1816. She acted there as a patron of the arts, and Canova – who was *principe perpetuo* of the Academy of St Luke – was a frequent visitor to her salon. See her letters from Rome in TD, p. 411 *ff*.

76 Letter of 1st March [1817], Biblioteca Civica di Bassano del Grappa, Epistolario Canova, V.550.3597. Lawrence goes on to express his apologies that he, Flaxman and Fuseli had not yet thanked Canova for making them members of the Academy of St Luke. Canova had sent them an official declaration of their election in November 1816 – see CELF, p. 425.

77 Among other people of note – for the most part artists – introduced by Lawrence to Canova in those years are Richard Westmacott, jun., Joseph Severn, Henry Wyatt and J.M.W. Turner – "our finest Landscape Painter, a man of the most powerful, the most elegant and comprehensive Genius in this Art, that has been known in Europe since the Days of Claude" (Biblioteca Civica di Bassano del Grappa, Epistolario Canova, V.550.3605). These and about twenty more letters from Lawrence to Canova dating from 1816 to 1822 are held at the Biblioteca Civica di Bassano del Grappa.

78 JSLM, p. 111.

79 Letter of 1st November 1820 to William Haslam, ROL2, p. 354. I can find no evidence of Miln after 1825. The Protestant Cemetery of Florence housed the tomb of a Robert Miln who died on 25th May 1828 and was buried two days later in the presence of Revd Taylor, chaplain of the English embassy, Horace Hall and Doctor Kissock, but I have been so far unable to ascertain whether it is the same person.

80 Letter of 23rd August 1820, ROL2, p. 331. The quotation "make a purse [...]" is from Keats's letter of 18th [?] August 1820 to Charles Brown.

81 Letter of 18th June 1820, ROL2, p. 295. The naturalist John James Audubon (1785–1851) had persuaded George to invest in his steamboat, the *Henderson*, plying the Ohio and Mississippi commercial routes. The boat, however, had already been sold by Audubon's brother-in-law, Thomas Bakewell, and the new owner – who had not paid for it – had disappeared down the Ohio River

and surrendered the craft to prior claimants. George appears to have been swindled out of his capital by Audubon and Bakewell, who, crushed by debt, were trying to fend off their creditors. For a full account and the background of this intricate affair, see FOR, pp. 100–8. I assume that George is referring to the *Henderson* and not another boat when writing to Keats in June 1820.

82   John Taylor's letter of 19th February 1821 to Michael Drury, KC1, p. 218. It is not clear who might have written to George. Charles Brown was in Scotland at the time, but on his return to England he told Haslam he was waiting for an important letter from George Keats. See Brown's letter of 30th September 1820 to William Haslam, KC1, p. 159.

83   Letter of 8th November 1820, ROL2, p. 356.

84   Keats's efforts to have loans repaid to him by Haydon and others appear to have been fruitless, except for £30 or £40 returned by Haslam in September 1819 (letter of 5th September 1819 to James Augustus Hessey, ROL2, p. 154 and note 2), perhaps money he had borrowed from George Keats.

85   See John Taylor's letter of 19th February 1821 to Michael Drury, KC1, p. 218.

86   For the debt to his publishers, see ibid. For the debt to Brown, see Brown's letter of 2nd May 1826 to Charles Wentworth Dilke, STIL, pp. 250–51. For the debts to the doctor and tailor, see Keats's 'Testament', ROL2, p. 319 and note 8. Keats's doctor was George Ramsay Rodd, who had looked after him before the spring of 1820.

87   'Assignment of Copyright by Keats', 16th September 1820, ROL2, pp. 334–37.

88   John Taylor's letter of 19th February 1821 to Michael Drury, KC1, p. 218.

89   Ibid.

90   MAM, pp. 19–20.

91   He moved to 2 Wesleyan Place, Kentish Town, on 4th May 1820; to Mortimer Terrace with the Hunts on 23rd June; and to Wentworth Place (the Dilkes' half) with the Brawnes on 12th August.

92   The two letters in question were written on 14th and 18th [?] August 1820. The second letter is dated on the basis of Brown's assertion that it was composed "a few days after" the previous one (KC2, p. 77). "A few days ago," Keats wrote on 23rd August 1820 to his sister Fanny, "I wrote to Mr Brown, asking him to befriend me with his company to Rome" (ROL2, p. 329). On the same day he wrote to Haslam: "I have written to Brown to ask

him to accompany me" (ROL2, p. 330). He seems to be referring in both instances to the second letter.

93 His 'Life of John Keats' is reproduced in KC2, pp. 52–97.

94 Letter of 14th August 1820, KC2, p. 78.

95 Letter of 18th [?] August 1820, KC2, pp. 78–79. The "secret" is in all probability his engagement to Fanny Brawne.

96 His smack passed the *Maria Crowther* at Gravesend, where the two vessels were moored for the night (KC2, p. 79). For Brown's claim regarding receipt of the letters on 9th September, see KC2, p. 77.

97 For Brown's protestations and the quotation "very early in the spring", see KC2, p. 80. In the afternoon of 18th September 1820, Fanny Brawne wrote to Fanny Keats that "in a very few weeks Mr Brown, who you probably know by name will follow him" (FBL, p. 2). I am not sure whether this came from Brown's own lips (Fanny might have been able to talk to him by then, as he arrived in London early on the morning she was writing), or whether this was what Keats was expecting of his friend. Brown did leave England with his son Carlino and lived in Rome for around twelve years, sharing accommodation with Severn from October 1823 to March 1824, but according to Dilke (ROL2, p. 329, note 3) he did not start for Italy until July or August 1822, fifteen or sixteen months after Keats's death.

For Brown's circumstances, see his letter of 21st December 1820 to John Keats: "I must tell you Abby is living with me again, but not in the same capacity,—she keeps to her own bed, & I keep myself continent. Any more nonsense of the former kind would put me in an awkward predicament with her. One child is very well. She behaves extremely well, and, by what I hear from Sam [Fanny Brawne's younger brother Samuel], my arrangements prevent the affair from giving pain next door. The fact is I could not afford to allow her a seperate establishment. [...] And so you still wish me to follow you to Rome? and truly I wish to go,—nothing detains me but prudence. Little could be gained, if any thing, by letting my house at this time of the year, and the consequence would be a heavy additional expence which I cannot possibly afford,—unless it were a matter of necessity, and I see none while you are in such good hands as Severn's" (ROL2, p. 365).

98 Letter of 27th March 1821, FBL, p. 21.

99 Ibid., p. 19. In 1877 Joseph Severn wrote that on his return to England "after 20 years Artistic sojourn in Italy" Fanny Brawne "was unable to receive [him] for deep emotion—for She with her mother had felt the most painful regret that they did not follow

Keats & [him]self to Rome" (letter of 13th November 1877 to Harry Buxton Forman, JSLM, p. 553).

100 Charles Wentworth Dilke, jun. (1810–69) went on to become an eminent Whig politician, and was one of the chief promoters of the Great Exhibition of 1851, for which he received a knighthood from Queen Victoria.

101 For Keats's letter to George of March 1819, see ROL2, p. 78. Haslam's "business" was "being one of Mr Saunders executors" (letter of 17th September 1819 to George and Georgiana Keats, ROL2, p. 187). Haslam had married his fiancée Mary on 16th October 1819 (JSLM, p. 94, note 8). Their daughter was born on 28th August 1820 (familysearch.org).

102 Identical ads had been run in the PLDA of 14th and 21st July, and 8th, 15th, 18th, 22nd and 25th August 1820. It is clear from John Taylor's letter of 13th September 1820 to William Haslam (ROL2, pp. 333–34) that he was quoting from one of these adverts. The *Maria Crowther* had been at first advertised (PLDA of 30th June and 4th July) as "Want[ing] only a few Tons of Goods, and [being] under positive Engagement to Sail on or before the 6th of July". Her departure was later moved to 13th July (PLDA advert of 7th July) and then postponed until August or September.

103 Keats's passport (plates, 1b, 1c) was signed on 16th September 1820 by the envoy for the Kingdom of the Two Sicilies in Britain, Costantino Guglielmo, Count von Ludolf (1758–1839). The passport is held by the Houghton Library, Harvard University (MS Keats 7). The copyright deal was signed by Keats in the presence of Haslam and Woodhouse on 16th September 1820 (ROL2, pp. 334–36). The quotation "be ready to go by the Vessel" is from John Taylor's letter of 13th September 1820 to William Haslam (ROL2, p. 333), which confirms Keats's arrival in London on that day. The date of the poet's departure from Wentworth Place is corroborated by Fanny Brawne's letter of 18th September 1820 to Fanny Keats (FBL, p. 2). In the same letter Fanny Brawne states that "the ship waited a few days longer than we expected", so perhaps it was meant at first to sail on 15th September.

104 See PMJ, Vol. 56 (July–December 1820), p. 240. The temperatures for 13th September 1820 (taken by William Cary from his shop at 182 The Strand, which sold globes and other philosophical and mathematical instruments) were 59 °F (15 °C) at 8 o'clock in the morning, 72 °F (22 °C) at noon and 59 °F (15 °C) at 11 o'clock at night. The weather was described as "Fair".

105 Keats's lock of hair was for his sister Fanny. His fiancée already had one "that was cut off two or three years ago" (see Fanny

Brawne's letter of 6th October 1820 to Fanny Keats, FBL, p. 5).
For Fanny Brawne's lock of hair see Keats's letter of 22nd October
1820 to Mrs Frances Brawne, ROL2, p. 350. Before leaving for
Italy, Severn gifted Fanny Brawne a miniature of Keats that had
been exhibited at the Royal Academy the year before ('Portrait
of J. Keats, Esq.', ERA, p. 39, No. 940). It is a watercolour on
ivory over a pencil outline (a lock of Keats's hair cut off by Severn
on the poet's deathbed was later enclosed in its frame). In 1848
Fanny Brawne sold it to Sir Charles Dilke, the son of Keats's
friend. It was later bequeathed by Sir Charles Dilke's son to the
Fitzwilliam Museum. In later years Severn wrote: "I was just
about to write to Mr Lindon [Herbert Valentin, Fanny Brawne
Lindon's son] at the War Office, presuming that he possesses my
miniature portrait of Keats which I presented to his Mother on
my leaving for Italy with Keats" (letter of 26th September 1877
to Harry Buxton Forman, JSLM, p. 552), and described the
painting as "[t]he one I presented to Miss Brawne" (letter of 21st
February 1878 to Sir Charles Dilke, JSLM, p. 556). See also Mrs
Frances Brawne's letter of 6th February 1821 to Joseph Severn:
"Mr Taylor sent me the Miniature beautifully set for which I
return you many thanks" (ROL2, p. 374).

For the travelling cap, see Keats's letter of 1st November 1820
to Charles Brown, ROL2, p. 351. For the pocketbook and knife,
see Keats's letter of 22nd October 1820 to Mrs Frances Brawne,
ROL2, p. 350. For the cornelian, see OAKF (JSLM, p. 613).

106 "As it was for 1819," Gittings points out, "she wrote it against
8 September, the second Wednesday in September for that year"
(GITT, p. 591, note 43).

107 William Haslam's letter of 13th September 1820 to John Taylor,
ROL2, p. 333. Haslam had spent the previous night at Wentworth
Place with his friend, and had slept there. "Keats seems comfort-
able & well at ease," he added in a postscript.

108 John Taylor's letter of 13th September 1820 to William Haslam,
ROL2, p. 333.

109 In his letter of 15th April 1830 to Charles Brown, Severn writes:
"I knew Keats as far back as 1813—I was introduced to him by
Haslam—he was then studying at Guy's Hospital, yet much
inclined to the muses" (JSLM, p. 303). Keats was at Guy's from
October 1815 to July 1816, so 1813 is much too early.

110 For the visit to the British Museum, see letter of 14th February
1819 to George and Georgiana Keats, ROL2, p. 68.

111 In 1817, Keats gave Severn a copy of his *Poems* with the playful
inscription: "The Author consigns this copy to the Severn with

all his Heart." Writing in July 1820, after a copious spitting of blood had confined his friend indoors, Severn asserts to "have seen him many times—particularly previous to this accident—once since". In the same letter he says he is "delighted" with the latest volume of poems (LAM), and plans to "continue to visit Keats very much at every opportunity—perhaps twice a week—" (letter of 12th [?] July 1820 to William Haslam, JSLM, pp. 93–94).

112 "When we left England," Severn wrote in his letter of 6th October 1845 to Richard Monckton Milnes, "I certainly was not aware of Keats's being more than a common acquaintance with this Lady" (KC2, p. 130). For Brown's disclosure concerning Severn's illegitimate son, see Keats's letter of 17th September 1819 to George and Georgiana Keats, ROL2, p. 205.

113 Letter of 21st September 1820, KC1, p. 157.

114 Letter of 4th December 1820 to Fanny Keats, FBL, p. 9.

115 Letter of 22nd October 1820 to Mrs Frances Brawne, ROL2, p. 349.

116 The medal was announced at a General Assembly of the Academicians on 10th December 1819, the anniversary of the date on which the Royal Academy was founded in 1768 (General Assembly of the Academicians minutes, RA).

117 MTL, fos. 16^r–17^r. Severn's recollections are confirmed by Charles Brown, who wrote, in his 'Life of John Keats': "In my absence, while the autumn was too far advancing, a dear friend, Joseph Severn, almost at a day's warning, accompanied him" (KC2, p. 80). In all likelihood the day referred to was 13th September 1820, if the memoir's account is correct. Haslam had spent the previous evening and night at Wentworth Place. Haslam lived in Bethnal Green and worked for Frampton's and Sons at 34 Leadenhall Street; Severn lived in Goswell Street Road (today's Goswell Road). All the Severn quotations in the rest of this chapter are taken from MTL, fos. 17^r–18^r.

118 Severn's parents were James Severn (1765–1833), a music teacher, and Elizabeth Severn (née Littell, 1762–1848).

119 The addressee of the second letter of introduction has not been identified by previous Keats biographers. Born in Bonn in about 1749, Metz had studied in London at the Royal Academy Schools. Since 1801 he had been in Rome, where he worked on a huge engraving, from fifteen plates, of Michelangelo's *Last Judgement*. He was a correspondent of Sir Thomas Lawrence, and died in Rome in 1827. Severn does not appear to have made use of this contact: he does not name Metz in MTL or mention Lawrence's second letter of introduction when writing to Richard Monckton Milnes in 1848 (letter of 5th May 1848, KC2,

p. 232). The German artist acted as a cicerone to Selina Martin in Rome: "Mr. Metz was one of the first foreigners introduced to me at Rome, and is certainly a desirable acquaintance for those who wish to be instructed in all that relates to fine arts, which in fact have been the subject of his laborious research for nearly threescore years and ten" (SEL2, p. 132). See also SEL2, pp. 131 *ff.*, 164 *ff.*

120 Biblioteca Civica di Bassano del Grappa, Epistolario Canova, V.550.3595.

121 Joseph Severn's letter of 19th September 1821 to Charles Brown, JSLM, p. 173.

122 Severn's parents' home was 4 Mason's Court, "Shoreditch High Street,—at 109, about twelve doors on the L. from the church, towards Bishopsgate", according to *Lockie's Directory of London* of 1810.

123 Severn's eldest and youngest brothers were Thomas Henry Severn (1801–81) and Charles Severn (1806–94), respectively.

VOYAGE TO NAPLES

1 See PMJ, Vol. 56 (July–December 1820), p. 240. London temperatures for 17th September 1820 were 54 °F (12 °C) at 8 o'clock in the morning, 64 °F (18 °C) at noon and 52 °F (11 °C) at 11 o'clock at night. The weather was described by Cary as "Cloudy".

2 For the members of the group, see John Taylor's letter of 19th September 1820 to Fanny Keats, ROL2, p. 338. Edmund Blunden writes that Taylor "took with him an apprentice, William Smith Williams, who was to become reader for Smith, Elder & Co. and friend of the Brontës" (KP, p. 79). In her letter of 18th September 1820 to Fanny Keats, the poet's fiancée writes that "[Keats] did not sail from London till 7 o'clock yesterday morning" (FBL, p. 2). This piece of information must have been included in one of the letters she received that afternoon "from two of his friends" (perhaps Haslam and John Taylor, who the following day wrote a similar letter to Fanny Keats "by Desire of her Brother" to communicate details of his departure). Fanny Brawne may have confused the time when Keats and his friends left Fleet Street for that of the ship's sailing.

3 MTL, fo. 18^r. If we compare the London maps for 1817 (Darton), 1822 (Thompson) and 1830 (C. and J. Greenwood, based on a survey conducted in 1824–26) with *Lockie's Directory of London* for 1810 and merchantmen's departure notices and adverts in contemporary newspapers, the most prominent wharves on that

stretch of the river appear to be (downriver from London Bridge) Cotton's Wharf, Beale's Wharf and Hay's Wharf. Other wharves (downriver from London Bridge up to Pickle Herring Stairs) include Bridge Wharf, Walton's Wharf, Yoxall's Wharf, Griffin's Wharf, Gun and Shot Wharf, Stanton Wharf, Symonds Wharf, Corder's Wharf and Clouder's Wharf. There was no "Tower Dock" or "Tower Wharf" – the usual denominations used by biographers for Keats's departure point – on that side of the river at that time. "Tower-Dock, Tower Hill" was, according to *Lockie's*, "on the W. side of the Tower, also about ten houses between Tower-st. and Lower Thames-st.", on the north side of the river.

4   He and his brother "arrived in time on the southward bank of the Thames where we found dear Keats, John Taylor the Publisher[,] Charles Brown & William Haslam" (MTL, fo. 18ʳ). Severn mistakes Woodhouse (or Williams, if he was there) for Brown.

5   From the following year, the word "new" was dropped in her PLDA adverts. "The remarkably fine, fast-sailing, coppered Brig MARIA CROWTHER. Thos Walsh, Commander. Lying at Yarmouth Chain. Burthen 130 tons," read the 12th December 1821 advertisement for the ship's January 1822 voyage to Naples, Palermo and Messina. This became "The well-known fine, fast-sailing Brig MARIA CROWTHER, coppered and copper fastened.— Thomas Walsh, Commander. Lying in the London Dock" in the 25th July 1822 advert for a trip to Naples.

6   LBP, pp. 260–62.

7   Ibid., pp. 260–61.

8   PLDA, 25th July 1822.

9   Here are a few examples from other contemporary PLDA adverts. FOR LEGHORN AND GENOA: *Albion*, 123 tons; *Felicity*, about 150 tons; *Harmony*, 120 tons; *Fortune*, 130 tons; *John*, 115 tons; *John Baker*, 124 tons; *Fanny*, 109 tons; *Henry*, 135 tons; *Sprightly*, 116 tons; *Jane*, 125 tons; *Symmetry*, 136 tons; *Waterloo*, 141 tons; *New Thomas*, 144 tons; *Margaret*, 105 tons. FOR NAPLES, PALERMO AND MESSINA: *Cordelia*, 109 tons; *Robert Fuge*, 135 tons; *Prince Regent*, 115 tons; *Arno*, 111 tons; *Victoria*, 117 tons; *Active*, 89. All these ships offered both freight and passage.

10 LBP, p. 262.

11 *Derby Mercury*, 3rd December 1812.

12 *Saunders's News-Letter*, 9th August 1815. She had left Liverpool on 4th April 1815 (*Liverpool Mercury*, 7th April 1815).

13 For the Liverpool–Dublin commercial route, see *Gore's General Advertiser*, 11th July 1816, and *Saunders's News-Letter*, 31st March 1817. The *Maria Crowther* is listed in Stewart's

Gentleman's and Citizen's Almanack for 1815 (p. 3) among the "Regular Trading Ships in the Bristol, Liverpool and Holyhead Trade". For Newfoundland, see *Star* (London), 19th August 1818. She was travelling from Liverpool.

14 *Lloyd's List*, 9th February 1819. See also *Derby Mercury*, 18th February 1819.

15 PLDA, 11th May 1820 and *Lloyd's List*, 12th May 1820. About a hundred chests of oranges from the *Maria Crowther* were being offered on sale at the Bell Tavern, Lower Thames Street (PLDA, 12th and 15th May 1820).

16 For "Captain Nicholas Walsh of the Kitty of Glasgow", see *Caledonian Mercury*, 9th December 1819.

17 For the *Sir George Prevost*, see *Lloyd's List*, 28th May 1813. The *Sir George Prevost* (574 tons register) was built in Quebec in 1811 (see PLDA, 15th February 1812). For the *James & Ann*, see *Lloyd's List*, 24th February and 19th May 1815. For the *Whim*, see *Star* (London), 16th September 1816.

18 Repeated in the *Caledonian Mercury* of 12th April and *Bell's Weekly Messenger* of 13th April 1817. The *Shamrock* was a 147-ton-register brig built in 1811–12 (*Liverpool Mercury*, 13th March 1818).

19 She arrived in Malta on 23rd May 1817 (*Lloyd's List*, 4th July 1817). For the arrival in Liverpool, see *Liverpool Mercury*, 27th February 1818, where his name is given as "T. Walsh". Another Walsh is reported as the commander of the *Mercury* in late 1817 to mid-1818 (at Oporto from London: PLDA, 11th November 1817; at Gravesend from Leghorn: PLDA, 1st July 1818). The contraction "hhds" means "hogsheads". Blain and Sandar were the Liverpool merchants who owned the ship.

20 For the arrival in Genoa, see *Lloyd's List*, 11th June 1819. For Leghorn and Smyrna, see *Liverpool Mercury*, 9th July 1819, and *Lloyd's List*, 31st August 1819. For the return to Liverpool, see *Lloyd's List*, 6th November 1819.

21 For the departure date of 17th February 1820, see *Liverpool Mercury*, 25th February 1820.

22 For the first published sailing date, see 'Before the Departure', note 102.

23 MTL, fo. 18[r]. The *Maria Crowther* had obtained customs' outward clearance the day before: see *Star* (London), 18th September 1820.

24 *The Sun* (London), 16th September 1820; *Statesman*, 18th September 1820.

25 For Severn's seeing Thomas off, see Severn's letter of 21st September 1820 to William Haslam, ROL2, p. 340. For the name

of the friends accompanying Keats and Severn to Gravesend, see John Taylor's letter of 19th September 1820 to Fanny Keats, ROL2, p. 338.

26 Letter of 9th April 1837, JSLM, p. 340.

27 Joseph Severn's letter of 21st September 1820 to William Haslam, ROL2, p. 342. For Mrs Pidgeon's first name, unknown to previous biographers, see FO 610/1: "July 13 [1820], 4526, M.ʳˢ Elizabeth Pidgeon, [Where going] Naples (by sea), [By whom recommended] M.ʳ Henry Minasi (Count Ludolf's)." Henry Minasi was an engraver and a diplomat. He is listed as vice-consul for Naples in *Pigot and Co's Commercial Directory of London* for 1825–26 (p. 24), and was nominated consul-general for the king of the Two Sicilies in 1832 (*Edinburgh Gazette*, 8th May 1832). For Count von Ludolf, see 'Before the Departure', note 103. It appears that Mrs Pidgeon applied for her passport through the Neapolitan consulate. For Walsh's cat, see Joseph Severn's letter of 21st September 1820 to William Haslam, ROL2, p. 340.

28 John Taylor's letter of 19th September 1820 to Fanny Keats, ROL2, p. 338, which also mentions the ship reaching Gravesend "about noon".

29 Letter of 16th September 1820, ROL2, pp. 336–37.

30 This is now at the Morgan Library & Museum in New York (MA 214.9). It is sewn to a piece of paper with the following signed inscription by Richard Woodhouse: "A lock of the hair of John Keats, which I cut off at Gravesend on Sunday the [17th] Septʳ 1820 on board the Maria Crowther, just prior to leaving him. He was to sail for Naples for the benefit of his health on the following day—"

31 Joseph Severn's letter of 21st September 1820 to William Haslam, ROL2, pp. 340–41.

32 BNK: "I was anxious about Keats who was in a birth opposite me" (KC2, p. 137); Joseph Severn's letter of 21st September 1820 to William Haslam: "Keats assended his bed" (ROL2, p. 342).

33 The quotation "some things from the Chymists" is from Joseph Severn's letter of 21st September 1820 to William Haslam, ROL2, p. 341. "[A] little basket of medicines", Severn recollects in OAKF (JSLM, p. 613). The quotation "bottle of Opium [...]" is from Severn's letter of 25th January 1821 to John Taylor, ROL2, p. 372. Laudanum was the normal remedy for seasickness at the time.

34 Joseph Severn's letter of 21st September 1820 to William Haslam, ROL2, p. 341. The goat Walsh tried to buy was presumably for a daily supply of fresh milk.

35 MTL, fo. 18ʳ.

36 The quotations are from Joseph Severn's letter of 19th September 1820 to William Haslam, ROL2, p. 339, except the last ("a sad martyr to her illness"), which is from his letter of 21st September 1820, also to William Haslam, ROL2, p. 341. The information in the rest of this paragraph, unless stated otherwise, is taken from the second of these letters, ROL2, pp. 341–42.

37 See plates, 2a. The caricature is now at the London Metropolitan Archives (KPM/S/72), as is the watercolour (KP/PZ/02).

38 The quotation "not so well" is from Joseph Severn's letter of 19th September 1820 to William Haslam, ROL2, p. 338.

39 MTL, fo. 18^r.

40 Since her passport was registered by the Foreign Office on 18th September 1820 – see FO 610/1, 4696, where she is described as "Miss Maria Cotterell (of Southampton) [Where going] Naples (for health)" – it appears that she joined on board at the very last moment.

41 Joseph Severn's letter of 1st November 1820 to William Haslam, ROL2, p. 354. Mrs Pidgeon is here called "our other passenger".

42 For Mrs Pidgeon's request, see Joseph Severn's letter of 21st September 1820 to William Haslam, ROL2, p. 340. William Taylor, a licensed victualler, is given as the keeper (from 1820 to 1827) of the Half Moon – a very old and established inn and chop house in Leadenhall Market (round the corner from where Haslam worked, at 34 Leadenhall Street) – in several documents, newspaper articles and directories of the time. As a reference for her passport application, Miss Cotterell didn't give her father's name, but "Mr F.N. Shaw 9 Richmond Terrace East Lane Walworth". Perhaps Shaw was the property's landlord.

43 See Laurie and Whittle's *New Map of London with Its Environs, 1809–10* (Richmond Terrace does not appear in their 1802 or 1807 *New Map of London*). Richmond Terrace was at the eastern end of East Street before its intersection with Dawes Street (called North Street/South Street at the time). The name that appears on maps is often "Richmond Place", which was on the same stretch of that street. It is indicated as "Richmond Terr." in C. and J. Greenwood's 1830 map of London (from a survey conducted in 1824–26).

44 *Morning Chronicle*, 23rd September 1819. East Lane was the old name of today's East Street.

45 Charles Cotterell (1767?–1828?) married Elizabeth White (*c.*1769–1808) on 26th April 1792 at St Mary's Church, Southampton (information from familysearch.org). He may have been the son of Charles Cotterell (born *c.*1735), "gent.", of St Maurice, Winchester. See William J.C. Moens, ed., *Hampshire Allegations*

for Marriage Licences Granted by the Bishop of Winchester,
1689–1837, Vol. I (London: Harleian Society, 1893), p. 185.

46   familysearch.org, Hampshire Parish Registers.

47   Charles Edward Cotterell (1793–1871) was baptized on 13th
     June 1793 at St Mary's Church. He was followed by Eliza Wilson
     (baptized 1st December 1794); Anne (baptized 4th June 1796);
     Martha White (baptized 3rd May 1798, buried 4th May 1801);
     William Henry (baptized 16th October 1799); George Stephen
     (baptized 25th October 1803); and John Nelson (baptized 17th
     November 1805, buried 5th January 1824). Sidney was buried on
     31st March 1808; Elizabeth Cotterell was buried a few days later,
     on 6th April 1808. She was thirty-nine years old. The information
     is taken from familysearch.org.

48   Marianne Jones (*c.*1785–1861) was the sister of Doctor Edwin
     Godden Jones (1775–1842), "Physician to His Royal Highness the
     Duke of York" and a man of substance (see *Hampshire Chronicle*
     of 1st March 1813, *Hampshire Telegraph* of 15th August 1842
     and *The Hampshire Advertiser* of 7th September 1861). Charles
     and Marianne Cotterell were married on 8th October 1809.
     The children born prior to Maria's departure were Louisa Anne
     (baptized 13th September 1810, buried 13th March 1811); Edwin
     Frederick (baptized 2nd January 1813); Emma Louisa (baptized
     12th September 1814); Walter Graindorge (baptized 11th January
     1817); and Louisa Augusta (baptized 14th May 1819). Two more
     children followed: Mary (baptized 2nd February 1821) and Emily
     (baptized 14th December 1824). Again, the information is taken
     from familysearch.org.

49   For Cotterell's marriage licence, see *Hampshire Allegations for
     Marriage Licences*, op. cit. Cotterell is not listed in the 1806
     Cunningham's Street Directory.

50   His office was on Suffolk Street East (now Great Suffolk Street),
     near Stones End Street, in Southwark (*Morning Advertiser*,
     12th March 1819; 21st to 23rd November 1825). A *Morning
     Chronicle* article of 14th January 1825 cites him as a resident
     in the "Borough" (Southwark) since at least the beginning of
     1823. He is listed in *Pigot's Commercial Directory of London*
     for 1825–26 as an auctioneer (p. 31).

51   Joseph Severn's letter of 21st September 1820 to William Haslam,
     ROL2, p. 341.

52   Unless stated otherwise, the information for the period 19th to
     21st September 1820 is taken from Severn's letters of 19th and
     21st September 1820 to Haslam, ROL2, pp. 338–39, 342–43.

53   MTL, fo. 19ʳ.

54 By "surgically" Severn meant that Keats gave medical orders.

55 The *Star* (London) reported on 22nd September 1820: "BRIGHTON,
    SEPTEMBER 20. This day the wind changed to the S.W. and blew
    a hurricane. His MAJESTY [George IV], therefore, will have had
    to encounter an equinoctial storm, if he did not take shelter last
    night in Cowes, or got this morning into Portsmouth." Sailing
    from Brighton, the *Royal George*, accompanied by a flotilla of
    four cruisers, had in fact arrived at Cowes at an early hour on
    Wednesday, 20th September. The king was in Portsmouth when
    the *Maria Crowther* landed there on 28th September. See *British
    Press*, 22nd and 23rd September 1820; *Morning Chronicle*, 29th
    September and 2nd October 1820.

56 A famous aria from Act III of *Artaxerxes* (1762) by Thomas Arne
    (1710–78). At the time, it was also a very popular concert piece.

57 They were lucky to come out unscathed. "In the storm on
    Wednesday last," reported the *Morning Chronicle* on 25th
    September, "two vessels were driven ashore at Brighton, and
    one of them was completely wrecked."

58 Severn's letter of 21st September 1820 is dated "Dungee Ness—
    near the Down's / on Deck—Thursday Mor^g / 20th Sept^r / 1820".
    Thursday was the 21st.

59 MTL, fo. 19^r.

60 Now at the Keats-Shelley House in Rome (KTS-1.8). His letter
    of 21st September 1820 to William Haslam began: "It will be
    best to make a kind of journal in my letters to you" (ROL2,
    p. 340). William Sharp quotes an excerpt from a letter Severn
    is supposed to have written to his sister Maria after Christmas
    1820, in which he says: "I am finishing a journal of our voyage
    so that you shall have every particular" (LLJS, p. 71). There is
    no evidence, however, that Severn continued to keep a journal
    on board the *Maria Crowther*, and the quoted letter, like many
    other documents published by Sharp in his biography, does not
    appear to exist in manuscript.

61 MTL, fo. 19^r.

62 Letter of 5th October 1820, ROL2, pp. 346–47. Mr and Mrs Snook
    were John (1780–1863) and Lætitia (1781–1865) Snook. Lætitia
    was Dilke's sister. Keats had stayed at their home in Bedhampton,
    Old Mill House, in late January 1819, and was very friendly with
    the family. Severn sketched a pen-and-ink drawing during their
    brief visit there, 'Acasia from Mr Snooks Garden Bedhampton',
    which is now at the Houghton Library, Harvard University (MS
    Eng 1460). The lady liked by Keats was Miss Cotterell; the one
    he had aversion for was Mrs Pidgeon. At this point, they must

have considered aborting the trip. In his letter of 22nd October 1820 to Haslam, Severn wrote: "I had determined on returning with [Keats] to London from the conviction that he would die on the passage" (ROL2, p. 348).

63　Letter of 30th September 1820, ROL2, pp. 344–46. "The very thing which I want to live most for" was his love for Fanny Brawne.

64　Ibid.

65　Portland Roads was "a natural anchorage [...] protected by Portland to the south, Chesil Beach to the west and mainland Dorset to the north" (The Encyclopedia of Portland History, available at https://www.portlandhistory.co.uk/portland-harbour.html). On the way to Portland Roads, Severn produced two watercolour drawings of the Dorset coast – 'Handfast Point, Dorsetshire / Studland Bay' (plates, 2b) and 'Sandwich Bay, Dorsetshire'. These are now in the Z. Smith Reynolds Library Special Collections and Archives, Wake Forest University, Winston-Salem, North Carolina (Joseph Severn Watercolors, MS651). "Sandwich Bay" was not Severn's mistake, but the name used on old maps for Swanage Bay.

66　'Sonnet by the Late John Keats', in The Union Magazine, Vol. 1, January to June 1846 (London: Barker and White, 1846), p. 157.

　　The edition being prepared by Monckton Milnes was MON. The poem had in fact already appeared in the Plymouth and Devonport Weekly Journal of 27th September 1838.

　　The edition of Shakespeare Keats gave to Severn was The Poetical Works of William Shakspeare (London: Thomas Wilson, 1806). This was the volume Keats had shared with his friend John Hamilton Reynolds, who gave it to him in 1819, as testified by an inscription on the title page of the book. It is now in the Keats House Museum.

67　JSLM, pp. 172–73.

68　Critical opinion varies on the dating of the sonnet, but there is a wide consensus that it was written sometime in 1819. Charles Brown had transcribed the poem and given it the title 'Sonnet (1819)'. Another transcription of 'Bright Star', almost identical to the one in Shakespeare's Poetical Works, was made by Fanny Brawne in her copy of Dante's Divine Comedy – according to Gittings, before the middle of April 1819. Gittings makes the point that the late transcript appears in Keats's firm earlier hand, but a comparison with the manuscript of his letter of 30th September 1820 to Charles Brown, written on board the Maria Crowther, does not show any striking dissimilarities.

69　See Michio Sugano, 'Was "Keats's Last Sonnet" Really Written on Board the "Maria Crowther?"', Studies in Romanticism, Vol. 34, No. 3 (Fall 1995), pp. 428–29.

70 MON, p. 72. William Sharp's further embellishments and out-and-out inventions in LLJS (pp. 54–55) helped perpetuate the myth.

71 The quotations in this paragraph are from MTL, fos. 19^r–20^r. Severn returned to this episode during a conversation with his son Walter in Rome on 17th September 1878. See Walter Severn's notes of this conversation in ECL1: "Sailed from Port of London & put in to Dorchester owing to bad weather. Keats shewed my father the beautiful coast which he knew & on returning on board Keats wrote that lovely Sonnet 'Bright Star' in the Vol. of Shakespeares Poems wh. he gave to ~~Severn~~ my father. 3 days storm in Bay of Biscay, but fortunately Keats did not suffer from sea sickness. My father suffered very much but during calm weather amused himself by drawing. Vide sketches of Keats & ship in scrap book."

72 Letter of 22nd October 1820, ROL2, p. 348. He was referring to his letter of 21st September.

73 Letter of 1st November 1820 to William Haslam, ROL2, pp. 354–55.

74 The quotation "carried by a good wind" can be found ibid., p. 355; "up and down like a roundabout" is from Severn's letter to his sister Maria of 21st January 1821, JSLM, p. 129. The letter continues: "5 Weeks on the seas—3 weeks of which I never saw land—this was the most entertaining time—we were beset with such rough seas—[…] we would sit down to breakfast—and on a sudden away would go the Coffe pot into a Lady's lap—a ham into mine and the Cabin boy who was set to hold the table up— would be lying on it—After this my breakfast would make another movement—retrograde—over the side of the Ship—But what I enjoyed most was the storms—mostly I was on deck with a great Coat—this was a treat to me—the grand sea—waves as long as your Shoreditch—in a valley—then rushing up like mountains— Another pleasant part was in passing the Inglish coast—here the wind was against us and we were many times obliged to land—I would ramble about in the most beautiful places—Studland in Dorset—that was the most beautiful" (JSLM, pp. 129–30).

75 Letter of 1st November 1820 to William Haslam, ROL2, p. 355.

76 MTL, 21^r. This is an anachronism. Don Carlos, Count of Molina (1788–1855), the brother of King Ferdinand VII, made a claim to the Spanish throne only after Ferdinand's death in September 1833. This resulted in a civil war – the First Carlist War of 1833–40 – in which the British (as well as the French and the Portuguese, who were also embroiled in a civil war – the Miguelite War – between liberal constitutionalists and conservative absolutists) provided military assistance to the liberal supporters of

Ferdinand's daughter Isabel II against the reactionary forces of Don Carlos. At the time the *Maria Crowther* crossed the Bay of Biscay, Portugal was in the middle of the so-called "Liberal Revolution of 1820", spearheaded by the merchant classes, who resented their diminished trade and the British control of the Portuguese armed forces. A few days later, on 10th October, the ex-commander-in-chief of the Portuguese army, Lord Beresford, returning from Brazil on HMS *Vengeur*, was not allowed to disembark in Lisbon by the revolutionary junta, fearful of any British involvement. "Most of the English Officers in the service of Portugal [have] been displaced," commented Admiral Sir Graham Moore in his diary (GMD, 17th October 1820), "at least those who did not think fit to swear to the new Constitution." The aim of the Portuguese men-of-war may have been either to gain intelligence about potential military preparations by the Royal Navy in Britain, since there were rumours of a possible British intervention in Portugal (see GGC, 13th October 1820), or to deter the pirate ships operating along those shores. On 18th September, the provisional government of Portugal had instructed the naval authorities to dispatch a frigate and a few other smaller ships to protect any traders arriving at Portuguese ports against the threat of corsairs (*Gazeta de Lisboa*, 20th September 1820). This would explain Thomas Walsh's initial fears that the *Maria Crowther* might be plundered.

77 BNK (KC2, p. 134). Keats's edition of Byron's poem was *Don Juan*, Cantos I–II (Paris: Galignani, 1819). The section referred to by Severn is II, xxvi *ff.*, based on the much-publicized shipwreck of the French frigate *Méduse* in July 1816, which also inspired Théodore Géricault's famous painting of 1818–19.

78 Letter of 17th September 1819 to George and Georgiana Keats, ROL2, p. 200.

79 The quotation "really popular among women" is from Keats's letter of 18th [?] August 1820 to Charles Brown, ROL2, p. 328.

80 MTL, 21ʳ.

81 For the drawing of the Barbary Coast, see ibid. For the drawing of the Malaga coast, see Severn's letter of 21st January 1821 to his sister Maria: "[P]assing through the Straits of Gibralter—is a grand treat—the mountainous coast of Africa—I made drawings I made puddings—and I made them all in good spirits" (JSLM, p. 130). The drawings are 'Ceuta [written "Ciutra"] / Coast of Barbary – from the Straits / passing [little drawing of a brig] / 16 Oct' (plates, 2c) and 'Coast of Malaga / 16 Oct'. They are now both at the Houghton Library, Harvard University (MS Eng 1460).

82   Letter of 22nd October 1820 to William Haslam, ROL2, p. 348.

83   GGC, 31st October 1820, p. 2: "*Ships arrived at the Port of Naples*: [...] on 22nd October. [...] From London, the English Brig Maria Crow[.], Capt. Thomas Walsh in 21 days [perhaps calculated from the time they cleared British waters], with goods for Mr Giuseppe Ascione." All previous biographers have followed Sharp in giving 21st October as the date of the *Maria Crowther*'s arrival. He must have deduced it backwards from the ten-day quarantine period imposed on the ship, which terminated on 31st October. It appears, in fact, that the quarantine came to an end on the tenth day from the day of their arrival (inclusive). Giuseppe Ascione was a merchant and a member of the Advisory Chamber of Commerce in Naples between 1817 and 1819 (see GRDS, 11th January 1820).

The voyage didn't last much longer than expected or than was usual. John Taylor had warned Fanny Keats that her brother would be at sea "about a Month" (ROL2, p. 338). Doctor Madden, who left Naples for England on the *Maria Crowther* in May 1822, writes in his memoirs that the passage took thirty-five days (MAM, p. 19). He also reports that his crossing from Naples to Plymouth on the schooner *Betsy* the following year lasted seventy-five days. Leigh Hunt, who also left London for Italy on a trader, the brig *Jane*, on 15th November 1821, and experienced an odyssey of a journey, wrote to the Shelleys three weeks later from Ramsgate: "Dearest friends,—Is not this monstrous? The 6th of December, and not yet got away from the coast! We were obliged to put in here from the Downs yesterday fortnight, owing to contrary winds, and a whole week after going on board, and here have we been kept by the same winds ever since. [...] Shelley told us of some happy person who was blown to Leghorn in little more than a fortnight. The mate tells me that he himself went from Liverpool to Naples in nineteen days. But these are blasts from heaven. The average passage is five weeks, sometimes six or seven, and it has been known to be twelve" (CLH, pp. 174–75).

The quotation "most horribly rough" is taken from Severn's letter of 22nd October 1820 to William Haslam, ROL2, p. 348.

84   Ibid.

85   RS.

86   "Between 1816 and 1819, typhus racked up 1.5 million cases and killed about 65,000 people in Ireland, according to estimates, with the greatest rate of mortality recorded in the summer of 1817" (*The Irish Times*, 15th March 2020). See

also *The Times*, 6th April 1820: 'Eighteenth Report of the Institute for the Cure and Prevention of Contagious Fever in the Metropolis, Feb. 11, 1820'. See also James Cowles Prichard, *A History of the Epidemic Fever Which Prevailed in Bristol, during the Years 1817, 1818, and 1819* (London: John and Arthur Arch, 1820) and William Harty, *An Historic Sketch of the Causes, Progress, Extent, and Mortality of the Contagious Fever Epidemic in Ireland During the Years 1817, 1818, and 1819* (Dublin: Hodges and McArthur, 1820).

The quotation from Severn is from MTL, 21^r.

87 See, for example, the *Caledonian Mercury* of 6th November 1819, 'The Yellow Fever at New York', and *Saunders's News-Letter* of 24th September 1819, 'Yellow Fever in Spain'. There were more outbreaks of yellow fever in Spain and America in 1820 (see *Gazeta de Lisboa*, 8th September and 25th October 1820). For the discussions between the health authorities, see 'Misure di precauzione per le provenienze dall'Inghilterra' (Archivio di Stato di Napoli, 'Regolamenti e disposizioni generali sul servizio sanitario', Vol. 503).

88 Ibid. See also ITA, p. 270, note 2, in reference to the late winter of 1820: "[Some of the] English merchants established at Naples [...] complained to us bitterly of their position, and of the annoyances to which they were subjected, from the government of Naples, and the neglect of their own. Ships from England were obliged to perform quarantine."

89 It might have been fourteen days in total (as Severn recalled in his memoir), including four of navigation. It is also possible that Charles Cotterell, Maria's brother, used his contacts to have the passengers' quarantine abridged.

90 Theodore Dwight, who sailed from New York to Naples and arrived there on 26th December 1820, around two months after Keats, was well aware that he would be subjected to a long quarantine on arrival – which his Italian travelling companion boasted he could help abridge (DWI, pp. 43–44). When his ship reached Naples, he wrote in his diary: "We learn, from the American consul, that we have been sentenced to a quarantine of twenty-one days, as a quantity of nankins, of which our cargo partly consists, are considered peculiarly susceptible of contagion: because no official accounts have lately been received from Spain, although the plague had entirely disappeared long before we left Gibraltar. We are to leave this harbour, therefore, as soon as possible, and go to Nisita, a small island in the bay of Pozzuoli, which is a recess in the great bay of Naples, about five miles distant" (DWI,

pp. 55–56). Nisita was then used as a lazaretto for longer-term quarantine of ships and maritime travellers.

91 MTL, fo. 22^r.

92 Letter of 1st November 1820 to William Haslam, ROL2, p. 353.

93 For the Naples weather, see the *Liffey* ship's log (ADM 53/794), 22nd to 31st October 1820: "Sunday 22^d[:] A.M. Fresh breezes and cloudy w^r […] noon Fresh breezes and cloudy weather[.] P.M. D^o weather […] 12. [midnight] Squally with rain at times[;] / Monday 23^d[:] A.M. Squally with rain at times […] 8 Moderate and clear weather […] Noon Moderate and clear weather[.] P.M. D^o weather […] 12. Moderate w^r. / Tuesday 24th[:] A.M. Moderate and cloudy weather […] Noon Fresh breezes and cloudy w^r[.] P.M. D^o weather […] 12. Fresh breezes and clear weather[.] / Wednesday 25th[:] A.M. Fresh breezes and cloudy. 8 D^o weather [..] Noon Fresh breezes and clear weather[.] P.M. D^o weather […] Midnight moderate with rain[.] / Thursday 26th[:] A.M. Moderate with rain. 8 Moderate & cloudy […] Noon Moderate & cloudy weath. P.M. D^o W. […] 12. Moderate & clear. / Friday 27th[:] A.M. Light breezes and clear weather. […] Noon Calm and clear weather. P.M. D^o W. […] Midnight Moderate and clear weather[.] / A.M. Moderate and clear weather. […] Noon Strong breezes & squally with rain […] P.M. Strong breezes with heavy rain. […] 12. Moderate & cloudy[.] / Sunday 29th[:] A.M. Moderate and cloudy weather. 8 D^o W^r. […] Noon Light breezes & cloudy weather. P.M. D^o weather […] 12. Light variable winds & cloudy[.] / Monday 30th[:] A.M. Light breezes with rain at times. 8 Light breezes and clear […] Noon Light variable winds and clear. […] P.M. D^o weather […] Midnight moderate with rain[.] Tuesday 31st[:] A.M. Moderate with light rain. 8 Calm & cloudy […] Noon Light breezes & cloudy w^r[.] P.M. D^o weather […] Midnight moderate with rain at times."

94 Alternatively, the *contumacisti* could unfold the letter themselves, place it between the prongs of an iron peg and give it to the guard for direct exposure to the fumes.

95 Letter of 1st November 1820 to William Haslam, ROL2, p. 354.

96 Letter of 22nd October 1820 to Mrs Frances Brawne, ROL2, pp. 349–50.

97 See previous note.

98 Ibid.

99 Charles Cotterell began his naval career on HMS *Thunder* (Captain Watkin Owen Pell), an eight-gun bomb vessel, during the Peninsular War. The master's log of 7th August 1812, from off Fort Catalina in the Bay of Cádiz, reads: "Joined the Ship

a Purser M.‍ C.E. Cotterell" (ADM 52/4636). On 9th October 1813, as she proceeded home from Spithead to Woolwich, the *Thunder* was approached by the French privateer *Neptune*. "[A]t half-past ten," wrote Captain Pell in a letter reporting the event, "she [the *Neptune*] came up on the larboard quarter, and hailed us to bring to and strike; her [written 'his'] decks were full of men, in readiness for boarding. She put her helm up to lay us alongside, we put ours down, and fired four guns and a volley of musketry; she fell on board, and was carried in the most gallant style by boarding. […] [T]he enemy had four men killed and ten wounded; five very severely, once since dead. I am happy to say, that we had only two men wounded" (NC, p. 438). Cotterell was part of a detachment led by Lieutenant Ambrose A.R. Wolrige of the Royal Marine Artillery which assisted the capture through the firing of mortars. For this action, service medals (and clasps) were issued long afterwards, in 1848, by the NGSM to Captain Pell and the six men of Wolrige's detachment (JGD, pp. 38–39). It appears that Cotterell was not present at that time to receive his medal, which is now held by the Royal Naval Museum. After the *Thunder* was paid out of commission on 5th November 1813 (ADM 35/3944), Cotterell joined the sloop HMS *Clio* on 24th March 1814, where he remained in service until she was decommissioned on 9th October 1815 (ADM 35/3400). See also ADM 6/195/398 for Cotterell's early-service record.

100 MTL, fo. 23ʳ.

101 Letter of 1st November 1820 to William Haslam, ROL2, p. 354.

102 BNK (KC2, p. 136). Severn writes "*No*, they" as "*No*, there".

103 Letter of 1st November 1820 to William Haslam, ROL2, p. 355.

104 The *Rochfort* was the flagship of the squadron. She arrived in Naples on the evening of 17th October (GMD, 20th October 1820). The *Liffey* and the *Active* arrived in Naples on 6th October (ADM 51/3252 and ADM 51/3005). The *Revolutionaire* reached the Bay of Naples on 11th October (ADM 51/3398) and was let out of quarantine on 19th October. The *Spey* moored in Naples on 20th September (ADM 51/3417). The *Aid* (a surveying vessel) came into the bay on 17th October in the course of the night and was sent to Malta on 19th October (GMD, 20th October 1820). Two more warships would soon join the British squadron in the Bay of Naples: the *Vengeur* (74 guns, ship of the line, Captain Frederick Lewis Maitland – the same officer who received Napoleon on his surrender at Rochefort in 1815, and the same ship that had just returned from Brazil with Lord Beresford) on 27th October (GMD, 29th October 1820) and the

Glasgow (40 guns, frigate, Captain Anthony Maitland) on 2nd December 1820.

105 GGC, 24th October, p. 2. In order to defuse the situation, the *Revolutionaire* and the *Spey* were sent to lie at Baia on the morning of 28th October (GMD, 29th October 1820).

106 He swore to the new constitution on 13th July 1820 and then renewed his oath on 1st October, at the opening of the Neapolitan parliament.

107 DCLC, p. 161 (18th September 1820).

108 Ibid., p. 170. Sir William had introduced Lord Colchester and Admiral Moore, the commander of the British squadron in the Mediterranean, to the King of Naples on 26th October (*Dublin Evening Post*, 21st November 1820) – an event that could not have gone unnoticed or failed to raise suspicion among the *carbonari*.

109 *The Sun* (London), 24th November; *Star* (London), 30th November; *Bell's Weekly Messenger*, 3rd December 1820. The rumour was unfounded, and the British issued a denial (PLDA of 21st December 1820, quoting a letter from Naples of 2nd December). For the British government's official position, reiterated in the dispatch of 20th October 1820 by the Foreign Secretary, Lord Castlereagh, see Lord Colchester's summary in his diary entry of 4th November 1820: "The conduct of Great Britain as to Naples is not a question of obligation, and alliance, and treaty; our conduct is to be that of 'strict neutrality' upon a 'condition declared,' viz. 'the personal security and preservation of the Royal Family.' We are to participate in their deliberations only to watch over the balance of power. You (Sir W. A'court) are authorised to require from the Royal Family a reasonable conformity to your wishes in the execution of our purpose for their safety, and your authority to employ force to that end does not extend to general hostilities" (DCLC, pp. 171–72).

110 *Morning Post*, 27th December 1820.

111 DCLC, pp. 152, 155 and 175.

112 MTL, fo. 22ʳ. No Lieutenant Sullivan can be found in the muster or pay books for the ships of the British squadron present in the Bay of Naples at the time – *Rochfort*, *Liffey*, *Spey*, *Active*, *Revolutionaire* and *Vengeur* (which arrived at 3.30 p.m. on 27th October and remained in quarantine until 1st November). Because of its size, the *Express* didn't have spare officers apart from its active commander. There is no reference to the incident in any of the captains' logs. In all likelihood Severn, writing over fifty years after the events he describes, misremembered the name of the officer. The closest-sounding match is Lieutenant Williams

Sandom of the *Liffey* (ADM 37/6095). There are many ordinary seamen called "Sullivan", "Sulivan" and "O'Sullivan" in the muster lists of the British squadron, and a Thomas R. Sulivan among the petty officers of the *Spey* (ADM 37/6282) – who, however, joined the ship on 3rd November 1820, aged only twenty.

113 Warships were subject to less stringent rules (see RS, pp. 40–41), but still had to undergo quarantine if they sailed from "suspect" ports. For example, Admiral Moore's *Rochfort*, which arrived in the Bay of Naples on 17th October, was released from quarantine on 21st, "which was, to a certain degree, an indulgence as the usual time for a Man of War to ride Quarantine from Malta is a fortnight, counting from the day she sails from Malta" (GMD, 26th October 1820).

Quarantined ships were required to display a yellow flag at the bow (see RS, p. 55)

114 See RS, p. 51.

115 MTL, fo. 22^r.

116 Letter of 5th January 1822, JSLM, p. 190.

117 BNK (KC2, pp. 134–35).

NAPLES

1 DOI, p. 187. The proverb, meaning "See Naples and then die", is mentioned in the accounts of several travellers of the time – among them Goethe's *Italian Journey*, which seems to have given it much of its notoriety.

2 "Travellers, on entering Naples, are obliged to deposit their pass-ports at the Police-Office; neither can they, till their departure, legally reclaim them" (TC, Appendix, p. 150, note). Keats's visa reads, in translation:

Regist^d with the Council of Public Security
Naples 31st Oct 1820
By the off^e of the 3rd Dep^t

F. MADIA

3 MTL, fos. 22^r–23^r.

4 John Willes Johnson, *The Traveller's Guide through France, Italy, and Switzerland* (London: Longman, 1828), pp. 153, 164.

5 IPRN1, pp. 16 and 18; Filippo Marzullo, *Guida del forestiere per le cose più rimarchevoli della città di Napoli* (Naples: Saverio Giordano, 1823), pp. 107–8. The sulphur spring is indicated in some old maps of Naples.

6   HOL, pp. 190–91; Louis Valentin, *Voyage en Italie fait en l'année 1820* (Paris: Gabon et Compagnie, 1826), p. 77. "*Acqua suffregna*" means "sulphurous water" (Neapolitan dialect). In Italian: "*acqua sulfurea*".

7   *Acqua ferrata* means "ferrous water" (Italian) – that is, "mineral water". The two waters had been drunk and sold for centuries across Naples and were one of the greatest sources of revenue for the inhabitants of Borgo S. Lucia. There were hawkers and kiosks of *acqua suffregna* and *acqua ferrata* in Naples until the early 1970s.

8   PEN, pp. 527–28.

9   Domenico Antonio Parrino, *Nuova guida de' forastieri* (Naples: Parrino, 1725), p. 76. Details of the individuals named are as follows: Don Tommaso, 5th Prince of Castiglione (1669–1753), from the family of the barons of Aquino; Philippe, Duke of Anjou (1683–1746), grandson of King Louis XIV of France, who became Philip V of Spain on 1st November 1700, the first member of the House of Bourbon to rule over Spain; Juan Manuel Fernández Pacheco, 8th Duke of Escalona (1650–1725), viceroy of Naples between February 1702 and July 1707, when a new viceroy was appointed by the Austrians; Don Giovanni Battista Amendola, state councillor and president of the Regia Camera della Sommaria (the Royal Treasury); and Ettore Fabio d'Alessandro (1694–1741), 4th Duke of Pescolanciano.

10   Enrique de Guzmán, 2nd Count of Olivares (1540–1607) was viceroy of Naples between 1595 and 1599.

11   Nicola Maria II d'Alessandro, 7th Duke of Pescolanciano (1784–1848); Pasquale Maria, 6th Duke of Pescolanciano (1756–1816).

12   TI calls the inn a "lodging house" (p. 93). Mariana Starke mentions the Aquila Nera in her letter dated September 1797. The inn is not listed in GVI (1791): "There are some very good hotels in Naples, in a delightful setting, such as Albergo Reale, Crocelle, Emanuele [Gaiola], Casa isolata, Stefano di Rosa" (p. 214). Stephen Moore, 2nd Earl Mount Cashell (1770–1822), and his wife spent nine weeks at the Aquila Nera between 1st January and 6th March 1803. Katherine Wilmot, who accompanied them in their travels, left a description of their time in Naples and the view from her balcony. See Thomas Sadleir, ed., *An Irish Peer on the Continent* (London: Williams and Norgate, 1920), pp. 135–71.

    For Don Ambrogio, see *Taurinen. seu Neapolitana beatificationis, et canonizationis ven. Servæ Dei Mariæ Clotildis Adelaidis Xaveriæ Reginæ Sardiniæ summarium super dubium* (1830), p. 818.

Marie Clotilde (1759–1802) was the younger sister of Louis XVI, the last King of France.

13 The street number for Palazzo d'Alessandro was 82 at the end of the eighteenth and the beginning of the nineteenth centuries (it is now No. 62), as confirmed by documents in the D'Alessandro family archive. I am indebted to Ettore d'Alessandro for this information and some of the details about the early history of the building.

14 *Monitore napoletano*, 9th August 1809.

15 *Giornale degli annunzj*, 2nd June 1814.

16 The Swiss historian Jacques Augustin Galiffe (1773–1853) was a guest there on 8th March 1817. Its address at No. 82 Strada S. Lucia is confirmed by an advert for a lost dog in the *Giornale del Regno delle Due Sicilie* of 6th April 1818.

17 TC, p. 439. See also GALI, pp. 398, 406.

18 Ewa Kawamura, 'Il soggiorno dei tisici inglesi negli alberghi italiani e svizzeri tra Ottocento e Novecento', in Annunziata Berrino, ed., *Storia del turismo: annale 2005*, Vol. 6 (Milan: FrancoAngeli, 2007), p. 21. See also TC, p. 438: "In the quarter of S. Lucia the vicinity of the sea, united with the dampness occasioned by a tufo mountain [Mount Echia], directly under which the houses are built, renders the air dangerous to Invalids, and not very wholesome even for persons in health."

19 QUA, p. 87; TE, p. 384.

20 It is not mentioned by Mariana Starke in TEUT8 (1833), p. 333.

21 For the Villa di Russia, see *Manuale del forestiero in Napoli* (Naples: Bobel e Bompard, 1845), p. 72, and *Guide to Naples and Sicily* (Rome: L. Piale, 1847), p. 175. The 1908 Baedeker guide to *Southern Italy and Sicily* (p. 22) lists the "Hôt. de Russie, Strada Santa Lucia 82" among the "second-class hotels [...] chiefly visited by commercial men". The 1911 Baedeker to the *Mediterranean* (p. 136) mentions the "Russie" among other "unpretending" hotels, describing it as "plain" – the sign of an irreversible decline.

22 GAL, p. 60. GALI (p. 406) confirms that the Hotel Villa di Londra charged "two ducats and upwards per night for lodgings, and other things in proportion". For a rough indication of extra charges for breakfast, dinner, carriages, etc., see *Guide du voyageur en Italie* (Paris: Audin, 1826), p. 488.

23 GAL, p. 60.

24 BER, pp. 213 and 167.

25 PEN, pp. 527–618. Pennington was in Naples from 20th October 1819 to 22nd February 1820.

26 GVSM, p. 168. Count Girolamo Silvio Martinengo (1753–1834) translated Milton's *Paradise Lost* (Venice: Antonio Zatta, 1801)

and *Paradise Regained* (unpublished) into Italian. He arrived at Villa di Londra on 29th February and left on 16th March 1820. His diary was kept and written down by Giuseppe Compagnoni, who travelled with the count's family and their staff. On 7th March, the Martinengos received an evening visit at the Villa di Londra from Antonio Canova, who was in Naples at the time. For further background material on their journey and their residence in Naples, see COM, pp. 131–201.

27 GVSM, pp. 232–33.
28 Letter of 1st November 1820, ROL2, pp. 353–54.
29 Letter of 1st November 1820 to Charles Brown, ROL2, pp. 351–52. Keats was "prisoner at Hunt's" from 23rd June to 12th August 1820. Keats stayed at 2 Wesleyan Place (where he moved on 4th May 1820), and at the Hunts' in Mortimer Terrace, both in Kentish Town.
30 Letter of 1st November 1820, ROL2, pp. 354–55.
31 GAL, p. 155; *Jettatura* (1856), Chapter 3.
32 See EB, pp. 30–32.
33 DCLC, p. 154.
34 EB, p. 23; DCLC, p. 159.
35 CLDR, No. 6, p. 209.
36 COL, p. 392.
37 CAR, p. 128.
38 PEP2, p. 31. Pepe and his *carbonari* supporters had tried, without success, to have the King's Guard disbanded. It had been objected to them that even in Spain this special squad had been preserved. See PEP1, pp. 279–80.
39 DCLC, p. 176.
40 CAR, pp. 217–22.
41 For the figure of 899 soldiers, see EB, p. 23. For the 3,000 more, see DCLC, p. 168.
42 Ibid., pp. 177–78.
43 *Dublin Evening Post*, 21st November 1820. See also GCRDS, 25th October 1820, which gives the correct date of Florestano's speech. For a fuller account, see *La voce del secolo*, 31st October 1820.
44 *Dublin Evening Post*, 21st November 1820. The "Quiroga of the Nation" is a reference to Antonio Quiroga (1784–1841), who was regarded, together with Rafael del Riego (1784–1823), as the leader of the January 1820 military uprising in Spain.
45 *Diario del Parlamento nazionale delle Due Sicilie* of 23rd October 1820 (Naples: Stamperia Nazionale, 1820), p. 2.
46 Both letters are reported in the *Dublin Evening Post* of 21st November 1820.
47 GGC, 3rd November 1820.

48 *Sheffield Independent*, 23rd December 1820, referring to reports in the *Gazette de France*.

49 GCRDS, 10th November 1820. News of this exemplary punishment was publicized in many local papers (see MRN, pp. 93–94) and had some resonance even abroad (see for example *Gazette de France*, 30th November 1820). On 2nd November the prince regent had a meeting with Pepe, Zurlo, Ricciardi and Siniscalchi about "the arrest of the *carbonaro* Fanini" (DDC, entry of 2nd November 1820).

50 The *Oesterreichischer Beobachter* published another anti-*carbonari* front-page piece on 19th November 1820, the day after its report of the 2nd November disorder in Naples.

51 PEP2, p. 48.

52 MTL, fo. 23ʳ.

53 For newspaper reports, see, for example, the long piece in the *Glasgow Herald* of 1st December 1820, quoting extracts from the liberal Neapolitan paper *La voce del secolo* of 7th November: "The review of Sunday last formed a magnificent spectacle. It consisted of 18,000 men superbly mounted, and exciting by their discipline the admiration both of citizens and foreigners. Of the latter were present, the Ambassador of Spain, and the Ministers [that is, the envoys] of Russia, England, and the Low Countries, with all the officers of the English squadron. The Prince Vicar General having mounted his horse, caused them all to pass in review, after which he expressed to General Caracoso, the Minister of War, his highest satisfaction at the excellent condition of the troops [...]. But let pomp and show give place, and actual operations commence. Let the divisions destined for Abruzzi receive instant orders to march." The grand review of 29th October had been announced in the GCRDS of 24th October.

54 The review was also reported by a number of other newspapers, such as the GGC of 7th November, the *Gazzetta piemontese* of 16th November and *Le Moniteur universel* of 24th November 1820. The *Gazzetta di Firenze* of 14th November 1820 adds, at the end of its short notice of the event: "H.R.H. expressed to General Carrascosa, the Minister of War, his satisfaction at the excellent condition of his troops." The prince regent wrote in his diary that day: "I got up, did a few things, went to the Field to pass in review the entire soldiery, which was most beautiful, I saw them perform an about-turn and then saw them parade, then we went back home" (DDC). Lord Colchester's son, a lieutenant serving on the *Liffey* (ADM 37/6095), was also at the parade that day (PRO 30/9/3/34), and later dined with Sir William à Court and the officers of the British fleet, and went to a ball organized

by the Duchess of Berwick (Rosalía Ventimiglia di Grammonte y Moncada). No doubt his father was with him that day.

Regarding the journalist's comment about the number of men in a division: an active division comprised 9,424 men (CLDR, No. 6, Quadro N.° VI). The words here are a bit of constitutionalist braggadocio.

"The last Italian war" refers to the Neapolitan War of 1815 between the army led by Joachim Murat, then King of Naples, and the Austrians. Carrascosa and Pepe had been involved, on the Neapolitan side, in some of the crucial phases of this conflict.

55 GGC, 7th November 1820.

56 MTL, fo. 23ʳ. As we have seen, it was the prince regent who was in command, not the king.

57 BNK (KC2, p. 136).

58 "Drove after breakfast to the Campo di Marte," wrote Henry Matthews in his *Diary of an Invalid*, "where, to my great surprise, I found myself transported ten years backwards, into the middle of old school-fellows. There was a regular double-wicket cricket match going on;—Eton against the world;—and the world was beaten in one innings!" (DOI, p. 171). For the Campo di Marte as a destination for day outings, see IPRN1, p. 148, and IPRN2, p. 51.

59 RLL, pp. 14–15. "Bourbon Museum" ("Real Museo Borbonico", also known at the time as "Studi", from the name of its building, Palazzo degli Studi) was the name of today's Museo archeologico nazionale di Napoli from its opening in 1816 to 1861.

60 Ibid., pp. xiii–xv.

61 Compare his portrait of Mathias with that left by Richard Robert Madden in MAAL1, pp. 422–25.

62 RLL, pp. 1–12.

63 According to his wife's journal, during his stay in Naples Shelley visited the Bourbon Museum on three occasions: on Saturday 19th December 1818, on Saturday 2nd January and on Friday 26th February 1819. See Shelley's short description of his first visit in his letter of 17th or 18th December 1818 to Thomas Love Peacock (PBSL, p. 63) and his longer comments in his letter of 25th February 1819, also to Peacock (PBSL, pp. 80–81).

64 Mary's journal and Shelley's letters to Thomas Love Peacock from Naples (see previous note) prove that the poet did not go to Pompeii the day after any of his visits to the Bourbon Museum.

65 For Macfarlane's interest in macaroni, see PCSR, pp. 9–17, 'Maccaroni-Eaters'.

66 For his piece on Shelley, Macfarlane recycled parts of his long account of an 1848 visit to Pompeii published in GRI, pp. 207–16,

which starts with an almost identical turn of phrase ("We entered the 'City of the Dead'—as it ought always to be entered—by *the Street of Tombs*") and includes a visit to a macaroni manufactory in Torre Annunziata on the way back.

67 MSJ, pp. 245 and 249. Mary's journal entry for Tuesday 22nd December 1818 reads: "Go to Pompeii—We are delighted with this antient city—read Montaigne—S reads Livy—"

68 PBSL, pp. 71–75.

69 In all likelihood, the Shelleys travelled from Naples by sea, not by coach. See Shelley's letter of 17th or 18th December 1818 to Thomas Love Peacock: "We are going to see Pompeii the first day that the sea is waveless" (PBSL, pp. 63–64). For a contemporary map of the Pompeii excavations, see 'Plan des fouilles de Pompéï, 1820', available at https://gallica.bnf.fr/ark:/12148/btv1b525054318.

70 PCSR, 'Some Recollections of the Easter Holidays', pp. 43–49. Mary's journal entries can be found in MSJ, p. 249. Shelley's account of their three-day excursion to Paestum, which is contained in his letter of 25th February 1819 to Thomas Love Peacock (PBSL, pp. 78–80), does not mention their stopping in Pompeii on the way back to Naples.

71 Macfarlane claims to have met Beau Brummel at a hotel in Calais, on his way to the south of Italy, in the autumn of 1820 (RLL, p. 269); to have been in Naples at the end of that year (RLL, p. 85); to have attended the debates of the Neapolitan parliament (between 1st October 1820 and 19th March 1821, GRI, p. 73); and to be travelling in the Abruzzi in 1821 (LEBR, p. 284).

Macfarlane knew Leigh Hunt very well, and had dealings with him over a long period of time (see RLL, pp. 102–5), so I doubt he could have mistaken him for someone else. A Macfarlane is mentioned in Hunt's correspondence in connection with a letter that George Lillie Craik (who was working with Charles Macfarlane at that time on the *Pictorial History of England*) was to send or deliver to him in person (see letter of 24th May 1839 to George Lillie Craik, CLH, pp. 314–15).

For the detail concerning Captain Medwin, see MSJ, p. 337.

72 RLL, p. xiii. He also says in his preface: "I have no intention of making any present use of these memorabilia; but they [...] may be published hereafter; and, if they are not, the books which contain them may interest my children, and recall to their memory the valuable friendships I have enjoyed, and the numerous acquaintances I have had from my boyhood upwards" (RLL, p. xiv).

73 See Mathias's letter of 26th May 1828 to Charles Edward Cotterell (State Library of New South Wales, A24/p. 59):

My dear Sir,
I am convinced that you will favour me by accepting the enclosed Canzone, or Ode, intended as a tribute to the memory of our late much lamented & accomplished friend Sir W. Drummond. I have printed several copies privately.

Yours sincerely,

T.J. Mathias

For Macfarlane's association with Mathias and Drummond, see RLL, pp. 84–92.

74 Macfarlane does not appear in Severn's letters.

75 See Severn's letters of 5th July 1822 to his brother Thomas (JSLM, pp. 202–8) and of August 1822 to his sister Maria (JSLM, pp. 208–11). Grant F. Scott identifies the "very kind Gentleman" of the August letter with the "kind Englishman" of the July letter, that is, Charles Cotterell, but Severn mentions that the former has a family, whereas we know that Cotterell was unmarried at the time. Severn was back in Rome by 24th October 1822 (letter to Sir Thomas Lawrence, JSLM, pp. 212–14). From his letter of 26th October 1822 to Charles Brown it appears that he had only just returned to Rome from his sojourn in Naples (JSLM, pp. 214–17). According to MTL, fos. 35–36, Severn met Lady Westmorland in Mola di Gaeta in the summer of 1825, and accompanied her and her friends to Naples, where he renewed his acquaintance with Thomas Uwins, who became a good friend of both Severn and Cotterell (see MTU1, p. 351; MTU2, pp. 191–288; MTU2, pp. 99, 153–54). He then visited the city again in September–October 1827, by which time Macfarlane had already left on his voyage to Sicily, Malta, Greece and Turkey (see GRI, p. iii, and CONS, p. 1).

76 For Macfarlane and the Bourbon Museum, see RLL, pp. 1, 86, and GRI, p. 220. On 17th September 1822 Severn applied for permission to reproduce some of the works in the Bourbon Museum (ASN, Ministero Affari Interni, Inventario II, folder No. 1993):

Your Excellency,
Giuseppe Severn, an English painter studying at the Royal Academy of Painting in London, wishes to copy Tiziano's *Danaë*, Schedoni's *Charity*, the *Holy Family* by Raffaello and the one by Giulio Romano, as well as a few other classical paintings in the renowned Royal Bourbon Museum, and begs Your Excellency to grant him permission, for which he will be very grateful   Joseph Severn

He was granted permission the following day, 18th September 1822.

77   During their journey from Naples to Rome, Severn "delighted Keats by gathering the wild flowers" (MTL, fo. 24ʳ). See also Severn's letter of 5th January 1822 to John Taylor: "One morning early in February, (before his death) I was delighted to find the Spring had commenced here—and when the poor fellow awoke I told him of it—I told him I had seen some trees in blossom—this had a most dreadful effect on him—I had mistaken the point— he shed tears most bitterly—and said—'The spring was always inchantment to me—I could get away from suffering—in watching the growth of a little flower—it was real delight to me—it was part of my very soul—perhaps the only happiness I have had in the world—has been the silent growth of Flowers[']" (JSLM, p. 190). In his letter to Rice of 14th February 1820 (ROL2, p. 260), Keats wrote: "I muse with the greatest affection on every flower I have known from my infancy—their shapes and colours are as [written 'coulours as are'] new to me as if I had just created them with a superhuman fancy—It is because they are connected with the most thoughtless and happiest moments of our Lives—I have seen foreign flowers in hothouses of the most beautiful nature, but I do not care a straw for them. The simple flowers of our sp[r]ing are what I want to see again."

For the coach drive, see IPRN1, p. 148; IPRN2, p. 51.

78   "A.M. Light breezes and clear weather. [...] Noon Moderate & clear w. P.M. Dᵒ weather" (ADM 51/3252). Temperatures: morning, 7.5 °C; noon, 11.9 °C (CASR, pp. 67 and 129).

79   Louis Simond, writing in April 1818, says: "There was to-day a grand review, at which the king of Naples was present [...]. All Naples was there; lords and lazzaroni in crowds repaired to the Campo Marzo to see the show. [...] This Campo Marzo stands high; a splendid road leads up to it" (SIM, pp. 426–27).

80   For Keats's aversion to the military, see, for example, his verse letter of August 1816 to his brother George (ROL1, p. 108), ll. 128–30:

> Through which the Poppies show their scarlet Coats;
> So pert, and useless, that they bring to Mind
> The scarlet Coats, that pester human kind.

81   Macfarlane's description is reminiscent of a passage in PCSR: "But your true-bred lazzarone, who scorns knives and forks, and puts his food into his mouth with his fingers, never breaks the strings at all until they are descending, *facili descensus*, down the wide throat to the Avernus of his stomach. He takes up a whole handful from his wooden platter, gives it a flourish in the air, and

then lets it gradually drop into his mouth. But this practice is rather picturesque than genteel or cleanly; and although I warmly recommend their manner of cooking it, I can scarcely recommend to the imitation of Englishmen the Neapolitans' mode of eating maccaroni" (p. 13).

The words attributed to Keats contain, I believe, a veiled quotation from Swift's *Polite Conversation* (Dialogue II), where Colonel Atwit, taking out some fritters with his hands before passing them to Miss Notable, quips: "Here, Miss; they say, Fingers were made before Forks, and Hands before Knives."

Porta Capuana is the north-eastern gate of the city. For the nearby macaroni shops, see PCSR, pp. 14–15.

82 MTL, fo. 23ʳ. In BNK, Severn inverts the order of the events, and has the review in the morning following the night at the theatre. However, there were no performances at the San Carlo on 3rd November. It could be argued that Keats went to the opera on Tuesday, 7th November, the day before leaving Naples, following Severn's assertion in MTL, fo. 24ʳ: "And the next day we were on our way to Rome ³¹ October 1820" (the date given by the painter is of course wrong). This is not beyond the bounds of possibility, because there were indeed performances at the San Carlo that night – Giovanni Pacini's opera *Il Barone di Dolsheim*, followed by the "anacreontic" ballet *Odio alle donne, ovvero Il trionfo di Amore*, by Louis Henry (1784–1836) – but less likely, for a number of reasons, including the following: the military review and the night at the opera appear to be in close chronological succession in both of Severn's accounts; Keats was very weak during his stay in Naples, and I doubt that he would have agreed to a late night out on the eve of an early-morning departure for Rome; the presence of soldiers described in Severn's account seems to be linked with the riots of 2nd November; anyone wanting to impress his guests, as Cotterell did, would have chosen a Saturday rather than a midweek performance, and an opera by an acclaimed in-vogue author such as Rossini, sung by a stellar cast, rather than a lesser-known work by a younger composer which was being performed at the San Carlo for the first time. *Il Barone di Dolsheim* enjoyed five performances at the Teatro del Fondo (now Teatro Mercadante) between 21st October and 6th November 1820, before moving on 7th November to San Carlo, where it was performed only twice (see TSC, p. 171, and GCRDS, 28th October and 7th November 1820).

83 See GAL, p. 64: "One of the first objects of our curiosity at Naples was, of course, the *Theatre of San Carlo*, of which we had heard and read so many magnificent descriptions: and unquestionably

our first sensation upon entering the house was that of delight and astonishment. The whole interior is so richly gilt from the top to the bottom, that it actually appears to be built of gold: and its shape and size give the fullest effect to this dazzling splendour." The rebuilt theatre was inaugurated on 12th January 1817.

84   Letter of 20th October 1822 to Georgiana Gell (Derbyshire Record Office, D258/50/110).

85   Count Martinengo's journal entry for 5th March 1820 reports: "In the evening we went to the opera at the Teatro di San Carlo, in a box provided by Baron Antonini in the fourth tier, No. 3. It is very difficult for tourists to get tickets for any of the boxes in the lower tiers, because the first-floor ones belong to freeholders who won't rent them out on any account; the second tier is allotted to the Court, the Ministers and the Head of Foreign Affairs, and the third one is always let on a six-month or yearly basis" (GVSM, pp. 177–78). See also GAL, pp. 65–66: "On [...] festivals the seats cost twelve or fourteen *Carlini*; (four or five shillings sterling). A ticket without a seat costs only eight *Carlini*: but the difference is ill saved at the expense of two great inconveniences; first, the fatigue of standing; and in the second place, the almost certainty of having one's clothes sprinkled with wax, from the chandeliers which hang outside of the boxes. On ordinary nights, the ticket costs only five *Carlini*. The seats are remarkably comfortable arm-chairs, to which you are directed by the number of your ticket. The latter is really a very agreeable regulation."

86   *Torvaldo e Dorliska* had a libretto by Cesare Sterbini, the librettist of *The Barber of Seville*, which made its debut in Rome at the Teatro Argentina (under the title *Almaviva, o sia l'inutile precauzione*) on 20th February 1816, less than two months after the premiere of *Torvaldo e Dorliska*.

    Music for *Otranto liberata* was by Pietro Raimondi and Luigi Carlini. Cast: Adélaïde Taglioni, Alfonso Demasier, Salvatore Taglioni, Giacomo Durante, Louis Henry. *Otranto liberata*, which had its premiere at the San Carlo on 4th October 1820 on the occasion of the prince regent's name day, proved to be very popular and had a run of twenty-six performances. For more information about this ballet, see Patrizia Veroli, 'Danza e letteratura. Alcune considerazioni sul ballo storico a Napoli nel processo risorgimentale sulla base dei libretti', in Antonio Caroccia, ed., *Arte e cultura al tempo di Francesco de Sanctis* (Avellino: Conservatorio di Musica Domenico Cimarosa, 2017).

87   TSC, p. 170.

88　For the full cast and the original libretto, see *Torvaldo e Dorliska, dramma semiserio, rappresentato in Napoli nel Real Teatro S. Carlo nell'Estate del 1820* (Naples: Tipografia Flautina, 1820).

89　See *La voce del secolo*, 31st October 1820: "Every night, the officers of the English men-of-war anchored in our bay go to see our shows from the boxes of the King's Navy, and they are exceedingly pleased with the cordial welcome given them by their Neapolitan compeers."

The prince regent wrote that day in his diary: "The family went to the Theatre tonight" (DDC, entry for 4th November 1820). It is safe to assume that he meant the San Carlo – the "theatre" par excellence in Naples – because elsewhere in his diary he specifies the names of the smaller theatres (see, for example, the entries for 6th, 7th and 8th November 1820). He didn't go himself that night, being occupied with an emergency meeting about parliamentary matters.

90　GAL, p. 65.

91　BNK (KC2, pp. 135–36). In his later memoir (MTL, fos. 23^r–24^r), Severn repeated the anecdote in similar terms: "[W]e [...] admired the fine scene painting but particularly two soldiers on each side the stage, when to our astonishment at the finish of the Act they moved off & we discovered that they were real men—Keats exclaimed in a frenzy, Severn "we'll go to Rome for as I am to die I should not be able to die comfortably ~~like to leave my Ashes~~ in the presence of a people with such miserable politicks." Severn went back to the San Carlo in the summer of 1822. "This Naples is great in Music," he wrote to his brother Thomas. "The Theatre here is the most beautiful in the world—the performance but so-so—" (letter of 5th July 1822, JSLM, p. 207). In his letter of 24th March 1822 to his father, Severn said that he had now become "a great admirer of Rossini" (JSLM, p. 196), and his passion for the works of the Italian composer was destined to last (see JSLM, pp. 279–82).

92　The work being rehearsed was *Chao-Kang*, by Louis Henry, which was performed the next day. Rosolio is a liqueur.

93　MTL, fos. 22^v–23^r. The first paragraph is an insertion written on the verso of fo. 22^r, to be added between the passage about the "grand review" (ending "they would never stand", see p. 87) and the second paragraph (both on 23^r). It is clear that this was an afterthought, and as a result the chronology here is rather muddled. According to contemporary newspapers, King Ferdinand had been busy pheasant-hunting in his royal park on 2nd November (*Gazzetta di Firenze*, 11th November 1820), and had spent the 6th (*Gazzetta piemontese*, 21st November 1820) – and perhaps also the morning of the 7th (*La voce del secolo*, 10th November 1820) – at his Vomero villa, then returning to his palace at Capodimonte. The king used to walk or ride around Naples without an armed escort, much to the surprise of many contemporary foreign travellers. "The numerous foreigners that are now in our capital," wrote *La voce del secolo* on 10th November 1820, "who have been fed many idle stories about the widespread disturbances that are supposed to reign among us, will be amazed to see our revered monarch pass through the crowded streets of Naples escorted by a single courier [a mounted servant who helped with travel arrangements] and without any protection other than the respect and love of his grateful people."

94 For the date of the king's departure, see GCRDS, 13th December 1820. In fact, King Ferdinand had left with the blessing of the Neapolitan parliament, on his solemn promise not to betray the constitution – which of course he did.

95 *Liffey* captain's log, 5th November 1820 (ADM 51/3252). James Ruthven, 7th Lord Ruthven of Freeland (1777–1853), was living in Naples at the time (see DCLC, p. 165). Severn met him and his wife, Lady Mary Ruthven, in Rome in April 1821. The Ruthvens became good friends of the young painter and introduced him to the beau monde of the capital. See JSLM, pp. 146, 155, 158, 162, 358.

96 For Cotterell's qualities, see MTU2, p. 222; DJM, pp. 390, 396; JSLM, p. 204.

97 For Cotterell's activity as an international art dealer and exporter, see Andrea Milanese, *In partenza dal regno* (Florence: Edifir Edizioni, 2014). Cotterell became a partner of John Freeborn (who was appointed British consul in Rome in 1831) before July 1822 (Severn's letter of 5th July 1822 to his sister Maria, JSLM, p. 208) and operated as a banker, wine merchant and shipping agent. Sometime between June 1825 and July 1828 he set up in business on his own (see MTU1, p. 262, BEW, p. 97, and TE, p. 503), and before 1836 (TEUT9, p. 579) he went into a partnership with William Iggulden, which was dissolved in 1846.

98 MAAL1, pp. 400–1. Details of the individuals named are as follows: "Dr. Quin": Frederic Hervey Foster Quin (1799–1878), the first homeopathic physician in England. He went to Rome at the end of 1820 as the travelling physician of the Duchess of Devonshire, moving to Naples the following year. See MAAL1, pp. 399–401.

"[T]he Honorable Keppel Craven": The Honourable Keppel Richard Craven (1779–1851), the youngest son of William Craven, 6th Baron Craven. He is the author of *A Tour through the Southern Provinces of the Kingdom of Naples* (1821). After his father's death in 1791, his mother married the Margrave of Brandenburg-Ansbach. See MAAL1, pp. 409–22.

"Sir Frederick Faulkner": An impoverished Irish gentleman. See MAAL1, pp. 401–2.

"[T]he Margravine of Anspach": Lady Craven, Keppel Craven's mother. See MAAL1, pp. 409–22.

"Abbé Campbell": The infamous Irish Catholic priest Abbé Campbell (*c.*1753–1830). See MAAL1, pp. 388–96.

"Sir Richard Acton and his lady": Sir Ferdinand Richard Edward, 7th Baronet Acton (1801–37) – son of Sir John Acton, a former prime minister of the King of Naples – and his wife Marie Louise Pelina von Dalberg (*c.*1812–60).

"Dr. Watson": Doctor John Watson. The name can be deduced from the will of Sir William Gell, quoted in MAEL2, p. 500. Very little is known about him. Since Gell tells us that he returned to Naples from Paris in 1834, after living there for five or six years (MAEL2, p. 76), he is perhaps to be identified with John Watson, the Irish librarian born in Rathfarnham, near Dublin, in 1799, who applied for French naturalization in 1830 (Archives nationales Paris, BB/11/300, Dossier n° 4333 B7). James Minet wrote in his diary: "[H]is fame appears to outstrip that of all his competitors: I dined with him a few days since, at Mr. Cotterell's, when I was so much pleased with his manner that, in case of need, I almost think I should give him the preference over your old friend [Doctor Roskilly]" (DJM, pp. 378–79); and "Dr. Watson [...] came here to take the cholera in hand, in which line, they say, he has been most successful, performing some remarkable cures" (DJM, p. 387). Doctor Watson is also mentioned in the letters of Thomas Uwins.

"Ramsay": James Ramsay, "a prosperous and very hospitable merchant, and fond of literature and men of letters", according to Charles Macfarlane (see RLL, p. 85). He was also an "old and valued friend" of Richard Robert Madden (MAAL1, p. 328).

"Francis": The Anglo-Irish clergyman Philip Francis (1708–73), famous for his translations of Horace.

"Reilly, the true Hibernian": The Irishman Charles Reilly, surgeon to the British legation. See MAM, p. 18, and MAAL1, pp. 396–98.

"[O]ld Walker": Not the famous Thomas Walker (1749–1817), but his younger brother Richard (c.1754–1833), who was also implicated in his youth in Manchester radical politics, later moving to Naples, where he lived as a merchant.

"Muir and Palmer": The political reformists Thomas Muir (1765–99) and Thomas Fyshe Palmer (1747–1802).

"General Wade": The Irish general Matthew Wade (1747–1829).

"Lever": The Irish physician, novelist and raconteur Charles Lever (1806–72). The surgeon Maurice Quill appears in his novel *Charles O'Malley, the Irish Dragoon* (1841), and is based on a real-life doctor of the same name, who was noted for his wit and humour.

99 LOW, p. 496.
100 See Archivio di Stato di Napoli, Ministero degli Affari Esteri, folder No. 6303. It is likely that the applications were not submitted in person, since some of the information provided is incorrect. Keats's age is given as "28 years"; status: "gentleman"; height: "average"; hair: "brown". Severn's name is spelt "Savera"; his age is recorded as "25 years"; status: "gentleman"; height: "average"; hair: "blond".

INTERLUDE

1 LLJS, pp. 45–101.
2 For a more in-depth analysis, see Grant F. Scott's edition of Severn's letters and memoirs, JSLM, pp. 6–7, 563–75, and his essay 'Writing Keats's Last Days: Severn, Sharp and Romantic Biography', *Studies in Romanticism*, Vol. 42 (2003), pp. 3–26.
3 The memoir from which chapters are supposedly missing is IML, although they may never have been written. There are ten "chapters" missing in all. See JSLM, pp. 563, 566.
4 LLJS, p. 58.
5 Ibid., p. 59.
6 Ibid., pp. 59–60.
7 PBSL, p. 590. Sharp appears to have derived the idea from Richard Monckton Milnes's biography: "He had received at Naples a most kind letter from Mr Shelley, anxiously inquiring about his health, offering him advice as to the adaptation of diet to the climate, and concluding with an urgent invitation to Pisa, where he could ensure him every comfort and attention. But for one circumstance, it is unfortunate that this offer was not accepted" (MON, p. 80). Milnes knew of Shelley's invitation of July 1820 (MON, p. 65) – which contains no dietary advice – so it is odd that he would mistake one letter for the other.

308

Shelley did in fact write a second letter to Keats when he heard that he was in Naples, but this was only around 18th February 1821, when the poet was nearing his death in Rome. In a postcript to a letter to Claire Clairmont written on that day (PBSL, p. 268), he said:

> Keats is very ill at Naples—I have written to him to ask him to come to Pisa, without however inviting him to our own house. We are not rich enough for that sort of thing. Poor fellow!

After the postcript there is a cancelled beginning of the letter to Keats, with no date:

> My dear Keats,
> I learn this moment that you are at Naples, & that

Shelley's second letter may have been forwarded or given to Severn after the poet's death, and it is possible that Milnes saw it and mistook its chronology, or that the painter only reported its contents to him from memory many years after the events. However, there is no mention of this letter in Severn's correspondence or extant memoirs.

In his letter of 4th April 1821 to Thomas Medwin, Shelley wrote: "I hear Keats is in Rome, & dangerously ill.—Should you happen to see him, or if you could take the trouble to call upon him, I should be very glad to know how he is, & where he directs his motions.—& that you would say every thing that is kind from me to him, & entreat to know if I can in any manner be of any service to him.—I am afraid poor fellow it is too late.—Apparently he did not receive my letter addressed to Naples.—" (PBSL, pp. 280–81)

8   LLJS, p. 63. Sharp replaces "Hotel Villa di Londra" with "Hotel d'Inghilterra" throughout his book.

9   The first two volumes (LLWS1 and LLWS2) appeared in 2018 and 2020, respectively. The third volume is forthcoming. The quotation here is from LLWS1, p. ix.

10   SHA, p. 7.

11   Ibid., p. 15.

12   In 1871 Sharp developed a severe case of typhoid fever. Between 1880 and 1886 he had several bouts of rheumatic fever and suffered from scarlet fever (LLWS1, pp. 10, 141).

13   SHA, p. 25.

14   Among the famous writers Sharp came to know and correspond with were George Meredith, Oscar Wilde, Walter Pater, Walt Whitman, Thomas Hardy, Robert Louis Stevenson and W.B. Yeats.

15 Letter of 24th January 1881, LLWS1, p. 30.
16 Sharp's book on Rossetti was *Dante Gabriel Rossetti: A Record and A Study* (London: Macmillan, 1882).
17 SHA, p. iii.
18 Letter of December 1885, LLWS1, p. 157. For an account of Walter Severn's meeting with William Sharp at Fancourt, the Surrey residence of his friends Sir Walter (1803–87) and Lady Sophia (1825–85) Hughes, on Saturday 28th June 1884, see ECL2.
19 For Sharp's comments on the *Life of Robert Browning*, see letter of 16th April 1890 to J. Stanley Little, LLWS1, p. 287. The anthology *Sonnets of This Century*, edited by Sharp, had been even more successful, selling over 15,000 copies in ten months, with an immediate reprint of 10,000 copies (Sharp's letter of 14th December 1886 to Robert Louis Stevenson, LLWS1, p. 173). The anthology included six sonnets by John Keats. For the "Romantic revival", see Sharp's 'Dedicatory Note' to RBPP, pp. v–xiii.
20 Letter of 20th December 1887 to Mr Clarke, LLWS1, p. 201.
21 LLWS1, p. 247.
22 See Sharp's letter of 17th June 1890 to Edmund Clarence Stedman, LLWS1, pp. 292–95. His dream was to abandon his "literary manufacturer" tag and "begin literary life anew", living abroad and focusing only on creative work.
23 SHA, p. 173.
24 "With all his faults—poetic and artistic, Walt Whitman is a noble and truly great fleshly or natural poet" (Sharp's letter of 17th [?] March 1881 to Violet Paget, aka Vernon Lee, LLWS1, p. 41). Sharp visited Whitman in Camden, New Jersey, in January 1892, two months before the poet's death.
25 Letter of 19th September 1891, LLWS1, p. 345.
26 SHA, p. 186.
27 Letter of mid-July 1891 to Bliss Carman, LLWS1, p. 339.
28 For the success of *The Life and Letters of Joseph Severn*, see letter of [14th?] October 1892 to Alfred Austin, LLWS1, p. 439.
29 "To her [Edith Wingate Rinder] I owe my development as 'Fiona Macleod' though, in a sense of course, that began long before I knew her, and indeed while I was still a child" (letter of 21st [?] October 1896 to Elizabeth A. Sharp, SHA, p. 222).
30 SHA, pp. 221–22.
31 *Pharais: A Romance of the Isles* (Derby: Moray Press, 1894), pp. viii–ix.
32 *Vistas* (New York: Duffield and Company, 1906). The quoted words are found on p. 2.
33 OSS, pp. ix, xxiii.

34 These words from the Introduction to *Lyra Celtica* are repeated in the introductory note ibid., p. xxiii.

35 Among her correspondents were W.B. Yeats, who became a friend of William Sharp.

36 William Sharp's letter of 18th August 1896 to John Macleay, LLWS2, p. 241.

37 OSS, p. ix.

JOURNEY TO ROME

1 See for example GALI, p. xxii, or William Cathcart Boyd's *A Guide & Pocket Companion through Italy* (London: Whittaker, Treacher & Co., 1830), pp. 239, 320. Using Google Maps calculations, stage by stage, of Keats and Severn's journey from the Naples toll barrier to the Lateran Gate, Rome, a similar figure is obtained.

2 See M.L. Dutens's *Itinéraire des Routes les plus fréquentées* (London: William Faden, 1779), pp. 68–70, for a detailed analysis of the route from Rome to Naples via Piperno, which totalled 152.5 miles. According to VAL (pp. 249, 252), in which the two routes are listed as identical in length (though the conversions from Italian to English miles appear to be erroneous), Roma–Terracina via Piperno was 9¼ stages and could be covered, riding by post, in 11 hours and 52 minutes. Roma–Terracina via the Pontine Marshes was 10¼ stages and could be travelled in 13 hours. Since the stretch from Terracina to Naples took a further 12 hours and 28 minutes (VAL, p. 255), the whole itinerary could be completed in just over a day. Travelling continuously by *cambiatura*, it was possible to reduce the journey time to twenty-two hours (see MTU1, pp. 253, 266)

3 Travelling from Rome to Naples in 1787, Goethe already used the new road over the Pontine Marshes (see *Travels in Italy*, entry of 23rd February 1787 from Fondi).

4 VAL, p. 252. See also GALI, p. 393.

5 Spalatro is the villainous accomplice of Schedoni in Ann Radcliffe's *The Italian*.

6 VADR, p. 200.

7 For the cost and duration of the journey from Naples to Rome by government courier see MHC, p. 192. Travelling from Rome to Naples by courier took forty hours and cost 20 scudi (GALI, p. xxii). Regarding hiring costs: some people even bought their coaches and then resold them at a much lower price at the end of their journeys. See for example Charles Brown's letter of 2nd May 1826 to Charles Wentworth Dilke, STIL, p. 250.

8   DWI, p. 172.
9   Ibid., p. 174. See also HOL, pp. 241–42.
10 TSI, p. 107.
11 For the use of trusted *vetturini*, see for example Sir William Gell's letter of 22nd February 1827 to Georgiana Gell (Derbyshire Record Office, D258/50/126).
12 In February 1821, the American tourist Theodore Dwight paid a fare of 70 carlins, all inclusive (with a seat at the front of the carriage), for the journey from Naples to Rome by *vettura*, and agreed to give the coachman a tip of 6 carlins and 25 cavalli (DWI, p. 174).
13 TSI, p. 109. Dwight concurs: "On account of the cheapness of the vettura, it is to be presumed that the poorest travellers would usually avail themselves of it, and therefore, that they would offer very little temptation to the avidity of banditti" (DWI, p. 173).
14 Joseph Severn's letter of 5th July 1822 to Thomas Severn, JSLM, p. 202. He was delayed seven hours in the Pontine Marshes by the breaking of a wheel (see note 100 below).
15 For Keats's fear of relapse, see his letter of 1st November 1820 to Charles Brown: "I have been more calm to-day, though in a half dread of not continuing so" (ROL2, p. 352).
16 Letter of 24th December 1820 to John Taylor, KC1, p. 182. "Italy" is "Jatatu[?]" in both KC1 and JSLM (p. 118), but the context and the similar shape of the words "Jatatu" and "Italy" (perhaps written "Iataly" by Severn) make my suggested reading plausible.
17 MTL, fo. 24ʳ. For Sharp's interpolations, see LLJS, pp. 63–64.
18 At times departures were delayed in order to travel together with other carriages. See for example GAL, p. 322, MHC, p. 43, and GVSM, p. 160.
19 Sir William Gell's letter of 22nd February 1827 to Georgiana Gell: "Generally the last 20 miles [to Naples] infernal road" (Derbyshire Record Office, D258/50/126).
20 The night of the 8th and the morning of the 9th were rainy in Naples. This may have made progress slow. MVI (1818) says that after heavy rains the road between Capua and Sant'Agata was "impassable" (p. 604).
21 In the entry for 28th February 1820, Martinengo's journal reports: "Despite bearing the name of city, Fondi was not a place where one could stay at night" (GVSM, p. 165). Either because there was no suitable lodging or because the place was reckoned too dangerous, the count and his retinue decided to hire three dragoons and travel in the dark all the way to the inn at Mola di Gaeta (Albergo di Cicerone), skipping Itri. Writing a year later, Theodore Dwight says: "It has been determined to stop here [at Mola] tonight, to avoid

the danger of passing the country between Fondi and Terracina in the evening; for there is no inn at Fondi" (DWI, p. 188). I could find no mention of any inn other than the post-house (see for example SEL1, pp. 54–55) – which might have been able to accommodate night guests, but was also a place where ransoms were delivered to brigands (see DCLC, p. 187) – and no record of any early-nineteenth-century traveller spending a night there. It should be pointed out that travellers – foreigners in particular – tried to avoid staying at post-house inns. The inevitable disturbance late at night and early in the morning, as well as the malodorous vapours from the stables, made them unsuitable for overnight stays. Because of the terrible reputation of Itri and Fondi, and their association with banditti, travellers tended to go through these towns as quickly as possible, trying to reach the safe haven of the Papal States' border before sunset. Lady Miller, James Edward Smith and Goethe spent a night at a run-down inn in Fondi, but that was in the second half of the eighteenth century. There is a mention of a Locanda Barbarossa in Fondi towards the mid-1830s by the anonymous author of NNE (p. 36), and its existence is confirmed by the 1853 Murray's *Handbook for Travellers in Southern Italy* (p. 62). It may also be that the *vetturino* knew of a small inn or private lodgings at Fondi (QUA, p. 131, observes that there are "woeful inns" in Itri and Fondi). In that case, it would have made sense for Keats and Severn to break the journey there, as it is halfway between Mola di Gaeta and Terracina, but there is no reason to suggest that they may have departed from the typical pattern of travel.

22   Doctor Clark's letter of 27th November 1820 to an unknown recipient, ROL2, p. 358. For Torlonia, see KSMB, p. 95. Torlonia's bank operated from its headquarters on the ground floor of Palazzo Bolognetti in Piazza Venezia and from a smaller branch in Via dei Condotti 43–46, in the L-shaped building at the corner of Via del Corso (now called Largo Carlo Goldoni), only 300 yards from Doctor Clark's house (see VDPR, p. 11; GASP, p. 30; and the land-registry map Catasto urbano, Rione Campo Marzio, III, No. 957).

23   VPRN. The engravings can be seen online on the Istituto Centrale per la Grafica website (www.calcografica.it).

24   The Strada del Gigante is now Via Cesario Console. The Piazza del Real Palazzo is now Piazza del Plebiscito.

25   Before the new toll barrier built at Capodichino between 1826 and 1831, the old turnpike was situated on the Via Foria, past the Albergo de' Poveri. See TEN, p. 17, ITA, p. 147, and Giuseppe Pignatelli, *Napoli: Tra il disfar delle mura e l'innalzamento del muro finanziere* (Florence: Alinea editrice, 2006), pp. 54–58.

26 GVSM, p. 167.

27 EI, p. 61.

28 SEL1, p. 56.

29 SIM, pp. 393–94.

30 DWI, pp. 181–82.

31 SHER, p. 316. Sherer visited Capua in the autumn of 1823.

32 *History of Rome* XXIII, 18, 10–12.

33 EI, p. 62.

34 TSI, pp. 109–10.

35 BER, p. 217 ("the sea opened […]"); DWI, p. 183 ("far behind […]"). It should be pointed out that what was described, by many travellers, as mountainous heights and picturesque country worthy of Salvator Rosa is in fact, for the most part, a landscape of sloping fields and gentle hills: the village of Cascano, the highest elevation on the road between Naples and Terracina, is only about 207 metres (680 feet) above sea level.

36 TEN, p. 21.

37 ITA, pp. 145–46.

38 DWI, pp. 183–84.

39 GAL, pp. 323–24.

40 EI, p. 63 ("scarcely more […]"); ITA, p. 146 ("in the midst […]"); TEN, p. 23 ("beautiful oaks […]").

41 ITA, p. 146.

42 TEN, pp. 23–25.

43 For the bridge of boats, see PEN, p. 521, and TEN, p. 27. The quotation "passed through a gate […]" is from DWI, p. 186. For the inscription, see VAS, p. 39, and others.

44 DWI, pp. 186–87.

45 TEN, p. 27.

46 PEN, p. 519.

47 The Albergo di Cicerone was housed in an elegant eighteenth-century palazzo called Villa Patrizi, which was destroyed during the Second World War. The building can be seen in pre-war postcards and nineteenth-century paintings, such as the one attributed to Pasquale Mattej (1813–79), dating from around 1850 (see plates, 4c). At the time of Keats's journey, the inn was probably owned (or simply managed) by Clemente Zaurini, who in the early 1830s left the Albergo di Cicerone to open a competing establishment in the nearby Villa di Caposele (now Villa Rubino). See TEUT8, p. 302, note h, and ACE, entries of 25th–26th October 1834. The inn was on the site occupied today by the two red-brick buildings located between Via Angelo Rubino and Via Olivetani in Formia.

48 BROC, p. 194.

49　The Shelleys, for example, rested for an entire day at the Albergo di Cicerone on 2nd March 1819 as they rode from Naples to Rome, and spent their time "playing at chess & st[r]olling about the woods & by the sea shore" (MSJ, p. 250). For their impressions of the inn and its surrounding scenery, see MSJ, p. 241 and PBSL, p. 83. In the summer of 1825, Severn returned to Mola to paint the local peasants in their traditional costume, and stayed at the Albergo di Cicerone, where he met his friend Lady Westmorland and attended her "pic nic parties down on the seacoast under Ciceros Villa" (see MTL, fos. 35–36).

50　This is in the Z. Smith Reynolds Library Special Collections and Archives, Wake Forest University, Winston-Salem, North Carolina, USA (Joseph Severn Watercolors, MS651). See plates, 4a.

51　See plates, 4b, 4c.

52　For more detail and background information about the rediscovery of Severn's three watercolours, see Grant F. Scott, 'New Severn Watercolours from the Voyage to Italy with Keats', *Romanticism*, Vol. 22, No. 2 (2016), pp. 213–29.

53　ITA, p. 143, note.

54　DWI, pp. 187–88.

55　KOTZ, pp. 222–23.

56　For Mola's evening attractions, see DWI, p. 190. J.M.W. Turner left several sketches of the Gulf of Gaeta seen from Mola and the Albergo di Cicerone, executed during his journey to Naples of 1819. See his sketchbooks (*Naples, Paestum and Rome*, fo. 19c; *Gandolfo to Naples*, fos. 25a–26, 27a–27), currently held at the Tate.

57　It was around six and a half miles from the Albergo di Cicerone, which was about a mile from Mola on the way to Itri.

58　SEL1, p. 54.

59　ITA, p. 141.

60　FAUL, pp. 182–83.

61　"*Sozzo e meschinissimo budello*", TEN, p. 31.

62　SIM, p. 392.

63　ITA, pp. 141–42.

64　FAUL, pp. 183–84. The words "crime" and "malady" are from ITA, p. 141.

65　BROC, p. 193.

66　ITA, p. 131 ("the true classic […]"); JOUS, p. 104 ("well fitted […]").

67　ITA, 140. On sentry posts, see also GVSM, pp. 240–41.

68　ITA, 140.

69　Ibid., p. 139.

70　Ibid., p. 140.

71　PEN, p. 517.

72 FAUL, p. 181.

73 For the information contained in this paragraph, see DOI, p. 170; SASS, p. 153; ITA, p. 139, GVSM, pp. 163–64. For the quotations "all filth, dirt [...]" and "*Carità, Cristiani*", see ITA, p. 140.

74 Monticello is now called Monte San Biagio.

75 ITA, p. 139.

76 GVSM, pp. 248–55.

77 DCLC, p. 168.

78 DWI, p. 192.

79 CARN, p. 357.

80 DWI, pp. 198–99.

81 TEN, p. 35.

82 The tales that make up 'The Italian Banditti' are included in Washington Irving, *Tales of a Traveller*, Vol. 2 (London: John Murray, 1824), published under the pseudonym "Geoffrey Crayon". For Joachim Murat and the Albergo Reale, see HERM, p. 262: "The King of Naples used to stay here, and mine host shows us the room where Murat slept."

83 For the story of the building, see Rosario Malizia, *Un mito letterario del Grand Tour: La Locanda di Terracina* (Terracina: Bookcart, 2017). The Albergo Reale and other buildings in this area were destroyed during the Second World War by the retreating Germans.

84 The porch can be seen in VPRN, plate 41.

85 See GREC, p. 310: "Our coach stopped in the yard of a large stone building: the Pontifical border douane. Two or three officers inspected our things in a quick, tactful manner, and were satisfied with a small tip. We breakfasted at the inn housed in the same building. Its peculiarity is that the rooms they rent out to travellers are not distinguished by numbers, but by the name of some Italian city – for example Milan, Naples, Rome, Venice." The quotation "enormous" is from DWI, p. 200.

86 F. de Romain, *Souvenirs d'un officier royaliste*, Vol. 1 (Paris: A. Égron, 1824), p. 263.

87 DWI, p. 191.

88 SIM, p. 391.

89 ITA, p. 136; PEN, p. 511. John Mayne, stopping at the hotel for the night in January 1815, declares: "The inn at Terracina is good, and my bedroom was situated over the roaring Mediterranean. Our supper well served, and beds, as everywhere else, excellent and clean" (MAYN, p. 255). Selina Martin, writing in 1819, says: "The inn is very comfortable" (SEL1, p. 54). Theodore Dwight recalls in his travel diary: "The inn where we have stopped is very large, and the hospitality of its inmates was redoubled in our

view, by the joy we experienced on finding ourselves delivered from the danger of banditti" (DWI, p. 200). Count Martinengo's journal reports: "The inn at Terracina was reasonably good, and certainly better than any we could have expected to find along the way if we had been forced to travel on and stay at some other place overnight before reaching Rome" (GVSM, pp. 242–43).

90 *Rome, Naples et Florence* (Paris: Édouard Champion, 1919), Vol. 1, p. 372. Stendhal claims to have met and talked to Gioachino Rossini there, which has been doubted by scholars.

91 FRAN, pp. 232–33. He adds: "I well remember how ill we were served here eight years ago, and the astonishment of the Camareire [for "Cameriere"] at the jobation he received from me, who took him for the Albergatore himself."

92 COBB, p. 201.

93 *Satires* I, 5, ll. 6–7, 14.

94 COBB, p. 198.

95 DOI, p. 171.

96 BER, p. 162.

97 COBB, p. 198.

98 DWI, pp. 201–2. The villages referred to are Piperno and Sezze.

99 For the advice to travel on a full stomach, see EI, p. 68.

100 In his journey of early July 1822, when he travelled to Naples with Maria Erskine and her daughters, an accident forced Severn to traverse the Pontine Marshes at night. He wrote: "I was the only Knight all the way—and had to keep [the ladies] awake in crossing the pestilential places so we chatted and chatted" (Letter of 5th July 1822 to Thomas Severn, JSLM, p. 203). In his memoir IML (No. 20, fo. 1^r) he adds: "We were stopd in the Pontine Marshes by the breaking of a wheel & had to stay some 7 hours in the most deadly malaria at night.—The air was heavy with ^{a} vegetable damp fog exhuding from the soil & the Canal had the largest toads crawling up & down the bank I ever saw & there were so many, at least 13 inches in length most loathsome beings—we kept ourselves awake by drinking tea, for sleep would have been fatal sooner or later."

101 See BROC, p. 189.

102 DWI, p. 202 ("the unhealthy exhalations [...]").

103 See for example DWI, pp. 201–2: they left "very early in the morning" from Terracina and "reached the post house, in the middle of the marsh" at noon.

104 George Hume Weatherhead gives an amusing description of the fare he was offered at Tor de' Tre Ponti: "I had eels served up for

supper [...]; a fowl so lean that it might have passed for a lizard metamorphosed; and water to drink that *smelt* of corruption" (PTFI, p. 208). Recounting his trip to Naples of July 1822, Severn says: "Bad food on the journey [threw] my Stomach into a false state" (letter of 5th July 1822 to Thomas Severn, JSLM, p. 203).

105 ITA, p. 127.

106 BER, p. 219.

107 SIM, p. 391.

108 COBB, p. 199. From "*ciocia*" is derived the word *ciociari*, a term applied to the mountain shepherds and farmers of a large area of south-eastern Lazio.

109 The quotation "made of straw or haulm" is from PEN, p. 512.

110 BER, p. 221.

111 ITA, p. 130.

112 FAUL, p. 180. The Latin term "*mapalia*" refers to huts used by African tribes.

113 BROC, p. 189. The reference is to famous engravings by Bartolomeo Pinelli (1781–1835).

114 EI, pp. 71–72.

115 This was regarded as "an ugly slovenly custom", as explained by Sir George Cockburn in *A Voyage to Cadiz and Gibraltar, up the Mediterranean to Sicily*, Vol. 2 (London: J. Harding, 1815), p. 206. The quotation is from Severn's letter of 21st January 1821 to his sister Maria, JSLM, p. 130.

116 The location of Tres Tabernæ is still disputed, but most biblical scholars and archaeologists believe that it was on the site or in the vicinity of Cisterna.

117 The bridge comprised two large arches and a smaller one to channel rainwater.

118 BROC, p. 187.

119 TEN, p. 38.

120 See for example VG, pp. 76–78. Talking about his trip from Rome to Florence in June 1823, Severn says: "I have had a most delicious journey on foot of some 200 Miles" (JSLM, p. 244).

121 For the bumps and jolts, see VG, p. 76.

122 TSI, p. 115.

123 PEN, pp. 507–8. The editor of the *London Magazine*, John Scott, also left a good description of Palazzo Ginnetti and Velletri in his *Sketches of Manners* (London: Longman, 1821), pp. 329–33. Four days after Keats's death Scott was killed in a duel by Jonathan Henry Christie, the London agent of John Gibson Lockhart of *Blackwood's Edinburgh Magazine*, in the wake of the "Cockney School" controversy.

Berrian concurred about the "superb marble staircase" – see
BER, p. 160.

For the poet (Horace) and the gnats and frogs, see note 93 above.

124 TSI, p. 116.

125 William Thomson employed eleven hours from Velletri to Rome
on his "slow machine" (TJIS, pp. 179–80).

126 For the southwards turn, see TEN, p. 39. The quotation "rather
nasty" is from GVSM, p. 244. See also FAUL, p. 178.

127 FAUL, p. 178.

128 COBB, p. 196.

129 TEN, p. 39.

130 Civita Lavinia was supposedly named after the daughter of King
Latinus and wife of Aeneas, who according to legend had a city
founded in her honour called Lavinium. The modern town is
called Lanuvio. See VADR, p. 186. The quotation "delightful
village" is from TEN, p. 39.

131 BER, p. 160.

132 *Impressions de voyage: Le Corricolo*, Vol. 2 (Paris: Michel Lévy
Frères, 1872), pp. 268–69.

133 Galloro is the site of a sanctuary between Genzano and Ariccia.

134 From 'La strada da Genzano ad Albano, sestine', ll. 115–216.
Gregorio Giannini (1815–d. before 1875) was a surgeon, a poet
and patriot. He played an active role in the establishment of the
short-lived Roman Republic of 1849, and after the restoration of
the pope was forced to go into exile to Turkey, where he died. For
the complete text of the poem in Italian and more information
about Giannini, see *Genzano sempre luccica* (London: Alma Books,
2018), pp. xxiii–xxvii, 155–66. The poem was recited by Giannini
on 16th October 1842, in the presence of Cardinal Tosti, during a
grand ceremony to celebrate the prelate as a protector of Genzano.

135 Joseph Severn's letter of 6th June 1821 to his sister Sarah, JSLM,
p. 162. The Infiorata was celebrated that year on Sunday, 24th June.
See the "Programma" of the festival signed by the *gonfaloniere*
Luigi Leoffredi. One of the "others" might have been Johann
Anton Ramboux (1790–1860), who left a beautiful painting of
the occasion (*Festa vulgarmente detta l'Infiorata nell'Ottavario
del Corpus Domini in Genzano 1821*), now in the Städel Museum
in Frankfurt am Main.

The "picture" referred to by Severn is *The Death of Alcibiades*.
The quotation "it [was] a miracle [...]" is from l. 114 of
Giannini's poem.

136 VADR, p. 172. KNI (p. 81) says it was called "la Fontana della
bugia, or 'the fountain of deceit,' from its being a resting place

for the people who bring wine from Gensano, and are here supposed to replenish the casks with water".

137 Rome temperatures for 14th November 1820 were 12.8 °C in the morning and 15.6 °C during the day (*Diario di Roma*, 15th November 1820).

138 For a visual impression of Porta Napoletana, Porta Romana and Piazza di Corte, see Giovanni Battista Camuccini's *The Porta Napoletana with the Palazzo Chigi* (Toledo Museum of Art) and Luigi Rossini's *Ingresso all'Ariccia* (VPRN, plate 29) and *Piazza dell'Ariccia* (VPRN, plate 30).

139 DWI, p. 208.

140 Although still known today under that name, the tomb in fact dates from the first half of the first century BC, and is thought to be the mausoleum of the Etruscan warrior Aruns.

141 No. 57 in the 1819 land-registry map for Albano (see CGCA, map and index).

142 Via della Posta is now Piazza Antonio Gramsci.

143 No. 404 in the 1819 land-registry map for Albano (CGCA). The registry index gives "Emiliano Giorni, son of the late Pietrantonio" as the owner. Villa di Londra's entry in the land registry says: "Lodging house used as an inn, with a portion inhabited by the owner and a courtyard."

144 IDTC5, p. 224.

145 See CRI1, p. 69. Pietrantonio Giorni (1731–1805) was a wealthy landowner and a prominent figure in the Albano of his time. For more details, see CRI2, pp. 19–20. *View of the City of Albano* was an engraved map of the town included in Giovanni Antonio Riccy, *Memorie storiche dell'antichissima Città di Alba-Longa e dell'Albano moderno* (Rome: Giovanni Zempel, 1787).

146 See CRI1, pp. 70–74. Mme Récamier was a guest of the Locanda in 1813, when she was invited by Canova to take up some of the rooms he kept there during the summer.

147 The building that housed the inn was demolished in 1932 during the redevelopment of Albano's town centre (CRI1, p. 69). Between 1823 – the year in which Emiliano Giorni died – and 1827, the inn became the Europa (see IDTC6, p. 260, which adds "wholesome wines" between the "good dinners" and the "tolerable beds"), under the management of Emiliano's widow Agnese Ferrari and their sons, and continued to be active under that name for decades (see, for example, HT43, p. 503; HT53, p. 276), although still referred to at times as "Hotel Ville de Londres" or "Hotel de Londres" (see CRI1, p. 69).

148 See Arcangelo Ferri, notaio e cancelliere, 'Atti e Decreti di Volontaria Giurisdizione dall'anno 1851 al 1852' (Albano, Archivio Storico Diocesano). Don Francesco Giorni was the author of a notable *Storia di Albano* (Roma: Puccinelli, 1842), a history of the town.

149 See the description left by Amelia Lenormant (the niece and adopted daughter of Mme Récamier): "Pompey's villa extended its magnificent shadows to the left – the sea lined the horizon, and on the vast plain that stretched under the large balcony of Mme Récamier's room, a thousand shifting variations of ground, vegetation and light created, depending on the time and the weather, one of the most beautiful views in the world. This room, which was used as a drawing room, was furnished with white calico curtains, and its walls were adorned with colour engravings of frescoes from Herculaneum" (SCT, p. 234). According to Lenormant (SCT, p. 235), Giambattista Bassi's portrait of Mme Récamier, *Ritratto di nobildonna*, dated Rome 1816, was painted at the hotel Villa di Londra in 1813. The landscape visible from the window, however, is hilly, and Villa Borghese and the Muro Torto can be glimpsed in the background. (For a full analysis of the painting, see https://paoloantonacci.com/it/artworks/categories/6/9429-giambattista-bassi-ritratto-di-nobildonna-in-un-interno-con-villa-1816/.)

150 See, for example, Severn's letter of 6th June 1821 to his sister Sarah: "The Palaces are nearly all deserted—many are in Ruins—for this reason—that a great part of the year in and about Rome—the air is poisonous—it produces deadly Fever's call'd Malaria—this lasts for the Summer—during all the hot weather (the place is quite deserted)—a great amount of poisons [fill the] air so that the place is thinned of people—This Malaria arises from the Marshes and small rivers—stagnating in the hot weather—the air becomes putrid—and to sleep in it is death certain" (JSLM, p. 160).

151 TEN, pp. 39–40.

152 *Rom, Römer und Römerinnen* (Berlin: Duncker und Humblot, 1820), p. 31. The excerpt is from Müller's letter of 16th July 1818 from Albano. Wilhelm Müller is the author, among other things, of the sets of poems *Die schöne Müllerin* and *Winterreise*, the basis for Franz Schubert's famous song cycles.

153 For the attractions of Albano, including the museum, see IDTC5, p. 224.

154 Rome temperatures for 15th November 1820 were 13.8 °C in the morning and 16.1 °C during the day (*Diario di Roma*, 22nd November 1820).

155 ITA, pp. 123–24. See also Shelley's impressions in PBSL, p. 84.

156 TEN, p. 40.

157 DWI, p. 210.

158 The gateway was the Porta Romana.

159 The "mountain" is the hill on which the town of Albano is built.

160 EI, pp. 75–78.

161 MTL, fo. 24ʳ. The stick was planted into the ground.

162 The Archivio Storico Luce has a short film from 1929, 'Caccia all'allodola nella campagna romana' ('Skylark-Hunting in the Campagna Romana'), which provides a visual idea of what Severn is describing. By that time artificial decoy birds ("*zimbelli*") and hunting callers were also being used alongside real owls.

163 A pulmonary affliction, according to one of his descendants (https://www.unicaumbria.it/raccontami-l-umbria/unazienda-non-convenzionale-in-umbria-le-terre-di-poreta/).

164 B. [Marie-Henri Beyle], 'Letters from Rome, II', NMM, p. 471. For the attribution of the piece to Stendhal, see Robert Vigneron, 'Du Stendhal retrouvé', in *Modern Philology*, Vol. 30, No. 1 (August 1932), pp. 82–83 (Chicago: University of Chicago Press, 1932).

165 From Artaud de Montor's *History of Pope Leo XII*. I am translating from the Italian version of the book, SPL (p. 18). For the French original, see HPL, p. 22.

166 MOR, p. 5.

167 Gaetano Moroni, *Dizionario di erudizione storico-ecclesiastica*, Vol. 38 (Venice: Tipografia Emiliana, 1846), p. 51. See also Antonio Nibby, *Analisi storico-topografico-antiquaria della carta de' dintorni di Roma* (Rome: Tipografia delle Belle Arti, 1848), p. 9.

168 See Alessandro Dani, 'La normativa di Annibale della Genga cardinale vicario di Roma', in Roberto Regoli, Ilaria Fiumi Sermattei and Maria Rosa Di Simone, eds., *Governo della Chiesa, Governo dello Stato: Il tempo di Leone XII* (Ancona: Consiglio Regionale Assemblea legislativa delle Marche, 2019), pp. 341–67.

169 Lorenzo Litta (1756–1820), Della Genga's predecessor as vicar general, served between 28th September 1818 and his death on 1st May 1820. For Della Genga's 'Invito sagro' of 11th November 1820, see Archivio di Stato di Roma, *Bandi*. His 'Inviti sagri' for 26th and 30th October are also endorsed by Antonio Argenti.

170 For the hunting edict, see Cesare De Cupis, *La caccia nella Campagna Romana secondo la storia e i documenti* (Rome: Attilio Nardecchia, 1922), pp. 122–24.

171 *"Quando il Papa è cacciatore / Le città diventan selve; / I ministri sono i cani, / Ed i sudditi le belve."* Anonymous, *Il governo pontificio in rapporto a legalità, legittimità ed influenza sulla religione* (Paris: Poussielgue, 1833), p. 10, note. See also Belli's sonnets 'La pissciata pericolosa', 'Le carcere', 'Le mura de Roma', 'Er linnesto', 'La porta dereto', 'Er dente der Papa', 'Li cancelletti', 'Li discorzi', 'Papa Leone' and 'Er mortorio de Leone Duodescimosiconno'.

172 *Dell'Acqua Santa e dei bagni di essa rinnovati, notizie storico-mediche* (Rome: Clemente Puccinelli, 1853), pp. 9–10. The book includes a floor plan of the Baths' building. The Casino (or Casale) del Papa and the Baths are now derelict.

173 MO, p. 1161. Chateaubriand's first audience with the pope took place around the middle of October 1828.

174 Ibid., p. 1215, from a letter of 12th January 1829 to the French foreign minister, Auguste de la Ferronays, in which Chateaubriand gives a detailed report of his audience with the pope of 2nd January 1829.

175 MTL, fo. 24^r. The brackets enclosing the word "Sir" appear to have been pencilled in by a later hand.

ROME

1 Clark is referred to as residing in Piazza di Spagna in IDTC5, p. 211.

2 ROL2, pp. 358–59.

3 LOW, p. 501, where she misnames him "Samuel Edward Gray". *A Supplement to the Pharmacopœias* was published in London by Thomas and George Underwood in 1818. The book was reprinted and updated several times, under the title *A Supplement to the Pharmacopœia*. Thomas and George Underwood also published James Clark's JCLA in 1820.

4 Clark's comment about "the Edinburgh Rev{iewe}rs" refers to Francis Jeffrey's in fact rather mixed review of *Endymion* and LAM in the August 1820 issue of the *Edinburgh Review* (Vol. 34, No. 67, pp. 203–13).

   The words "throw medicine to the dogs" are taken from *Macbeth*, Act v, Sc. 3, l. 47.

5 JCLA, p. 76.

6 The quotation "so that he might [...]" is from MTL, fo. 24^r. See also Severn's Letter of 5th May 1848 to Richard Monckton Milnes: "Sir J. Clark began by getting Keats a lodging just opposite to him so that he might attend him even at night" (KC2, p. 233). The houses opposite No. 26 Piazza di Spagna were Nos. 70 to 75.

7   For a history of the building and its setting, see Richard Haslam, 'The House by the Barcaccia', in *Keats and Italy: A History of the Keats-Shelley House in Rome* (Rome: Il Labirinto, 2005), pp. 75–80.

8   Catasto urbano di Roma, Rione Campo Marzio, IV, No. 1157.

9   Alessandro Angeletti is the author of the engraved frontispiece of *Opere di Niccolò Machiavelli, Cittadino e Segretario Fiorentino*, Vol. 1 (Florence: Gaetano Cambiagi, 1796).

10   A colourful figure among the English expatriates in Rome, Revd "Colonel Calicot" Finch later became friends with Joseph Severn and travelled with him to Florence in 1823. Finch's reputation was tarnished by his love of fibbing. See Severn's letter of 11th January 1824 to his brother Charles, JSLM, pp. 248–50. For his own testimony that he "had [...] more than once inhabited" the lodgings at No. 26, Piazza di Spagna, see PBSL, p. 300n.

11   Bodleian, MS Finch e.15 (13th April–8th May 1815), e.16 (9th May–12th June 1815). "Signor Vasi" is Mariano Vasi (1744–1820), son of the famous engraver Giuseppe and author of the most influential and popular guidebooks for travellers to Rome and Naples of the time, whose shop was at "Via del Babuino, near the Piazza di Spagna, No. 122" (VAS, title page). Vasi had married Maria Caffuro from Corfu (Anna Angeletti's aunt) in 1778 (COEN, pp. 43 and 56n).

12   The census data are taken from the *Stati delle anime* (S. Andrea delle Fratte) for the years 1819, 1820 and 1821. The registers are kept at the Archivio Storico Diocesano in Rome.

13   The house at 26/27 Piazza di Spagna was sold at auction on 11th March 1843 by "Signora Virginia Angeletti Palmieri" and "Mr and Mrs Cappuccini" (Lucrezia and her husband Agostino Cappuccini), owners of an equal share in the building. Bids started at 1,500 scudi (*Supplemento al Num. 12 del Diario di Roma*, 11th February 1843).

14   Joseph Severn's letter of 24th December 1820 to John Taylor, KC1, p. 184.

15   ROL2, pp. 359–60.

16   MTL, fo. 27ʳ. In the same paragraph, Severn dates Keats's recovery to "the beginning of the year 1821", but by then the poet was already bedridden. For Clark's opinion, see extract of a letter of 3rd January 1821 from Doctor Clark to an unknown recipient [Doctor Gray?], ROL2, p. 367.

17   Day temperatures in Rome between 15th November and 14th December 1820 (as reported by the *Diario di Roma*) were between 10 °C and 14.5 °C, with the exception of 3rd December (9.2 °C).

18 This is mentioned in Severn's letter of 17th December 1820 to Charles Brown, ROL2, p. 363. Since Monckton Milnes – who had been lent all of Severn's letters to Haslam (see Haslam's letter to Milnes of 5th February 1847, KC2, pp. 188–89) – doesn't quote from it in his biography of the poet, we can assume it was lost.

19 KSMB, p. 95.

20 KC2, p. 92. See also Keats's letter of 30th November 1820: "My stomach continues so bad, that I feel it worse on opening any book" (ROL2, p. 359). The verse can be translated as follows: "Alas! No other respite I'm allowed / Than shedding tears – and even tears are sinful" – Vittorio Alfieri, *Filippo*, Act I, Sc. 1, ll. 19–20. Perhaps the edition he bought was *Opere scelte*, 4 vols. (Milan: Società Tipografica de' Classici Italiani, 1818).

21 MTL, fos. 27^v–28^r. The first paragraph ("The return of apparent health [...]") is an insertion written on the verso of fo. 27^r, to be added on 28^r before "He even talkd [...]". The word "characteristic" is written "charec^{ter}tic".

22 Letter of 19th September 1821 to Charles Brown, JSLM, p. 172. See *Comus*, l. 859 ff.

23 Letter of 5th January 1822 to John Taylor, JSLM, p. 190. See also BNK: "He intended to write a long Poem on the story of Sabrina as left by Milton & often spoke of it at Rome but never wrote a line" (KC2, p. 138).

Una is a character from Edmund Spenser's *The Faerie Queene*.

24 Geoffrey of Monmouth, *Historia regum Britanniæ* II, 4.

25 For the horse, see Severn's letter of 24th December 1820 to John Taylor, KC1, p. 182. Keats's letter of 30th November 1820 (ROL2, p. 360) suggests he was already going horseback-riding. In Clark's letter of 27th November 1820 (ROL2, p. 358) this was still only a plan, so in all likelihood Keats hired the horse at about the same time as he rented the piano, on 29th November 1820.

The Keats-Shelley House holds an autograph receipt for Keats's piano signed by the landlady: "The undersigned has received from Messrs Jos eph Pecurn [sic] and John Keats [s]even [written "*ette*" rather than "*sette*" in Italian] Scudi for a month's rental of a piano up until and including 28th December next. — Anna Angeletti" (KTS-1.18).

26 MTL, fo. 27^r. For William Sharp's novelistic elaboration of these two paragraphs, including the spurious 'Æolian Harp' anecdote, see LLJS, pp. 81–83. Severn's claim that Keats went horseback-riding in "the middle of January" is incorrect: this must in fact have been between 28th November and 9th December 1820. It is

also untrue that Elton "survived Keats nearly a year": in fact, he survived Keats by more than two years.

27   Hyder E. Rollins, 'Louis Arthur Holman and Keats', *Harvard Library Bulletin*, Vol. 4, No. 3 (Autumn 1950), p. 381.

28   Shorter notices were published in the *London Packet and New Lloyd's Evening Post* of 18th–20th June and *Baldwin's London Weekly Journal* of 21st June 1823, and a mention appeared in the 'Military Obituary' section of *The Sun* (London) of 7th August 1823. Elton had left England in early 1819 (see FO 610/1: "Jany 15 [1819], 3777, M! Marmaduke Elton (Royal Eng.^{rs}) [Where going] The Continent"). Regarding "Coire [Chur], in Switzerland": consumptive patients who had passed the winter in Italy were recommended a summer sojourn in Switzerland before returning to Italy for the colder seasons. See JCLA, p. 91 *ff.*

Gais is a Swiss village, famous at the time as a whey health resort, about 45 miles north of Chur.

29   See, respectively, *The London Gazette*, No. 16584, 17th March 1812, p. 520 ("Gentleman Cadet [trainee officer] Isaac M. Elton, vice Hulme, promoted. Dated December 14, 1811"), and No. 16623, 14th July 1812, p. 1366 ("Second Lieutenant Isaac M. Elton to be First Lieutenant, vice Dixon, promoted, Dated July 1, 1812").

30   Elton's account of the death of Captain Edward Parker at the Battle of Orthez (27th February 1814) survives in a letter written by Parker's elder brother Thomas:

July 27th, 1814
   Captain Parker was attached to the 3rd division. He rode out to join it the morning of the battle after breakfasting with me, and remained with Sir Thos. Picton [the commander of the 3rd division] during the action until the minute of his death. In the act of galloping to the rear to carry an order from the General, a cannon shot struck him in the body, when he fell from his horse and instantly expired. His body was buried by an officer of artillery, in the rear of whose guns he was killed, having previously been rifled by some Spanish muleteers under a heavy fire. His watch and what cash he had about him were thus irrecoverably lost; but his horses, mules &c., were disposed of by auction to the best bidder by direction of the brigade-major, and the produce lodged in the pay-master's hands. A *will was also found*, made during his stay at Lisbon.

   His sword I endeavoured in vain to recover, though I discovered it in the possession of a Spanish officer. He had purchased it from an English hussar. General Alava [Miguel Ricardo de Álava y Esquivel, Wellington's Spanish liaison officer], to whom I applied, promised to restore it, but neglected to keep his word. Had I before known how to address any of Captain P.'s relatives, I should not have delayed informing them of the handsome way in which General Picton mentioned him, and also that had he survived that day it was the General's intention to have recommended him strongly for his majority.

(Quoted in LNC, pp. 188–89)

On Elton's role in the Peninsular War, see Mark S. Thompson, *Wellington's Engineers: Military Engineering in the Peninsular War 1808–1814* (Barnsley: Pen and Sword, 2015), p. 212, and 'The Rise of the Scientific Soldier as Seen through the Performance of the Corps of Royal Engineers during the Early 19th Century' (doctoral thesis, University of Sunderland, 2009), pp. 263–69.

31   G.R. Gleig, *Story of the Battle of Waterloo* (London: John Murray, 1849), pp. 306–7, 317. A miniature on ivory of a distinguished-looking man survives, inscribed on the reverse "To E. Elton Esqr / from Joseph Severn / Rome April 22nd 1823", which could be a portrait of a member of the young officer's family who accompanied him on his journey to Switzerland. See Daphne Foskett, *Miniatures: Dictionary and Guide* (Woodbridge, Suffolk: Antique Collectors' Club, 2000), p. 406. A Bible (now in the possession of Ross Severn), inscribed "Joseph Severn from Lieut Elton", also survives.

32   JCLA, p. 75. The only exception to Doctor Clark's rules about churches in Rome was St Peter's: "From the immense body of air which it contains, it is always of a mild temperature, and always safe for the invalid" (ibid.).

33   MTL, fo. 27^r. See also BNK (KC2, p. 138).

34   MTL, fos. 24^r–25^r. Lord Colchester returned to Rome from Naples on Tuesday, 5th December 1820 (DCLC, p. 185), so Severn must have visited Gibson's study after that date, not "at once", "straight" after his arrival in Rome.

35   MTL, fo. 26^r.

36   Hilton was elected Royal Academician on 10th December 1819 at a General Assembly of the Academicians. During the same meeting, it was announced that Severn was to be awarded a Gold Medal in the category of historical painting (see 'Before the Departure', note 116). Severn wrote about this incident in his letter of 17th July 1821 to Charles Brown (STIL, pp. 79–80), who replied: "I cannot believe Hilton would be so base as you suspect. There must be some guiltless mistake. [...] I must correct an error that you have fallen into respecting Hilton. Those illiberal expressions

concerning your prize picture were not used by Hilton, nor at his house, nor even in his presence; but by Hilton's friend De Wintd (or Windt, or what?) at Taylor's house. It is true we all imagined that Hilton was his anonymous authority" (letter of 13th August 1821, published in the new, revised edition of NLBS).

37 MTL, fos. 26ʳ–27ʳ. Severn revisited this anecdote during a conversation with his son Walter in Rome on 17th September 1878. See Walter Severn's notes of this conversation in ECL1: "Talking of the difficulty I had about getting his pension increased, he got upon his early life & described how after the award by the R.A. of the Gold Medal for my fathers picture of the Cave of Despair Hilton and his brother in law De Wint on the occasion of a dinner set to & abused Severn in such a manner that Keats the poet who was present left the Table. He said he could not hear his friend abused so unfairly & from shere jialosy & left the house. Sir Thos. Lawrence afterwards awarded the Travelling Pension to Mʳ Severn. Mʳ Keats the poet was dying and his greatest anxiety seemed to be lest his friend should not succeed with the R.A. He begged my father to get all the influence he could to bear on Sir T. Lawrence."

38 MTL, fos. 27ʳ–28ʳ. The same anecdote is narrated by Severn in BNK: "On our arrival in Rome we were sadly servd with dinners and as the price was great Keats determined to set it right.— Neither of us could speak Italian sufficiently to do it, but Keats told [me] he had found an effectual way of doing it without words—When the dinner came in the basket as usual, he went & opend it & finding [it] bad as usual, he opened the window & calm[l]y & collect[ed]ly emptyd out each dish into the Street & then pointed to the Porter to take the basket away—Keats was right, in a quarter the man returned with an excellent dinner nor did we ever have a bad one again.—We were not chargd for the condemned one" (KC2, p. 135). Sharp turned this into a comic set piece by adding detail and weaving in material from later unrelated letters by Severn (see LLJS, p. 67, and JSLM, pp. 568–70).

39 MTL, fo. 28ʳ. The date is deduced from Severn's letter of 14th December 1820 to Charles Brown, in which he affirms: "This is the fifth day [from the haemorrhage]" (KC1, p. 176).

40 Letter of 14th December 1820, KC1, pp. 175–76.

41 Severn wrote "Dec. 17 4 Morning" before continuing the letter started on the 14th. From what Severn says in the second part of the letter ("the first for 8 nights", "This is the 9th day"), it looks as though the date may be an error for 18th December. The 17th was a Sunday.

42 See 'Voyage to Naples', p. 45 and note 33.

43 Letter of 14th December 1820, KC1, pp. 176–79. Severn added in a postscript: "I have just looked at him—this will be a good night."

   The quotation "can he administer to a mind diseased" is from *Macbeth*, Act v, Sc. 3, l. 40.

   Regarding "a certain kind of fish", see MTL, fo. 28^r: "[Doctor Clark] ordered the scanty food, of a simple anchovy a day with a morsel of bread."

   Regarding Severn's lack of contact from his family, see his letter of spring 1821 to his mother: "O—what a many times I went down to [the] Post Office for the Letter—" (JSLM, p. 141).

44 I follow the text given in KC1, pp. 179–84, and the suggested readings of Hyder Edward Rollins and other editors, as well as my own, for the damaged parts.

   The readings given in braces in the following instances are conjectural: "he is now under the {impression that poison} was administered to him" (para. 1); "the book he has set his mind upon all through this last {week}" (para. 1); "and then seeing no face but min{e around} him he {will} say it makes him worse" (para. 2).

45 Severn named "the works of Jeremy Taylor" as "Holy living & dying" in his late memoirs (OAKF and MTL) – that is, *The Rule and Exercises of Holy Living* (1650) and *The Rule and Exercises of Holy Dying* (1651), two devotional works by the Church of England divine Jeremy Taylor (1613–67), which were very popular in Keats's day. In OAKF, an early draft for an article for the *Atlantic Monthly*, Severn portrays his friend's request as a wish to reconnect with religious faith:

> [H]e now felt convinced that every human creature required the support of Religion that he might die decently—"Here am I with desperation in death that would disgrace the commonest fellow—Now my dear Severn I am sure if you could get some of the work of Jeremy Taylor to read to me I might become really a Christian & leave this world in peace[.]" [...]
>
> He was a great lover of Jeremy Taylor & it did not require much effort in him to embrace the holy spirit in these sublime works. Thus he gained strength of mind from day to day just in proportion as his poor body grew weaker & weaker & at last I had the consolation of finding him more prepared for his death than I was. [...] In all he then uttered he breathed a calm Christian spirit, indeed I always think that he died a Christian, that Mercy was trembling on his dying lips, that the tortured soul was received by those blessed hands which could alone receive it (JSLM, pp. 614–15).

Keats's supposed deathbed conversion, however, sounds inauthentic, and is at odds with the account given by Severn in the letters preceding the poet's death and in MTL: "'Severn he said I now understand how you can bear all this, 'tis your Christian faith—How I should like [it] if it were possible to get some of Jeremy Taylors works for you to read to me & I should gain consolation for I have always been a great admirer of this devout author['.] [...] I read to poor Keats both morning & evening from this pious work & he received great comfort" (MTL, fo. 29ʳ).

"Madam Dacier's Plato" refers to *The Works of Plato Abridg'd* (London: A. Bell, 1701; French edition: 1699) by the French scholar and translator Anne Le Fèvre Dacier (also known as "Madame Dacier", 1647–1720). Keats would no doubt have been interested in the Greek philosopher's arguments for the immortality of the soul.

"Miss Edgeworths Novels" refers to the work of the popular Anglo-Irish novelist Maria Edgeworth (1768–1849).

The quotation "mind's eye" is from *Hamlet*, Act 1, Sc. 2, l. 185.

46 "He does not like any one—he says—a strange {face makes} him misera{ble.}" (SEVERN'S NOTE). See also letter of 13th August 1820 to Fanny Keats, ROL2, p. 314; letter of 14th August 1820 to Charles Brown, ROL2, p. 321; and Leigh Hunt's letter of 8th March 1821 to Joseph Severn, MON, p. 95.

47 Although he says "this is my 5ᵗʰ Letter", no other Severn letter dated 24th December 1820 survives. One might have been to Charles Brown, since Severn wrote to him in May 1821 of an incident he had mentioned in a previous letter during Keats's illness (letter of 2nd May 1821, JSLM, pp. 151–52).

48 "Scots Monastery" is *The Monastery: A Romance*, an 1820 historical novel by Walter Scott.

49 "[T]he very air we breathe is loaded with contagion. We cannot even sleep without risk of infection. I say infection – this place is the rendezvous of the diseased. You won't deny that many diseases are infectious – even the consumption itself is highly infectious. When a person dies of it in Italy, the bed and bedding are destroyed, the other furniture is exposed to the weather, and the apartment whitewashed before it is occupied by any other living soul. You'll allow that nothing receives infection sooner, or retains it longer, than blankets, feather beds and mattresses – 'sdeath! How do I know what miserable objects have been stewing in the bed where I now lie? I wonder, Dick, you did not put me in mind of sending for my own mattresses" (HC, p. 82).

50   DOI, p. 187. To get an idea of the stringent process of sanitiza-
     tion after the removal of a contagious invalid from a room, see
     RS, pp. 79–80: "All the furniture, beds and linen from an invalid's
     room (except for glass, metal and solid-wood furnishings), includ-
     ing any fabric or paper covering the ceiling, must be taken out
     to the yard [...] using iron hooks and immediately burnt. Floors
     and walls must be brushed with brooms, and any dirt collected
     therefrom must be carefully burnt. [...] After which, walls (and
     stairs, if applicable) must be treated three times with whitewash,
     whereas floors must be rubbed and scraped using sand or wet
     sawdust. Any residue from this cleaning process must be buried
     underground.
        "Once the room is totally dry, it must be subject to fumigation
     for three days by means of copious fumes of oxygenated hydro-
     chloric acid, making sure all doors are shut. At the end of this
     term, the room can be reopened and left exposed to draughts,
     humidity and light for 15 days in a row. Finally, a certain quan-
     tity of sulphur, gunpowder and small bits of tar must be burnt
     in the room."

51   TPC, p. 181. "Morgagni" is the Italian anatomist Giovanni
     Battista Morgagni (1682–1771).

52   Angeletti's petition, with Del Drago's covering letter, can be
     found in SC1.

53   The police register in question is DGP1. Keats's name was entered
     under the letter X, and the entry reads: "Xeats John, Measures
     to be taken against him, being affected with consumption." The
     entry in the same register for Anna Angeletti reads: "Angeletti
     Anna, She demands that measures be taken against a man affected
     with consumption." The *registro di protocollo* (DGP2) shows the
     following entry on 18th December 1820: "[Case number] 14330.
     [Date in which the case has been registered and time in case of
     urgency] d., [Document produced / number, date] 3576. 18 d.
     [Person who has produced or written the document] Campo
     Marzo President, [Subject Matter of the case or of the document
     produced and number of enclosed documents] He wishes that
     some measures be taken about the foreigner John Xeats affected
     with consumption in the house of Anna Angeletti], [Referring
     to the Section] 7, [Register] Public Health, [Manner in which
     the documents have been processed and execution of immediate
     ministerial orders: Date, Addressed to, Content] 19th Dec., Sacra
     Consulta, Angeletti's petition is forwarded so that the necessary
     steps may be taken."

54   SC1. A draft of the letter in Bernetti's hand is preserved in DGP3.

55 Most of the information contained in this biographical portrait of Domenico Morichini is drawn from IAN, RAC1 (pp. III–ILIV) and VIS, unless otherwise indicated.

56 RAC1, pp. IX, 45–55.

57 Ibid., pp. XXX–XXXI.

58 RAC1 and RAC2.

59 For Morichini's consultation about Napoleon's health, see RAC1, p. XXXIII. Sir Humphry Davy met Morichini in Rome in 1814 and was impressed with the latter's experiments in magnetism. In two letters written that year, Davy described the Roman doctor to his friends as "a modest & enlightened man" (DAV1, p. 292) and "a very candid & enlightened man" (DAV1, p. 300). The two scientists developed a strong friendship, and Morichini became Davy's personal physician, treating him until the end of his life in May 1829. Davy signed off a letter he wrote to his doctor less than three months before his death with a tender compliment: "*Morichini buono per tutti e sempre ottimo per me*" ("Morichini, good to everyone and always the best for me", DAV4, p. 178). He left Morichini £50 in his will (RAC1, p. XXXIV). After being treated and cured by Morichini, Christian, the Prince of Denmark, bestowed on him the prestigious Order of the Dannebrog. Giacomo Leopardi, Italy's most famous and studied poet after Dante, was treated by Morichini when he stayed in Rome in late 1831 and early 1832. For Leopardi's sympathetic portrayal of the doctor, see his letter of 21st January 1832 to Giovan Pietro Vieusseux (LEO, p. 85).

60 Archivio Segreto Vaticano, Segreteria di Stato, 1816, rubrica 155, 'Regolamento per impedire la propagazione del contagio fisico'.

61 IAN, p. 267.

62 Morichini's letter can be found in SC1.

63 Letter of 3rd January 1821 to an unknown recipient (perhaps Samuel Frederick Gray – see p. 175 and note 3 above), from a transcript by James Augustus Hessey, ROL2, pp. 366–67.

64 TPC, pp. 10, 17, 20–21.

65 Ibid., p. 254.

66 Ibid., p. 279. See also p. 286.

67 Given the time at which it was composed, the correct date could be 12th January.

68 In the letter of 24th December 1820 to John Taylor, KC1, p. 183.

69 KC1, pp. 186–92.

70 Letter of 6th February 1821 to Joseph Severn, ROL2, pp. 374–75.

71 Letter of 1st February 1821, FBL, pp. 14–15.

72 Letter of 26th February 1821, FBL, p. 18.

73   KSMB, p. 95. The remaining 260 scudi were cashed in five instalments after the poet's death: 28th February 1821 (50), 8th March (50), 14th March (50), 31st March (50) and 14th April (60).

74   Letter of 13th January 1821 to [Samuel Frederick?] Gray, KC1, pp. 193–95.

75   The last line of this mutilated letter reads "I must now attempt to fill {up this} sheet tho' 'tis past {...} my head is a", suggesting that it was written at night.

76   The five individuals are named in John Taylor's letter of March 1821 [?] to Richard Woodhouse, KC1, p. 235. The quotation "Five of those [...]" is from John Taylor's letter of 3rd April 1821 to Joseph Severn (JSLM, p. 143). Joseph Bonsor (1779–1835) was a wholesale stationer in Salisbury Square, Fleet Street. He was Master of the Girdlers' Company in 1820, and a friend of Taylor and Hessey. For his obituary notice see the *Morning Post* of 16th November 1835. Revd John Percival (1788–1832), Fellow of Wadham College, Oxford, preferred to the ministry of the Oxford Chapel (St Peter, Vere Street, Marylebone) by the king in 1826, was a long-time friend of John Taylor. For a notice of his death, see the *Norfolk Chronicle* of 24th November 1832 and *The Edinburgh Gazette* of 18th December 1832.

77   Charles Wentworth-Fitzwilliam, 3rd Earl Fitzwilliam (1786–1857).

78   Taylor sent a reassuring letter to Joseph Severn on 6th February 1821 telling him that the bill would be paid and that he and Hessey would continue to provide financial support: "Torlonia's will not only let you have the rest of the money, which I hope is done ere this, but you may further draw upon us for Fifty Pounds more (as I told Dr Clarke in my last Letter[)], and after that if necessary for 50£ more still—" (MLP, p. 109). In the same letter he wrote: "Reynolds sent 50£ a fortnight since[.] Did you receive it?" (MLP, p. 111). The painter wrote to Taylor in reply: "I have not received the 50£ you mention at least Tolonias have had no notice of it" (letter of 6th March 1821, JSLM, pp. 139–40). Taylor then informed Severn on 3rd April 1821: "Reynolds I find did not send the 50£ after all. {I} did not know that till very lately—he wrote {to me of his} desire Keats would draw upon him for that Sum" (JSLM, p. 144).

79   Taylor's letter of 3rd February 1821 to his father, KC1, p. 207, note. Woodhouse had offered Keats financial support before his departure. See his letter of 16th September 1820 to Keats, ROL2, pp. 336–37.

80   £30 was paid to Torlonia on 10th January 1821 and £120 on 17th February 1821. See Taylor and Hessey's letter of 17th February 1821 to George Keats, KC1, p. 215.

81 Ibid. See also John Taylor's letter of 19th February 1821 to Michael Drury, KC1, pp. 217–20.

82 Letter of 18th April 1821 to John Taylor, KC1, p. 235.

83 See George Keats's letter of 20th April 1825 to Charles Wentworth Dilke, KC1, p. 287. In the spring of 1821, Taylor asked Woodhouse if he could help him realize £1,000 through the sale of some of his family's shares in the Regent Canal. See letter of March [?] 1821, KC1, p. 234.

84 The letter has not survived. Hunt's letter of 8th March 1821 to Severn makes no mention of it, suggesting it was never written.

85 ROL2, pp. 367–70. The quotation "dash the cup from his lip" is from Matthew 26:39.

86 BNK (KC2, p. 138).

87 OAKF (JSLM, p. 613). A carnelian (or "cornelian") is "a variety of chalcedony, a semi-transparent quartz, of a deep dull red, brownish-pink, or reddish-white colour; used for seals, etc." (OED). See Byron's Don Juan I, cxcviii, ll. 6–8.

88 ROL2, pp. 371–73. The reading "easy" in "the only {easy} comfort" (para. 1) is conjectural. The quotation "smell of mortality" is from King Lear, Act IV, Sc. 6, l. 136. The underlining of "<u>dare</u>" follows Grant F. Scott's reading in JSLM, p. 132.

89 Now at the Keats-Shelley House in Rome (ART-008).

90 Letter of 5th January 1822 to John Taylor, JSLM, p. 190.

91 KC1, pp. 200–1. For Severn's letter of 17th December (started on 14th December), see pp. 186–89.

92 This letter has survived in a transcript used by Brown for his 'Life of John Keats' (KC2, pp. 90–94).

93 For Alfieri, see p. 180, and note 20 above.

94 "[T]here are so many English here (about 200) that is almost like London" (Severn's letter of 21st January 1821 to his sister Maria, JSLM, p. 128). By the British consul's account (DCLC, p. 195), the English in Rome were about five hundred, a considerable number for that time of year.

    The "Porta Santa Giovanna" is Porta San Giovanni – that is, the Lateran Gate.

95 DCLC, p. 200.

96 DCLC (11th December 1820), p. 185.

97 The quotation "[a] general arrest […]" is from DCLC (2nd December 1820), p. 184. See also the Duchess of Devonshire's letter of 16th December 1820 to Sir Thomas Lawrence: "[N]o foreigner hardly dare to stay in Naples, here they arrive each day, and frequently in the day—" (RA archive, LAW/3/239), which also contains the quote "epidemic [of] Carbonarism".

98 See also Severn's letter of 21st January 1821 to his sister Maria, passage written on 19th February 1821: "[P]oor Keats has lived on bread and milk for a month past[—]it is the only thing he can take—[...] I make bread and milk three times a day for Keats" (JSLM, p. 128).

99 Perhaps George Keats for not remitting any money, or Miss Brawne for her apparent coldness.

100 Letter of 21st January 1821 to his sister Maria, JSLM, pp. 126–30.

The English architect Lewis Vulliamy (1791–1871) had been awarded a Royal Academy Gold Medal for architectural design in 1813 and was the recipient of a three-year travelling scholarship which was coming to an end in July 1821. "He seems certain I shall succeed him," Severn wrote to his sister Maria, "he says it depends intirely on myself" (ibid., p. 126).

In the same letter, Severn wrote of Canova: "[H]e was exceedingly kind to me—the letter of recommendation gave me a most friendly welcome—I mean our Presidents letter—he has promised me his service at any time—and has already written to his holiness the Pope to permit me to study in any of his palaces—he seems to think highly of my views" (ibid., p. 127).

Of Lord Colchester, Severn wrote: "A Gentleman has offered me the use of his study" (ibid., p. 130).

Regarding his dinners, he said: "[M]y dinner now I go out for—I have for 1st dish macarona—it is like a dish of large white earth worms—made of Flour with butter &c—very good—my 2nd dish is fish—and then comes Roast Beef or Mutton—a cutlet of Pork or wild boar—their vegetables here are beautiful—cabbage—cauliflower—brocola spinach—every thing good—and very well cooked—then I have pudding every day—[...] the puddings are beautiful—rice particularly—plum pudding delicious—they even call it by its English name" (ibid., p. 128).

101 Ibid., p. 130. The "young Lady" is Maria Cotterell. This suggests that her brother Charles had been in contact with Severn.

102 Letter of 6th March 1821 to John Taylor, JSLM, p. 138.

103 MTL, fo. 30. See also Severn's earlier memoir, IML, fos. 5ᵛ–6ʳ: "During Keats's lingring illness he made me go twice to see the place where he was to be burried & he was so pleasd with my descriptions that at times it seemd almost his only consolation—"

104 Letter of 17th or 18th December 1818 to Thomas Love Peacock, PBSL, pp. 59–60. William died on 7th June 1819.

105 SEL2, p. 127. Between 1816 and 1821, the Protestant community in Rome gathered in rented rooms for the celebration of daily

services. At the time of Keats's sojourn in Rome the rooms were by Trajan's Column (ibid., p. 128).

106 Ibid., pp. 125–26. See also DCLC, pp. 195–97, 209 and 256.

107 See GRJK, pp. 1–21, and IPP, pp. 157–69. See also Severn's letter of 21st January 1823 to Charles Brown: "I have just returned from the funeral of poor Shelly—[…] You must know a new burial ground has been made—well walled in to protect us Heretics against the Catholics who had most wantonly defaced many of the Protestant Tombs[—]the old ground they would not wall—because it would spoil the view of the Pyramid of Cajus Cestus—so this new one is given and the Old one protected with a Ditch—and with an Order that not more shall be burried there—" (JSLM, p. 227). The sunken fence remained the only protection of the Old Cemetery until the turn of the twentieth century (GRJK, p. 17).

108 GRJK, pp. 9–15.

109 Ibid., p. 16; IPP, pp. 177–80.

110 ROL2, pp. 375–76.

111 KC2, pp. 94–95, dated "Rome. 27 February 1821". A draft of this letter survives, with some variants: "He is gone—he died with the most perfect ease—he seemd to go to sleep—on the 23rd (Friday) at ½ past 4 the approaches of death came on— 'Severn—S—lift me up for I am dying—I shall die easy—dont be frightened—thank God it has come'—I lifted him up in my arms—and the phlegm seemd boiling in his throat—this increased until 11 at night whe[n] he gradually sunk into death—so qui[e]t that I still thought he slept—but I cannot say more now—I am broken down beyond my strength—I cannot be left alone—I have not slept for 9 days—I will say—I will say the days since—On Saturday a Gentlem[a]n sent to cast the face—hand and foot— On Sunday the body was opened—the lungs were completely gone—the Doctors could not conceive how he had lived in the last 2 Months—Dr Clark will write you on this head—~~Since then—the Police has been to take away all the furniture—and has ordered that—~~" (JSLM, pp. 136–37).

Regarding "Three days since": in fact, on Sunday 25th. It may be that Severn wrote his fair copy of the letter to Brown on 28th February.

For more about the letters in Keats's coffin, see MTL, fo. 30: "I duly performed my promise that I would place the 3 unopend letters within the winding sheet on his heart." It is unclear which letters were buried with the poet. Severn mentions two unopened letters – perhaps both by Fanny Brawne, or one by Fanny and one by Keats's sister – in his letters of 11th January (to Mrs Brawne) and 15th January 1821 (to William Haslam). On 14th February,

Severn mentioned to Brown that he had received another letter from Fanny, which was left unread. Keats's instructions, at that time, were to place only his sister's purse and unopened letter, with some hair, in his coffin. These, of course, may have changed over the following days, prior to the poet's death.

112 Letter of 6th March 1821, ROL2, p. 379.

113 Ibid., p. 139. "Dr Luby" has been identified with Lieutenant Thomas Luby, an ex-army surgeon. He was made lieutenant in 1814 (*London Gazette*, 22nd January 1814, p. 185). He served in the Peninsular War in 1814 as an assistant surgeon of the Provisional Battalion of Militia: see SOSC, p. 162.

No doubt Clark did write to Taylor, but the letter has not survived.

114 The note was copied by Poynter's daughter Henrietta May Poynter on 24th October 1921. See Dorothy Hewlett, *Adonis: A Life of John Keats* (London: Hurst & Blackett, 1937), p. 426.

115 Joseph Severn's letter of 6th March 1821 to John Taylor, ROL2, p. 379. William Ewing was a sculptor and ivory carver who had lodgings in Piazza di Spagna and was later the secretary of the British Academy at Rome, founded by Severn and Richard Westmacott, jun. (among others) in late 1821. In a letter of introduction to Charles Brown dated 2nd May 1821 (JSLM, pp. 151–52), Severn wrote:

> I have great pleasure in introducing to you this Gentleman—Mr William Ewing for his kind services to our poor Keats and myself—
>
> Altho' we came here strangers to him—he gave us all the attention of an old friend—and that of the most valuable kind—You will remember my mention of a Gentleman who sought all over Rome—for an Ice Jelly when it was told me none could be got—It was this Gentleman who procured one—and who rendered me many other like services on the like dreadfull occasions—I have no other soul to help me—
>
> Except Dr Clark and myself—he saw more of Keats than any one—he will inform you on many points—as yet—too dreadfull for me to write— [...]
>
> You will find this Gentleman to possess extraordinary skill as Sculptor—his works in Ivory are to me the most beautiful things of the kind I ever saw— [...]
>
> Be so kind as [to] introduce him to Mr Hunt and also to Mr Taylor—and Haslam.

See also Severn's letter of 16th May 1821 to John Taylor: "You will [see] a Gentleman in London soon—a Mr Ewing who has been very kind to me here—he knew more of Keats than any other person here—he will give you much information—this is a great pleasure to me—he is a very good fellow—" (KC1, pp. 249–50).

When in London, Ewing had a brief meeting with Fanny Brawne (and, perhaps, with Fanny Keats too). Fanny Brawne wrote to the poet's sister in the second half of 1821: "Did you tell Guiterez you had seen a gentleman from Italy? If so, I suppose Mr Ewing has called on you. My mother thinks it probable, but I imagine it his mistake—I have only seen Mr Ewing for a few minutes almost in the dark but he seemed so fluttered and confused that I could make nothing of him; but he has claims on us both from his great kindness in Italy" (FBL, pp. 35–36). For Valentín Maria Llanos y Gutiérrez, who married Fanny Keats in 1826, see KC1, cix–cxi. According to the Irish novelist and playwright Gerald Griffin, Llanos "was intimate" with Keats in Rome and "spoke with him three days before he died" (letter of 21st June 1825 to his sister Lucy, LGG, p. 190), but there is no evidence to support this very credible testimony in Severn's letters.

Richard Westmacott, jun. (1799–1872), the son of a famous sculptor of the same name, had arrived in Rome on 15th December 1820 with a letter of introduction by Sir Thomas Lawrence to Antonio Canova (Biblioteca Civica di Bassano del Grappa, Epistolario Canova, V.550.3594, 7th September 1820). Although he had met with the architectural student Vulliamy – "I have seen but little of him but that little has not pleassed me much; this entre nous," he said in a letter of 24th March 1821 to his brother William (Henry Moore Institute, Wes/C/C2/7) – and was later involved in setting up the British Academy at Rome (Severn letter of 26th December 1821 to his sister Maria, JSLM, p. 181, and MUN, p. 46), he doesn't seem to have known Severn very well at the time. Surprising at it may seem, there is no mention of Keats, Severn or the funeral in his letters of 30th January, 23rd February (the day of the poet's death) and 24th March 1821 to his brother William (Henry Moore Institute, Wes/C/C2/5–7).

"Henderson" could be either the amateur artist and wealthy patron of the arts John Henderson (1764–1843), the husband of the painter Georgiana Keate (1771–1850), or, more likely, their son, also called John (1797–1878), who would later become a renowned art collector. After the sudden death of their daughter Jane (b. 1799) in early December 1819, the Hendersons decided to take their family on a journey abroad, perhaps as a means to recover from the trauma of their loss. There is a record of two passport applications linked to this trip: FO 610/1 ("Sept. 13 [1820], 4683, Mr John Henderson—Mrs H. / 2 daughters 1 son

& 3 servants, [Where going]———, [By whom recommended:] M:
John Henderson, 3 Montagu / Street Russell Squ.") and FO 610/1
("Oct. 12 [1820], 4724, M: John Henderson and his suite, [Where
going] D.º [The Continent], [By whom recommended] M: Jefferd
Downing Street"). The "son" must be the youngest of the chil-
dren, Charles Cooper (1803–77), later a well-known painter,
who had been withdrawn from Winchester College sometime
in 1820 (*The Wykehamist*, No. 316, October 1895, p. 139),
and the "John" travelling separately with his suite must be his
older brother. The two surviving daughters were Georgiana
("Georgy", 1798–1881) and Harriet (1801–45). For Jane's death,
see the letter of 8th December 1819 from John Henderson, sen.,
to Thomas Monro, V&A, NAL Special Collections, 86.W.15.

"Pointer" is the sculptor Ambrose Poynter (1796–1886).

Richard Wolfe was the English chaplain at Rome (see SEL1,
p. 356). Selina Martin praises him for his great kindness (SEL2,
pp. 241, 260). He was one of the "two young clergymen" – the
other being Revd Spencer Knox (SEL1, p. 356) – who officiated
at the funeral of Selina Martin's niece Anny on 8th January
1821. She writes: "Never was our beautiful burial service read
in a more impressive manner" (SEL2, p. 261). Wolfe must have
left Rome by 26th July 1821, since Selina Martin writes on
that date: "We have no English clergyman here at present"
(SEL2, p. 335).

Poynter mentions in his 1850 note that "The party consisted
of his friend Severn [...], Henry Parke, the Architect, the English
Chaplain and myself [...], we four in one carriage and the COFFIN
in another" (see above, note 103). It is possible that Severn forgot
to mention Parke among the "many English" present. We know
that Parke was in Italy at that time (FO 610/1: "July 27 [1820],
4572, M: Henry Parke (architect)[,] his father, mother & sister,
[going to] The Continent"; SALM, pp. 169–70). Seymour Kirkup
was supposed to be among the mourners, but that day "[he] was
in bed with the fever" (AM, p. 748).

"D' Bell" was the Scottish anatomist and surgeon John Bell
(1763–1820).

POSTHUMOUS JOURNEYS

1   Letters of 1st February and 23rd May 1821 to Fanny Keats, FBL,
    pp. 15, 25.
2   Letter of 27th March 1821 to Fanny Keats, FBL, p. 21.
3   Letter of 5th August 1819 to Fanny Brawne, ROL2, p. 138.

4   For the period of mourning and trauma, see FBB, p. 112 (and note 15); LGG, pp. 190, 298. For an insight into Fanny's feelings after the death of the poet, see the draft of her letter of 29th December 1829 to Charles Brown, reproduced in LJK, pp. lxii–lxiv.

5   KC2, pp. 95–96.

6   Severn's letter of 24th December 1820 to John Taylor, KC1, p. 180.
    The Hawthorne quotation is from his story 'P.'s Correspondence', which is contained in *Mosses from an Old Manse* (1846).

7   IML, No. 15, fo. 5ʳ. There is an illegible deleted word before the proposed insertion "[arrived]".

8   OAKF (JSLM, p. 611). The quotation "with all his imperfections on his head" is from *Hamlet*, Act 1, Sc. 5, l. 85.

9   For Keats's half-formed plans to travel to America, see his letter of 18th July 1818 to Benjamin Bailey: "I intend to pass a whole year with George if I live to the completion of the three next—" (ROL1, p. 343). See also his letter of 13th January 1820 to Georgiana Keats: "I could almost promise that if I had the means I would accompany George back to america and pay you a Visit of a few Months" (ROL2, p. 239).
    For Tom Keats's plan to leave for Italy, see his letter of 17th May 1818 to Marianne Jeffery, ROL1, p. 286.
    Severn attended Queen Victoria's coronation in Westminster Abbey on 29th June 1838.

10 'Ego Dominus Tuus', ll. 56, 58.

11 T.S. Eliot, 'The Romantic Generation. If It Existed', *The Athenæum*, 18th July 1919, p. 616.

12 As we have seen, Keats had just turned twenty-four when he wrote his last poem, *The Cap and Bells*.

13 Letter of 10th May 1817 to Leigh Hunt, ROL1, p. 139.

14 KC2, p. 97. For "moulting", see his letter of 10th [?] January 1819 to Benjamin Haydon: "I have been writing a little now and then lately: but nothing to speak off—being discontented and as it were moulting—yet I do not think I shall ever come to the rope or the Pistol: for after a day or two's melancholy, although I smoke more and more my own insufficiency—I see by little and little more of what is to be done, and how it is to be done, should I ever be able to do it—" (ROL2, p. 33).

15 Sonnet written before 30th April 1819 and included in Keats's letter of 14th February 1819 to George and Georgiana Keats (ROL2, p. 105 for the original draft contained in that letter).

16 Notices appeared in *The Morning Chronicle* (22nd March); *The Public Ledger and Daily Advertiser* (23rd March); *The Champion* (24th March); *The Mirror of the Times* (24th March);

The Examiner (25th March); *Bell's Weekly Messenger* (25th March); *The News* (25th March); *The Weekly Intelligencer, and British Luminary* (25th March); *The Tyne Mercury* (27th March); *Kentish Chronicle* (27th March); *The Bath Chronicle* (29th March); *Caledonian Mercury* (29th March); *Inverness Courier* (29th March); *The Lincoln, Rutland and Stamford Mercury* (30th March); *The Hull Advertiser and Exchange Gazette* (30th March); *The Norfolk Chronicle and Norwich Gazette* (31st March); *The Edinburgh Magazine and Literary Miscellany* (1st April); *Belfast Commercial Chronicle* (7th April), etc.

17 John Taylor's letter of March 1821 [?] to Richard Woodhouse, KC1, p. 234.

18 Some argue that it is unclear from Severn's letter of 14th December 1820 to Charles Brown (entry of 14th February 1821, KC2, p. 91) whether Keats wanted only the inscription on his tombstone, without any of his personal details, but I doubt that Keats would have wanted to dilute the poetic effect of that line by adding a name and dates. See also Charles Brown's letter of 21st August 1821 to Joseph Severn: "[I]n obedience to his (Keats) will I would have his own words engraven there, and <u>not</u> his name, letting the stranger read the cause of his friends' placing such words" (published in the new, revised edition of NLBS).

19 In fact, Charles Brown had tried to get the epitaph written by Leigh Hunt. See his letter of 21st August 1821 to Joseph Severn, ibid.

For Taylor's belief regarding Keats's dying wish, see his letter of August 1821 to Joseph Severn quoted in LLJS, p. 107: "I can conceive none better than our poor friend's melancholy sentiment, 'Here lies one whose name was writ in water.' It is very simple and affecting, and tells so much of the story that none need be told. Neither name nor date is requisite. These will be given in his life by his biographer. So, unless something else is determined on, let this line stand alone. I foresee that it will be as clear an indication to posterity as the plainest, every-day inscription that one may find in Westminster Abbey." I cannot trace the original of this letter, and although there is no reason to doubt its substance, it may have been edited by Sharp.

See also Charles Brown's letter of 21st August 1821 to Joseph Severn: "Mr Taylor sets his face against [...] any words except what Keats himself desired to be put on his tombstone [...] [A]n epitaph must necessarily be considered as the act of the deceased's friends and not of the deceased himself" (published in the new, revised edition of NLBS).

For Brown's professed intimacy with Keats, see his letter of 13th August 1821 to Joseph Severn: "I fear Taylor may do Keats an injustice,—not knowingly, but from the want of knowing his character" (published in the new, revised edition of NLBS).

20 See Severn's letter of 1st June 1823 to William Haslam, JSLM, p. 242. In the end, according to Charles Wentworth Dilke, despite being in very reduced circumstances, Severn footed the entire bill and refused to accept money from Brown (DIL, p. 17). For Severn's ideas, see his letter of 1st January 1823 to Charles Brown, JSLM, p. 228.

21 The original draft of the epitaph, to be found in Charles Brown's letter of 21st August 1821 to Joseph Severn, reads: "This Grave contains all that ~~mortal was~~ was mortal of a young English Poet, who, on his death-bed, in bitter anguish at the neglect of his Countrymen, ~~& desired the following words to be engraven on his tomb-stone~~ desired these words to be engraven on his tomb-stone: 'Here lies one whose Name was writ in water.'" Brown himself was not satisfied with his wording (published in the new, revised edition of NLBS).

For the date of erection, see Severn's letter of 1st June 1823 to William Haslam, JSLM, p. 242.

22 The lyre had been Keats's idea before he left for Italy. See Severn's letter to William Haslam of 5th May 1821, JSLM, p. 156.

23 OAKF (JSLM, p. 616).

24 JLSM, pp. 468–69. In the same letter, the painter proposed the following amended inscription (the errors in the dates are Severn's): "This grave / Contain[in]g the mortal remains of / John Keats / a young English Poet / who died at Rome Feb 20 1820 aged 23 years / his short life / was so imbitterd by discouragment & sickness / that he desired these words to mark his grave / 'Here lies one whose name was writ in water' / Time / Having reversed this sentence / His friends & admirers / now inscribe his name / in Marble / 1859" (ibid., pp. 469–70). Dilke, however, did not agree with Severn. On 5th February 1859, he wrote to Monckton Milnes, one of the subscribers for the proposed new memorial to Keats: "If you are of opinion that a monument should be erected to Keats, whether in Rome or in London, I shall be most happy to subscribe, but to *destroy the existing monument*, and erect another on its site, seems to me very like falsifying history. If, as Mr. Severn says, this unseemly stone was erected when Keats's memory was cherished by few, and his genius known to fewer; and if Keats was so embittered by discouragement that he desired those words to mark his grave, then the unseemly stone

tells the story of his life. If the fame of Keats be now world-wide the anomaly is another fact, and I for one am willing to join in recording it on another monument. As to the proposed inscription, it is certainly not to my taste; but if you approve I will waive my objections, and will hope you are right" (DIL, pp. 11–12).

25 Letter of 3rd April 1821, JLSM, p. 143.

26 *New Times* (29th March); *The Bath Chronicle* (26th April); *The Morning Chronicle* (4th June), etc.

27 Letter of 16th May 1821, KC1, p. 249.

28 Letter of 17th July 1821, STIL, p. 78.

29 Brown's letter of 15th August 1821 to Thomas Richards, STIL, p. 88, and of 21st August 1821 to Severn (published in the new, revised edition of NLBS).

30 Letter of 13th August 1821 (LLJS, p. 109, reproduced in STIL, pp. 85–86).

31 "I rejoice you sent me the papers," Brown wrote to him in his letter of 21st August 1821 (published in the new, revised edition of NLBS).

32 Letter of 5th January 1822, JSLM, p. 190.

33 Letter of 21st August 1821 (published in the new, revised edition of NLBS).

34 For Brown's belief that Clarke was planning a biography of Keats, see his letter of 13th August 1821 to Joseph Severn (published in the new, revised edition of NLBS). Nothing came of it until January 1861, when Clarke published his 'Recollections of Keats, by an Old School-Fellow' in the *Atlantic Monthly* (Vol. 7, No. 39, pp. 86–100).

35 On Brown's first meeting with Keats, see KC2, p. 57.

36 Taylor's great-niece Olive M. Taylor in the *London Mercury*, Vol. 12 (1925). In the same article she said that in her youth she "read this manuscript, but [...] it ha[d] now been lost sight of".

37 Fanny Brawne, however, gave her reluctant consent (see LJK, pp. lxii–lxiv).

38 Milnes was born in 1809 and educated at Trinity College, Cambridge, where he became a member of the famous "Apostles Club", which included Alfred Tennyson, Henry Lushington, John Sterling, Joseph Blakesley, R.C. Trench and Arthur Hallam, among others. As a student, he defended the merits of Shelley over Byron in a debate in Oxford (see LLMM, pp. 77–86).

39 For the fragment of a draft of *Lamia*, see 'John Keats 1795–1821', in Barbara Rosenbaum, ed., *Index of English Literary Manuscripts*, Vol. 4, Part 2 (London: Mansell, 1990), p. 369. For Severn's painting of Keats, see Milnes's letter of 21st June 1832 to his father (LLMM, p. 127).

40　See Charles Brown's letter of 9th April 1841 to Richard Monckton Milnes, KC2, p. 100.

41　After his initial predicaments, George became one of the wealthiest and most influential citizens of Louisville, Kentucky. Alongside his business activities, he played an active role in the running of local schools, charities and cultural societies. Following another major crisis in his personal finances, he died of tuberculosis on Christmas Eve, 1841, aged forty-four. His widow Georgiana remarried in January 1843 to a young Scotsman, John Jeffrey, who was twenty years her junior and often unfaithful to her. Jeffrey provided great assistance to Milnes in the preparation of his biography. Georgiana died in her eighties in April 1879. For a biographical sketch of the George Keatses, see KC1, pp. xcvi–cviii. After spending almost thirteen years in Italy with his son Carlino, Brown returned to England in March 1835, settling near Plymouth and writing articles for magazines, lecturing on Keats and publishing a book of some merit called *Shakespeare's Autobiographical Poems* (London: James Bohn, 1838). Having sent his son ahead of him, he sailed for New Zealand on the *Oriental* in June 1841, arriving in New Plymouth in October of that year. Dissatisfied with the wild aspect of the land and already failing in health, he decided to return to England, but before he could do it he died of apoplexy on 5th June 1842, at the age of fifty-five. His son Carlino (Charles C. Brown) went on to become a prominent New Zealand businessman and politician. For a biographical sketch of Charles Armitage Brown see LJK, pp. xlix–li.

　　For Dilke's dislike of Brown's memoir, see his letter of April [?] 1841 to Joseph Severn, KC2, pp. 103–6.

42　See Reynolds's letters of 27th November and 15th December 1846 to Edward Moxon (KC2, pp. 162, 166–67), and his letter of 22nd December 1846 to Richard Monckton Milnes (KC2, pp. 172–73).

43　For the date of publication, see Charles Cowden Clarke's letter of 7th August 1848 to Richard Monckton Milnes, KC2, p. 235.

44　Ibid.

45　Letter of 24th August 1848, BMM, p. 122.

46　For the agreement between John Taylor and Edward Moxon, see KC2, pp. 128–29.

47　GGC, 28th November 1820; PLDA, 6th March 1821.

48　*Carlisle Journal*, 18th and 25th November 1837.

　　For the *Maria Crowther*'s voyages under Walsh's command, see *Lloyd's List*, 2nd March 1821; PLDA, 9th April 1821; *Lloyd's List*, 23rd October 1821; PLDA, 12th December 1821; *Lloyd's List*, 11th January 1822; PLDA, 18th March 1822; PLDA, 25th

July 1822; *Lloyd's List*, 24th September 1822; *Lloyd's List*, 1st October 1822; *Gore's General Advertiser*, 1st May 1823.

For its becoming leaky, see *Lloyd's List*, 1st October 1822.

Later captains were Buckley (August 1823), Redmond (January 1824), Wood (November 1824), Higgins (January 1826). After being repaired in 1827: Rae (February 1828), Pearson (November 1828) and Dawes (April 1832).

For its repair, see *Cumberland Pacquet*, 1st May 1827.

49 *Gore's General Advertiser*, 3rd May 1827.

50 For Walsh's command of the *Naples Packet*, see PLDA, 14th May 1824; *The Sun* (London), 21st June 1825; *Lloyd's List*, 17th February 1826; *Gore's General Advertiser*, 3rd May 1827; PLDA, 13th February 1828; PLDA, 28th August 1829; *Star* (London), 15th May 1830; *Lloyd's List*, 16th August 1831; PLDA, 6th February 1832; and *Evening Standard*, 22nd August 1833, which reports: "STANDGATE CREEK, Aug. 21.—Arrived [...] the Naples packet, Walsh, from Naples."

His replacement was Captain Cotterell, who arrived in Naples from Swansea and Leghorn on 25th December 1833 (*Morning Advertiser*, 21st January 1834).

51 Letter of 10th April 1821, JSLM, p. 147.

52 Archivio di Stato di Napoli, Stato civile della restaurazione, Quartiere San Ferdinando, Morti, 1821. The death certificate says "Died in her own house [...] at Largo del Castello No. 7 / unwedded daughter of Carlo [Charles], absent". The first of the two witnesses who made the declaration is Giovanni Ivar, "clerk" (born *c.*1770), who perhaps worked for the British legation, since his name often appears in the Neapolitan registers as a witness in connection with the deaths of British subjects, including that of Charles Cotterell's nineteen-month-old daughter Elizabeth Mariana on 2nd October 1836. This could be the same "Giovanni" mentioned by Keats in his letter of 22nd October 1820 to Mrs Frances Brawne (ROL2, p. 349).

53 For Cotterell's commercial activities, see 'Naples', note 97.

54 MAEL2, pp. 122–23; MTU2, pp. 217, 222; Severn's letter of 5th July 1822 to his brother Thomas: "[H]e makes open house to me whenever I may like to come to Naples" (JSLM, p. 204).

55 For Cotterell's marriage, see *The Sun*, 29th July 1831; *The Observer*, 31st July 1831. A marriage declaration for a potential Royal Navy widow's pension gives the date as 5th July 1831 (ADM 13/70/51).

Enoch Hodgkinson Warriner (1784–1861) was rector of All Saints from 1823 until his death in 1861. See DJM, p. 3.

56 See E.H. Warriner's letter dated Rome 21st April 1830 to his brother George: "Least you should begin to think I have traveled out of the land of the living I have this day determined to notify you that we are all alive & well (Elis.^{ths} lameness excepted)" (Warwickshire County Record Office, CR1635-38-1).

57 E.H. Warriner's letter of 10th September 1830 to his brother George (Warwickshire County Record Office, CR1635-38-2).

58 James Lewis Minet (1807–1885) was the scion of a notable Huguenot family. He married Elizabeth, the younger daughter of Cotterell's business partner, William Iggulden, and acted, with Mariana Starke, as godparent to Cotterell's first daughter, Elizabeth Mariana, who died as an infant (DJM, pp. 217). See also ibid., pp. 2–3.

59 Ibid., p. 227.

60 25th February 1845 (CDL4, pp. 274–75), 14th November 1845 (CDL4, p. 434) and 23rd March 1846 (CDL4, p. 524). A fourth one, dated early March 1850 and mentioned in a letter to John Auldjo of 9th December 1850, is now lost: "I am sincerely sorry to hear of the death of poor Le Gros [W.B. Le Gros (see next note), who – unbeknownst to Dickens – had left Italy and died], who interested me greatly when I was at Naples, and whom I had hoped to walk and talk with again, one day. [...] [I] had written to our common friend the Banker on the Chiaja [Charles Cotterell], only a few days since, charging him with many friendly messages and reminders to him" (CDL6, p. 228).

61 The manuscripts were by W.B. Le Gros (d. 1850), an Englishman living in Naples, who worked as a Vesuvius guide and was the author of a book of poems called *Fables and Tales: Suggested by the Frescos of Pompeii and Herculaneum* (London: Richard Bentley, 1835). He is the "Mr Pickle of Portici" who tumbled down the slope of Mount Vesuvius, emerging "sound in limb", as narrated in hilarious fashion by Dickens in his *Pictures from Italy* (London: Bradbury & Evans, 1846), pp. 249–54.

62 Letter of 25th February 1845, CDL4, p. 275. "Miss Hogarth" is Georgina Hogarth (1827–1917), Dickens's sister-in-law. She had been in Naples with the Dickenses in February 1845.

63 Letter of 14th November 1845, CDL4, p. 434.

64 Letter of 23rd March 1846, CDL4, p. 524. "Here" is Devonshire Terrace, London.

65 *Mr. and Mrs. Charles Dickens: His Letters to Her*, ed. Walter Dexter (London: Constable, 1935), p. 203.

66 *The London Gazette*, No. 20648, 9th October 1846, p. 3566: "NOTICE is hereby given, that the Partnership lately existing

between the undersigned, Charles Edward Cotterell and William Iggulden, of Naples, Merchants and Bankers, carrying on business under the firm of Cotterell, Iggulden, and Co. was dissolved, on the 1st day of May 1846, by mutual consent; and that the liquidation will be arranged by Mr. Iggulden, who will continue the business under the firm of Iggulden and Co.—Dated this 18th day of August 1846. / C.E. Cotterell. / William Iggulden."

67 Among his multifarious activities, in June 1838 Cotterell served as vice-consul of Brazil during the absence of the consul general, Cavaliere Colonnello Luigi dell'Hoste (Archivio di Stato di Napoli, Ministero degli Affari Interni, Inventario II, 438.14).

Regarding his sons: according to the 1851 census, Charles Edward, jun. (17, late pupil) and George (13, pupil) were living on the Isle of Wight, and Thomas (11) was a student at Christ's Hospital.

68 For Cotterell's appointment to HMS *Prince Regent*, see *The Navy List* (London: John Murray, 1850), p. 152; *Colburn's United Service Magazine and Naval and Military Journal*, Part 1 (London: H. Hurst, 1848), p. 152; ADM 38/4515. For his appointment as secretary to the commander, see ADM 196/74/774 and *The Hampshire Advertiser* of 12th April 1851.

69 ADM 196/74/774. During her husband's absence, Elizabeth Cotterell resided at Foots Cray with her parents (DJM, p. 550) and with her family at Ryde, on the Isle of Wight.

70 According to Revd Warriner's will, Elizabeth Cotterell and her two siblings (Sophia May and Thomas Warriner) were to take one third each of the entire estate after the death of their mother. His granddaughter Elizabeth Caroline Sophia was given, "in addition to any legacy or benefit she may have or take under my said Will", the sum of one hundred pounds. The other trustee was Revd Warriner's nephew Henry (Warwickshire County Record Office, CR1635-73).

71 National Library of New Zealand, Thomas Warriner Cotterell, Notebooks (MS-0614-0616). Charles Cotterell's presence in Nelson is confirmed by his attendance, later that year (3rd December 1858), at a dinner for E.W. Stafford and C.W. Richmond at Freemasons' Hall, Trafalgar Street, in which "MR. COTTERELL responded on the part of the Navy" (*The Colonist*, 7th December 1858).

72 *Lyttelton Times*, 14th September 1859; *The Colonist*, 27th September 1859; *Nelson Examiner*, 28th September 1859.

73 For receptions and dinners, see *The Colonist*, 6th December 1859; *Nelson Examiner*, 4th May 1867. For Prince Alfred's visit, see *Nelson Examiner*, 21st April 1869.

74 "Of oil-paintings perhaps the choicest were exhibited by Mr. Cotterell, being two of Hogarth's 'Rake's Progress;' 'Grotto;' 'Roman Vintage;' 'Satyr and Tamborine Player,' and some others" (*The Colonist*, 10th May 1861).

75 For the will, see Archives New Zealand, Nelson Probate case files, Charles Edward Cotterell (1872). For the obituary notice, see *Nelson Evening Mail*, 13th March 1871.

76 For his mother's will, see Archives New Zealand, Nelson Probate case files, Elizabeth Cotterell. His notebooks and collection of photos are held at the National Library of New Zealand. In his will he bequeathed his estate to his nephews and nieces (Archives New Zealand, Nelson Probate case files, Thomas Warriner Cotterell).

77 "Crayfield" was located at the corner of Collingwood Street and Brougham Street. An advert published on a local newspaper soon after Cotterell's death gives the following details: "To Be Sold or Let / THAT DESIRABLE PROPERTY known as CRAYFIELD, being Town Acre No. 195 [...] / The Property comprises a VILLA containing Six Good Rooms and Hall; Outbuildings and a Good Garden and Orchard well stocked with carefully selected Fruit Trees of every description. / It commands one of the most extensive views of Nelson and the Bay, and is within fifteen minutes' walk of the Post Office" (*Nelson Evening Mail*, 26th April 1871).

78 IML, No. 15, fo. 1ᵛ.

79 For a biography of the painter, see JSB, and for his letters and journals JSLM.

80 In Greek: "ὃν οἱ θεοὶ φιλοῦσιν ἀποθνήσκει νέος".

81 See Keats's letter of 10th June 1818 to Benjamin Bailey: "Life must be undergone" (ROL1, p. 293).

82 DIL, p. 17.

83 See MTL, fo. 30: "The burning of the furniture of the death room took place in the Piazza di Spagna & the walls were restored & I had scarcely payd the shamful demand, when the brute of a Landlady sent for me to pay for the crockery broken in my service & I was amused to find a long table covered with the broken crockery of what must have been all the parish—I assum'd to be in a mad rage & with my stick I dashd & smash'd every thing that was on the table & singular enough I frightened the vile creature of a landlady & I never heard any more about the crockery."

84 At one point he even considered writing a historical romance, *The Dead Hand*, set in the time of Titian and the Inquisition, drafting a general plan for it in 1839 (see LLJS, pp. 237–46).

He also penned a short ghost story, 'The Pale Bride' (reprinted in LLJS, pp. 231–37), and tried his hand at a series of imaginary letters between great artists and their contemporaries, in the manner of Walter Savage Landor (see LLJS, pp. 221–27). The manuscripts of these works are in the Houghton Library, Harvard University: MS Eng 1434 (480–81), (492) and (485), respectively.

85 Severn died on 3rd August 1879 and was buried in a nondescript area of the Non-Catholic Cemetery (also known as the Protestant Cemetery), after a low-key ceremony that was not attended by family members or official representatives from the British embassy or consulate. It was only in February 1882 that his remains were moved next to Keats's grave, and a few weeks later a monument was erected, identical in style, shape and size to that of the poet (see JSLM, pp. 58–59).

Index